SOCIAL
REGISTER
2 0 2 3

THE SOCIALIST REGISTER
Founded in 1964

EDITORS
GREG ALBO
NICOLE ASCHOFF
ALFREDO SAAD-FILHO

FOUNDING EDITORS
RALPH MILIBAND (1924-1994)
LEO PANITCH (1945-2020)
JOHN SAVILLE (1916-2009)

ASSOCIATE EDITORS
COLIN LEYS
STEPHEN MAHER
ALAN ZUEGE

CONTRIBUTING EDITORS
GILBERT ACHCAR
PATRICK BOND
ATILIO BORON
JOHANNA BRENNER
MICHAEL CALDERBANK
VIVEK CHIBBER
MADELEINE DAVIS
BARBARA EPSTEIN
NATALIE FENTON
BILL FLETCHER JR
ANA GARCIA
SAM GINDIN
ADAM HANIEH
BARBARA HARRISS-WHITE
DAVID HARVEY
JUDITH ADLER HELLMAN
CHRISTOPH HERMANN
NANCY HOLMSTROM
URSULA HUWS
RAY KIELY
MARTIJN KONINGS
HANNES LACHER
SASHA LILLEY
LIN CHUN
MICHAEL LOWY
BIRGIT MAHNKOPF
ŞEBNEM OĞUZ
BRYAN PALMER
ADOLPH REED JR
STEPHANIE ROSS
SHEILA ROWBOTHAM
JOHN S. SAUL
JOAN SANGSTER
MICHALIS SPOURDALAKIS
HILARY WAINWRIGHT

To get online access to all Register volumes visit our website
http://www.socialistregister.com

SOCIALIST REGISTER 2023

CAPITAL AND POLITICS

Edited by GREG ALBO, NICOLE ASCHOFF AND ALFREDO SAAD-FILHO

THE MERLIN PRESS
MONTHLY REVIEW PRESS
FERNWOOD PUBLISHING

First published in 2022
by The Merlin Press Ltd
Central Books Building
Freshwater Road
London
RM8 1RX

www.merlinpress.co.uk

© The Merlin Press, 2022

British Library Cataloguing in Publication Data is available from the British Library

ISSN. 0081-0606

Published in the UK by The Merlin Press
ISBN. 978-0-85036-779-9 Paperback
ISBN. 978-0-85036-780-5 Hardback

Published in the USA by Monthly Review Press
ISBN. 978-1-58367-986-9 Paperback

Published in Canada by Fernwood Publishing
ISBN. 978-1-77363-553-8 Paperback

Printed and bound in the UK on behalf of Stanton Book Services

CONTENTS

Greg Albo Nicole Aschoff Alfredo Saad-Filho	Preface	ix
Adam Hanieh	World oil: Contemporary transformations in ownership and control	1
Nicolas Graham William K. Carroll	Climate breakdown: From fossil capitalism to climate capitalism (and beyond?)	25
Rafeef Ziadah	Logistical landscapes: Corporate power and capital in the maritime industry	47
Patrick Bond	Multilateralism at a crossroads: Vaccine apartheid, climate wars, geopolitical turmoil	64
Stephen F. Diamond	The 'corporate governance' myth	90
Charmaine Chua Spencer Cox	Battling the behemoth: Amazon and the rise of America's new working class	120
Kyle Bailey	The illusions of 'stakeholder capitalism': The case of Unilever	141

Richard Saunders	Transnational capital and regulating African extractives: Zimbabwe's blood diamonds	165
Minqi Li	From '996' to 'lying flat': China's regime of accumulation	190
Pun Ngai Chen Peier	Infrastructural capitalism: High-speed rail and class conflict in China	210
Armando Boito	Political divisions and neo-fascism in Brazil	225

LEO PANITCH AND THE SOCIALIST CHALLENGE

Stephen Maher Scott M. Aquanno	Capitalist restructuring, state transformation: Leo Panitch and capitalism today	247
Panagiotis Sotiris	Mass parties, dual power, and questions of strategy: A dialogue with Leo Panitch	274
Madeleine Davis	Leo Panitch on British Labourism and the prospects for a 'Labour new left'	289
Leo Panitch Rafael Khachaturian	Against pessimism: A life on the left	313

CONTRIBUTORS

Scott M. Aquanno is Associate Professor of Political Science at Ontario Tech University in Oshawa.

Kyle Bailey is a PhD Candidate at York University in Toronto.

Armando Boito is Professor at the State University of Campinas in Brazil.

Patrick Bond is Professor of Sociology at the University of Johannesburg.

William K. Carroll is Professor of Sociology at the University of Victoria in Victoria, Canada.

Chen Peier is a PhD student in the Department of Cultural Studies at Lingnan University, Hong Kong.

Charmaine Chua is Assistant Professor of Global Studies at the University of California, Santa Barbara.

Spencer Cox has a PhD in Geography, Environment and Society from the University of Minnesota and organizes with Amazonians United.

Madeleine Davis is a Reader at the School of Politics and International Relations, Queen Mary University of London.

Stephen Diamond is Associate Professor of Law at the Santa Clara University School of Law in Santa Clara, California.

Nicholas Graham teaches in the Department of Sociology at the University of Victoria in Victoria, Canada.

Adam Hanieh is Professor of Development Studies at the School of Oriental and African Studies, University of London.

Rafael Khachaturian is a Lecturer in Critical Writing at the University of Pennsylvania, and Associate Faculty at the Brooklyn Institute for Social Research.

Minqi Li is Professor of Economics at the University of Utah.

Stephen Maher is a Visiting Professor at the Institute of Political Economy, Carleton University in Ottawa.

Leo Panitch was Professor Emeritus of Politics at York University in Toronto.

Pun Ngai is Professor of Cultural Studies at Lingnan University, Hong Kong.

Richard Saunders is Associate Professor of Politics at York University in Toronto.

Panagiotis Sotiris teaches at Hellenic Open University in Patras, Greece.

Rafeef Ziadah is Lecturer in Politics and Public Policy at King's College London.

PREFACE

It has been almost four decades since Leo Panitch's name did not appear on the cover of the *Socialist Register*. His tenure of editorial leadership surpassed even that of Ralph Miliband, Leo's mentor, comrade, and founding editor of the *Register*. While Leo's death in December 2020 was acknowledged in the preface of last year's volume, he remained listed as editor, in recognition of his role in conceiving and commissioning the set of essays that became *New Polarizations, Old Contradictions: The Crisis of Centrism*. We gave ourselves the remit to return in this year's volume to an appreciation of Leo's contributions – both to the *Register* and to socialist thought more generally – while continuing to take up the themes that Leo and Greg Albo had mapped out earlier, in meetings with the wider editorial grouping. Both commitments are reflected in the contents of this volume, our 59th annual, as we first take stock of 'capital and politics' at this enormously complex moment in global capitalism, and then reflect on Leo's writing and political engagements in the context of the socialist challenge today, in a special section which includes one of the final interviews he gave on his life, the *Register*, and socialist theory.

The title of this year's volume, *Capital and Politics*, is borrowed, in homage, from the title of one of Leo's more recent essays. It also captures the dual track we set out for ourselves: to dissect capitalist organization and power in this fraught moment defined by the Great Financial Crisis, the global pandemic, and war; and to reconsider Leo's own assessment of the making of global capitalism and its consequences for state power and socialist strategy.

In Leo's review essay with the same title, he surveyed major social democratic accounts of the explosion of social inequality and the crisis of democratic capitalism, arguing there was much to support the 'neo-Marxist concern to show how and why, despite quite different historical and institutional legacies, all states in capitalist societies have come to act in ways that promote capital accumulation and the reproduction of class inequality' ('Capital and Politics', *Perspectives on Politics*, December 2015). Coming to his critique of Thomas Piketty's *Capital in the Twenty-First Century*, with its focus on the 'decile struggle' over income inequalities as opposed to 'class struggle', Leo noted with consternation that 'what is especially remarkable is that corporations, the central institutional forms of capitalist investment, production and distribution, are mentioned only in passing, and then mainly to highlight the exorbitant incomes that the "super-managers" of these corporations came to pay themselves by the twenty-first century … That multinational corporations should earn only one entry in the index of a book on capitalism in the twenty-first century is strange indeed.' Looking for a way forward for socialist analysis and politics, beyond the unimaginative reformism of Piketty, and the abject pessimism of social democratic thinkers like Wolfgang Streeck and Colin Crouch who lament the bleak prospects of the 'post-democracy' impasse, Leo returned to Miliband and Nicos Poulantzas for inspiration. Finding common ground in the frequently juxtaposed thinkers, Leo argued that both envisioned a 'central task' for socialists: to investigate 'how common commitments among various state and business actors to the reproduction of capitalist social relations came to be forged – with all the limits this necessarily imposed on reducing, let alone ending, class inequality'. This required combining a socialist politics with 'a political science that would seek to develop and contribute its knowledge of institution building to aid in the process of developing popular capacities to enter and transform the state so that democracy can in fact prevail against capitalism'. This is, in good part, the task we set for ourselves in assembling this volume.

Socialist analysis has always placed emphasis on a careful accounting of the organizational means by which capitalists accumulate assets and wealth to understand the parameters of power in capitalist society. The arc of crisis, from the financial implosion of 2008-10 to the Covid pandemic from 2020 on, has demonstrated the necessity of examining the concrete, material ways capital is financing and organizing the modern corporation, from its place-specific labour processes in factories and warehouses to the global logistics networks that manage global supply chains. This requires continual evaluation of the uneven processes of accumulation, of endless differentiation followed by replication of processes and products, in specific sectors and states, the ever-shifting financial contours of formal ownership and real possession and control of firms and productive assets, and the constant searching out by individual corporations, business associations, and the political parties of distinctive forms of social legitimation. Our objective is not to marvel at the latest examples of capitalist ingenuity or to seek out 'community stakes' or 'partnerships' in modern firms. It is to insist on seeing class as a social process, continually made and remade through struggle and the competitive imperatives of capitalist society. Such assessments are about building the capacity of working classes to collectively organize and strategize about overturning the inequalities inherent in capitalist class relations and confronting the limits imposed by the concentrated power of capital on democratic governance over the state and workplaces.

From the outset, the *Register* has insistently returned to the themes of capitalist organization and power in its pages, at times to map the leading sectors of accumulation that are restructuring production, the world market, and the state, and at others to debunk reformist claims that ownership structures and labour processes were evolving into a 'responsible capitalism' that were making socialist politics an unnecessary distraction. It was in the *Register* in the 1960s that Ernest Mandel published his first thoughts on 'neo-capitalism', which would later culminate in his renowned text on 'late capitalism', with its retrieval of Marxist political economy's laws of accumulation to refute postwar Keynesianism's view that corporations and the state provided new structures of economic stability; and Ralph Miliband presented his classic critique of John Kenneth Galbraith's contention that control over the modern corporations was being passed from capitalist shareholders and top executives to a technostructure of managers and engineers. Similarly, the *Register* took on the claims of an emergent participatory post-Fordism, and adjacent social democratic assertions of a 'progressive competitiveness' strategy of corporations deploying new technologies, as oppositional to neoliberalism and even tilling the soil of socialism, as many in progressive circles began proposing in the 1990s. These themes became preoccupations of the *Register* in numerous essays over the years examining the new organizational forms of capitalist firms and global value chains. The 2014 volume *Registering Class* and the recent *Beyond Digital Capitalism* of 2021 expanded the focus to include examinations of new digital platforms for managing labour and production, and the adjoining concentration of power in finance and the supporting departments of industry inside the state.

In our invitation to contributors this year, we set out the assignment as follows: 'In surveying capitalist power and the functioning of contemporary capitalism at the end of the first quarter of the twenty-first century, fifteen years after the Great Financial Crisis and on the heels the global pandemic of 2020-22, we want to address the restructuring of corporate organizational forms, alliances and power, and the new relations between the capitalist classes and state power. We envision this volume covering such topics as the new forms of "asset-manager capitalism"; the new stakeholder ideologies focusing on corporate social responsibility and the environmental, social and governance

(ESG) agenda; capital mobility and the questions of logistics, supply chains and re-shoring …' Capitalist organizations, in firms and networks, always take particular institutional forms, across time and space, and in relationship to states. As such, social struggles against capitalist power continually emerge in many forms and there is a need for 'a critical assessment of anti-corporate campaigns, strategies for nationalization/re-municipalization, new methods of organizing and struggles against corporations in the gig economy, and struggles for industrial conversion with respect to climate change …'. We hoped our contributors would draw out linkages to classical socialist themes, including working-class organization and socialist strategy, that would also find parallels in the essays we were collating in memory of Leo.

Understanding corporate structures, including the relationship between industrial capital and the financial system, as well as the forms of capitalist internationalization they organize, is essential for grounding socialist strategy. Corporate organization represents the historical articulation of the capitalist class at a given point in time. It is here where we must look to examine the 'practical form' of the accumulation process, and to discover the emerging contradictions and crises that are the generative force of historical change. This intuition has led scholars to argue for the importance of the logistics sector in enabling the global circulation of commodities in global supply chains and the mammoth warehouses of Amazon. Rafeef Ziadah's essay on the 'Logistical Landscapes' of maritime transport, and Charmaine Chua and Spencer Cox's account of 'Battling the Behemoth' of Amazon, provide us with remarkable insights into these key forces in global accumulation, but also the union organizing and class struggles that are critical to making a new working-class movement. China is pivotal to both global logistics and Amazon, and Minqi Li's essay on labour struggles in 'China's Regime of Accumulation' provides a rich perspective from which to examine corporate structure and workplace struggles at this juncture.

Looking at the practical form of accumulation in specific firms is the basis on which we can hope to answer fundamental questions of whether the 'neoliberal' phase of capitalism, and patterns of international integration that underpinned US-led globalization, are now coming to an end, or to assess intensifying international rivalries and geopolitical conflicts. It allows us to see that although capitalism may be in the throes of a serious legitimacy crisis, it is by no means 'on its last legs', and the shifting balances of power in the state system cannot be equated with a US empire in terminal decline. Moreover, an analysis of contemporary corporate structures helps to situate fossil capital, a central pivot of the world market, within the economic structure of accumulation, and thus the political formation of capitalist class power.

To these ends, Adam Hanieh's essay on 'World Oil' and its shifting patterns of ownership and control, and Patrick Bond's essay on 'Multilateralism at a Crossroads', provide a global scan of the fissures in the inter-state system at this moment through a reading of key sectors of accumulation and critical axes of confrontation.

Particular capitalist interests emerge from the imperatives of reproducing corporate forms, and their place within the structures of accumulation. Clarifying these dynamics points to the implausibility of a politics of 'class compromise' around matters ranging from welfare state programs to the existential climate crisis – a central theme of Nicolas Graham and William Carroll's 'Climate Breakdown' essay on fossil capitalism. That competitiveness remains so central to the contemporary form of finance capital, for instance, reveals how wrongheaded are hopes that the giant asset management companies, which today have amassed unprecedented ownership power, will, by virtue of their role as 'universal owners', undertake to decarbonize the economy or break with neoliberalism. It also reveals the extent to which talk of a turn to 'stakeholder capitalism', or the growth of 'sustainable' investment vehicles which place a greater emphasis on 'environmental, social, and governance' (ESG) factors, are merely the latest bottles for very old wine. Indeed, Stephen Diamond's essay probes 'The "Corporate Governance" Myth' that has dominated debates about ownership and control and insists that the imperatives of capital accumulation and profits remain central to the analysis of capitalist firms. This theme is further underscored by Kyle Bailey's look at the case of Unilever and 'The Illusions of "Stakeholder Capitalism"'. In a detailed and spirited look at 'Transnational Capital and Regulating African Extractives', Richard Saunders comes to similar conclusions on the failures of international regulatory processes to protect workers, communities, the surrounding ecology and the need for new struggles to meaningfully regulate the global mining industry.

In our assessments of whether the climate crisis, for example, can be resolved *within* capitalism, or whether we are, indeed, facing a stark choice between 'socialism or barbarism', it is crucial to look at corporate power and its relationship to the state. The limits of reforms in the face of globalized structures of corporate power, the disciplines of competition, and – perhaps above all – the weakness of the working class and the left, highlights not only that the socialist project remains relevant, but is in fact more vital than ever for securing an alternate democratic and equal future. Pun Ngai and Chen Peier's contribution on 'Infrastructural Capitalism' in China with respect to high-speed rail and class conflict, and Armando Boito's essay on 'Political Divisions and Neo-Fascism in Brazil', provide two studies where globalized structures of corporate power are expanding and internationalizing, working classes are attempting to regroup, and where the outcomes of these class conflicts are of global significance for any alternative to capitalism.

Leo Panitch often argued vehemently that capitalism was not likely to collapse 'on its own' as the inevitable end-stage of financialization. On the contrary, capitalism remains dynamic and competitive, persistent crisis tendencies and disturbing social and ecological polarizations notwithstanding. The essays in our forum on 'Leo Panitch and the Socialist Challenge', pay tribute to Leo but also enter current debates with original – and indeed important – contributions to the challenges facing the left. The outstanding essay by Stephen Maher and Scott Aquanno, 'Capitalist Restructuring, State Transformation', bridges the essays addressing 'capital and politics' and those taking up ideas running across Leo's writing. Maher and Aquanno move from Leo's discussion (with Sam Gindin) in *The Making of Global Capitalism* to look at the new forms of financial capital that have arisen over the last decades, notably asset management firms, to look at corporate organization and power in the current moment. Panagiotis Sotoris offers a critical engagement with Leo on the question of the state and the left in power in his 'Mass Parties, Dual Power, and Questions of Strategy'. And Madeleine Davis offers a remarkable historical perspective in her essay on 'British Labourism and the Prospects for a "Labour New Left"', spanning the early studies of 'parliamentary socialism' by Ralph Miliband to the most recent contributions of Leo and Colin Leys on the left's 'searching for socialism'. If there is a theme across these engagements with Leo's writing, it is that if capitalism is going to come to an end, let alone be replaced by socialism, its end must arrive through the active agency of the working classes. In the absence of this struggle, it is the far right which stands to gain most, at least in the short term, from a delegitimated global capitalism. Leo often expressed this concern in his writing, his speeches, and the volumes of the *Register* he edited. It is fitting, then, that we close with one of the final interviews Leo gave with Rafael Khachaturian, titled 'Against Pessimism', where he discusses capital and politics, the state and power, and the working class and socialism.

The agenda we set out for this volume, of exploring capital and power and the socialist challenge today, has gained additional salience and even urgency. The waning of the Covid pandemic is matched by an easing of fiscal and monetary stimulus, on the one hand, and the horrifying war in Ukraine, which is entangling the world's leading imperialist powers, and giving a fresh mandate to both NATO and its antagonists to instigate a new arms race of frightening destructive power. Another round of fiscal austerity attacking workers' wages and social provisioning to contain government debt and make room for increased military spending now seems all but inevitable in the coming period. As much as we might wish differently, the themes of this annual volume will have to be resumed in new ways in the future, but hopefully in the context of a resurgent left able to exercise its own agenda of a radical democratization and socialization of production.

This is a difficult period of transition for the *Register*. In preparing this volume we have leaned heavily on the advice and solidarity of the Contributing Editors, notably, Sam Gindin, Michalis Spourdalakis, Sebnem Oguz, Ursula Huws, Hilary Wainwright, Barbara Harriss-White, and Lin Chun. The political judgement and editorial skills of Associate Editors Colin Leys, Stephen Maher, and Alan Zuege have been an invaluable resource. Their help in constructing and executing the volume from the scattered ideas Leo had passed on was crucial at every stage. We are also immensely grateful to our sympathetic and patient publishers at Merlin Press, Adrian Howe and Tony Zurbrugg, and to Louis Mackay, who has once again demonstrated his design skills and wonderful imagination in crafting this year's cover design.

Finally, it is necessary to acknowledge the deaths of two of our longstanding Contributing Editors, George Comninel and Aijaz Ahmad. George was a colleague of both Leo and Greg at York University since the 1990s and an active participant in discussions of the plans of the *Register* as well as at the numerous workshops and talks organized at York. Aijaz was also a colleague at York during an extended stint as a Visiting Professor, and an irreplaceable essayist over many years, writing in the *Register* on imperialism in our time, Islam and the West, India and the extreme right, post-colonial theory, and the national question. It is hard to overestimate the influence his essays had on our editorial thinking and on socialist politics and strategy across the globe. George and Aijaz's commitment to socialist education and politics, and day-to-day movement-building, was never wavering and an inspiration to countless intellectuals and activists.

GA, NA, AS-F
September 2022

WORLD OIL: CONTEMPORARY TRANSFORMATIONS IN OWNERSHIP AND CONTROL

ADAM HANIEH

To many observers, Russia's invasion of Ukraine in February 2022 has brought into sharp relief a central characteristic of world oil today: the rise of national oil companies (NOCs), on one hand, and the relative decline of privately-owned, international oil companies (IOCs) on the other. For most of the twentieth century, corporate power in oil had been defined by the almost complete dominance of the IOCs, a handful of vertically-integrated firms located in North America and Europe, who collectively controlled each stage in the production, refining, and marketing of the world's most important commodity (including the ability to set its price). Over the last two decades, however, this dominance has sharply eroded, with NOCs run by governments in Saudi Arabia, Russia, China, and elsewhere now surpassing IOCs in their levels of oil production, refinery outputs, market capitalization, and export quantities. The significance of this shift is said to go far beyond simple questions of energy supply – in much of the contemporary writing on oil and politics, the rise of the NOCs has been linked to the consolidation of authoritarianism, the spread of corruption, and increased geopolitical instability.[1] The war in Ukraine has highlighted the importance of these debates, most directly through the heavy reliance of Europe on energy supplied by Russian NOCs.

At a purely descriptive level, there can be little doubt that this IOC/NOC rift captures much of what has changed in world oil over recent decades. Nonetheless, academic and industry discussion around this shift is often frustratingly superficial, tending to uncritically assume a fundamental distinction between private and state (capitalist) ownership, and implicitly linking 'Western democracies' with a 'free market' in oil. As one astute observer notes, an overemphasis on whether – and to what degree – NOCs pose a threat to private companies and the established market-order has skewed writing on oil away from 'systematic research into the configuration of social power at the commanding heights of the petroleum sector'.[2] A deeper mapping of this 'social power' – including its regional specificities and extensive cross-border linkages – requires a broader analysis of oil's place within capitalism, and its connection to the changing forms of accumulation across the world market. Without this, we lack an understanding of the fundamental drivers of the oil industry today – a gap with serious political implications, not least in terms of organizing against the catastrophic threat of anthropogenic climate change.

Departing from these points, this essay makes two key methodological claims. The first of these is that an understanding of world oil needs to begin from the recognition that crude oil is a commodity with little practical use prior to its transformation into various kinds of liquid fuels or raw materials (such as petrochemicals and plastics). It is the ability to produce these diverse forms of 'circulating constant capital' that has made crude oil so essential to capitalism since the mid-twentieth century. The necessity of this transformation into circulating constant capital means that crude oil must move through its own commodity circuit before it enters the wider valorization of industrial capital – it needs to be extracted, transported from oil fields to refineries, processed, and then marketed to the final customer. For this reason, the oil industry incorporates much more than simply the upstream extraction of crude oil; downstream segments of the industry (refining, petrochemicals, transportation, storage, etc.) are no less consequential to patterns of control within world oil. Too much work on oil – typified in those 'geopolitical' analyses that fixate on inter-state competition for allegedly scarce crude resources – ignores the significance of these downstream activities (especially refining).

Given the importance of crude oil's transformation and subsequent circulation, the second key claim of this essay is that corporate forms of control in world oil need to be understood through the changing spatial configuration of the global oil circuit. A key element to this is the emergence of China as a core zone of global value production over the past two decades, which has dramatically altered how forms of circulating constant capital derived from oil flow through the world market. China's rise – linked to a broader regional reconfiguration of East Asian capitalism – has driven growing interdependencies between East Asia and the oil-rich countries of the Middle East. At the same time, two other major zones of global oil consumption have consolidated: a regionally integrated North American bloc, mostly centred around the US and Canada, and the European Union (EU), dependent upon energy flows from Russia and Central Asia. The interdependencies that have emerged around this particular spatialization of world oil – including both upstream crude production and downstream refining – are essential to understanding the apparent rise of NOCs and the changing corporate structures of the leading IOCs.

FROM THE SEVEN SISTERS TO OPEC

Oil would not definitively displace coal as the world's primary fossil fuel until the 1950s, but the early decades of the twentieth century were crucial to shaping the industry's later structure.[3] Stretching across the roughly seventy-year period between 1870 and the eve of the Second World War, a handful of large oil companies emerged in the US and Western Europe. More than in any other comparable industry, these firms were marked by an extreme degree of vertical integration, through which crude oil was transferred internally within the same company to be refined and sold. Vertical integration enabled the largest firms to exert pressure on competitors and shift profit-making activities down the value chain depending on price fluctuations and market demand.[4] Rapidly expanding beyond their domestic markets, these vertically integrated firms would come to control a densely interlocked network of oil fields and circulatory infrastructure stretching across the globe. By the mid-twentieth century, just seven of these firms would dominate virtually all the world's production and trade in oil.[5] Dubbed the 'Seven Sisters' by industry rivals in the 1950s, the leading IOCs that remain at the centre of global debates around energy use and the climate transition – ExxonMobil, Chevron, BP, Royal Dutch Shell and so forth – are today the direct descendants of these firms.[6]

While these Western firms would remain the controlling force in world oil until well into the 1970s, they were not themselves equally balanced. Despite the considerable international reach of the main European IOCs (especially Royal Dutch Shell and BP), the world oil industry became increasingly American-centred throughout the first half of the twentieth century. One reason for this was the presence of large oil reserves inside the US itself, which made the US the core centre of crude production and consumption.[7] The reality of US oil dominance also reflected the wider transformation in global economic and political power away from Western Europe towards an American capitalism increasingly fuelled by crude oil and its derivatives. Oil's emergence as the principal source of circulating constant capital was crucial in inaugurating and pushing forward this transition to a US-centred global capitalism – a shift that was decisively concluded in the aftermath of World War II.

The post-war era saw US oil companies finally break into the main oil-rich areas of the Middle East – ending the previous stranglehold of European firms – and further entrenched the dominance of the US within world oil. Nonetheless, burgeoning anti-colonial and radical nationalist movements in the main oil-producing states in the Middle East and Latin America began to upset the control of Western oil firms over oil production, refining, pipelines, and pricing.[8] These movements would eventually culminate in the formation of the Organization of Petroleum Exporting Countries (OPEC) in 1960, initially made up of Saudi Arabia, Venezuela, Iraq, Iran, and Kuwait. At that time, the five countries constituting OPEC produced around 37 per cent of world crude and a majority of all oil outside of the US. Over the following decade, the organization's membership would continue to expand. Today, most major oil producers – excepting the US, Russia, and Canada – are members.

With the establishment of OPEC, the longstanding structures of world oil would begin to irrevocably change. From the 1960s onwards, governments across the Middle East and Latin America gradually nationalized oil resources and state-owned oil companies took over much of the exploration and production of crude outside of the US. The largest IOCs retained their dominance in downstream activities but would increasingly have to contend with powerful non-Western NOCs in the upstream sectors across the main oil-producing states. Crucially, IOCs gradually lost their ability to set the *price* of oil, which increased significantly in 1973-74 and again in 1978-1980. Rising oil prices, coupled with the changes in the structure of ownership in the oil industry, massively increased the financial surpluses flowing to oil producing states (especially in the Middle East Gulf).[9] By the end of the 1970s, IOCs would own less than a third of the crude oil located outside of the United States.

Facing significant restrictions on their ability to earn profits on upstream crude oil, IOCs initially sought to respond to these changes by shifting their activities towards downstream refining, marketing, and petrochemical production. Nonetheless, these structural measures were unable to prevent growing financial pressures on these firms, further compounded by increasing competition in the oil market and a lengthy period of low oil prices that extended through most of the 1980s and 1990s. Reflecting these pressures, a major wave of corporate consolidation took place among Western oil firms in the late 1990s. The most important example of this was the merger of the two US oil giants, Exxon and Mobil, in 1999 – creating ExxonMobil, the biggest private company in the world.[10] At the time, this was the largest industrial merger in history, surpassing an earlier oil sector deal – BP's acquisition of the American firm, Amoco, in 1998 – which had previously held that record. Other significant corporate consolidation at this time included Chevron's takeover of Texaco in 2001, and the merger of Conoco Inc. and Phillips Petroleum Company to create ConocoPhillips in 2002. Outside of the US, the large French oil firm, Total, merged with Petrofina in 1999 and then later took over Elf Aquitaine to create Total S.A (now known as TotalEnergie). The net result of these mergers was a reconfiguration of the Western oil industry around a handful of so-called 'supermajors' that remain the dominant IOCs today: ExxonMobil (US), BP (British), Royal Dutch Shell (British/Dutch), Chevron (US), Eni (Italy), TotalEnergies (France), and ConocoPhillips (US).

This wave of industrial consolidation was accompanied by a set of other important changes to how Western oil companies functioned. As the largest privately-owned firms in the world, the oil supermajors were deeply implicated in the wider turn to financialized capitalism that took place through the 1980s and 1990s, particularly in US financial markets. Of particular note was their increasing emphasis on share buybacks and the prioritization of dividend payments to shareholders – a feature of Western oil firms that has continued through to the current day.[11] The financialization of oil firms was accompanied by an unprecedented wave of job-shedding – indeed, 60 per cent of the global workforce of the international majors were made redundant between 1980 and 1997 (a fact often overlooked in discussion of the oil industry in this period).[12] With reduced access to conventional onshore oil fields (now controlled by the largest non-Western NOCs), Western oil majors moved towards environmentally-risky, technologically-intensive oil production in areas where oil was difficult to extract (e.g. deepwater drilling) and continued to emphasize downstream activities, especially the production of petrochemicals. Several of the leading Western supermajors also sought to project themselves as 'energy companies' and even began distancing themselves (misleadingly) from oil in their corporate branding.[13]

IOCs AND THE SHALE REVOLUTION

Throughout the 1990s, the refining of oil and the final consumption of oil products continued to be weighted towards North America and Western Europe, where the largest Western IOCs were overwhelmingly dominant. Beginning in the early 2000s, however, a major shift occurred in the geography of oil consumption alongside China's integration into the world market. As a core site of world manufacturing, China's seemingly insatiable demand for energy drove a 30 per cent global increase in oil consumption between 2000 and 2019. In 2000, China consumed around 6 per cent of the world's oil; by 2019, this figure had risen to 14 per cent (second only to the US with 21 per cent of oil consumption). China's increased consumption of oil was part of a wider trend across Asia, with the region's consumption of oil reaching more than one-third of the world's total in 2019, greater than Europe, Russia, Central Asia, Africa, and Central and South America combined.[14]

Increased oil demand from China and wider Asia helped drive a prolonged boom in oil prices from the early 2000s onwards.[15] From an average monthly price of around $27/barrel in 2000, global oil prices eventually peaked at just over $147/barrel by mid-2008. A short downturn followed the global economic crash of 2008, but oil prices resumed their upward trend from January 2009, reaching more than $110 in April 2011. Despite considerable global economic uncertainty because of the eurozone sovereign debt crisis through 2012, the oil price continued to fluctuate around $100 until mid-2014. This extended period of rising prices was a boon for most oil exporters (especially in the Middle East), but it also incentivized the production of so-called 'non-conventional' oil and gas supplies – reserves that are difficult and significantly more expensive to extract than conventional fossil fuels. Of particular importance here was US shale, crude oil that is held in shale or sandstone of low permeability and which is typically extracted through fracturing the rock by pressurized liquid (hence the term 'fracking'). Between 2007 and 2014, the production of US shale oil grew more than ten-fold, propelling the United States into the top rank of oil producers globally.[16] Remarkably, the US became a net exporter of oil in early 2011, overtaking Saudi Arabia to become the world's largest producer in 2014[17] – a position it has maintained until this day, and a far cry from the panicked predictions of 'energy dependence' that had marked US energy policy debates in the early years of the new millennium. Over the same period, Canadian oil production also grew massively, increasing by 70 per cent between 2009 and 2019 as a result of tar sands extraction and fracking.[18] Since 2015, Canada has ranked as the fourth largest producer of oil in the world.

This increase in North American oil production has been immensely profitable for the largest Western IOCs who remain the dominant players in the US and Canadian markets. Indeed, around one-third of all the oil produced globally by IOCs comes from North America, more than any other region of the world.[19] For some of the leading IOCs such as ExxonMobil, Chevron, and BP, the share of North American oil in their total global production is even higher (around 40 per cent).[20] By contrast, most oil produced by NOCs comes from the Middle East (51 per cent) and Russia/Central Asia (22 per cent). The centrality of North America to the crude base of the largest IOCs has been a major reason behind the expansion in some of the most ecologically and socially destructive types of oil extraction over the last decade, notably shale, tar sands, and deepwater drilling. IOCs now spend a majority of their upstream investment on these forms of oil extraction, whereas around 90 per cent of NOC upstream investment is spent on conventional onshore fields.[21]

Alongside this close link with North American oil production, other changes have taken place in the corporate behaviours of the largest IOCs. Most important is the continuing deep connection between US financial markets and the oil industry. Virtually all leading oil firms in the US are publicly-listed, and in keeping with the trends towards financialization that began in the 1990s, place a strong emphasis on short-term shareholder returns and stock market valuation rather than spending on long-term physical production (let alone investment in a low-carbon transition).[22] This is reflected in the high proportion of oil company cash flow that goes towards share buybacks and dividend pay-outs; indeed, between 2015 and 2019, around 40 per cent of IOC cash flow was returned to investors in these ways.[23] The US oil industry now spends more on share buybacks than any other business sector, a trend that has accelerated sharply following the rapid rise in oil prices through early 2022.[24]

These various indicators of financialization also point towards the significant weight of finance capital within the ownership structures and directorship positions of the leading IOCs.[25] The three biggest US oil companies by market capitalisation – ExxonMobil, Chevron, and ConocoPhillips – have between 60 to 80 per cent of their share-ownership controlled by various forms of finance capital (such as investment banks, asset management firms, private equity funds and so forth).[26] Prominent here is the role of the world's 'Big Three' asset management firms – Vanguard, Blackrock, and State Street – which occupy the top three shareholder positions for around one-third of the largest publicly-listed oil and gas firms in the US (including ExxonMobil, Chevron, and ConocoPhilips).[27] The strong presence of these and other financial conglomerates indicates that when we consider *how and where* accumulation takes place in the Western oil industry, it is not enough to focus simply on the outward form of the large IOCs. While firms such as ExxonMobil, BP, and Chevron appear to be driving much of the physical extraction of crude oil in North America, the dynamics of oil production are ultimately tied to the accumulation imperatives of large finance capital groups that act simultaneously in both financial markets and the day-to-day 'real world' of energy production. Through their deep involvement in the ownership of IOCs and the wider North American and European oil industry, this class of finance capital needs to be viewed as a leading beneficiary of the carbon economy.

INTER-REGIONAL FLOWS AND WORLD REFINING

The close connection between the accumulation of the leading IOCs and North American crude production needs to be situated within the wider dynamics of the global oil market. To this end, Tables 1 and 2 provide a snapshot of cross-border flows of both crude oil and refined oil products in 2019, the year preceding the Covid-19 pandemic. The data illustrate the highly regionalized character of North American oil production: most oil exports (crude and refined products) from the US, Canada, and Mexico tend to circulate as cross-border flows within the North American bloc itself. In the case of crude oil, Canadian exports to the US account for around half of all the North American exports shown in the table (the other half is mostly made up of Mexican exports to the US, and US exports to Europe, Other Asia, and Canada).[28] Canadian crude exports feed into the US refining industry (along with US domestic crude) and the resulting products are exported back to Canada, Mexico, and the wider Americas (Table 2). Canada itself also has a significant refining sector, with almost all exports of refined products going to the US. Only a small proportion of North American refined products end up exported beyond the Americas. These intra-regional flows of oil and refined products within North America are largely superintended by the largest IOCs (both American and European) who profit from both the upstream and downstream components of this trade.

Unlike the predominantly self-contained North American oil circuit, the rest of the world depends much more heavily upon inter-regional imports to satisfy oil demand. For Europe, which consumes around one-fifth of the world's crude oil imports, the Russia/Central Asia region supplied around 40 per cent of crude oil imports and half of imported refined products in 2019.[29] The MENA region is also an important source of European crude, although in much lower quantities than Russia/Central Asia. As the destination for roughly half of all Russia's oil exports (up until the war in the Ukraine), Europe is thus crucial to the Russian oil market. Most of these Russian exports (around 70-85 per cent) enter the EU by maritime routes, while the remainder is transported via Belarus and Ukraine through the world's longest oil pipeline, the Druzbha pipeline.[30] The Russian oil industry is dominated by a handful of NOCs (Gazprom, Rosneft, Transneft, etc.) whose origins lie in the dismantlement of the Soviet-era property relations and their reconstruction around state bureaucrats and a small layer of wealthy oil capitalists.[31] Leading IOCs – especially BP, Shell, and ExxonMobil – have also had longstanding relationships with Russian NOCs and the Russian oil industry, although most of these have been terminated

Table 1 Crude Oil Inter-Regional Trade Flows, 2019
(million tonnes)

To \ From	North America	Central and South America	Europe	Middle East and North Africa	Africa	India	China	Other Asia
North America	243.9	8.5	60	2.6	0.2	20	9	48.3
Central and South America	40.2	neg	12.6	0.4	0.3	18.7	67.2	6.7
Russia and Central Asia	9.4	0.5	221.1	10.5	0.3	6.5	81.9	27.7
Middle East and North Africa	53.5	6.8	163.8	23.5	15	138.4	236	370.4
West Africa	15.2	4.7	65.1	1.7	10	30.2	77.8	12.7
Total	362.2	20.5	522.6	38.7	25.8	213.8	471.9	465.8

Adapted by author from BP, *Statistical Review of World Energy – 69th Edition 2020*, p. 31, available at: www.bp.com. Totals are only of the regions included in the table, not the entire world.

Table 2 Refined Products Inter-Regional Trade Flows, 2019 (million tonnes)

To From	North America	Central and South America	Europe	Middle East and North Africa	Africa	India	China	Other Asia
North America	114	85.1	25.4	2.5	8.7	10.3	3.8	39.9
Central and South America	19.6	n.a	3.8	0.6	2.6	0.4	1.3	4.4
Europe	30.7	9.6	n.a	13.6	43.9	0.6	2.4	21.9
Russia and Central Asia	19.6	2.9	114.3	3.4	5.4	1	3.5	21.9
Middle East and North Africa	9.1	3.2	43.4	29.4	30.5	27	21.1	58.6
China	2.1	3.7	2.5	1.6	2.8	0.8	–	45.9
Other Asia	11.3	2.6	6.7	3.6	9.1	4.3	42.3	109.8
Total	206.4	107.1	196.1	54.7	103	44.4	74.4	302.4

Source: See Table 1.

following Russia's invasion of Ukraine in 2022.

By far the most significant driver of the world oil trade today, however, is demand from China and the wider Asia region. By 2019, around 45 per cent of all the world's oil exports were flowing to Asia – with more than half of these destined for China alone.[32] Between 2000 and 2019, the increase in China's oil imports was equivalent to a 'second US' entering the world market. This large growth in demand has reconfigured the long-established patterns of world oil exports. Rather than flowing predominantly to Europe or the US, Middle East crude oil exports have turned decisively eastwards, and now meet just under half of China's oil import demand (up from 34.5 per cent in 2001).[33] China's booming consumption of oil is part of a wider increase in Asian energy imports that have also largely been met by the Middle East – by 2019, nearly 70 per cent of all the Middle East's crude oil exports (mostly from the Gulf states) were going to Asia. As Table 2 indicates, the Middle East has also become the leading external source of exported refined products to both China and Asia, although the bulk of Asia's demand for refined imports is met through pan-regional trade flows (see below for further discussion).

This huge increase in Chinese/Asian crude imports has been closely connected to a corresponding shift in world refining away from North America and Europe. As Table 3 shows, in the early 1990s, nearly two-thirds of the world's refining capacity was located in North America, Russia/Central Asia, and Europe. Over the 1990s and 2000s, however, this structure of the refining industry changed fundamentally. On one side, the collapse of the Soviet Union led to a precipitous fall in Russian refining capacity, which essentially halved between 1992 and 2005. At the same time, there was a marked increase in Asian refining activity associated with the rise of China. Indeed, Asian refining capacity tripled between 1992 and 2020, and the absolute number of refineries grew more than 2.5 times. By 2020, Asia's share of world refining capacity stood at 37 per cent of the world's total, confirming the region's centrality to the global manufacture of refined oil products.

Table 3 also indicates that the only other region of the world that has seen a growth in its share of world refining capacity is the Middle East, where absolute capacity more than doubled between 1992 and 2020, and which now holds a 10 per cent share of the world's total. As with exports of crude oil, this growth in Middle East refining has been almost entirely driven by the rise of China and the wider Asia region. A key illustration of this is the export of ethylene, a basic petrochemical often described as 'the world's most important chemical', which forms an essential input for the manufacture of packaging, construction materials, and automobile parts. Led by Saudi Arabia, the Middle East has become the world's second largest producer of ethylene over the last decade (just behind North America).[34] This vital chemical is manufactured in massive integrated refineries and petrochemical complexes located in Saudi Arabia, the UAE, and elsewhere in the region, and then exported eastwards – indeed, just under half of all China's ethylene imports now come from the Middle East. The outward-oriented character of the Middle East's refinery industry is reflected in the fact that the average capacity per refinery in the region is now the largest in the world, far exceeding any domestic needs.[35] China's emergence as 'workshop of the world' would not have been possible without these massive refinery complexes that guarantee flows of refined petroleum products from the Middle East to Asia.

Table 3: Share of World Refining Capacity (%)

	1992	2020
Asia	18	37
North America	25	21
Europe	19	15
Middle East	7	10
Russia and Central Asia	20	8
Central/South America	8	6
Africa	4	3

Source: ENI, *World Energy Review*, 2021; Oil & Gas Journal, *Worldwide Refinery Survey*, various issues.

The Middle East and Asia account for two-thirds of all oil refineries that have been built over the past five years, and over 80 per cent of those currently under construction.[36] This geographical repivoting of the world refining industry is indicative of the interdependencies that are forming between the two regions: crude oil is either extracted in the Middle East and exported to Asia for refining; or it is extracted and refined in the Middle East, and then exported to Asia. In both cases, the refining process is dominated by large NOCs headquartered in the Middle East, China, and wider Asia. The refined fuels and chemicals produced from Middle East oil by these companies enter as circulating constant capital into Asian production chains. Western IOCs hold a relatively marginal position within the oil commodity circuit that links these two regions.

These regional interdependencies are driving significant changes to corporate power throughout the world refining industry. Much like upstream crude production, there is a pronounced concentration of ownership in the refining industry, with the largest fifteen refining companies controlling around half of all the world's refining capacity (up from a 40 per cent share in 1999). These fifteen firms have remained mostly the same over the last two decades; however, there has been a major shift in their relative ranking (see Table 4). In 1999, three out of the top four refiners were Western IOCs (Royal Dutch Shell, Exxon, and BP Amoco). Today, only ExxonMobil remains within the top four and the first, second, and fourth spots are taken by Chinese and Saudi NOCs (Sinopec, CNPC, Saudi Aramco). More broadly, among the top 15 refining firms, around half of all refining capacity is now held by NOCs, up from 37 per cent in 1999.

Much like the export of crude, the rising power of Sinopec, CNPC, and Saudi Aramco in the refining of oil is largely a reflection of the interdependencies emerging between the Middle East and Asia across the oil commodity circuit. And crucially, as with the earlier historical evolution of the largest Western oil majors, these NOCs are themselves increasingly adopting a vertically integrated structure that spans the entire petroleum value chain. A clear illustration of this is the case of Saudi Aramco, which, following the largest IPO in history in 2019, has now reached a market capitalization of nearly $2.4 trillion – surpassing Apple as the biggest company in the world in May 2022.[37] Saudi Aramco produces more crude oil than any other company in the world, and in 2020 took a major step towards downstream integration when it became the controlling shareholder of the Saudi Basic Industries Corporation (SABIC), the third largest petrochemical firm in the world. As part of this move to integrate its crude production, refining, and petrochemical activities, the firm has also established several trading arms in Asia (mostly located in Singapore) and is the second largest shareholder in Bahri, a Saudi logistics and shipping company that owns and operates the world's biggest fleet of double-hulled Very Large Crude-Oil Carriers (VLCCs). Similar trends of vertical integration are also evident among the other NOCs listed in Table 4.

Nonetheless, we should qualify this apparent shift towards NOCs within the world refining industry. As Table 4 indicates, large privately-owned Western companies still hold half the refining capacity of the top 15 firms in the world, and thus remain major players in the transformation of oil into circulating constant capital. Reflecting the patterns discussed above, however, the refining activities of these Western companies tend to be overwhelmingly concentrated in North America and Europe. In these traditional geographic centres of oil refining, NOCs control less than 10

Table 4: Top 15 Refining Companies in the World, 1999-2020

Firm	Country	1999 Refining capacity (kkbl/day)	Firm	Country	2011 Refining capacity (kkbl/day)	Firm	Country	2020 Refining capacity (kkbl/day)
Royal Dutch Shell	UK/NL	5.2	ExxonMobil	USA	5.78	Sinopec	China	5.7
Exxon	USA	4.5	Royal Dutch Shell	UK/NL	4.51	CNPC	China	4.793
BP Amoco	UK	3.4	Sinopec	China	3.9	ExxonMobil	USA	4.765
PDVSA	Venezuela	3.2	BP	UK	3.33	Aramco	Saudi Arabia	3.559
Sinopec	China	3.1	ConocoPhillips	USA	2.78	Marathon	USA	3.252
Mobil	USA	2.6	Chevron	USA	2.76	Rosneft	Russia	3.179
Saudi Aramco	Saudi Arabia	2.4	PdVSA	Venezuela	2.68	Shell	UK/NL	3.024
CNPC	China	2.2	Valero	USA	2.62	Valero	USA	2.826
Petrobras	Brazil	2.2	CNPC	China	2.62	PDVSA	Venezuela	2.504
Petroleos Mexicanos	Mexico	2	Total	France	2.45	Phillips 66	USA	2.313
Total Fina	France	1.9	Saudi Aramco	Saudi Arabia	2.43	Petrobras	Brazil	2.211
NIORDC	Iran	1.8	Petrobras	Brazil	2	Total	France	2.138
Texaco	USA	1.8	Petroleos Mexicanos	Mexico	1.7	NIORDC	Iran	1.99
Chevron	USA	1.7	NIORDC	Iran	1.45	BP	UK	1.905
Repsol	Spanish	1.4	JX Nippon Oil & Energy Corp	Japan	1.42	ENEOS	Japan	1.837

Sources: Energy Intelligence, *Petroleum Intelligence Weekly*, various issues; McKinsey, *Energy Insights*, various issues.

per cent of refining capacity – in contrast to Asia, the Middle East, South America, and Russia/Central Asia, where NOCs control the largest share. The pattern of refining across the world market is thus sharply bifurcated: divided between North America and Europe on one side (36 per cent of world refining capacity), where IOCs and other privately-owned companies are dominant, and the emerging zones of refining in Asia and the Middle East on the other hand (47 per cent of world capacity), where NOCs control the market.

These patterns confirm the ways in which the IOC/NOC division embodies a deeper spatialization of the world oil market today. On one side, the large Western IOCs tend to be dominant in North American and European markets. Their upstream production is centred upon unconventional, shale, and deepwater extraction (with a heavy emphasis on North America), which feeds their downstream refining activities that are also predominantly located in North America or Europe.[38] The resultant fuels and chemical products are mostly consumed in Western markets or exported to South/Central America and Africa (see Table 2). On the other side, the trajectories of East Asian capitalism depend fundamentally on the steady and ever-increasing flow of circulating constant capital derived from the Middle East, and it is these East-West regional interdependencies that have helped constitute the growing power of NOCs. In this sense, the rise of Middle East and Asia NOCs can be viewed as one expression of the profound spatial restructuring that has taken place within the capitalist world market over the last two decades.

EAST ASIA AND THE MIDDLE EAST

Given the significance of the Middle East and East Asia linkages to the configuration of the contemporary world oil industry, it is useful to look more closely at the cross-border investments in oil emanating from these two regions. Between 2012 and 2021, China made more than US $76 billion in outward investments in oil-related activities.[39] The first phase of these Chinese investments in oil infrastructure (2012-2016) followed the announcement of the Belt and Road Initiative (BRI), and focused mainly on North America, Western Europe, and Russia/Central Asia. Following 2016, however, there was a major reorientation in Chinese overseas oil investment. Between 2017 and 2021, more than 30 per cent of Chinese investments in oil-related activities went to the Middle East region, greater than any other world region and a five-fold increase in the Middle East's relative share compared to 2012-2016 period. This has given Chinese firms a prominent role in oil related industries across the Middle East. In the

UAE, for example, Chinese firms are leading partners of the state-owned oil company, the Abu Dhabi National Oil Company (ADNOC), and hold major stakes in onshore and offshore oil fields. In Iraq, a privately-owned Chinese firm now operates one of the largest oil fields in the world, the 'supergiant' Majnoon oil field. And in Kuwait, a Sinopec subsidiary has become the largest oil drilling contractor, controlling 45 per cent of drilling contracts in the country. The largest deal involving China in the Middle East oil sector was finalized in 2021, with Chinese participation in a multinational joint venture (JV) that owns a 49 per cent equity stake in Aramco Oil Pipelines Co., a company that will have rights to 25 years of tariff payments for oil transported through Aramco's crude pipeline network in Saudi Arabia. These kinds of relationships have developed alongside myriad political and diplomatic initiatives connected with China's BRI in the Middle East region.

Concurrent with China's pivot to the Middle East, the Gulf states have become the leading foreign presence in the Chinese oil sector through numerous JVs with Chinese firms. These projects aim at securing market share for the Gulf's crude exports and include refineries, petrochemical plants, transport infrastructure, and fuel marketing networks. An important example of this is the Sino-Kuwait Integrated Refinery and Petrochemical Complex, a 50:50 JV between Sinopec and Kuwait Petroleum Corporation that is the biggest refinery joint venture in China, incorporating within it the country's largest petrochemical port (completed in May 2020). Both the refinery and port are viewed as an integral component of China's BRI, enabling China to import crude oil from the Gulf to manufacture fuels and other basic chemicals that are then exported to neighbouring Asian countries. Saudi Arabia's significant presence in China is evident through several large JVs between Saudi Aramco and Chinese firms in the refining and petrochemical sector, as well as a network of over 1000 service stations in Fujian province that was the first province-level fuel retail joint venture in the country. These partnerships involve NOCs, such as Sinopec, as well as leading privately-owned refining companies in China (which control around 30 per cent of China's crude refining volumes). Qatar has also been a prominent Gulf investor in China's energy sector, focusing particularly on securing markets for its LNG exports.

This expansion of the Gulf into China is helping extend the activities of the largest Gulf NOCs beyond upstream production into each moment of the oil commodity circuit – in this sense, the deepening vertical-integration of Gulf oil firms is occurring *through* their internationalization into China. Crucially, however, this process needs to be viewed through the lens of the wider pan-Asian regional scale. With the reorientation of East Asian capitalism around Chinese production networks, Gulf NOCs have also taken significant positions in the oil-related sectors of other Asian countries. Indeed, between 2012 and 2021, nearly half of all foreign investments from outside of Asia (by value) into Asian oil-related assets came from the Gulf, including the four largest deals during this period.[40] Through these investments, Gulf firms have sought to expand their production of refined oil products and basic chemicals within Asia itself (utilizing crude feedstocks imported from the Gulf), which are then circulated within Asia by the trading arms of Gulf firms. Key regional targets for this downstream diversification of Gulf oil firms are South Korea, Singapore, Malaysia, and Japan. Across these four countries – which each possess established industrial capacity that is often closely linked to the accumulation of domestic business conglomerates – Gulf firms have fully or partially acquired leading companies as well as undertaken other kinds of partnerships such as JVs.

Unsurprisingly, the chief Gulf firm in this respect has been Saudi Aramco, which now holds considerable weight across key Asian states. In 2015, for example, Saudi Aramco acquired control over the South Korean firm S-Oil, which is the third largest refining company in the country (with about 25 per cent market share) and operates the sixth largest refinery in the world (located in Ulsan, South Korea). This acquisition enabled S-Oil to expand its petrochemical capacity in Korea, and the firm is now a major producer of various refined fuels and basic chemicals that Saudi Aramco's regional trading arm (Aramco Trading Singapore) then exports to other Asian countries. Also in South Korea, Saudi Aramco became the second largest shareholder of Hyundai Oilbank in 2019 following the purchase of 17 per cent of the company's shares. Hyundai Oilbank is the fourth largest refining company in Korea, and is majority owned by the Hyundai industrial conglomerate. In Malaysia, Saudi Aramco is currently building a refinery and petrochemical plant that is projected to be the largest downstream petrochemical plant in Asia following its completion; the project is a 50:50 JV with the Malaysian NOC, Petronas. And in Japan, Saudi Aramco became the second largest shareholder in Idemitsu Kosan in 2019 – the firm is the number two refiner in Japan, controlling roughly one third of the domestic oil products market through six refineries and a network of 6,400 retail service stations.

These patterns confirm the strong interdependencies that are emerging between East Asia (especially China) and the Middle East (especially the Gulf region). In each area, capitalist development is increasingly interlaced through an integrated oil commodity circuit that straddles both regions. This is much more than the simple export of Middle East crude to Asia –

the internationalization of oil capital is occurring in both directions and, crucially, encompasses all moments of the oil commodity circuit: refining, petrochemical production, and the onward circulation of oil products to the consumer. These interdependencies involve the large Gulf and Asian NOCs as well as major privately-owned conglomerates in both regions. In this manner, processes of capital accumulation (and thus class formation) are also increasingly interlinked across regions, and to posit a simple opposition between state ownership and the accumulation of private capital is misleading.[41]

THE FUTURE OF OIL

The Covid-19 pandemic that spread so rapidly across the world from early 2020 onwards delivered a profound shock to oil markets and the broader fossil fuel industry. With demand for energy in freefall during the initial months of the pandemic, world oil markets were simultaneously hit by a March 2020 'Oil Price War' between Russia and Saudi Arabia, which promised to significantly increase global supplies. Global oil prices fell to multi-decade lows, and producers rushed to find storage space on land and sea for their oil rather than sell it at a loss. In mid-April 2020, the price of West Texas Intermediate (WTI) oil turned negative as traders holding contracts for physical delivery were forced to pay others to take oil off their hands due to lack of storage space. At that moment, some commentators speculated that this might all be a bit of good news in the context of the Covid-19 calamity – the pandemic could 'kill the oil industry and help save the climate', as an April 2020 headline in the UK's *Guardian* newspaper exclaimed, with the demise of many smaller oil producers and the weakening of oil majors bringing the world one step closer to a transition away from fossil fuel use.

Any hope of such a rosy scenario quickly unravelled, however. While the oil industry did face a severe crisis through most of 2020, the eventual outcomes were by no means negative for the leading firms. In the US, low oil prices and high debt levels led to a wave of consolidation in the shale industry, with the largest US oil firms (and other financial investors) buying up assets on the cheap. Simultaneously, the Trump administration loosened environmental regulations and provided up to $15.2 billion in direct economic support to the fossil fuel industry.[42] These corporate subsidies were not limited to the US – the EU and individual European governments also provided billions of euros in direct support to major oil and gas companies throughout the worst months of the pandemic. As demand for oil resumed with the relaxing of pandemic restrictions, the price of oil increased sharply, reaching a five-year peak in October 2021. By the end of 2021, oil company profits had returned to their highest levels in nearly a decade.⁴³

With the Russian invasion of Ukraine on 24 February 2022 – which pushed oil prices up to over $100/barrel by May 2022 – the revenues of the leading oil companies have further exploded. But perhaps even more significant than this financial windfall has been the war's impact on the prevailing political discourse, with policy discussions moving away from tackling climate change and limiting fossil fuel production towards a prioritization of 'energy security' and the practicalities of ending EU reliance on Russian energy. Such discussions have raised the possibility of Russia pivoting its energy exports away from Europe to seek a greater market-share in countries across East and South Asia.

Nonetheless, new energy transport infrastructures take time to build and given the heavy dependence of many European states on Russian oil it is hard to envisage an immediate break. Globally, those countries that moved initially to place an embargo on Russian oil – notably the US and the UK – were never major importers to begin with. After months of discussion, the EU agreed in June 2022 to a partial embargo on Russian crude oil and oil products, but these measures are only scheduled to take effect at the end of 2022, and imports through the Druzbha pipeline are exempted.⁴⁴ Another major complicating factor is the presence of Russian NOCs in the European refining industry itself. In Germany, for example, the Russian NOC Rosneft is the second biggest refiner in the country, and responsible for a quarter of all Germany's oil imports.⁴⁵ Likewise, Italy's largest refinery is owned by Lukoil, and Russian firms have a strong presence in the refining sectors of the Netherlands, Romania, and Bulgaria. These Russian-owned refineries are typically set up to process Russian oil, and it takes time and expense to switch them over to processing oil from the Middle East or elsewhere.

Despite these complexities, Russia's energy exports have become a major target of US and European policymakers. Alongside a partial embargo against Russian oil, the EU agreed in June 2022 to ban European companies from providing insurance (or reinsurance) to ships carrying Russian oil (after a six-month phase-in period). Because of the importance of maritime transport to the Russian oil trade, this step has the potential to significantly hinder Russian exports.⁴⁶ In the face of these kinds of sanctions, the volume of Russian oil exports to Europe has dropped. Nonetheless, buyers from China, India, Turkey, and elsewhere have stepped in to purchase Russian oil at a discount, with China overtaking Europe to become the largest importer of Russian oil in June 2022. At the same time, the spike in world oil prices has meant that Russian oil earnings have increased despite a reduction in export volumes, leading the International Energy Agency to note in August

2022 that sanctions against Russia have had 'limited impact'.[47]

In this context, we may well be witnessing the emergence of what some well-placed Western strategists have described as two 'decoupled' energy blocs – China and Russia on one side, and Europe and the US on the other – a development that would embody many of the wider geopolitical schisms now evident across the world market.[48] However, within this structure, the interweaving of the Gulf, Chinese, and East Asian oil circuits will be of fundamental importance. As discussed, these Middle East-East Asia linkages run deep and have taken many years to build; crucially, they extend far beyond the simple export of crude oil from the Gulf. While Russian energy exports to Asia will undoubtedly expand in the short to medium-term, there is little likelihood that Russia will successfully dislodge Gulf NOCs from East Asian markets. At the same time, despite its weakened position, the US remains the pre-eminent power in the Middle East, with American hegemony resting primarily upon its decades-long political, military, and economic relationships with Israel, Saudi Arabia, and the other Gulf states. These dynamics bind the future of world oil to the Middle East's place in global capitalism – and make it ever more important to take the region, and especially the Gulf states, seriously as a site of capitalist accumulation and not simply conflict.

Of course, the crucial underlying issue here is not the patterning of world oil exports but rather the urgency of phasing out oil production altogether. While scientific consensus now states unequivocally that no new oil and gas projects can be brought online, and that carbon emissions must be halved within the next seven years, the major oil companies are embarking on exactly the opposite course of action. A recent investigation found that the twelve largest global oil firms, led by Saudi Aramco, are planning to collectively spend $103 million *each day* for the rest of the decade on *new* oil and gas projects.[49] The leading firms have made final financial commitments for new projects over the next seven years that would ultimately deliver 116bn barrels of oil – equivalent to about two decades worth of US oil production at 2020 levels.[50] In this respect, the current moment is one of extreme danger: amidst the travails of pandemic and war, on one hand, and the logics of profit and 'energy security', on the other, the major oil companies – NOCs and IOCs alike – are driving us squarely towards ecological collapse.

NOTES

1. For a recent example, see Paasha Mahdavi, *Power Grab: Political Survival through Extractive Resource Nationalization*, Cambridge: Cambridge University Press, 2020.
2. Naná de Graaff, 'Oil elite networks in a transforming global oil market', *International Journal of Comparative Sociology*, 53(4), 2012, p. 276. In numerous works, de Graaff and her colleagues have presented a meticulous and highly revealing mapping of directorship interlocks and other linkages between (and among) IOCs and NOCs.
3. Many illuminating accounts of this history are available, see especially, Timothy Mitchell, *Carbon Democracy*, New York: Verso, 2011; Matthew Huber, *Lifeblood*, Minneapolis: University of Minnesota Press, 2013; Guiliano Garavini, *The Rise and Fall of OPEC in the Twentieth Century*, London: Oxford University Press, 2019.
4. An early and brilliant analysis of the IOCs is presented in John Blair, *The Control of Oil, New York,* NY: Pantheon Books, 1976.
5. In 1949, around two-thirds of the world's known crude reserves, and more than half of the world's crude production and refining, were controlled by these companies. Outside of the US, the Seven Sisters held more than 82 per cent of all known crude reserves, 86 per cent of crude production, 77 per cent of refining capacity, and 85 per cent of cracking plants (used in the manufacture of petrochemicals). Between them, it was estimated that the Seven Sisters owned at least half of the world's tanker fleet in 1949, and around two-thirds of privately controlled tankers. See: Federal Trade Commission, United States Congress, Senate Select Committee on Small Business, Subcommittee on Monopoly, *The International Petroleum Cartel*, Washington: U.S. Government, 1975.
6. The original 'Seven Sisters' were Anglo-Iranian Oil Company (originally Anglo-Persian, now BP); Royal Dutch Shell; Standard Oil Company of California (SoCal, later Chevron); Gulf Oil (now merged into Chevron); Texaco (now merged into Chevron); Standard Oil Company of New Jersey (Esso, later Exxon, now part of ExxonMobil); and the Standard Oil Company of New York (Socony, later Mobil, now part of ExxonMobil).
7. See: Huber, *Lifeblood*; Blair, *Control of Oil*.
8. Christopher Dietrich, *Oil Revolution*, Cambridge: Cambridge University Press, 2017; Garavini, '*The Rise and Fall of OPEC*'.
9. Adam Hanieh, *Money, Markets, and Monarchies: The Gulf Cooperation Council and the Political Economy of the Contemporary Middle East*, Cambridge University Press, 2018.
10. United States Congress. House Committee on Commerce. Subcommittee on Energy and Power, *The Exxon-Mobil Merger: Hearings before the Subcommittee on Energy and Power of the Committee on Commerce, House of Representatives, One Hundred Sixth Congress, first session*, 10 and 11 March, Washington: U.S. G.P.O., 1999, p. 4.
11. In 1982, a rule change by the Securities and Exchange Commission permitted companies to repurchase their own shares on the open market within certain limits dependent on trading volumes (often financed through debt). The reduction in the number of shares led to an increase in the company's stock price, allowing senior executives to make millions through the exercise of their stock options. US oil companies were at the forefront of this practice; indeed, between 2003 and 2012, ExxonMobil was the largest stock repurchaser on US financial markets. See: William Lazonick, 'Profits Without Prosperity', *Harvard Business Review*, September 2014.

12   United States Congress, *Exxon-Mobil Merger*, p. 22.
13   Perhaps the most notorious example of this was British Petroleum's rebranding of itself as BP in 2000, under a new tagline 'Beyond Petroleum' and with a new green sun-burst logo. At the time, BP remained the second largest oil company in the world and spent more on the corporate rebrand than they did on renewable energy.
14   Figures in this paragraph drawn from ENI, *World Energy Review*, 2021, available at: https://www.eni.com/assets/documents/eng/scenari-energetici/2021/World-Energy-Review-2021.pdf
15   The debate around this boom in oil prices is complex and cannot be reduced to simply increased Asian demand. The financialization of oil has played a major role in the determination of oil prices. See: Mazen Labban, 'Oil in parallax: scarcity, markets, and the financialization of accumulation', *Geoforum*, 41(4), 2010, pp. 541–552, and Adam Hanieh, 'The Commodities Fetish? Financialisation and Finance Capital in the US Oil Industry', *Historical Materialism*, 29(4), 2021, pp. 70-113.
16   Lutz Kilian, 'How the shale oil revolution has affected US oil and gasoline prices', *VoxEU*, 14 January 2015, available at: https://voxeu.org/article/shale-oil-and-gasoline-prices.
17   BP, *Statistical Review of World Energy – 70th Edition 2021*, p. 18, available at: https://www.bp.com/en/global/corporate/energy-economics/statistical-review-of-world-energy.html. World ranking of oil production varies according to whether non-conventional and Natural Gas Liquids (NGLs) are included (as they are in BP's statistics), and whether production is measured by barrels, million tons, or energy.
18   Tar sands are a mix of sand, clay and water from which bitumen is extracted and processed into petroleum products. They are an extremely expensive, and ecologically damaging form of oil production, with significantly higher levels of carbon emissions than conventional oil. The largest tar sands reserves are located on indigenous lands in Alberta, Canada, and indigenous communities have faced the worst impacts of this form of oil extraction and associated pipeline development.
19   Calculated by author from ENI, *World Energy Review*, 2021, available at: https://www.eni.com/assets/documents/eng/scenari-energetici/2021/World-Energy-Review-2021.pdf. The other major sources of IOC crude production are Russia/Central Asia (through equity participation with Russian state-owned firms), Europe (in the UK North Sea, Denmark, and the Netherlands), and Central/South America. Collectively, these regions make up another 44% of IOC crude production globally.
20   Calculated by author from ExxonMobil, Chevron, and BP annual reports.
21   IEA, *World Energy Investment Report*, International Energy Agency, 2020, p. 42.
22   Labban 'Oil in parallax'.
23   Calculated by author from: Rystad, *Rystad Energy Data, Upstream Report*, 22 May 2022, p. 7.
24   Geoffrey Morgan, 'Oil and Gas Share Buybacks Boomed Before Energy Prices Hit Highs', *BloombergUK*, 15 March 2022.
25   For a mapping of these ownership patterns in the context of the financialisation of oil see: Hanieh, 'The Commodities Fetish?'.
26   IEA, 'World Energy Investment' p. 161. Some of the most important firms in this respect are JP Morgan, Goldman Sachs, Morgan Stanley, Vanguard, Blackrock, State Street, and the Blackstone and Carlyle private equity groups. See: Hanieh 'Commodities Fetish'.

27 Hanieh, 'Commodities Fetish'.
28 Canadian exports to the US made up 96 per cent of all Canada's crude exports in 2019.
29 BP, 'Annual Statistical Review 2020', p. 32.
30 Transport and Environment, 'How Russian oil flows to Europe', *Briefing*, 7 March 2022, p. 11, available at: https://www.transportenvironment.org/discover/how-russian-oil-flows-to-europe.
31 Publicly listed companies also play an important role in the Russian oil industry, most notably the country's second-largest oil producer, Lukoil. Ownership and control of these private firms are typically held by Russian billionaires with close links to the Kremlin.
32 BP, 'Annual Statistical Review 2020', p. 30.
33 BP, 'Annual Statistical Review 2020', p. 30.
34 For a discussion of petrochemicals and their place in the study of oil, see Adam Hanieh, 'Petrochemical Empire: The Geo-Politics of Fossil-Fuelled Production', *New Left Review*,130, July-August 2021, pp. 25-51.
35 In 2020, the average capacity per refinery in the Middle East stood at 164 thousand barrels/day, compared to 140 kbbl/day in Europe, 131 kbbl/day in North America, and 116 kbbl/day in Asia Pacific. See: ENI 'World Energy Review', p. 71.
36 IEA, 'World Energy Investment', p. 48.
37 In the IPO, 1.5 per cent of Aramco's shares were listed. The rest are held by the Saudi government and a Saudi sovereign wealth fund, the Public Investment Fund.
38 For ExxonMobil, for example, around 75 per cent of the company's refineries, 88 per cent of its retail sites, and 70 per cent of its chemical sales were located in North America and Europe in 2019. See: ExxonMobil, *Annual Report* 2020, pp. 44-46.
39 The figures in this paragraph are calculated by author from Orbis Database, available at: https://www.bvdinfo.com/en-gb/our-products/data/international/orbis. They include investment in both upstream production as well as refining, petrochemical production, and oil and gas services (drilling, pipelines etc).
40 Calculated by author from Orbis Database. Asia is defined here as China (including Hong Kong), Taiwan, Korea, Malaysia, Indonesia, Japan, Thailand, Singapore, and the Philippines.
41 In Asia, we can point to the Hyundai and Idemitsu conglomerates, as well as the large private refineries in China. In the Gulf, most of the leading private conglomerates are linked to the oil sector in some way, often through partnerships with the large NOCs in activities such as petrochemical production. See: Hanieh, *Money, Markets, and Monarchies*.
42 Bailout Watch, 'Bailed Out & Propped Up', November 2020, available at: https://report.bailoutwatch.org.
43 Bailout Watch, 'Fossil Fuel Profits Surged in 2021', 24 February 2022.
44 The ban applies only to maritime imports of Russian crude (by 5 December 2022) and petroleum products (by 5 February 2023). Hungary, Slovakia, and the Czech Republic will continue to receive Russian oil transported through the Druzbha pipeline but are not allowed to re-sell this oil in Europe.
45 Robert Perkins and Elza Turner, 'European oil refineries exposed as fears of Russia invading Ukraine grow', *S&P Global*, 21 January 2022.

46   The EU's eventual adoption of this ban rested heavily upon the agreement of the City of London, which remains the centre of global maritime insurance. The move is not without its critics, with some analysts predicting that an effective halt to Russian oil exports could lead to a large increase in the price of oil. Another unintended consequence of the measure might be the increased involvement of Chinese and other non-Western financial institutions in the provision of shipping insurance.

47   Tom Wilson, 'Western sanctions have had 'limited impact' on Russian oil output, says IEA', *Financial Times*, 11 August 2022.

48   James Fernyhough, 'Russia to permanently 'decouple' with west on energy, gas producers say', *Financial Times*, 17 May 2022.

49   Damian Carrington and Matthew Taylor, 'Revealed: The 'carbon bombs' set to trigger catastrophic climate breakdown', *Guardian*, 11 May 2022.

50   Carrington and Tayler, 'Carbon Bombs'.

CLIMATE BREAKDOWN: FROM FOSSIL CAPITALISM TO CLIMATE CAPITALISM (AND BEYOND?)

NICOLAS GRAHAM AND WILLIAM K. CARROLL

By spring 2022, climate politics was back in the spotlight after having been displaced from mainstream news by the Covid-19 pandemic. On 25 March, youth around the world began a wave of school strikes, reviving the movement spearheaded by Greta Thunberg in 2018.[1] On 4 April, the IPCC released part 3 of its Working Group II *Sixth Assessment Report*, focusing on mitigation. Climate scientist and WGII Co-chair Jim Skea observed that to avoid runaway climate change, 'it's now or never … Without immediate and deep emissions reductions across all sectors, it will be impossible'.[2] Responding to the report, UN Secretary-General António Guterres decried the 'litany of broken climate promises' from business and government, adding, 'simply put, they are lying. And the results will be catastrophic.'[3] Three days later, climate scientists joined Extinction Rebellion in protests in Madrid, London, Los Angeles, and other cities, calling for 'radical change in the face of the ecological crisis'.[4]

The catastrophic impact of climate change is registering strongly in the streets and in union halls, among natural scientists and at the pinnacle of global governance. Yet on 6 April, the Canadian government greenlit Bay du Nord, an oil megaproject offshore of Newfoundland, issuing a 'slap in the face to climate scientists … tantamount to denying that climate change is real and threatens our very existence', as Julia Levin of Environmental Defence Canada put it.[5] The next day, the Canadian government released its budget. Framed as a major emissions-reduction initiative, the budget promoted electric cars, largely ignoring the source of emissions in ever-increasing oil and gas extraction. Its big-ticket item was a carbon capture investment tax credit,[6] incentivizing corporate Canada to develop and deploy a technology which to date seems more useful in capturing public opinion than in capturing carbon.[7]

As the only G7 country whose emissions have increased since the 2015 Paris Accord, Canada presents an interesting case of a climate laggard, posing incongruously on the international stage as a climate leader.[8] Beneath ambitious climate targets (none of which has ever been met), a *regime of obstruction*, cutting across the various political scales of the integral state, protects revenue streams issuing from carbon extractive development, while bolstering popular support for an accumulation strategy in which fossil capital figures as a leading fraction. In our view, this regime includes the economic relations through which fossil capital accumulates (including its financing), the political relations in policy-planning, state regulation and subsidization of fossil capital, and the cultural-ideological relations through which consent to the regime is secured in various sectors of civil society. As elsewhere, this regime, however, appears to be in transition. Fossil-fuelled consumer capitalism remains paradigmatic, yet spurred by the deepening climate crisis, alternatives are emerging. On the one hand, to borrow Gramsci's terms, a 'passive revolutionary' project of climate capitalism is gaining momentum, portending a molecular recomposition of the historical bloc and reconfiguration of forces of production, while protecting relations of production. On the other hand, the crisis opens space for transformative alternatives. Energy democracy, which constitutes a bundle of sectorally-focused radical reforms, holds potential for the formation of an alternative historical bloc, and opens political space for eco-socialism.

In this essay, we first focus on capitalism's deep dependency on fossil fuels, before outlining recent carbon extractive development in Canada, centred upon the tar sands. Through this development, Canada has become a major oil producer and a climate laggard, and is marked by a regime of obstruction that seeks to sustain the accumulation of fossil capital for as long as possible, while slowly transitioning to renewable energy under corporate control.

FOSSIL CAPITALISM

Fossil capitalism is a form of capitalism 'predicated on the growing consumption of fossil fuels and therefore generating a sustained growth in emissions of carbon dioxide'.[9] The term names the deep symbiosis between fossil fuels and capital accumulation since the mid-nineteenth century, and the key role of fossil capital fractions – the coal, oil, and gas industries – in that relationship.

Elmar Altvater first introduced the term in the *Register*, providing a pathbreaking analysis of the 'tight fit' between fossil fuels and the logic and spatio-temporality of capitalist development.[10] Matthew Huber furthers this analysis by homing in on the 'energy/labour' nexus, analyzing the industrial revolution as an energy transition, from *muscle power* to power via fossil fuelled *machinery*.[11] While capitalism predates the Industrial Revolution, this shift 'hastened the *generalization* and *extension* of the wage labour relationship on a scale hitherto unseen'.[12] Following on this work, Malm provides a deep historical analysis of the transition from energy 'flows' (energy from water or wind) to mineralized energy 'stock' (condensed inanimate energy contained in the crust of the earth).[13] He shows that nineteenth-century mill owners switched from water to coal power not because coal was cheaper, more reliable, or more abundant, but because coal offered the ability to relocate production to settings with a high surplus population, enabling capital to seek out the most profitable pools of labour power and to level down wages (thereby increasing absolute surplus value). Later, it served as a means of increasing the productivity of labour through technological means (in pursuit of relative surplus value), accelerating the use of fossil fuels. Hydrocarbons had become a 'general lever for surplus value production'.[14]

The relationship between fossil fuels and capital accumulation has only deepened through subsequent phases of capitalist development. Indeed, the consolidation of monopoly capital in the post-war period required and accelerated the production and consumption of fossil fuels, particularly petroleum, as hydrocarbons became embedded in products from plastics to fertilizers to pesticides to napalm, as well as in a host of new household commodities encouraged by the corresponding 'sales effort'.[15] Indeed, oil became fundamental to the growth of the 'American way of life'. The entire 'electric-oil-auto complex' reconfigured the geographies of social reproduction, while oil provided the *ecological foundation* for post-war social construction of a 'peculiarly privatized sociospatial existence', based on single-family housing, suburban consumerism and automobility.[16]

The enhanced globalization of production and consumption that since the 1980s has accompanied the recent phase of neoliberal capitalism has likewise only occurred through expanding fossil-powered productive forces.[17] In particular, the enlarged 'production-consumption' disconnect and elongated supply chains that accompanied fully-fledged globalization beginning in the late-twentieth century have greatly accelerated the burning of carbon, whether in trucks, trains, or super tankers. In little more than two centuries fossil capital has become embedded in the entire economic structure, from industrial production to plastics and petrochemicals, to the agro-industry, to transportation, and all else. New oil and gas projects and pipelines add to this mass of infrastructure, 'locking-in' carbon in an era of deepening climate crisis.

While the literature on fossil capitalism tends to focus on the qualities of fossil fuels as 'abstract energy' (i.e., its unique density and ability to be stored and transported), oil is not only fuel to power machines or move commodities; it is simultaneously an embodiment of exchange value that must be realized.[18] Indeed, the role of fossil fuels in powering productive capital assumes the prior business of extracting coal, oil, and gas. In this circuit, fossil fuels are not accessories consumed in the production or circulation of other commodities, but that which is '*produced as its own immediate object of profit-making*'.[19] As the case of Canada confirms, this valorization and realization process, central to the expanded reproduction of fossil capital fractions and to the revenue streams of petro-states, is a crucial force in the maintenance of a social metabolism dependent on fossil fuels.

CANADA AND EXTREME EXTRACTION

In the same period during which the climate crisis has become an existential threat, the Canadian economy has become more focused on carbon extraction, especially bitumen from the Alberta tar sands, along with fracked shale gas and offshore oil. Although Canada's oil industry had its origins in mid-nineteenth century Ontario, after the 1947 discovery of massive oil deposits in Alberta the industry moved decisively westward, with Calgary becoming its corporate command centre. New technologies for extracting oil from tar sands brought bitumen production on stream by 1967; four decades later, in his first speech abroad as Prime Minister, Stephen Harper announced intentions to transform Canada into a 'global energy powerhouse'[20] on the strength of the burgeoning bitumen sector. This vision was soon matched by policy initiatives to rapidly expand the tar sands, build pipelines to transport diluted bitumen, and withdraw (in 2011) from the Kyoto climate accord. By 2015, enormous fixed-capital investments in bitumen mining and pipelines had pushed Alberta ahead of Ontario as a locus for the country's capital stock. Alberta had become 'the new centre for capital accumulation in Canada and thus an important source of employment and income'[21] and, not incidentally, foreign exchange for a Canadian state mindful of current account deficits.

Because of bitumen's high carbon intensity compared with conventional oil and the vast reserves (comparable in magnitude to the world's total proven reserves of conventional petroleum), Alberta's tar sands epitomize 'extreme fossil fuels':[22] their appropriation entails greater environmental, labour-related, and social risks and costs. As Pineault explains, the vast majority of these fuels cannot be burned if we are to avert catastrophic, and ecocidal, climate change.[23]

Other features of the extreme extraction model in Canada include the high local environmental costs of extraction and transport (in particular, to water systems) and the fact that accessing and transporting these sources expands the carbon extractive frontier over treaty and traditional Indigenous lands. Indeed, Canada's carbon-extractive development occurs in a context of settler colonialism, entailing an ongoing process of accumulation by dispossession.[24] The expansion of the carbon-extractive industry provokes frequent and ongoing clashes with Indigenous rights, title, and sovereignty.[25] First Nations and other communities in extraction zones and downstream from them continue to suffer in many ways from fossil fuel development.[26] As a result, new fossil capital projects often face strong opposition from a combination of Indigenous communities, environmental groups, and some segments of labour.

This resistance is conjoined with broader political economic challenges facing the industry. Indeed, the collapse of oil prices beginning in 2014-2015 spelled trouble for the extreme extractivist business model. Bitumen's high costs of production and its low quality as 'dirty oil' brought a flood of divestment from Canada's oil patch. Capital spending among Canada-based majors dropped 40 per cent between 2014-2015, while several global majors, including Total, Shell, and Statoil sold off major oil sands assets.[27] A second price collapse in 2020, triggered by the Covid-19 pandemic, again hampered tar sands production, as prices for Canadian bitumen dropped to a record low of US $3.50 per barrel.[28] At the time of writing, prices have rebounded, yet long-term demand for bitumen remains doubtful. Indeed, divestment from tar sands reflects increasing investor scepticism about the future of bitumen in the global 'energy mix'. As McCreary asserts, these low-grade and costly reserves are among the most likely to remain in the ground as global decarbonization and energy transition advances.[29] Yet rather than sunset a climate-threatening and economically risky industry, Canadian business has pursued a sell-out strategy designed to valorize carbon assets by pushing them in volume to market while they still hold value.[30]

MAPPING THE REGIME OF OBSTRUCTION IN CANADA

The struggle to transform fossil capitalism requires critical analysis of the various social relations that enable the fossil fuel industry to thrive when carbon emissions pose an urgent existential challenge for humanity. Focusing on the case of Canada, this has been the remit of the Corporate Mapping Project (CMP), which views these relations as a *regime of obstruction* with a distinctive political-economic architecture. The regime is sustained through modalities of corporate power – both economic and cultural-political – that protect revenue streams issuing from carbon extractive development.

Using methods that include social network analysis, ethnographic fieldwork, and critical discourse analysis, the CMP has examined the organization of fossil-capital power (including its financial enablement) within and beyond the economy. This includes investigating how Canada-based fossil-capital firms link into the broader national and global power structure via interlocking governance relations. Paralleling the structure of corporate-elite *integration*, the CMP has documented a pervasive pattern of fossil-capital *reach* into several domains of political life and civil society, shoring up a modicum of popular support for the regime. The distinctive regime of obstruction that has developed in Canada offers lessons also for climate-justice activism as it confronts what are highly sedimented hegemonic relations.

Our mapping of power relations within Canada's fossil-capital sector uncovered an extreme concentration of capital under the control of an 'oligopolistic bloc' of five bitumen-producing firms.[31] Although bitumen production grew frenetically from 2000 through 2018, by 2019 the industry had reached a state of 'maturity', with the big producers able to turn a profit even at relatively low prices, but with much slower growth.[32] Given its very high capital intensity, oil and gas production's contribution to employment has always been relatively modest,[33] but in the 'mature' phase a number of technological innovations, such as driverless trucks, now enable the industry to massively boost productivity while shedding jobs. The productive nucleus of fossil capital also includes giant pipeline companies whose profits derive from the flow of hydrocarbons, from the point of extraction to processing facilities, and here we can observe obstruction cutting both ways. Even as fossil capital obstructs political and economic initiatives that might jeopardize its self-expansion (and even as the state backstops failing pipeline projects, as in the Canadian government's purchase of the TransMountain Pipeline in 2018), anti-pipeline campaigns strive to obstruct the flow of carbon energy that is the basis for that self-expansion.[34]

Closely articulated with fossil capital's productive nucleus is financial capital. This includes the blocs of corporate shares that give major investors a significant stake (sometimes amounting to strategic control), as well as the flow of credit from aligned financial institutions. On the former, our research has shown that, 'as concentrated as the sector is, so are its owners concentrated: a small group of actors has control over much of the sector'.[35] Although wealthy Canadian families own controlling interest in some mid-sized fossils, key shareholders of the majors tend to be institutional investors (including asset managers and banks), and in some cases, foreign transnational parent companies such as ExxonMobil. Yearly reports from Oil Change

International and its collaborators consistently rank Canada's five big banks near the top of fossil-capital financing. In 2021, all five ranked among the global top twenty fossil banks, and (with JP Morgan Chase) were among the six leading funders of the tar sands. Between 2020 and 2021, Canada's big five banks were all among the world's ten 'worst culprits', each having increased their financing of fossil companies by more than $4 billion US.[36]

Capital relations of these kinds underline the organic integration of fossil and financial capital, within Canada and globally. At another level, integrative ties link corporate directors and executives into elite networks. A mapping of the Canadian network of interlocking directorates as of 2015 revealed a tightly knit corporate community, as fossil-capital companies share directors with each other and with leading banks and other corporations.[37] In more recent research, Hudson and Bowness tracked the loans, shareholdings, and directorate interlocks linking major financial and fossil-capital players in Canada, and concluded that these complex networks form 'the enabling structure' for a power bloc enforcing 'what appears to be a unified, hegemonic, capitalist interest in the long-term maintenance of the fossil energy sector'.[38]

That bloc forms the core of Canada's regime of obstruction, furnishing a cohesive base for fossil capital's reach into civil and political society. In mapping that reach, the CMP has attended to a range of relations, each conveying power and influence into the political and cultural fields and thereby exercising *hegemonic* power alongside the power that inheres in the accumulation of capital. At the level of interlocking governance boards, we documented a pervasive pattern of fossil-capital reach into several domains of political life and civil society, including policy-planning think tanks, business councils, industry associations, university governance boards, and research institutes. As fossil-capital executives and directors serve on these boards, their cross-affiliations create a single, connected network, enabling the fossil-capital elite 'to define, defend, and advance its profit-driven concerns as "common sense", in the "public interest"'.[39]

Working in tandem with the elite network that reaches from fossil boardrooms into civil society is a dense network of lobbying relations between industry and various bodies comprising the state apparatus. In this instance, fossil-capital reach is accomplished through lobbyists in the employ of corporations and industry associations such as the Canadian Association of Petroleum Producers (CAPP), as they meet with state managers – whether elected parliamentarians or senior public servants. Covering the last years of the regime of the Conservatives led by Stephen Harper and the first years of the Liberal government of Justin Trudeau, our research uncovered a remarkably dense network of lobbying contacts, averaging just over six per working day, from the beginning of 2011 through early 2018. Reflecting the massive concentration of fossil capital, a few large corporations and key industry associations accounted for most of the contacts throughout the period. Our findings pointed to 'the existence of a "deep state," a form of co-government, far outlasting election cycles whereby key state institutions and actors within them develop long-term relationships with leading corporations and private interests that contribute extensively to policy formulation'.[40] At the extreme, such 'partnerships' entail institutional capture, as in the secret process through which CAPP and the British Columbia government crafted a 'Climate Leadership' plan at CAPP's Calgary offices in 2016, even as official public consultations were underway.[41]

Importantly, networks of hegemonic power extend beyond longstanding practices of business leadership, lobbying, and regulatory capture. Our studies of emergent online networks of 'extractive populism' mapped the use of social media by fossil capital and its proponents to convert passive industry stakeholders into engaged publics. As they recruit mass support, organizations such as CAPP's 'Canada's Energy Citizens' dispense accessible and shareable narratives and frames, contributing to the echo chambers that provide validation for climate-change denial.[42] The sources that support these narratives often emanate from the wider network of fossil-capital connected civil society organizations, thereby 'interfac[ing] supporters with material from ... networks of industry advocates that industry has itself helped cultivate over decades'.[43]

Case studies of strategic initiatives by fossil capital to build support in key constituencies give us another angle on hegemonic power. In northern British Columbia, as it learned from the defeat of the Northern Gateway pipeline proposal (2016), fossil capital enticed local mayors and Indigenous band councils through donations and financial arrangements while redefining natural gas as 'clean energy'. This strategy was successful in fragmenting the anti-pipeline coalition that had contributed to the demise of Northern Gateway. The petro-bloc thereby created a modicum of 'social licence' for BC Coastal Gaslink, currently under construction amid trenchant opposition from hereditary chiefs and Indigenous activists and their allies.[44]

In communities within extraction zones, CAPP and individual fossil firms build 'hegemonic community economic identity' through corporate social responsibility (CSR) initiatives, funding local amenities that create a sense of psychological identification among locals.[45] The oily fingerprints of CSR are also discernible in the curriculum gifted by industry-funded 'third party' organizations to schools struggling after years of neoliberal austerity. Purporting to 'balance' pro-environment perspectives by giving 'equal representation to industry', this strategic initiative recruits support for business-as-usual among the next generation.[46] Meanwhile at Postmedia and similar mainstream outlets, a fossil-friendly press dispenses 'petroganda' – 'journalism that treats Big Oil with kid gloves, and environmentalists and climate scientists with hostility'.[47]

Whether in schools, in mainstream media, or in policy discourses, such efforts exemplify a 'new climate denialism'. The latter no longer denies the reality of climate change or the causal role of carbon emissions, but denies the need to decarbonize at a pace commensurate with scientific knowledge, and advocates technological and market-based 'solutions' that create new avenues for accumulation.[48] New denialism, as we will see below, is at the core of the 'clean growth' project the Canadian government announced in 2016, which a network of corporate-funded ENGOs helped shape and promote.[49]

The image that emerges of the strategies of accumulation of the Canadian fossil fuel sector is that of a multi-scalar regime of obstruction, in which fossil capital's power over labour and non-human nature co-mingles with the power of finance while a variety of practices in civil and political society bolster the common sense of business-as-usual. The regime reaches from the shop floor and everyday worlds of local communities to the transnational level through a wide range of organizational forms and venues, forming an historical bloc in support of climate capitalism.[50] But the bloc is not homogeneous. For instance, extractive populism and new climate denialism tell different stories, to different publics. However, the tensions between them are hardly a liability. In postmodern times of cultural fragmentation, ideological diversification can mobilize a range of elite, mainstream, and fringe constituencies, satisfying the basic hegemonic requirement to organize consent, without building a uniform national consensus.[51]

Yet at each scale, the regime faces resistance and opposition in Canada. Anti-pipeline activism, for example, has been the most charged field of social struggle and has created 'flashpoints of resistance' along vital corridors of fossil capital's commodity chains, revealing power at work and thereby disrupting hegemony by expanding 'people's sense of what is possible, and what is desirable, as well as pointing to some of the blockages obstructing the needed transition'.[52] In view of fossil capital's dependence on financing for enormous fixed-capital investments, divestment campaigns have emerged as political interventions at the antecedent of fossil commodity chains. Divestment campaigns do not transform property relations, but they weaken fossil capital's hegemonic grip, and amount to non-reformist reforms that disturb the capitalist status quo, building popular power.⁵³ At the local level, in cities like Regina that have committed to becoming completely 'renewable' by 2050, activists have pushed for participatory planning and the adoption of an equity lens within the city's energy and sustainability framework.⁵⁴

Canada's status as a settler-capitalist formation means that decolonization has been pivotal in many struggles against extractive capitalism. Across Canada, Indigenous-led activism has been crucial, but it is also the case that the colonial apparatus of the Canadian state, combined with capitalist intrusions onto Indigenous land, has cultivated a stratum of Indigenous elites aligned with fossil sector development, creating 'deep political divisions between the grassroots and the Indigenous establishment'.⁵⁵ Ultimately, in settler-capitalist formations, any serious movement toward socialism will require substantial Indigenous leadership in addressing the horrific legacy of ongoing colonization. Yet Indigenous resurgence can only succeed as part of a broader historical bloc. 'Without mass movements for structural transformation of the colonial/capitalist state, Indigenous self-determination cannot be realised.'⁵⁶ One such front of opposition has been the Indigenous Climate Action's Decolonizing Climate Policy Project (supported by the CMP), a two-stage project that begins with an analysis and critique of recent federal climate plans, followed by the formulation of Indigenous-led climate policy, as Indigenous climate leaders consult Indigenous peoples across Canada.⁵⁷

CLIMATE CAPITALISM

Climate capitalism is an emergent accumulation strategy to redirect investments from fossil fuels towards decarbonization and renewable energy,⁵⁸ strategically supported by both the federal government and fossil capital in Canada. Climate Capitalism centres the search for 'cost effective' market solutions, such as carbon taxes or offsets, alongside technological developments, like efficiency enhancement and carbon capture and storage (CCS), to reduce emissions and incentivize an energy transition. Proponents frame climate change as a market transition that will lead to new fields of economic growth, working to reconcile the need to decarbonize with the continued imperative to locate new sites for capital accumulation.

As a project, climate capitalism fits the Gramscian notion of passive revolution – 'a condition of rupture in which processes of revolution are at once partially fulfilled and displaced'.⁵⁹ It entails 'reformist changes adopted by dominant groups to accommodate pressure from challengers' and which stabilize power relations.⁶⁰ Passive revolutionary projects *partially* accommodate change and satisfy oppositional demands from below, while *simultaneously* denying subaltern classes the initiative and disrupting alternative projects.[61] Climate capitalism offers such partial changes, advocating a fine-tuning of the productive forces, without transforming social relations of production, including the concentration of power and decision-making in large corporations. It seeks to draw subaltern groups (like unions and ENGOS) into the project by offering material and symbolic concessions, while simultaneously mediating tensions between fractions of capital and constructing an elite consensus.

Climate capitalism is a strategy still under construction, promoted within elite networks that bring corporate leaders together with policy communities and other organic intellectuals. Sapinski analyzes the construction of climate capitalism at the global level, identifying key policy-planning organizations that have shaped and promoted the project.[62] He finds that these organizations interlock extensively with key policy actors and the world's largest corporations, constituting a 'climate capitalist corporate-policy elite', small in size but positioned at the heart of a global network with European firms most involved. These findings are consistent with Carroll's mapping of the transnational network of fossil capital, which reveals that the segment of the global corporate elite network centred upon fossil capital is divided between a large, integrated community of mainly American corporations, a smaller Franco-German-Canadian configuration, and a third, loosely-knit, diverse community in which British capital predominates.[63] Fossil capital continues to occupy a central position in the American corporate community, as it does in Canada. Yet, the mapping also reveals a weaker presence of fossil fractions on the European continent, providing conditions more conducive to the emergence of an accumulation regime decoupled from fossil fuels. Indeed, climate capitalism appears to have gained greatest traction among European elites, as seen in the European Commission's (EC) 2019 European Green Deal, which provides a legislative roadmap for making the EU 'climate neutral' in 2050, combining decarbonization with green economic growth, particularly in the energy field.[64]

Nevertheless, for Sapinksi, the presence of major fossil fuel firms at the climate capitalist network's centre suggests a 'weak climate capitalism' – a slow transition to ecologically modernized production that averts stranded assets, while potentially allowing fossil firms to expand control of emerging renewable energy sources.[65] In the German context this reading is shared by Tadzio Müller: 'The short-term goal of the energy companies and their government allies is to delay the transition just long enough so that the companies can gain a good foothold in the renewables sector that allows them to be as dominant in the new energy system as they were in the old.'[66]

Recent pledges made by global carbon majors, such as Shell and British Petroleum (BP) to become net zero by 2050 through scaling up renewables and clean technology investments (and in the case of BP, wind down fossil fuel production) suggest that 'transition capture' may now be underway. Yet closer examinations of actions and investments of global majors (including these Europe-based firms) find little evidence that transition to a clean energy business model is imminent. Examining the climate policy political stances of the ten largest global fossil firms, Green et al. discern a more 'pro-climate' orientation among European majors compared to American ones, but find that all majors 'steadfastly deny the end of fossil fuels'.[67] Likewise, the investigation by Li and his colleagues of the four largest-emitting global oil and gas firms (accounting for over 10 per cent of total global carbon dioxide emissions since 1965) finds 'no evidence any major [is] comprehensively transitioning its business model away from fossil fuels', and a fundamental 'mismatch' between discourses and pledges on the one hand and investments on the other.[68] A form of greenwashing, decarbonization pledges play an important legitimation function: 'companies want stakeholders, including governments, to trust that a government-led phase out of fossil fuels is unnecessary and that they should be left to pursue their own emissions reduction and renewable energy targets at the speed and scale they want.'[69]

While carbon capital slowly hedges into renewables, Sweeney[70] and Christophers[71] elucidate key contradictions of an energy transition on the model of the market. Christophers critiques the hegemonic 'price and demand' interpretation of energy transition, reminding us that in a market-led transition, it is profit and investment return that is in the driver's seat, not the relative affordability of different energy sources. This poses a problem because, as Sweeney points out, current renewable energy deployments are nowhere close to the required scale, but *from a profit-perspective there is a surplus*. In the case of solar, for example, significant new production capacity emerging in China 2017 and 2018 encountered a stagnant global market. Apparent oversupply or 'overcapacity' subsequently depressed prices to the point that producers have been withholding part of their production in the face of falling profit margins, leading to a wave of bankruptcies.[72] In addition to problems of supply-demand disequilibrium, the major players in renewable energy continue to distance themselves from *energy generation* and are instead focusing on technology manufacturing and services.[73] The problem, for capital, is that since '[renewable] fuel is not hidden away in a separate chamber, but rather hangs like a fruit for anyone to pick, there is little surplus-value to extract in its production'.[74] The subsequent shortfall in renewable deployment 'draws attention to how climate targets are completely incompatible with the profit-focused framework'.[75] Or, as Graham asserts: renewable energy, which is part of the advancement of ecologically sane productive forces, is fettered by capitalist relations of production.[76]

Given fossil capital's weight in Canada's economy and in the ruling bloc, and as a concession to extractive populist forces, in Canada a hybrid project of fossil and climate capitalism, evident in federal and provincial 'clean growth' climate plans, has taken shape.[77] Gutstein notes the 'eerily similar'[78] nature of the federal Liberal's climate plans and the recommendations of the Canadian Council of Chief Executives (now Business Council of Canada), long recognized for its role in shaping state policy.[79] As early as 2007, the Council recommended a national energy strategy based on federal-provincial agreements, government subsidies for 'clean technology', and 'rational' carbon pricing – all initiatives later encouraged by the Canadian Association of Petroleum Producers. While CAPP's endorsement of a carbon tax produced some discord within the petro-bloc, the strategic gambit was laid bare by then-Council-president John Manley, who explained that 'Acquiescence to a price on carbon really is looked as one side of a grand bargain that would see pipelines built in return'.[80]

In their capacity to shape clean growth climate policy and discourse, the Council and CAPP are joined by a set of recently formed ENGOs, such as Canada's Ecofiscal Commission, which emerged during the oil price slump in 2014-15, and Smart Prosperity, whose formation coincided with the 2016 announcement of the federal government's *Pan Canadian Framework on Clean Growth and Climate Change*. These groups help stitch together a 'tightly-knit configuration of corporate, state, and civil-society actors' (including major fossil-capital players) who aspire to meet the country's international climate commitments, while supporting a robust rate of capital accumulation.[81] The policy discourses and frameworks trumpeted by this coalition of forces enable the valorization of existing fossil capital, while 'market forces' (that is, investors, including 'incumbent' corporations), incentivized by carbon taxes, cap-and-trade measures, and state-subsidized technological changes (from efficiency improvements to carbon capture utilization and storage, to geoengineering) usher in a lower-carbon future. The program postpones confrontation with fossil capital into the distant future, averting transformative measures that may threaten short-term profitability.

That clean growth frameworks convey a commitment to tackle climate change while delaying meaningful climate action is evident in the business strategies of Canadian carbon majors. In his study of transition capture in Canada, Graham reveals 'signposts' of an orientation towards climate capitalism by some major fossil fuel firms, but finds that these firms prioritize efficiency enhancement and emissions reduction of fossil fuel operations and use, not renewable energy.[82] Efforts to render each barrel of oil less 'carbon intensive' (including though CCS) are supported by extensive state funding and facilitated by a host of interlinked corporate, government, and university institutes, including industry innovation collaborations, such as Canada's Oilsands Innovation Alliance and the Oil Sands Pathway to Net Zero initiative.[83] While the role of CCS in decarbonization should not be dismissed,[84] under corporate hegemony these technologies actually prolong dependence on fossil fuels, while detracting from (rather than potentially complementing) more *bona fide* solutions. This contradiction is only poised to sharpen under the current rhetoric of 'net-zero', which as Lee suggests, 'means less incentive to get to "real zero" emissions from fossil fuels, an escape hatch that perpetuates business as usual and delays more meaningful climate action'.[85]

Our reading of a nascent transition to climate capitalism points to two key challenges facing the project. First, in the long term, the possibility of decoupling capitalism's growth imperative from emissions remains doubtful; and second, even in the short term, success is by no means assured. Indeed, the pace of change offered by climate capitalism is too slow, compared to the reality of the climate emergency. Forward-looking fossil majors, both in Canada and internationally, have begun shifting some investments to renewables in a process of 'transition capture' and financial institutions have become increasingly wary of the 'climate risks' associated with fossil fuel loans and asset holdings. Yet, a decisive shift to a green growth model still appears distant. A hegemonic capitalist interest in the managed decline of fossil capital, and development of renewable-energy substitutes, is far from certain or secure.

BEYOND CLIMATE CAPITALISM: ENERGY DEMOCRACY?

Attuned to some of the shortcomings of climate capitalism is its present form, momentum has developed across North America and Europe for a Green New Deal (GND). Propelled forward by social movement activism, the GND has metamorphosed over the last decade from a climate capitalist eco-modernist strategy into a more transformative project.[86] More capacious versions entered mainstream politics through proposals such as the Democratic Party's Green New Deal Resolution introduced by US Representative Alexandria Ocasio-Cortez, and Senator Bernie Sanders' yet more transformative Green New Deal Plan. These incorporate direct regulatory measures, large-scale public investments in green infrastructure, and a generally expanded role for the state in catalyzing changes at the speed and scale that is required. They promote stronger just transition measures for workers and frontline communities, including relocation assistance and green job guarantees, amounting to a 'class-focused environmentalism' that is more readily understood as improving people's lives and less easily cast as elites imposing costs on working people.[87]

Resistance to fossil capital expansion in Canada is conjoined with similar projects for green transformation. These remain at the political margins but have gained significant support across civil society. One such initiative was the Leap Manifesto – a proto-GND plan that linked ambitious climate action with social and economic justice – catalyzed by the 2015 oil price crash. It was launched through the initiative of activist-author Naomi Klein and documentary filmmaker Avi Lewis, who helped convene a gathering of labour, Indigenous, climate, and other movements that shaped and defined the project.[88] The Leap was a significant intervention in redefining the national interest, and provided groundwork for currents pressing for a 'made in Canada' GND. This includes the Pact for a Green New Deal launched in 2019 by a coalition of scientists, labour unions, Indigenous, and youth organizations, calling for rapid and comprehensive energy transition, a phase out of the oil sands, the creation of one million new green jobs, and reconciliation with Indigenous Peoples, and which convened hundreds of town hall meetings across the country.[89] Indigenous Climate Action has recently developed a grassroots-based critique of the federal climate plan and an Indigenous-led alternative that breaks from the logic of 'clean growth'.[90]

These broad initiatives have been accompanied by worker-led green transition campaigns, like that of Alberta-based Iron and Earth,[91] and green conversion campaigns like Green Jobs Oshawa, which aims to convert the General Motors (GM) plant to a facility for assembling fleets of electric vehicles. This follows GM's announcement of plant closures across North America, the largest of which was in Oshawa, leading rank-and-file workers, joined by community allies, to mobilize in an effort to realize a just transition of the plant, thereby sustaining productive capacity for the needed shift.[92]

While GND frameworks typically emphasize the demand-side, there is increasing recognition of the need to address the supply-side – i.e., direct limits on the exploration, extraction, or transportation of fossil fuels and a 'managed wind-down' of the sector.[93] This requires a strong state, employing 'command-and-control' environmental regulation (i.e., economic planning). A managed wind-down amounts to a direct confrontation with fossil capital, while also challenging the strong vested interest of financial fractions in valorizing (fixed) fossil capital investments and the flow of hydrocarbons they represent.

Strategically, then, a key issue is how to channel the Green New Deal (or wind-downs) into more transformative alternatives, going beyond both redistributive reform as panacea and technocratic wind-down which repress deeper issues of corporate power. Inflecting these currents with a salient concern for energy democracy is promising. Energy democracy is a bundle of sectorally-targeted 'non-reformist reforms'[94] that address both relations and forces of production in the process of decarbonization. It condenses the double power shift, from fossil-fuel power to renewables (decarbonization) and from corporate oligarchy to democratic control of economic decisions (democratization). It is guided by three overarching goals – '*resisting* the fossil-fuel-dominant energy agenda while *reclaiming* and democratically *restructuring* energy regimes'.[95]

A broad vision of energy democracy connects the dots between movements for green jobs and industrial conversion, divestment initiatives, Indigenous protectors, anti-fracking protests, community solar projects, renewable energy co-ops, re-municipalization efforts, and so on, providing grounds for building a counter-hegemonic historical bloc. Yet to encompass deep transformation, the bloc must extend beyond energy democracy per se. Decarbonization and democratization must be conjoined with decolonization. Likewise, the close relationship between financial and fossil fractions means that banks and other sectors of allocative power must be brought under greater democratic control. The reforms offered by energy democracy are steps towards system change, disturbing the capitalist status quo in ways that simultaneously build popular power. They open space for yet broader transformations, wherein corporate control over production and allocation is replaced with participatory democratic planning.

As Cohen asserts, 'Climate politics are *the* field of struggle on which the central social and economic struggles of the coming decades will be decided'.[96] Within this field, the case of Canada illuminates substantive and strategic issues in the urgent battle for a world beyond fossil capitalism. The view from above envisages hegemonic transition as climate-capitalist passive revolution, a formula for climate catastrophe. From below, the view is different: prospects for a transition powered by energy democracy are currently uncertain at best, but are fundamental to any ecologically-sustainable and egalitarian path forward.

NOTES

1. Damien Gayle, 'Fridays for Future School Climate Strikes Resume across the World', *The Guardian*, 25 March 2022.
2. Fiona Harvey, 'IPCC Report: "Now or Never" If World Is to Stave off Climate Disaster', *The Guardian*, 4 April 2022.
3. Frank Jordans and Seth Borenstein, 'Newest IPCC Climate Report Reveals "a Litany of Broken Climate Promises": UN Secretary-General Antonio Guterres', *Canada's National Observer*, 4 April 2022.
4. Extinction Rebellion, 'Rebellion Begins Tomorrow. Will You Step Up?', *Extinction Rebellion UK*, 8 April 2022.
5. Mitchell Beer, 'Ottawa Issues "Slap in the Face" to Climate Science, Approves Bay Du Nord Offshore Oil Megaproject', *The Energy Mix*, 8 April 2022.
6. Natasha Bulowski, 'Carbon Capture Tax Credit Is Budget 2022's Big-Ticket Climate Item', *Canada's National Observer*, 7 April 2022.
7. Kyla Tienhaara and Jeremy Walker, 'Lessons from Australia Show CCUS Is about Capturing Public Opinion and Public Finances, Not Carbon', *Canada's National Observer*, 6 April 2022.
8. Canada has one of the highest per capita levels of carbon emissions in the world. See E. Schaaf et al., 'Fossil CO2 and GHG Emissions of All World Countries', Luxembourg: Publications Office of the European Union, 28 March 2018. Meanwhile, a recent ranking of 61 countries on climate change performance in reducing emissions placed Canada 58th. See: Jan Burck et al., 'Climate Change Performance Index 2021', Berlin: German Watch, 7 December 2020.
9. Andreas Malm, *Fossil Capital: The Rise of Steam Power and the Roots of Global Warming*, London: Verso, 2016, p. 11.
10. Elmar Altvater, 'The Social and Natural Environment of Fossil Capitalism', in Leo Panitch and Colin Leys, eds, *Socialist Register 2007: Coming to Terms with Nature*, London: Merlin Press, 2006, pp. 37–59.
11. Matthew Huber, 'Energizing Historical Materialism: Fossil Fuels, Space and the Capitalist Mode of Production', *Geoforum* 40(1), 2009, pp. 105–15.
12. Huber, 'Energizing Historical Materialism', p. 110.
13. Malm, *Fossil Capital*.
14. Malm, *Fossil Capital*, p. 353.
15. Ian Angus, *Facing the Anthropocene: Fossil Capitalism and the Crisis of the Earth System*, New York: Monthly Review Press, 2016.
16. Matthew Huber, *Lifeblood: Oil, Freedom, and the Forces of Capital*, Minneapolis: University of Minnesota Press, 2013.
17. Altvater, 'The Social and Natural Environment of Fossil Capitalism'; Malm, *Fossil Capital*.
18. Eric Pineault, 'The Capitalist Pressure to Extract: The Ecological and Political Economy of Extreme Oil in Canada', *Studies in Political Economy* 99(2), 2018, pp. 130–50.
19. Malm, *Fossil Capital*, p. 291.
20. Jane Taber, 'PM Brands Canada an "Energy Superpower"', *The Globe and Mail*, 15 July 2006.

21 Geoffrey McCormack and Thom Workman, *The Servant State: Overseeing Capital Accumulation in Canada*, Black Point, Nova Scotia: Fernwood Books, 2015, p. 42.
22 Michael T. Klare, *The Race for What's Left: The Global Scramble for the World's Last Resources*, New York: Metropolitan Books, 2012; Pineault, 'The Capitalist Pressure to Extract'.
23 In a recent calculation of unburnable carbon under a 1.5C scenario, Welsby et al., find that Canada must leave 82-83 per cent of its entire fossil fuel reserves and 84 per cent of its tar sands in the ground. See Dan Welsby et al., 'Unextractable Fossil Fuels in a 1.5 °C World', *Nature* 597(7875), 2021, pp. 230–34.
24 Glen Sean Coulthard, *Red Skin, White Masks: Rejecting the Colonial Politics of Recognition*, Minneapolis: University of Minnesota Press, 2014.
25 Clayton Thomas-Muller, 'The Rise of the Native Rights–Based Strategic Framework', in Stephen D'Arcy et al, eds, *A Line in the Tar Sands*, Toronto: Between the Lines, 2014, pp. 240–52.
26 Dayna Nadine Scott, '"We Are the Monitors Now": Experiential Knowledge, Transcorporeality and Environmental Justice', *Social & Legal Studies* 25(3), 2016, pp. 261–87.
27 Ian Hussey et al., 'Boom, Bust, and Consolidation: Corporate Restructuring in the Alberta Oil Sands', in William K. Carroll, ed., *Regime of Obstruction: How Corporate Power Blocks Energy Democracy*, Edmonton: Athabasca University Press, 2021, pp. 35–59.
28 Oil Prices are drawn from the Alberta Economic Dashboard: economicdashboard.alberta.ca/OilPrice.
29 Tyler McCreary, 'Crisis in the Tar Sands: Fossil Capitalism and the Future of the Alberta Hydrocarbon Economy', *Historical Materialism* 30(1), 2021, pp. 1–36.
30 See: Gregor Semieniuk et al., 'Stranded Fossil-Fuel Assets Translate to Major Losses for Investors in Advanced Economies', *Nature Climate Change* 12(6), 2022, pp. 532–38, who provide a recent global assessment of potential stranded oil and gas assets – assets that face unanticipated write-downs, devaluations, or conversions to liabilities – based on what investors currently expect from their investments on the one hand and policy and technological changes to prevent more than 2 C of warming on the other hand. They estimate US $1.76 trillion in potential stranded assets globally, and US $100 billion in Canada, based on oilfield assets and production equipment alone (excluding pipelines and refineries).
31 Hussey et al., 'Boom, Bust, and Consolidation'.
32 Ian Hussey, 'Oil Sands Spending and Productivity Figures Indicate Majority of Lost Jobs Not Likely to Return', Edmonton: Parkland Institute, 2020.
33 Greg Albo and Lilian Yap, 'From the Tar Sands to "Green Jobs"? Work and Ecological Justice', *The Bullet*, 12 July 2016.
34 Jamie Lawson, 'Lines of Work, Corridors of Power: Extraction, Obstruction, and Counter-Obstruction Along Fossil-Fuel Production Networks', in William K. Carroll, ed., *Regime of Obstruction: How Corporate Power Blocks Energy Democracy*, Edmonton: Athabasca University Press, 2021, pp. 61–90.
35 William K. Carroll and Jouke Huijzer, 'Who Owns Big Carbon? Mapping the Network of Corporate Ownership', in William K. Carroll, ed., *Regime of Obstruction: How Corporate Power Blocks Energy Democracy*, Edmonton: Athabasca University Press, 2021, p. 134.

36 Rainforest Alliance Network, 'Banking on Climate Chaos 2022', Rainforest Alliance Network, 2022.
37 William K. Carroll, 'Canada's Carbon-Capital Elite: A Tangled Web of Corporate Power', *Canadian Journal of Sociology* 42(3), 2017, pp. 225–60.
38 Mark Hudson and Evan Bowness, 'Finance and Fossil Capital: A Community Divided?', *The Extractive Industries and Society* 8(1), 2021, p. 3.
39 William K. Carroll et al., 'Fossil Capital's Reach into Civil Society: The Architecture of Climate Change Denialism', in William K. Carroll, ed., *Regime of Obstruction: How Corporate Power Blocks Energy Democracy*, Edmonton: Athabasca University Press, 2021, p. 191.
40 Nicolas Graham, William K. Carroll, and David Chen, 'Carbon Capital's Political Reach: A Network Analysis of Federal Lobbying by the Fossil Fuel Sector from Harper to Trudeau', *Canadian Political Science Review* 14(1), 2020, p. 3.
41 Shannon Daub et al., 'Doing Things Better Together: Industry Capture of Climate Policy in BC', in William K. Carroll, ed., *Regime of Obstruction: How Corporate Power Blocks Energy Democracy*, Edmonton: Athabasca University Press, 2021, pp. 249–71.
42 Shane Gunster et al., '"Our Oil": Extractive Populism in Canadian Social Media', in William K. Carroll, ed., *Regime of Obstruction: How Corporate Power Blocks Energy Democracy*, Edmonton: Athabasca University Press, 2021, pp. 197–224.
43 Robert Neubauer and Nicolas Graham, 'Fuelling the Subsidized Public: Mapping the Flow of Extractivist Content on Facebook', *Canadian Journal of Communication* 46(4), 2021, p. 905.
44 Fiona MacPhail and Paul Bowles, 'Toward a Typology of Fossil Fuel Flashpoints: The Potential for Coalition Building', in William K. Carroll, ed., *Regime of Obstruction: How Corporate Power Blocks Energy Democracy*, Edmonton: Athabasca University Press, 2021, pp. 429–52.
45 Emily Eaton and Simon Enoch, 'The Oil Industry Is Us: Hegemonic Community Economic Identity in Saskatchewan's Oil Patch', in William K. Carroll, ed., *Regime of Obstruction: How Corporate Power Blocks Energy Democracy*, Edmonton: Athabasca University Press, 2021, pp. 307–30.
46 Simon Enoch and Emily Eaton, 'Crude Lessons', Saskatchewan: Canadian Centre for Policy Alternatives, 2019, p.10.
47 Robert Hackett and Hanna Araza, 'The Oil Blotter: Postmedia & Big Oil's Symbiosis', *The Monitor*, May 1, 2021.
48 Shannon Daub et al., 'Episodes in the New Climate Denialism', in William K. Carroll, ed., *Regime of Obstruction: How Corporate Power Blocks Energy Democracy*, Edmonton: Athabasca University Press, 2021, pp. 225–48.
49 William K. Carroll, Nicolas Graham, and Mark Shakespeare, 'Foundations, ENGOs, Clean-Growth Networks and the Integral State', *Canadian Journal of Sociology* 45(2), 2020, pp. 109–42.
50 William K. Carroll, 'Fossil Capitalism, Climate Capitalism, Energy Democracy: The Struggle for Hegemony in an Era of Climate Crisis', *Socialist Studies/Études Socialistes* 14(1), 2020.
51 David Tetzlaff, 'Divide and Conquer: Popular Culture and Social Control in Late Capitalism', *Media, Culture & Society* 13(1), 1991, pp. 9–33.
52 Karena Shaw, 'Flashpoints of Possibility: What Resistance Reveals About Pathways Toward Energy Transition', in William K. Carroll, ed., *Regime of Obstruction: How*

Corporate Power Blocks Energy Democracy, Edmonton: Athabasca University Press, 2021, p. 412.

53   Emilia Belliveau, James K. Rowe, and Jessica Dempsey, 'Fossil Fuel Divestment, Non-Reformist Reforms, and Anti-Capitalist Strategy', in William K. Carroll, *Regime of Obstruction: How Corporate Power Blocks Energy Democracy*, Edmonton: Athabasca University Press, 2021, pp. 453–77.

54   Emily Eaton, Simon Enoch, and Shanon Zachidniak, 'Renewable Regina', Saskatchewan: Canadian Centre for Policy Alternatives, 2020.

55   Arthur Manuel, *The Reconciliation Manifesto: Recovering the Land, Rebuilding the Economy*, Toronto: Lorimer, 2017, pp. 133–34.

56   Roxanne Amanda Dunbar-Ortiz, 'The Relationship between Marxism and Indigenous Struggles and Implications of the Theoretical Framework for International Indigenous Struggles', *Historical Materialism* 24(3), 2016, p. 86.

57   Indigenous Climate Action, *Decolonizing Climate Policy in Canada: Report from Phase One*, Ottawa: Indigenous Climate Action, 2021.

58   Peter Newell and Matthew Paterson, *Climate Capitalism: Global Warming and the Transformation of the Global Economy*, Cambridge: Cambridge University Press, 2010.

59   Adam David Morton, 'The Continuum of Passive Revolution', *Capital & Class* 34(3), 2010, p. 316.

60   Adrian Ford and Peter Newell, 'Regime Resistance and Accommodation: Toward a Neo-Gramscian Perspective on Energy Transitions', *Energy Research & Social Science* 79, 2021, p. 6.

61   Anne Showstack Sassoon, 'Passive Revolution and the Politics of Reform', in Anne Showstack Sassoon, ed., *Approaches to Gramsci*, London: Writers and Readers, 1982, pp. 127–48.

62   Jean Philippe Sapinski, 'Constructing Climate Capitalism: Corporate Power and the Global Climate Policy-Planning Network', *Global Networks* 16(1), 2016, pp. 89–111; Jean Philippe Sapinski, 'Climate Capitalism and the Global Corporate Elite Network', *Environmental Sociology* 1(4), 2015, pp. 268–79.

63   William K. Carroll, 'Fossil Capital, Imperialism and The Global Corporate Elite', in Vishwas Satgar, ed., *BRICS and the New American Imperialism: Global Rivalry and Resistance*, Johannesburg: Wits University Press, 2020, pp. 30–57.

64   European Commission, 'The European Green Deal', Brussels: European Commission, 2019, p. 2.

65   Sapinski, 'Constructing Climate Capitalism', p. 106.

66   Tadzio Muller, 'Of Energy Struggles, Energy Transitions and Energy Democracy', New York: Rosa Luxemburg Foundation, 2013.

67   Jessica Green et al., 'Transition, Hedge, or Resist? Understanding Political and Economic Behavior toward Decarbonization in the Oil and Gas Industry', *Review of International Political Economy*, 2021, p. 17.

68   Mei Li, Gregory Trencher, and Jusen Asuka, 'The Clean Energy Claims of BP, Chevron, ExxonMobil and Shell: A Mismatch between Discourse, Actions and Investments', *PLoS ONE* 17(2), 2022, p. 19.

69   Dario Kenner and Richard Heede, 'White Knights, or Horsemen of the Apocalypse? Prospects for Big Oil to Align Emissions with a 1.5 C Pathway', *Energy Research & Social Science*, 2021, p. 8.

70 Sean Sweeney, 'Sustaining the Unsustainable: Why Renewable Energy Companies Are Not Climate Warriors', *New Labor Forum* 30(3), 2021, pp. 104–10.
71 Brett Christophers, 'Fossilised Capital: Price and Profit in the Energy Transition', *New Political Economy* 27(1), 2021, pp. 1–14.
72 Sweeney, 'Sustaining the Unsustainable'.
73 Christophers, 'Fossilised Capital'; Malm, *Fossil Capital*.
74 Malm, *Fossil Capital*, p. 372.
75 Sweeney, 'Sustaining the Unsustainable', p. 106.
76 Nicolas Graham, *Forces of Production, Climate Change and Canadian Fossil Capitalism*, Leiden: Brill, 2021.
77 Carroll, 'Fossil Capitalism, Climate Capitalism, Energy Democracy'.
78 Donald Gutstein, *The Big Stall: How Big Oil and Think Tanks Are Blocking Action on Climate Change in Canada*, Toronto: Lorimer, 2018, p. 205.
79 David Langille, 'The Business Council on National Issues and the Canadian State', *Studies in Political Economy* 24, 1987, pp. 41–85.
80 Gutstein, *The Big Stall*, p. 204.
81 Carroll, Graham, and Shakespeare, 'Foundations, ENGOs, Clean-Growth Networks and the Integral State', p. 109.
82 Nicolas Graham, 'Canadian Fossil Capitalism, Corporate Strategy, and Post-Carbon Futures', *Canadian Review of Sociology/Revue Canadienne de Sociologie* 56(2), 2019, pp. 224–50.
83 Nicolas Graham, 'Fossil Knowledge Networks: Science, Ecology and the "Greening" of Carbon Extractive Development', *Studies in Political Economy* 101(2), 2020, pp. 93–113.
84 Given current climatic overshoot, some deployment of large-scale CCS (reducing atmospheric concentrations to historic levels), alongside radical reductions in emissions, is likely necessary. The key issue is who will control these emergent forces of production. Thus, Malm and Carton's injunction to 'seize the means of carbon removal' has merit. See Andreas Malm and Wim Carton, 'Seize the Means of Carbon Removal: The Political Economy of Direct Air Capture', *Historical Materialism* 29(1), 2021, pp. 3–48.
85 Marc Lee, 'Dangerous Distractions: Canada's Carbon Emissions and the Pathway to Net Zero', Vancouver: Canadian Centre for Policy Alternatives, 2021, p. 19.
86 John Bellamy Foster, 'On Fire This Time', *Monthly Review* 71(6), 2019, pp. 1–17; Naomi Klein, *On Fire: The (Burning) Case for a Green New Deal*, New York: Knopf Canada, 2019.
87 Matthew T. Huber, *Climate Change as Class War: Building Socialism on a Warming Planet*, London: Verso Books, 2022.
88 The Leap, 'Leap Manifesto - A Call for a Canada Based on Caring for the Earth and One Another', 2015, leapmanifesto.org/en/the-leap-manifesto. For a commentary on the potentials and limits of the Leap, see: Socialist Project, 'A Leap Toward Radical Politics?', *Socialist Project*, 7 June 2016, available at: socialistproject.ca/2016.
89 Climate Action Network, 'A Green New Deal for Canada – Climate Action Network', climateactionnetwork.ca/a-green-new-deal-for-canada.
90 Eriel Tchekwie Deranger et al., 'Decolonizing Climate Research and Policy: Making Space to Tell Our Own Stories, in Our Own Ways', *Community Development Journal* 57(1), 2022, pp. 52–73.

91 Iron & Earth, www.ironandearth.org.
92 Socialist Project, *Take the Plant, Save the Planet*, Toronto: Socialist Project, February 2020, at www.socialistproject.ca.
93 Emily Eaton, 'Approaches to Energy Transitions: Carbon Pricing, Managed Decline, and/or Green New Deal?', *Geography Compass* 15(2), 2021.
94 Andre Gorz, *Strategy for Labor: A Radical Proposal*, Boston, Massachusetts: Beacon Press, 1967.
95 Matthew J. Burke and Jennie C. Stephens, 'Energy Democracy: Goals and Policy Instruments for Sociotechnical Transitions', *Energy Research & Social Science* 33, 2017, p. 35.
96 Daniel Aldana Cohen, 'The Last Stimulus', *Jacobin*, 15 August 2017, p. 88.

LOGISTICAL LANDSCAPES: CORPORATE POWER AND CAPITAL IN THE MARITIME INDUSTRY

RAFEEF ZIADAH

The Covid-19 pandemic has highlighted both the significance and fragility of internationalized supply chains. With shortages in personal protective equipment, discussions of vaccine production and rollout, and even the rush on supermarkets, the largely invisible operations of business logistics became part of daily conversations. The labour of those in the transport and logistics sector – dockworkers, drivers, those in warehousing and food packing – was deemed essential, with these workers forced to carry a disproportionate risk of virus exposure to ensure continued access to commodities from basic necessities to the frivolous. Concurrently, the alarm over supply chain disruptions brought with it a debate on worker safety and precarity, graphically demonstrated by the thousands of seafarers 'abandoned at sea' and unable to return home for months on end due to travel restrictions.[1] Nonetheless, as the public health crisis unfolded and logistics workers faced unprecedented pressure, companies such as Amazon, who were completely immersed in global circulation and supply chains, were experiencing booming sales and record profits.

For the left, this conjuncture of emergency confirms the need to better understand the 'logistics revolution' and its place in contemporary capitalism. It is still too early to assess the full impact of the pandemic on supply chains (including the culpability in the subsequent inflationary surge), but the experience of the last two years has sharply highlighted how deeply daily consumption is now mediated through the corporate management techniques of business logistics. Logistics has come to permeate every aspect of our everyday lives – from managing access to the basic commodities we consume, to organizing emergency responses to natural disasters and humanitarian relief.[2] Yet, the rise of logistics has also raised the spectre of new forms of worker resistance and organizing. Despite the promises of 'seamless' trade and fully automated circulation, the pandemic – and now the war in Ukraine with its supply shocks to global oil and agricultural markets – has illustrated the fragility of these commodity movements and their ultimate dependence on human labour.

Maritime transport remains the backbone of global trade, with around 80 per cent of the volume of international trade and 65 per cent of commodity value carried by sea. The world's seas act 'as surfaces for the circulation and realisation of value'.[3] Maritime ports constitute key nodal points within increasingly integrated logistical networks that underpin the globally structured character of commodity circulation. This may seem like the arcane trivia of the global transport industry, but exploring the specific corporate landscapes of container shipping, the key trends mobilizing global supply chains, and the major concentration and consolidation of port operators and shipping liners reveals key points of political contestation in capitalism today.[4] Logistical networks are indeed differentially integrating states and labour regimes into processes of production and circulation.

THE 'LOGISTICS REVOLUTION'

A burgeoning critical literature amongst researchers and union activists has stressed the so-called 'science of business logistics', the management of commodity circulation through complex, networked infrastructures and internationalized supply chains, underpins contemporary capitalism.[5] Of course, attempts to expand, speed-up, and coordinate commodity circulation at a global scale are not new; however, the logistics revolution of the 1960s and 1970s was undoubtedly a significant turning point in the standardization of circulation and management of 'goods in motion'. The system-wide thinking of business logistics has worked to collapse production and distribution into one integrated unit that is mapped onto internationally networked infrastructures, trade gateways, corridors, and logistics clusters.[6] Although seemingly technical, business logistics is more than a set of management techniques; it is the organizing mechanism of what Tsing has termed 'supply-chain capitalism'.[7] As Khalili succinctly puts it: 'Maritime trade, logistics, and hydrocarbon transport are the clearest distillation of how global capitalism operates today.'[8] This logic is well captured in Marx's oft-quoted line: capital strives to 'annihilate this space with the time, i.e. to reduce to a minimum the time spent in motion from one place to the other'.[9]

A crucial dimension to this logistics revolution were the techno-scientific transformations associated with maritime trade. A marked shift took place with standardization of commodity shipping through the introduction of the container, which facilitated the movement of commodities across different modes of transport (known as inter-modality). Computer technologies were also essential to monitoring and managing commodities in motion.[10] Indeed, '[w]ithout a "revolution" in ocean-going cargo-handling technology, the global factory would not exist, nor the phenomenon of globalization itself'.[11] This backdrop of logistics acted to integrate new markets and manage commodity circulation, adding extreme pressure on labour to be more 'agile' and flexible in overseeing 'lean' supply chains.

As Campling and Colas note, however, much of the contemporary writing on logistics can fall into a kind of 'presentism', with an overemphasis on what is supposedly new and revolutionary, or a reification of particular turning points, such as the moment of containerization. In their analysis: 'The origins of "seamless" logistics lie not in containerisation per se but in the interpenetration of "national" capitals and inter-firm alliances linking colonial and non-colonial shipping and port complexes for acceleration and reliability in the transfer of commodity capital and against organised labour.'[12] They posit that the shifts to bulk and tanker shipping that preceded containerization were essential to pushing the maritime industry towards integrated logistics. For them, the logistics revolution is prefigured in the earlier legacies of colonialism and imperialism.[13]

The shift to end-to-end logistics provision is not, for these reasons, a rupture in the logic of capital expansion but an acute intensification of longstanding patterns of accumulation. This has involved a noticeable move towards an integrated 'whole systems' approach to managing commodities through each moment of the circulation of capital: production, transport, storage, and the realization of value. Logistics thus encompasses a wide range of activities including the management and planning of supply chains, the operations of transport infrastructures, through to forwarding and warehousing – all of which are increasingly managed by computer modelling and surveillance technologies. Business logistics puts emphasis on standardization and systems management of goods in motion, while minimizing and disciplining the labour time necessary to move them. As such, it has driven new and expanded geographies of accumulation, and reconfigured relations between corporations, the state, and labour.

MARITIME PORTS: CORPORATE CONSOLIDATION AND VERTICAL INTEGRATION

Maritime shipping and ports are critical nodes within this broader logistical architecture of commodity circulation. Most of what we consume reaches us through the movement of goods across oceans; in this respect, the internationalization of capital is in large part actually the story of the sea.

Today, the majority of global trade in manufactured commodities is carried on container ships, while bulk carriers transport essential raw materials such as iron ore and coal, and tankers transport crude oil, chemicals, and petroleum products. Most mega-ports will have a mix of terminals to accommodate these different commodities and various types of vessels. A complex array of shipping companies, port operators, and different kinds of labour underpin these maritime movements.

Over recent decades there has been a significant eastward shift in maritime trade, reflecting the movement of the centre of world manufacturing to China and East Asia. In 2021, the five countries with the highest Liner Shipping Connectivity Index (LSCI) were in Asia – China, Singapore, South Korea, Malaysia, and Hong Kong.[14] At port level, eight of the most connected ports were also in Asia, led by Shanghai; the remaining two are in Europe – Rotterdam and Antwerp. It is from these Asian ports that much of the world's commodity production is moved to North America and Europe, with the largest container ships and most densely used shipping routes tracking Asia-Europe and Asia-North America trade and supply-chain linkages. In contrast, Africa and Latin America are much less connected to these global routes.

In this manner, as states are inserted differentially into the structures of global trade, a clear hierarchy of mega-ports emerges along the core trade routes, influenced by state and corporate investment patterns, as well as technological factors like ship size and levels of automation. Maritime ports themselves are integrated into an environment of complete supply chain management and transport intermodalism. In the 1990s, with the policy frameworks of trade facilitation, corporate port operators saw an opportunity to expand and venture outside their flagship ports.[15] The increasing privatization of state operated infrastructures allowed port operators to expand their portfolios, relying upon concession agreements and public-private-partnerships (P3s) to construct, finance and manage expanded physical assets.[16]

At the same time, there has been a clear tendency towards reducing unit costs by increasing ship sizes, with the average size (per port) of the largest container ships increasing by 125 per cent between 2006 and 2020.[17] In turn, ports that can accommodate the enormous new vessels are further advantaged. Ever-larger vessels necessitate both a corresponding investment in port facilities, but also a reduction in the number of ports of call. This creates competitive pressures between ports, pushes out smaller regional ones and, at the same time, increases the power of the major ship liners. While the size of container ships has increased, the average number of shipping companies has decreased, reflecting patterns of capital concentration and market consolidation through mergers, acquisitions, and corporate alliances.

Today, there is a staggering concentration of control in terms of port operators, with just five companies controlling 50 per cent of container trade through ports at the world level. These companies are: (1) PSA International (Singapore), one of the first to pursue an international strategy; (2) Hutchison Port Holdings (Hong Kong); (3) APM Terminals (although headquartered in the Netherlands, this is a unit of the Danish shipping company Maersk); (4) COSCO Shipping Ports (China); and finally (5) Dubai Ports World (UAE). As this list indicates, there has been a significant shift in the geography of corporate control over the last two decades, with the port operators sector expanding beyond North American and European companies.

A similar concentration of ownership can also be seen in the shipping industry. Sixty-five per cent of the container ship market is currently controlled by just five companies: Mediterranean Shipping Company (Switzerland/Italy); APM-Maersk (Denmark); CMA CGM (France); COSCO (China), and Hapag-Lloyd (Germany).[18] Although these companies are dominated by European ownership, the ships owned and operated by these companies may be registered under 'flags of convenience' – loosely regulated jurisdictions such as Panama, Liberia, and the Marshall Islands – which allows them to minimize labour costs, taxation, and other regulations.[19] More recently, there has been a definite trend towards increasing interdependencies between the largest port operators and shipping companies, with many of the leading shipping companies also expanding into port operations (see Table 1). This trend towards vertical integration takes place in the context of increased acquisitions and mergers among shipping companies, and their consolidation in three large global shipping alliances that now control about 80 per cent of the global container market.[20]

The increasing concentration and centralization of ownership across shipping and port operations is being extended into other moments of commodity circulation, notably logistics companies that are involved in the transport of goods from ports to warehouses and then to the final consumer.[21] Such integration is in line with the foundational rationale of business logistics – a strategy of optimizing corporate control over integrated systems of production and circulation. By evolving towards end-to-end service providers that operate shipping, terminals, gateways, and inland logistics services, the corporate control of massive, geographically dispersed conglomerates over the basic sinews of global circulation is further consolidated.

Table 1: Relationship between ship liners and port operators

Shipping Company	Operator	Relationship	Number of Terminals operated
APM-Maersk	APM Terminals Terminal Investment Limited (TIL)	APM-Maersk and APM Terminals are owned by The Maersk Group	76
Mediterranean Shipping Company	Terminal Investment Limited (TIL)	TIL is fully owned by Mediterranean Shipping Company	40
COSCO Shipping Co Ltd	COSCO Shipping Ports	COSCO Container Line and COSCO Shipping Ports are owned by The COSCO Group	37
CMA CGM	CMA Terminal	CMA Terminal Fully owned CMA CGM	29
CMA CGM	Terminal link	Joint venture 51 per cent owned by CMA CGM and 49 per cent owned by China Merchants Port.	33

Source: Data drawn from company websites by author.

The growing power of a handful of firms is not only reconfiguring relations within the shipping industry, but also recalibrating the relative strength of corporations and capitalist states. The largest corporations in the maritime industry gain significantly increased bargaining power vis-à-vis states with less developed infrastructures. Shipping alliances, for example, can influence decisions about which ports survive simply by moving shipping elsewhere. Industry consolidation also has serious implications for the ways port concessions are negotiated and structured, forcing countries to build much more expensive ports that can accommodate large ship sizes and specialized terminals. All of this widens the geographical unevenness of global trade.

LOGISTICS AS DEVELOPMENT

Growing corporate consolidation in the maritime industry has been strengthened through the diffusion of neoliberal strategies that emphasize export-led development and trade liberalization, and thus the development of transport infrastructures and logistics as foundational to economic growth. In 2004, UNCTAD developed the Liner Shipping Connectivity Index (LSCI) to determine a country's position within global liner shipping networks, linking port performance to a country's trade competitiveness. This was followed in 2007 by the World Bank's Logistics Index, which served as a benchmarking tool to compare countries across metrics such as quality of transport infrastructures, timeliness, tracking and tracing, customs, and logistics services. Through these mechanisms, logistics has been elevated to a key measure of 'development' itself.

International development agencies and financial institutions, like the World Bank, which developed a global Logistics Performance Index, encouraged poorer countries to enhance their logistics sectors, privatize transport assets, and secure financing for ever larger transport projects and associated logistics spaces.[22] Integration into existing shipping lanes requires investments in infrastructures including terminals, cargo handling facilities, and associated warehousing. This has been facilitated through private investments and P3 arrangements aimed at overcoming what the World Bank has termed the 'logistics lag'. Within these models, the success of a port is measured by its level of automation and inland services, access to free trade areas, inland distribution routes, and connections to other transport modes. In practice, this also means the provision of necessary land to establish these large circulatory projects through either upgrading existing ports or building new ones. This confirms that although corporations advocate for and shape the increased logistical 'connectivity' along global trade routes, the capitalist state remains vital to guaranteeing legal regimes, investment, and financing arrangements.

But among port operators there is still a considerable role played by large state-owned enterprises (SOEs). Of the five port operators noted earlier, two are majority state-owned (COSCO and Dubai Ports World). A significant part of recent maritime infrastructural expansion and investment is financed by states and fuelled by SOEs. The major contemporary example of this is of course China's Belt and Road Initiative (BRI), which 'accelerated an ongoing trend of increasing Chinese investment in overseas ports that began in the early 2000s'.[23] Led by Chinese SOEs and backed by a host of development and private banks, the project is already impacting transport developments across the maritime sector in other countries. Likewise, the UAE's Dubai Ports World is also a major actor in the global maritime industry, a position that is simultaneously linked to the UAE's considerable weight in the global airport industry.

Maritime infrastructures are thus a vehicle through which countries such as China and the UAE are attempting to reconfigure their place within the hierarchies of states within the contemporary world market. Indeed, these transport investments are generating a multiplicity of geopolitical tensions – described by some as an 'infrastructure scramble' – that are forming in the context of 'multi-polar, competitive capitalist globalization'.[24] For example, it is worth noting here that concern over control of infrastructures has prompted the US to establish an International Development Finance Corporation with a mandate to consolidate the US capacity to finance infrastructures in developing countries. Other similar concerns are expressed in initiatives like the European Union's Global Gateway.[25] In a different context, the UAE's investments in maritime infrastructures in East Africa have inserted it forcefully into local politics, and has come hand-in-hand with investments in military bases and support for local allies willing to grant long term concessions.[26]

Such geopolitical tensions have a direct impact on emergent maritime infrastructures. This is illustrated, for example, in discussions around the African Continental Free Trade Area (ACFTA) agreement, which is embedded in notions of connectivity and logistics as development. ACFTA advances a spatial-economic restructuring that links the continent's markets internally and deepens their integration into international trading routes. The agreement entered into force in 2019, and its stated aim is to increase regional trade and eliminate trade barriers. It sets out measures to enhance market access and increase liberalization. One of the five priority sectors is the transport sector, with an emphasis on developing and financing integrated end-to-end logistical networks. The UN Economic Commission for Africa even noted that if the necessary infrastructure projects are fully implemented, Africa's maritime fleet is projected to increase by 188 per cent for bulk and 180 per cent for container cargoes.[27]

Although there is a tendency to focus solely on Chinese investments in upcoming port projects in the context of the BRI, the UAE is also keenly invested in linking up its logistical networks to African markets by strategically building up DP World's portfolio of ports and gateways in African states. As noted above, DP World does not have a shipping arm like its competitors, and it has tended to invest heavily in terminals, logistics, and free trade areas. The company has several projects across Africa with operations in Senegal, Mozambique, Egypt, Algeria, Rwanda, DR Congo, and Somaliland. A major focus of the UAE's activities in Africa is Senegal, where DP World has been operating since 2008. A concession agreement was signed for the construction of a $1.13bn deep-water port at Ndayane, situated approximately 50 km from Dakar, Senegal's capital.[28] This is being promoted as the project to make Senegal the logistics hub and maritime gateway to West Africa. Similarly, DP World has recently launched a new global e-commerce platform in Rwanda, aptly named DuBuy.com, which aims at boosting trade and business between Rwanda and UAE.[29] This major initiative is designed as an initial hub for expanding e-commerce across East Africa and will be linked to DP World's port infrastructure across the continent.

Investments such as these illustrate the growing focus by China and the UAE on mega-infrastructural projects in non-Western spaces. These projects are closely linked to the existing maritime logistics networks of firms such as COSCO and DP World; they envisage a wider logistical space that includes other kinds of transport infrastructures – such as road, rail, and air – linked through logistical gateways and corridors. In this manner, the 'logistics as development' mantra is not only serving to rewire the nature of global trade and capital flows, but also to alter the key actors that superintend these flows. We can see here an increasing entanglement of state and corporate power that is developing alongside the growing consolidation and vertical integration of the top tier corporations in the sector.

LABOUR, UNION ORGANIZING, AND DISRUPTION

Much of the labour involved in the maritime industry is hidden from view, and strikingly concentrated in East and South Asia. At the very base of the industry is the process of making ships themselves. Here, the last decade has witnessed an extraordinary geographical concentration, with just three countries – China, South Korea, and Japan – responsible for 94 per cent of global ship-building activity in 2020.[30] The labour on ships is also highly concentrated, with workers from the Philippines, Russia, Indonesia, China, and India making up nearly half of the global seafarer workforce. The labour involved in the end-life of shipping is as important, although often missed from the triumphalist accounts of the maritime industry. Here, Bangladesh and India jointly account for 71 per cent, and Pakistan for an additional 17 per cent of ship scrapping (tearing the massive cargo ships apart for recyclable materials after they have reached the end of their operational life) – a hugely labour-intensive process with highly unsafe working conditions.[31] In short, human labour remains crucial to the ways ports and ships operate – a fact crucial to remember in the face of threats of 'full automation' often deployed against workers. It is automation that also subordinates and controls labour that the industry seeks.

Elsewhere, the promotion of integrated maritime logistics is routinely couched in the language of development and 'win-win' scenarios. New port projects are promoted as job creation opportunities and investments allowing for more efficient trade. Swept away in these positive scenarios is the environmental degradation necessary for ever larger tracts of lands and oceans to be remade in the interest of commodity trade. For labour, on the other hand, the 'agile' and 'lean' supply chain ethos of business logistics is reflected in the greater precarity of flexible labour regimes across the maritime industry. Demands for port productivity and efficiency add pressure on transport labour, while surveillance technologies are increasingly used to measure and trace the productivity of individual workers.[32]

Historically, maritime workers have had high levels of unionization and led important campaigns against driving down labour standards. Dockworkers in particular have a long history of being at the forefront of labour, anti-militarist, and anti-racist struggles.[33] There are two international labour federations representing dockworkers: the International Transport Workers' Federation (ITF) with 700 affiliated unions from 150 countries, and the International Dockworkers Council (IDC). The (ITF) is by far the larger, more mainstream organization. It boasts on its official website that this size allows for stronger bargaining and lobbying power. The ITF has challenged the 'flags of convenience' system in the shipping industry and worked to enshrine maritime labour protections in international conventions.[34] The IDC, in contrast, came out of locals formerly affiliated to the ITF who accuse it of mishandling two critical dockworker disputes at the Port of Liverpool (1990s) and the Port of Charleston in 2000.[35] While much smaller, the IDC has focused on building a rank-and-file organizing model with a view towards coordinated industrial action.

Although historically there has been high levels of unionization among dockworkers, providing them with important leverage, the shift in global grade eastward and the consolidation of corporate power in the maritime industry have meant that new ports have emerged in states that did not allow unionization or had very weak labour standards. There has therefore been a long-term and consistent assault on working conditions, including through legal mechanisms that help the industry evade accountability. Beyond dockworkers and seafarers, union density varies extensively across the logistics sector. Warehousing for example, has low unionization rates and has been marked by short-term and zero-hour contracts and growing use of digital technologies to monitor and discipline labour. In a revealing expose of an Amazon warehouse in Montreal, Mostafa Henaway explained how the company uses a badge system that 'created an internal temp system' leading to a 'desperate and docile workforce among those hired as seasonal workers'. He goes on to describe the hyper-surveillance of workers and the ways technology is 'merged' with the human body to 'turn workers into industrial robots'.[36] Although at a difference pace and scale, such technologies are being mainstreamed across the global transport and logistics industry.

While it is important to trace these overarching trends, we need to be mindful that logistics chains contain different forms of labour – warehouse workers, dock workers, and seafarers have different histories of unionization and protections, but also work to different patterns. For example, seafarers are generally out at sea for six-month periods, while warehouse workers can be working shifts on zero-hour contracts. One of the challenges for labour organizing is how to work across such integrated logistics chains, operating on different geographical scales, while still attending to the different types and tempos of labour necessary in the sector. There has been a compelling argument to focus on unionizing last-mile delivery drivers and in-house warehouse workers – this work can advance faster if coordinated with truck drivers and dockworkers, sections of the logistics chain with higher levels of unionization.

An important thread in current debates on logistics and union power has stressed labour's unique structural ability to disrupt supply chains despite worsening labour conditions.[37] A striking contradiction of the modern 'lean', global system of production is its extreme vulnerability to disruption. Moody, for example, has forcefully argued that the logistics sector is a strategic arena for labour struggles because it has the potential to disrupt key nodes in a global system of circulation.[38] Much of this analysis has thus far tended to focus on labour contestation in the warehousing sector and major unionized ports. However, the varied geographies of maritime logistics integrate very different working conditions, forms of corporate organization, and a plethora of racialized labour regimes.[39]

It is thus important to understand how the transnational logistics space operates and the key corporate powers within it, but also the very place-specific labour regimes that shape class struggles that can be very localized in form and substance. For instance, many specialized logistics zones are promoted precisely due to their lack of labour regulations. Part of the strategy of global port operators has been specifically to expand to new locations with 'either historically weak or altogether illegal' unionization.[40] The geography of mega-port projects are constructed as securitized industrial complexes, which can in itself be a hindrance to labour organizing by both isolating labour from the broader community and extensively surveilling workers. The vast concentration of corporate power in the maritime industry is making it increasingly difficult for labour in territories with relatively decent labour protections to impact the major operating conglomerates. This was illustrated in the recent incident when P&O Ferries (owned by DP World) fired 800 British-based seafarers without consultation.

Nonetheless, important campaigns, discussions, and modest gains are being won in the logistics sector – most notably in recent unionization drives at Amazon warehouses and attempts to democratize the Teamsters union and launch sustained actions taking on UPS.[41] However, union branch actions tend to be localized and focused on immediate short-term gains. As Katy Fox-Hodess has convincingly illustrated, the challenge of linking local, national, and international campaigns, and most importantly the issue of democratic trade union structures, remains a complicated matter in the sector.[42]

While a focus on enhancing labour organizing and democratizing labour structures is crucial, it is important to stress that supply chain disruptions are not only a tool of the labour movement. Indigenous and anti-militarist campaigners have sought to disrupt critical logistical nodes (ports, trainlines, pipelines) as a key form of protest. These actions have been most effective when communities organize with trade unions to ensure action coordination and support. For example, in the summer of 2021, against a backdrop of yet another Israeli military assault on Gaza and ongoing forced displacement in Jerusalem, Palestinians appealed to trade unions internationally to halt material support for Israel. The Italian union, L'Unione Sindacale di Base (USB) in the Tuscan city of Livorno, led the way by refusing to load a shipment of weapons onto a vessel bound for Israel. A week later, the South African Transport and Allied Workers' Union (SATAWU) refused to offload the Zim Shanghai owned by Israeli company Zim Lines. Dockworkers in Oakland, California were also set to refuse to offload another Israeli-owned ship before it was diverted. Such actions highlight the potential for community-labour forms of contestation, but as with labour organizing more broadly, these are not spontaneous moments; they require time for open discussions, coordination, and education.

NEW TRENDS, ORGANIZING CHALLENGES

The Covid-19 lockdowns and slowdown in global trade put the spotlight on the politics of transport infrastructures. Restrictions led to commodity shortages and congestion and delays at key ports. Continuing outbreaks are closing some of the world's busiest ports in China, including Terminals Shenzhen and Ningbo-Zhoushan. The pandemic exposed the inherent fragility of internationalized supply chains, leading to debate about new ways of coping with disruptions. At the same time, the logistics industry experienced a major boost in e-commerce activities alongside soaring freight rates.[43] These high freight rates have bolstered profitability for the top tier conglomerates, but have also placed significant pressure on less connected regions (such as South America and West Africa) where price rises have been much higher than the core shipping routes to North America and Europe.[44] These uneven outcomes of the current crisis indicate the importance of understanding the structures of corporate power and their global modalities within the logistics sector.

At the same time – despite much speculation around the likelihood of increasing protectionism, reshoring, and nearshoring – there is little systematic evidence that significant manufacturing activity has shifted or that longer term patterns of global trade have been permanently impacted by Covid-19 (or the more recent war in Ukraine and proliferating sanctions). While labour-intensive and low-value production may be shifted more easily, mid-and high-value-added manufacturing is difficult to move. There is more likely to be mixed supply chain models, in which companies build contingency plans and maintain warehouse stocks in different locations to ensure less impact from unexpected disruptions. In contrast, e-commerce is increasing the demand for distribution facilities and warehousing in urban centres – this is partly why we see more organizing drives in warehousing facilities connected to on-line platforms like Amazon or mass retailers like Walmart. While there are small shifts in the US import trade away from China to places such as Cambodia or Mexico, it is often Chinese capital or products that are being assembled in these different locations, rather than a reshoring of production to the core capitalist countries.

It is crucial, then, that the left better understand the pivotal role of operational logistics for the global circulation of commodity capital. Uneven power relations permeate the production of trade routes, infrastructure investment, and construction. New geographies of control are emerging, with major ramifications for development processes in much of the Global South and evolving geo-political rivalries over markets and military alignments. While the extreme concentration of corporate power and authoritarian state practices are formidable obstacles that confront union organizing, there is nonetheless a burst of significant and innovative work taking place around warehouse and delivery driver unionization, sectors where informal work is rampant. The challenge remains linking these experiences and building solidarities across the entire logistics chain – especially within the pivotal maritime sector.

NOTES

1. See Laleh Khalili, 'Abandoned at Sea: Sailors and COVID-19', *Verso Blog*, 1 May 2020, available at: www.versobooks.com.
2. This is evident in the newly cohering field of humanitarian logistics. See: Rafeef Ziadah, 'Circulating power: Humanitarian logistics, militarism, and the United Arab Emirates', *Antipode*, 51(5), 2019, pp. 1684-702.
3. Liam Campling, and Alejandro Colás, *Capitalism and the Sea: The Maritime Factor in the Making of the Modern World*, London: Verso Books, 2021, p. 215.
4. Container shipping and ship size has grown significantly in the last two decades, and it is how the bulk of manufactured goods are handled and moved through logistical chains from maritime to rail and truck transport networks. However, bulk carriers and tankers (carrying oil and grains, for example) constitute the majority of trade in commodities going through oceans. While similar trends of concentration and centralization of corporate power are evident in these shipping sectors, there are specificities to each.
5. See: Charmaine Chua, Martin Danyluk, Deborah Cowen, and Laleh Khalili, 'Introduction: Turbulent circulation: Building a critical engagement with logistics', *Environment and Planning D: Society and Space*, 36(4), 2018, pp. 617-29.
6. See: Edna Bonacich, and Jake B. Wilson, *Getting the Goods: Ports, Labor, and the Logistics Revolution*, Ithaca: Cornell University Press, 2008; Deborah Cowen, *The Deadly Life of Logistics: Mapping Violence in Global Trade*, Minneapolis: University of Minnesota Press, 2014: and Neil Coe, 'Missing Links: Logistics, Governance and Upgrading in a Shifting Global Economy', *Review of International Political Economy*, 21(1), 2014, pp. 224–56.
7. Anna Tsing, 'Supply chains and the human condition', *Rethinking Marxism*, 21(2), 2009, pp. 148-76.
8. Laleh Khalili, *Sinews of War and Trade: Shipping and Capitalism in the Arabian Peninsula*, London: Verso Books, 2021, p. 3.
9. Karl Marx, *Grundrisse: Foundations of the Critique of Political Economy*, London: Penguin, 2005 (1939), p. 539.
10. Theo Notteboom and Jean-Paul Rodrigue, 'The future of containerization: perspectives from maritime and inland freight distribution', *GeoJournal*, 74(1), 2009, pp. 7-22.
11. Alan Sekula and Noël Burch, 'The Forgotten Space,' *New Left Review*, 69, 2011.
12. Campling and Colás, *Capitalism and the Sea*, p. 424.
13. It is important to underline that the logistics revolution is deeply entangled with the nature of modern war, and the management of supplies to front lines. It is often noted, for example, that the container itself was a US military creation, and the entire field of operations research that logistics management has deep origins in military planning and operations. This historical connection also means there are embedded notions of security, surveillance, and regulation that permeate logistical management.
14. UNCTAD, *Review of Maritime Transport* 2021, available at: unctad.org. The *Review of Maritime Transport* is an UNCTAD flagship report, published annually since 1968. It provides data and analysis seaborne trade, ports and shipping, and statistics on maritime trade and transport.

15 Theo Notteboom and Jean-Paul Rodrigue, 'The corporate geography of global container terminal operators', *Maritime Policy & Management*, 39(3), 2012, pp. 249-79.
16 Matti Siemiatycki, 'The global production of transportation public–private partnerships', *International Journal of Urban and Regional Research*, 37(4), 2013, pp. 1254-72.
17 Jan Hoffman and Julian Hoffmann, 'Bigger ships and fewer companies – two sides of the same coin', Article No. 70, *UNCTAD Transport and Trade Facilitation Newsletter*, N°89, First Quarter 2021.
18 '10 Largest Container Shipping Companies in the World', *Marine Insight*, 11 January 2022, available at: www.marineinsight.com.
19 This system has its roots in the 1920s and was massively expanded in the 1970s. One of the key reasons for the expansion was that it allowed companies to internationalize their labour forces, evading requirements to employ more expensive local labour, and, in turn, weakening the power of unionized labour.
20 The three major alliances are 2M (MSC, Maersk, HMM), Ocean Alliance (CMA-CGM, Cosco Group, OCCL and Evergreen), and THE Alliance (Hapag Lloyd, NYK, Yang Min, MOL, and K-line). These alliances allow the companies to share routes, networks, and port terminals.
21 For example, CMA-CGM within the Ocean Alliance purchased CEVA Logistics one of the top logistics firms. CEVA is headquartered in Marseille, France with some 800 locations worldwide.
22 See: World Bank, 'Logistics Performance Index', at pi.worldbank.org. The World Bank regularly notes that 'logistics performance both in international trade and domestically is central to the economic growth and competitiveness of countries, and the logistics sector is now recognized as one of the core pillars of economic development.' See: J.F. Arvis, D. Saslavsky and L. Ojala, *Trade Logistics in the Global Economy: The Logistics Performance Index and Its Indicators*, Washington, DC: World Bank, 2016.
23 The BRI chimes with the Chinese governmental initiative '*Made-in-China 2025*' meant to enhance and internationalize China's manufacturing sector. The BRI is an expansive project aiming to construct infrastructures and integrated trade corridors which would link back to China's existing trading hubs.
24 Miguel Kanai and Seth Schindler, 'Peri-urban promises of connectivity: Linking project-led polycentrism to the infrastructure scramble', *Environment and Planning A: Economy and Space*, 51(2), 2019, pp. 302-22.
25 For more information on both initiatives see: *International Development Finance Corporation*, available at: www.dfc.gov; Europe Commission, *Global Gateway*, available at: ec.europa.eu/info/strategy/priorities-2019-2024/stronger-europe-world/global-gateway_en.
26 See: Rafeef Ziadah, 'The UAE and the Infrastructure of Intervention', *Middle East Report*, 290, Spring 2019.
27 It is not accidental that the best-connected ports in Africa are those located at the north-eastern, north-western, and southern edges of the continent, namely ports in Morocco, Egypt, and South Africa. This reflects both colonial legacies and contemporary route-making that prioritizes connections to core international routes. Other African ports that lie outside the major Asia-North America/Asia-Europe routes have lower connectivity.

28 D. Ba, 'Construction begins at DP World's $1.1bln port in Senegal', *ZAWYA*, 3 January 2022, available at: www.zawya.com.
29 'DP World launches wholesale e-commerce platform with focus on Africa', *Arabian Business*, 29 April 2021, available at: www.arabianbusiness.com.
30 The three economies accounted for 94 per cent of shipbuilding in terms of gross tonnage, with China accounting for 40.3 per cent, South Korea 31.5 per cent, and Japan 22.2 per cent. Data on shipbuilding is available from: UNCTAD, *Maritime Review 2021*; UNCTAD, *Statistics Database*, available at: www. unctadstat.unctad.org.
31 Data on shipbuilding, seafarer workforce and ship scrapping based on: UNCTAD, *Maritime Review 2021*; UNCTAD, *Statistics Database*, available at: www.unctadstat. unctad.org.
32 See: Anja Kanngieser, 'Tracking and tracing: Geographies of logistical governance and labouring bodies', *Environment and Planning D: Society and Space*, 31(4), 2013, pp. 594-610.
33 On dockworker organizing see: Peter Turnbull, 'Dock strikes and the demise of the dockers' "occupational culture"', *The Sociological Review*, 40(2), 1992, pp. 294–318. For the role of dockworkers in anti-racist struggles see: Peter Cole, *Dockworker Power: Race and Activism in Durban and the San Francisco Bay Area*, Champaign: University of Illinois Press, 2018.
34 Jeremy Anderson, 'Transport workers and global supply chain governance', *International Union Rights*, 21(4), 2014, pp. 22-23.
35 For a detailed history and analysis of the differences between the two federations see: Katy Fox-Hodess, '(Re-)Locating the Local and National in the Global: Multi-Scalar Political Alignment in Transnational European Dockworker Union Campaigns', *British Journal of Industrial Relations*, 55(3), 2017, pp. 626-47; Katy Fox-Hodess, 'Worker Power, Trade Union Strategy, and International Connections: Dockworker Unionism in Colombia and Chile', *Latin American Politics and Society*, 61(3), 2019, pp. 29-54.
36 Mostafa Henaway, 'Infiltrating Amazon: What I learned going undercover at the corporate giant', *The Breach*, 11 November 2021. See also: Alessandro Delfanti, *The Warehouse: Workers and Robots at Amazon*, London: Pluto Press, 2021.
37 See: Cowen, *The Deadly Life of Logistics*; Brett Neilson, 'Five Theses on Understanding Logistics as Power', *Distinktion: Journal of Social Theory*, 13(3), 2012, pp. 322–39.
38 Kim Moody, *On New Terrain: How Capital is Reshaping the Battleground of Class War*, Chicago: Haymarket Books, 2017.
39 Jake Alimahomed-Wilson, 'Unfree shipping: The racialisation of logistics labour', *Work Organisation, Labour & Globalisation*, 13(1), 2019, pp. 96-113.
40 Jeremy Anderson, 'Intersecting Arcs of Mobilisation: The Transnational Trajectories of Egyptian Dockers' Unions', *European Urban and Regional Studies*, 20(1), 2013, p. 129.
41 Jake Alimahomed-Wilson and Immanuel Ness, eds, *Choke Points: Logistics Workers Disrupting the Global Supply Chain*, London: Pluto Press, 2018. On the Teamsters union see this compelling analysis by Dan La Botz, 'Prospects for the Teamsters Under New Leadership', *The Bullet*, 16 February 2022, available at: socialistproject.ca.
42 See: Katy Fox-Hodess, 'The "iron law of oligarchy" and North-South Relations in Global Union Organisations: A case study of the International Dockworkers Council's expansion in the Global South', *Labor History*, 29 April 2022, pp. 1-20.

43 UNCTAD estimates that between October 2020 and June 2021, the Shanghai Containerized Freight Index (SCFI) from Shanghai to Dubai rose by 176 per cent and from Shanghai to the Mediterranean ports by 400 per cent. This index reflects the fluctuation of spot freight rates on export container transport from Shanghai.

44 Based on UNCTAD data, by early 2021 freight rates from China to South America had jumped 443 per cent compared with 63 per cent on the route between Asia and North America's eastern coast. Freight rates went even higher when the Evergiven container ship blocked the Suez Canal in March 2021, wreaking havoc on international supply chains with a disruption at a critical chokepoint.

MULTILATERALISM AT A CROSSROADS: VACCINE APARTHEID, CLIMATE WARS, GEOPOLITICAL TURMOIL

PATRICK BOND

In late June 2022, Chinese President Xi Jinping frantically called the Brazil-Russia-India-China-South Africa (BRICS) bloc into a virtual meeting for their annual heads-of-state session. The anticipated gathering in China was originally scheduled for September in person, but quick consultations and consensus were needed to upend the G7's gathering in Germany, four days later. At the Bavarian G7 summit, German Chancellor Olaf Scholz won in-person attendance by the Indian and South African leaders, Narendra Modi and Cyril Ramaphosa, although neither conceded changes to their 'neutrality' in the Russia-Ukraine war.

In contrast, from Beijing, Xi was far more ambitious, restating China's agenda for BRICS expansion, accompanied by new anti-Western economic strategies relating to the development of trade and currency blocs. Countries whose leaders appeared amenable to joining the BRICS in March 2022 at Beijing's request initially even included Saudi Arabia, although US President Joe Biden's obsequious visit in July appeared to negate that threat of political realignment. Another traditional US ally, Egypt, plus major second-tier regional powers Indonesia and Argentina, were also courted as potential additions to the BRICS bloc. Ideological divisions remained acute throughout, given the five countries' very different orientations. The Sino-Indian turf war in the Himalayan mountains and greater Kashmir remained intractable. But *realpolitik* had evidently shifted in unpredictable ways that reflect tug-of-war diplomacy, apparently unhinged from durable geopolitical and economic alliances.

The West had little new to offer, and a general sense prevailed across many societies and regions in 2022, and seemingly into the foreseeable future, that 'end-of-history' liberal project of conjoining free markets and democratic politics had run into insurmountable troubles. There are today too many sites of systemic stress, and too few successes that could be claimed by the neoliberal economic and political circuits of power. Indeed, there are any number of fractures and ongoing sub-imperial tendencies within the emerging alternative geopolitical pole centred on Moscow and Beijing, to allow for the degree of Third Worldist triumphalism that was witnessed at the Shanghai Cooperation Organization (SCO) Samarkand summit oriented to Eurasian economic integration in mid-September of 2022.[1]

One reason was sustained weakness in the multilateral institutions that had proven profitable sources of power for the wealthiest powers, including the BRICS. But by 2022, the West's control of the global institutional architecture seemed to matter only in negative forms, especially protection of narrow corporate interests such as those of Big Pharma (and indeed all holders of Intellectual Property), greenhouse gas emitters, financiers, Big Data, mega-retailers, the arms industry and financiers. Where positive social and ecological stewardship were concerned, there were only failures to report. In multiple sites of struggle, the multilateral opportunities – and indeed survival-necessities – failed to generate coordinated interstate action.

Consider a few examples. First, from the standpoint of the most immediate public-good objective, health, the worst case was at the June 2022 World Trade Organisation (WTO) summit. At the Trade-Related Property System (TRIPS) negotiations, the rejection of de-commodified Covid-19 vaccines and treatment was imposed on the body by the British, German, Norwegian and Swiss governments, in the wake of 15 million 'excess deaths' (nearly entirely due to Covid) over the prior 30 months. Because of the refusal to waive Big Pharma's Intellectual Property (IP), notwithstanding a campaign led by the South African and Indian governments starting in late 2020, profits recorded by the world's ten largest pharmaceutical corporations in 2021 were $131 billion, nearly 100 per cent higher than in 2020, as more than 12 billion mostly state-subsidized Covid-19 vaccines were administered by mid-2012 (with huge variance in coverage).[2]

Second, when it came to the most vital long-term global public good, a livable planetary atmosphere, there was ongoing failure from November 2021 in Glasgow to June 2022 in Bonn within the United Nations Framework on Climate Change, in negotiations over emissions cuts and climate reparations (known as 'Loss and Damage' payments). Meanwhile, fossil fuel corporations recorded extraordinary profits: for example, in 2021, Saudi Aramco with $105 billion (on revenues of just $400 billion), itself 114 per cent higher than 2020; followed by Russia's Gazprom with $28 billion in profits. But in 2022, with the Brent Crude oil price moving from a pre-invasion level below $80/barrel to a peak of $126, the rewards were even more obscene, with several Western oil firms anticipating profits in the $50-$70 billion range.³

Third, at the apex of geopolitical crisis-management, the escalating failures of multilateralism became acutely obvious from February 2022 in both the United Nations Security Council and General Assembly when the Russian invasion of Ukraine failed to garner consensus on resolving the war, even as 100,000 civilians and soldiers from both sides were killed over the subsequent six months. The invasion in turn catalyzed an unprecedented US-led international campaign of financial, trade and investment sanctions, and asset seizures against Russia and its oligarchs, marking another step in global economic 'decoupling' and reversal of the longstanding trends of capitalist interdependence.⁴

The Ukraine War was only the most recent and spectacular failure of geopolitical crisis-management. The West's 'permanent war' project since the outset of the twenty-first century – eradicating Islamic extremism in hotspots including Afghanistan, the Sahel, and the Horn of Africa – continues to unravel and more such conflicts have emerged, including at the site of the world's largest gas field, offshore Mozambique. Multilateralism in the economic sphere, for its part, has served only to compound regional and local instabilities as debt crises spread across the world. With the International Monetary Fund (IMF) and World Bank proving incapable of shifting from their neoliberal debt-collection dogmas,⁵ there arose intense protests in scores of countries during 2022, most notably in Argentina, Sierra Leone, Sri Lanka, and Pakistan. Catalysts were the local rising cost of living, fiscal austerity policies, and curtailment of vital imports.

Three ways to interpret this global conjuncture have gained some prominence. One is to promote ongoing reforms of the existing world order, with its imperialist underpinnings, so as to make the multilateral system more effective and legitimate. This is often discussed in elite venues as a 'Great Reset,' a phrase those connected to the World Economic Forum (WEF) advocate.⁶ In its 2022 *Global Risks Report*, the WEF recognized several key areas as requiring a major strategic shift – with due recognition of the class politics involved to sustain elite political legitimacy – included what it terms climate action failure, extreme weather, biodiversity loss, debt crises, geoeconomic confrontations, digital inequality, and cybersecurity failure.⁷

A very different approach, coming from outside the dominant Western power circles, is to optimistically view the various vectors of crisis in global governance as a part of a historical progression in which 'the outlines of a multipolar world order are taking shape. An increasing number of countries and peoples are choosing a path of free and sovereign development based on their own distinct identity, traditions and values.' But such approaches 'are being opposed by Western elites, who provoke chaos, fanning long-standing and new conflicts and pursuing so-called containment policy of opponents, which in fact amounts to the subversion of any alternative, sovereign development options'. Thus, they are doing all they can to keep hold onto Western hegemony and power – 'essentially a neocolonial order'.[8]

Russian President Vladimir Putin's argument just above, made at the Moscow Conference on International Security in August 2022, represents a classic Third Worldist stance that could well have been uttered at the peak of Soviet power (though ideologically he stands comfortably on the far right).[9] It is obviously incorrect in that the capitalist bulldozers of 'commodification-of-everything' continue to roll over sovereignty (as revealed by the cases of Covid-19 vaccines and climate catastrophe, discussed below). But the opposition of the Western powers to transforming the multilateral mechanisms of their power is clear enough. What Putin leaves unmentioned is his own defences of Russia's elites and his own intervention in the brutal Ukraine invasion. In Russia's actions, there is something of a resurrection of an 'Empire of the Steppe'. Putin scathingly referred to 1922 when Vladimir Lenin granted the region of Ukraine nationhood within the USSR, and he then warned that Russia will 'not stop halfway. We are ready to show you what genuine de-communization means for Ukraine.'[10]

A third approach is a refutation of both the other two: a left internationalism that desires neither alliance with the Washington-London-Berlin-Paris axis, nor with a Beijing-Moscow pole, nor even a broader BRICS alternative. It is the need to work such an alternative approach out, especially in relation to public health, climate justice, and geopolitical alliance-building, with which the next pages are concerned.

Barriers to multilateral problem-solving coordination in these crucial areas are not necessarily economic, nor purely a reflection of the immediate self-interest of the most powerful actors. There was, after all, no shortage of funding available to the richer countries' policy-makers in 2021-22. They spent trillions to counteract the internal Covid-19 lockdown disruptions, through unprecedented monetary and fiscal stimulations in the form of quantitative easing, low interest rates, and debt-based spending. Moreover, corporate profits could have been taxed to address all these manifestations of global crises, with Fortune Global 500 firms' revenues in 2021 up 19 per cent on the prior year, at $37.8 trillion, especially thanks to retail, petroleum, and pharmaceutical industry growth.[11]

Indeed in 2022, the 'West-versus-the-rest' conflict over how to punish Russia meant multilateralism frayed further and faster. One symptom was that the BRICS, which before 2022 was facing the risk of itself falling apart due to internal contradictions,[12] became more ambitious in discussing alternative systems. These included not only belated vaccine collaboration, but Putin's proposed non-USD currency exchange systems, a free trade zone (in part incentivized by discounted Russian oil and gas sales), and other strategies to draw West-leaning India, Brazil, and South Africa towards Russia and China.[13] Moreover, prospects looked grim for reversing the centrifugal forces within capitalist multilateralism at two sites scheduled for November 2022: Sharm El-Shaikh, the Egyptian host city for the next climate summit, and the G20 gathering in Bali, Indonesia, where Putin and other BRICS leaders would confront their counterparts. However, two vital processes – Covid vaccine access and climate-crisis management – revealed how little scope there would be for compromise.

VACCINE APARTHEID AS MULTILATERAL POLICY

It is fair to estimate that several million deaths due to Covid-19 could have been prevented had vaccines been rolled out fairly and rapidly across the world instead of clustering in the West.[14] Tragically, while a 'BRICS Vaccine Centre' was promised in 2018 at the bloc's Johannesburg summit by the South African host, Ramaphosa, no steps were taken towards its implementation until 2021, and then only half-heartedly in virtual mode, long after the potential for collaboration had peaked.

Such an initiative, based on sharing knowledge unhindered by the profit motive, has been even more necessary as the pandemic wears on. The WTO leadership and the body's leading Western powers have reinforced the sanctity of IP, especially for Big Pharma, supported by states backing the industry and the most effective single influence in global health policy, philanthropist Bill Gates. The wealth of Microsoft's founder was based on Internet Explorer software intellectual property rights (illegally tied to personal computer hardware, for which in 1994 he was prosecuted under the US Sherman Act prohibiting monopolization). Long known as the world's main 'philanthro-capitalist' and social engineer, Gates' hostility to generic medicines dates to campaigns waged by HIV-positive activists during the early 2000s with the aim of releasing AIDS drugs from IP restrictions due to the scale of that pandemic.[15] Gates was firmly opposed and set up alternative non-state branded dispensaries in several African countries. But the activists won and the IP for AIDS drugs was waived during a WTO Doha summit in 2001.

South Africa is a useful place to consider the implications of vaccine nationalism.[16] In the world's most unequal country, reflecting so many of the world's most extreme social contradictions, the private healthcare system remains world-class, serving the wealthiest 14 per cent of the population of 60 million (whose employers subsidize their health insurance). The bottom 86 per cent are faced with a depleted public healthcare system under attack from the Treasury's extreme austerity, including a $260 million health budget cut in late February 2020 (even as the Covid pandemic was bearing down), and deeper cuts since. With the public healthcare system in such a state of neglect, it could not prevent extremely high levels of mortality. Officially, South Africa registered 100,000 Covid-caused deaths over the following two years, with the more accurate 'excess deaths' measurement three times as high (with South Africa among the world's top dozen countries at nearly 500 excess deaths per 100,000 population). As *The Economist* remarked in May 2022, 'Among developing countries that do produce regular mortality statistics, South Africa shows the grimmest picture, after recording three large spikes of fatalities'.[17] India's fatalities were certainly the highest in absolute terms with an estimated 4.7 million excess deaths among its 1.4 billion residents, or 336 per 100,000, according to the World Health Organization, although reliable data are impossible to acquire.[18]

The injustices of the pandemic were reflected in differential access to the vaccines across the world – 63 per cent of adults across the globe had at least one shot by mid-2022, but in Africa only 21 per cent (and this was even in a South Africa where the roll-out of AIDS medicines in the public sector had once been praised for raising life expectancy dramatically). Although state authorities never released breakdowns of class and race incidence of Covid, in mid-2022 a study confirmed that in South Africa black Africans had a far higher risk of Covid-19 mortality, higher hospitalization rates (and with more ventilation and Intensive Care Unit treatment required), yet decreased rates of treatment for those needing tertiary care, compared to white South Africans.[19] All manner of excellent technical supports for the wealthier citizens, including oxygen supply and cutting-edge Covid-19 treatment, were not available for the broader society. When the crisis broke in March 2020, the leader of the third party, the radical populist Julius Malema of the Economic Freedom Fighters party, suggested South Africa should follow the Spanish government's lead in nationalizing – even temporarily – the private healthcare system. The immediate response from Ramaphosa was scornful laughter.[20]

Ironically, in October 2020 at the WTO, it was Ramaphosa who led a group of four governments (South Africa along with India, Kenya, and Eswatini), to request IP waivers for Covid vaccines and treatment, and the sponsors soon gained the support of more than 100 countries. Had the IP waiver been granted, the strategy would have been to immediately produce generic versions in countries with production capacity. The UK government, mindful of profits from medicines not only for this pandemic but ones certain to arise in the future, joined European pharmaceutical powers from Germany, Switzerland, and Norway to persistently veto the idea of such a waiver. Thus the charge of 'vaccine apartheid'.

In the case of the IP waiver for AIDS drugs two decades earlier, once free generic medicines (not branded and relatively inexpensive) became available for free through the public health system (instead of costing $10,000 in private care), South Africa's life expectancy rose from below 54 in 2002 to above 65 just before Covid-19.[21] In mid-2021, Gates offered a technicist objection to allowing generic Covid-19 medicines: 'The thing that's holding things back, in this case, is not IP. It's not like there's some idle vaccine factory, with regulatory approval, that makes magically safe vaccines.'[22] In reality, India did indeed have massive productive capacity, as its Serum Institute showed in its branded production joint venture with AstraZeneca.

In contrast to their occasionally militant rhetoric, the delegates from New Delhi and Pretoria found themselves in May 2022 writing a compromise agreement alongside those from Washington and Brussels, coordinated by WTO Director-General Ngozi Okonjo-Iweala. Her prior jobs included Nigerian finance minister and World Bank managing director, and critics soon considered her bias during IP negotiations as excessively pro-corporate, even descending into bullying proponents of the IP waiver.[23] In this particular alliance between imperial and sub-imperial powers, the best reform that could be achieved was 'compulsory licensing' (for only a five-year period) to allow local manufacturers access to Big Pharma vaccine formulas with compensation.[24]

In short, Ramaphosa and Modi acquiesced to the core capitalist states defending the big pharmaceutical companies. A leading South African activist, Fatima Hassen, condemned the US and European Union (EU) governments for divide-and-conquer strategies and leading the 'various blockers, attackers, and detractors who refused to even temporarily consider lifesaving medicines and vaccines as public goods, opting instead to continue down the path of commodification and excessive profit.'[25] As veteran anti-WTO organizer Deborah James put it, 'what was agreed was not a real waiver, due to EU, US, UK, and Swiss determination to protect Big Pharma's profits,' despite the countervailing pressures from progressive forces:

> The People's Vaccine Alliance have mobilized a massive campaign on this issue for nearly two years … Civil society organizations denounced the

(in)action of the EU, UK, US, and Switzerland for stalling any effective action in the WTO during the entire Covid-19 pandemic by staging a first-ever 'die-in' in the WTO. One by one, activists symbolically 'died' as they explained how these four members prioritized patents over vaccines, leading to millions of deaths around the world ... A Medicines sans Frontières headline best summarized the outcome: 'Inability to agree a real pandemic intellectual property Waiver at WTO is a devastating global failure for people the world over ... and will set a negative precedent for future global health crises and pandemics.'[26]

Still, compared to 2001's AIDS medicines battle, pressure from social movements and healthcare workers was too little, too late, partly because so many activists had hunkered down in survival mode in 2020-21, and because protests at Western embassies and consulates were difficult to pull off during Covid-19 lockdowns and restrictions on gatherings.

As for the BRICS, the lack of a collaborative vaccine centre also reflected self-interested fragmentation tendencies within the bloc. Although Beijing's distribution of vaccines to poor countries was generous, it did not include the sharing of production technology. An alliance with Russia's Sputnik V vaccine – as well as use of the vast capacity for production of generic-medicines in India, South Africa, and Brazil – might have contained the pandemic in many countries, and maybe even helped prevent China's subsequent Covid crises. By early 2022, that stance appeared short-sighted because, even though 45 per cent of the world's vaccines were either Sinovac or Sinopharm, these were ineffective against the fast-spreading – albeit less lethal – Omicron variant. China's extreme lockdowns revealed the weakness of pre-mRNA vaccine technology. However, in 2022 state-owned China Resources (a conglomerate which in 2021 had $120 billion revenue) announced the belated development of China's own mRNA vaccine, with potential production capacity of 800 million annual doses.

Meanwhile, the Sputnik V owners (the Russian Direct Investment Fund and Gamaleya Institute) claimed up to 92 per cent efficacy for the vaccine, but this came into dispute in part because of opacity in Russian data and unusual homogeneity across age groups.[27] South Africa's Health Product Regulatory Authority banned Sputnik in late 2021 because it 'may increase the risk of vaccinated males acquiring HIV'.[28] In contrast, South Africa's locally-owned Aspen Pharmacare partnered with Johnson & Johnson to 'fill and finish' its Janssen vaccine, with an annual plant capacity of 300 million doses, requiring construction of a special new facility in late 2021. However, by mid-2022 there were so few orders that Aspen began closing the plant.

Ramaphosa blamed the Aspen-J&J deal's collapse on the failure of the Global Alliance for Vaccines and Immunisation (GAVI) – set up by Gates and chaired by Okonjo-Iweala – and other 'international organisations responsible for procuring vaccines for the continent. This immediately just devalues the whole process of local manufacturing and local production of vaccines.'[29] Two thirds of the 'Covax' program vaccines GAVI and its allies procured went to Africa, if belatedly. Canada, for example, muscled to the front of the vaccine queue, with its Prime Minister, Justin Trudeau, aiming to have five vaccines available per adult, in the world's most selfish case of vaccine apartheid. Covax was also committed to giving the Big Pharma manufacturers of vaccines protection from legal liability in the event of adverse side effects. A *New York Times* exposé found that Covax 'struggled with delays and infighting … bureaucratic barriers imposed by its leadership have held up the disbursement of $220 million to help countries administer vaccines', with many African countries running out early in the process and with nothing to fall back on.[30] All of this transpired on a public-private partnership basis that reflected not only the bias increasingly built into the initiative's sponsoring agencies – the World Health Organisation, UNICEF, and the World Bank – but also the institution's nefarious driving force, Bill Gates.

Other BRICS countries also failed. Throughout the pandemic, India's Serum Institute was still mainly a Western-oriented producer of branded vaccines. Brazil's President Jair Bolsonaro was not only pro-US and dedicated to corporate capital, but also flirted with Covid-denialism. Still, with the death rate at such high levels, his Congress passed legislation to break vaccine and medication patents during pandemics, although Bolsonaro refused to sign part of the law requiring Big Pharma to transfer knowledge and supply raw materials. Notwithstanding the urgency of vaccine distribution and the campaign for IP exemptions, the BRICS acted in consort with corporate-dominated multilateralism, blocking the idea that vitally-needed medicines were 'global public goods' that should fall outside IP protections.

CLIMATE INJUSTICES AND MULTILATERAL FAILURES

The most profound multilateral failure over the past three decades has been, without a doubt, the United Nations Framework Convention on Climate Change (UNFCCC). In November 2021, at the UNFCCC's Conference of the Parties (COP) 26, the 'Glasgow Climate Pact' confirmed a critique by Indigenous activist Ta'Kaiya Blaney (from the Tla A'min Nation in western Canada): 'COP26 is a performance. It is an illusion constructed to save the capitalist economy rooted in resource extraction and colonialism.'[31] Swedish climate action youth leader, Greta Thunberg, bitterly delegitimized the entire multilateral process: 'The COP26 is over. Here's a brief summary: Blah, Blah, Blah.'[32]

From two decades of climate justice advocacy, activists had a half-dozen concrete demands that any multilateral environmental-regulatory project serious about addressing the crisis should have endorsed.

Cut greenhouse gases: adopt sufficiently ambitious and binding global greenhouse gas emissions reduction requirements to keep temperatures below 1.5C; ensure the cuts are fairly distributed; impose accountability mechanisms including substantial penalties; and incorporate military, maritime and air-transport sectoral emissions.

Transition gracefully: ensure job-rich 'just transitions' from carbon-addicted economies for all affected workers and communities in what, during decarbonization, become radically transformed – and increasingly localized, public- and worker-controlled – systems for energy, transport, tourism, agriculture, urbanisation, production, consumption, and disposal.

Redress social injustices: empower oppressed constituencies in racial-justice, indigenous, Global South, feminist, LGBTQI, and especially youth communities; and provide formal rights for nature, for climate migrants and refugees, and for future generations.

Manage green technology as a global public good: allow dissemination of climate-friendly technology and localized production techniques without IP restrictions; commit to universal clean-energy and public transit access; adopt far-reaching agricultural and food-sovereignty reforms; avoid tech-fix 'false solutions' based on geoengineering fantasies, timber-plantation sequestration, dangerous genetic modification or nuclear energy; and prevent damaging 'extractivist' supplies of green economy mineral inputs that wreck local ecosystems.

Leave fossil fuels underground: compel owners or managers of oil, gas, and coal reserves to cease new exploration (and most current extraction); simultaneously revalue their 'unburnable carbon' accordingly – to be accounted as 'stranded assets'; and end trillions of dollars' worth of annual government fossil fuel subsidies.

Finance planetary and social survival: apply carbon taxation and pricing judiciously (not with regressive results, such as the taxes that caused revolts by working-class French and Ecuadoreans in 2018-19); dispense with failed emissions trading and offset gimmickry; replace debt-based finance with grants; and honor historical responsibilities for the 'climate debt' that large emitters owe so as to fully cover 1) 'loss and damage' reparations, 2) costs of climate-proofing adaptation and resilience, and 3) compensation for the low-emissions countries' use of carbon space now precluded from being utilized due to high-emitter overuse.

The Glasgow document gave *lip service* to a few of these demands,[33] but most were considered outside the realm of reasonable discourse. To illustrate, it was typical that at the last moment, an alliance of the US, China, and India pushed for 'phase-down' – not 'phase-out' – language on coal, a stance supported by South Africa's delegates. The actual *halt* to further exploration and exploitation of gas and oil was still not mentioned by the UNFCCC, notwithstanding scientists' badgering through the Intergovernmental Panel on Climate Change and even the International Energy Agency.[34]

Crucially, the alliance between the three largest polluters also regularly included Brazil and South Africa, starting in 2009 when at the 15th UNFCCC summit, Barack Obama famously barged into a room where the 'BASIC' countries' leaders were meeting: Lula da Silva, Jacob Zuma, Manmohan Singh, and Wen Jiabao. Obama tabled the brief 'Copenhagen Accord' and it was agreed upon and then imposed on the rest of the United Nations, setting the tone for future 'bottom-up' UNFCCC deals (in Orwellian tone, meaning voluntary and proposed by states without any accountability, since Obama himself had inadequate Senate support to sign a binding, full-fledged treaty). As activist Bill McKibben explained, it was a 'league of super-polluters and would-be super-polluters' who 'blew up the UN' and 'gutted progressive values'.[35] When Donald Trump walked out of the UNFCCC in June 2017, there was no punishment nor attempt to discipline the US, in spite of calls to do so from voices as diverse as Naomi Klein and former French president Nicolas Sarkozy.[36]

Another example of collaboration between high emission countries in quasi-multilateral form, in late 2021 on the sidelines of the Glasgow summit, was the much-celebrated finance deal that South Africa's state-monopoly power utility Eskom arranged with the US, UK, Germany, and France. Western agencies would lend South Africa $8.5 billion in additional funds under the guise of 'Just Energy Transition Partnership' decarbonization, thus leaving tens of billions of tons of coal underground by shutting coal-fired power plants early.[37] While the new financing will go, in part, to convert some Eskom power plants from coal-to-renewable energy, an anticipated 44 per cent would also fund coal-to-methane, thus increasing reliance upon imports from the war-riddled Mozambique gas fields.[38] This is one reason for a boycott call by local climate activists.[39]

What the imperial powers making these new 'concessional' (lower-interest) loans – yet inappropriately in *hard currency,* hence more expensive as the Rand declines – appeared to require most was the repayment of what many label Eskom's 'Odious Debt': the 2010s loans of $24 billion weighing down the power utility, which were mainly contracted to pay for the two largest coal-fired power plants under construction in the world (Medupi and Kusile). Even setting aside the climate implications, the plants' main contractor, Hitachi, had blatantly corrupted South Africa's ruling party, the African National Congress, a fact well known to a variety of Western lenders (led by the World Bank with its largest-ever project loan) by the time in 2009 they began offering Eskom more than $20 billion in credits.[40]

Contradictions emerged, however, as not only did South Africa aim to violate the spirit of decarbonization finance by developing more than 12 billion barrels-equivalent of offshore gas by the mid-2020s, mainly through infrastructure constructed by Total and Shell. More worrying was a Cape Town-based Russian exploration ship which in late 2021 discovered what it claimed were 500 billion barrels of oil and gas offshore of Antarctica.[41] If Gazprom, with its extensive experience drilling in the Arctic, or other oil majors eventually extract these fossil fuels, such a 'carbon bomb' would be devastating.[42]

To prepare for such extraction, in mid-2022 Russia announced another initiative. It would attempt to bring the other four BRICS members into a new fossil-energy alliance focused on coordinating oil and gas refining that would 'reduce the five-country bloc's dependence on what it called unreliable energy partners'.[43] Meanwhile, two of the BRICS continued to witness extremely high and rising emissions levels: China of more than 11 billion tons of CO_2 a year and India at 2.5 billion. The other three stagnated due to persistent deindustrialization over the last few decades: Russia at 1.5 billion tons, and both South Africa and Brazil at 450 million tons. But in all cases there were no major initiatives to cut CO_2 and methane emissions by anywhere near the levels required to stabilize the environment. Hence in the UNFCCC, multilateral posturing equally by the imperialist core state and the BRICS that characterized Glasgow would continue to be required.

The US was even more hypocritical. In mid-2022, Biden's congressional allies finally acquired sufficient votes to pass a climate bill that included $45 billion in 2023 state spending (60 per cent more than in 2021) to begin – rather tokenistically – greening the $24.5 trillion US economy. This contrasted with 2022 spending of $782 billion on the US military, the world's single largest CO_2 emitter. Biden's misnamed 'Inflation Reduction Act' was considered by most in the climate justice movement to have surrendered far too many concessions to coal-region West Virginia Senator Joe Manchin, including dramatic increases in oil and gas drilling on federal lands. The Indigenous Environmental Movement condemned 'destructive climate false solutions designed to line the pockets of the fossil fuel and energy industries and cultivate the growth of the extractive industries'. There were only,

> ... meager amounts of grants and loans as 'environmental justice investments' – dangling a carrot in the face of Tribal communities to open up their lands to harmful practices like carbon capture and storage, hydrogen, nuclear, forest and agriculture offsets, and biofuel development. Similar tactics to gain the support of the labor movement by haphazardly attaching boilerplate 'prevailing wage requirements' are seen throughout the bill, without providing any meaningful pathways to a Just Transition for workers and frontline communities.[44]

Across the Atlantic, climate commitments were even worse. As sanctions against the invasion of Ukraine hit both Russia and Europe hard in 2022, the leader of the main industrial economy affected, Germany's Scholz, also courted Ramaphosa. Scholz invited the South African leader – and Modi from India – to the G7 in Germany in June, and a month earlier Scholz visited Pretoria to lobby the South African leader for a pro-West stance on the conflict.[45] His late-May trip followed brief stopovers in Dakar, Senegal and Abuja, Nigeria. These West African states possess major fossil fuel deposits which Scholz needed, in order to halt methane gas imports from Russia's Nord Stream pipeline as quickly as possible. Berlin's vulnerability had worsened when Scholz's predecessor Angela Merkel encouraged more trade, investment, and finance in the hope not only for gas supplies but a tighter Russia-European alliance.

Due to Berlin's increasingly urgent need for replacement gas sources, industrial Germany's fossil addiction will result in major infrastructure capital costs to accommodate new demand. Scholz remains a pernicious ally. Speaking directly to Ramaphosa (himself a former coal tycoon) during the May 2022 press briefing in Pretoria, Scholz explained that the West's anti-Russian sanctions, strenuously opposed by the South African government, will prevent Europe's import of Russian coal in the fall: 'This will work because there are a lot of suppliers all over the globe that are willing and ready to sell their coal to those countries that have got them so far from Russia and obviously there are some as South Africa for instance where we will do so.'[46]

Just a month earlier, Ramaphosa had visited the coastal city of Durban a day after a 'rain bomb' of 351 millimeters in 24 hours that killed 500 people.

He sounded genuinely ready to make a U-turn on South Africa's own fossil addiction: 'This disaster is part of climate change. It is telling us that climate change is serious, it is here. We no longer can postpone what we need to do, and the measures we need to take to deal with climate change.' Ramaphosa was forgetting (not unlike the EU and the BRICS as well) about his own massive CO_2 and methane-intensive mega-projects, such as increasing the export of coal to 18 billion tons.[47]

The anticipated expansion across Africa of oil and gas drilling will, in turn, benefit mainly Western oil companies, especially France's Total, the UK-Netherlands' Shell and Italy's ENI. But it will leave the continent with 'stranded assets' that may well result, later in the 2020s, in the imposition of 'Carbon Border Adjustment Mechanism' (CBAM) climate sanctions.[48] There are ongoing debates among progressive activists regarding the CBAM's merits, given that the primary power relations reflect Western imperialist and protectionist interests. Yet, many climate activists would welcome such pressure against their primary local high-emitting corporate enemies, reminding of an era of international solidarity that had characterized struggles for justice, against colonialism and apartheid. Subsequent examples included 'Boycott Divestment Sanctions' against Israel, and even the widespread 'divest/invest' boycotts of fossil financiers by even establishment forces (such as corporate foundations and pension funds with climate portfolios).

The climate financing alternative to the current trajectory of endless emissions by the leading capitalist states proposed by the climate justice movement is, as noted above, payments by Global North high-emitting countries and corporations to poorer countries to compensate them for *not* using fossil fuels, whether the source is domestic resources or imports. To claim this was a fantasy ignores the core principle established in the $8.5 billion deal for South Africa to pay the country's energy parastatal, Eskom, *not* to keep using coal, but to decarbonize. Even with Eskom's desired regassification ambitions giving merit to critiques of the deal by climate activists, it does not counteract the underlying demand (and Western concessions) for that component of reparations.

GEOPOLITICAL TURMOIL AND MULTILATERAL DIVISION

The impasse of capitalist multilateralism in vaccine provisioning and reducing carbon emissions needs to be placed in the context of the most intense geopolitical turmoil besetting interstate relations over the neoliberal period. Alongside general economic fragility in the world market, even the briefest of political tallies would note the bursting financial markets in, for example, cryptocurrencies and Chinese real estate debt, the innumerable logistics bottlenecks threatening global supply chains (emanating in part from Beijing's zero-tolerance Covid policy), and speculative bubbles leading to extreme price gyrations in agricultural and energy commodities. The faltering of multilateral coordination is, in part, a function of economic crises unfolding over decades, punctuated by increasingly acute financial meltdowns, starting with the early-1980s global recession and Third World debt crises, through the various housing, emerging markets and tech stock crashes of the 1990s and early 2000s, to the global financial crisis of 2007-10. The last decade has seen no let up in the turmoil from the turbulence in the euro of 2011-13, followed by the crash of mining capital as the commodity super-cycle phased out in 2014-15, and then the 2020 Covid lockdowns.

The dilemma confronting multilateral economic coordination can be seen as the perpetual problem of how to displace 'over-accumulated capital', driven by new 'over-productive' factories relative to existing demand and capital stocks, in the case of China. This is a process which has intensified uneven and combined development everywhere across the world market.[49] Global overcapacity problems can be seen in disproportionalities (between sectors), bottlenecks (in production systems and trade routes), bursting bubbles (in finance and real estate), volatile commodity markets (e.g. oil prices falling 30 per cent from May-July 2022), and other modes of devalorization that reflect the tentative post-Covid capitalist 'recovery' in 2022.

The unevenness of capitalist expansion in the current period can be seen by considering the 'output gap' measuring an economy's 'excess capacity' (as a register of the overaccumulation of capital). Russia had one of the worst output gaps in 2020-21, but China and the five other large semi-peripheral economies – Brazil, Indonesia, India, Mexico, and Turkey (all of which can be termed the Emerging Markets 7, or EM7) – were also suffering from output gaps still at more than 2 per cent of GDP in 2021 in spite of the global 'recovery' from Covid. Because they exhibited some of the world's worst such economic characteristics, the BRICS offered no alternative to a world system where, driven by overaccumulation of capital, territorial tensions continue worsening over how to defend against diverse forms of wealth devaluation. The EM7 layer contained some of the most elaborate 'spatial fix' strategies, such as Chinese capital's 'going out' via the Belt and Road Initiative to displace its overaccumulation crisis. In this sense, the BRICS bloc represents a false alternative multilateral agenda.

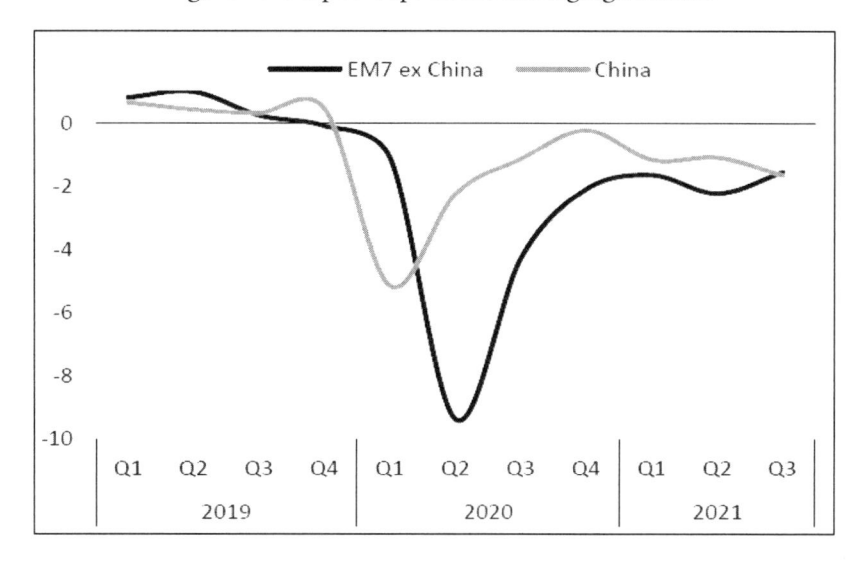

Figure 1: Output Gaps in the Emerging Markets

[Chart showing output gaps for EM7 ex China and China from Q1 2019 to Q3 2021, with values ranging from 0 to -10. EM7 ex China shows a sharp drop to approximately -10 around Q2 2020, recovering to around -2 by Q3 2021. China shows a drop to around -6 in Q1 2020, recovering sooner.]

Source: World Bank, *Rebalancing Act,* Washington: World Bank, December 2021.[50]

Early on in the process of the formation of the new trade and monetary architectures of neoliberal globalization, David Harvey observed that,

> The opening up of global markets in both commodities and capital created openings for other states to insert themselves into the global economy, first as absorbers but then as producers of surplus capitals. They then became competitors on the world stage. What might be called 'sub-imperialisms' arose … Each developing centre of capital accumulation sought out systematic spatio-temporal fixes for its own surplus capital by defining territorial spheres of influence.[51]

It was this inter-state competition for outlets for surplus capital and 'spheres of influence' that further set-off geopolitical turmoil in the form of the Russian 'special operation' in Ukraine in February 2022. The brutal intervention could be imagined, as Putin sometimes alluded, to a re-booting of a 'Russian empire' with its state-expansive logic following Harvey's search for spatio-temporal fixes that are both market-based and geopolitical. The IMF had already recognized the issue in its February 2021 survey of Russia's economy, of which one aspect of the slowdown was 'the impact of the decline in investment during the crisis on the productive capital stock' reflecting 'a large and persistent output gap'. The gap worsened steadily from -0.1 per cent of GDP in 2018, to -0.2 per cent in 2019, to -2.8 per cent in 2019, to –3.0 per cent in 2020.⁵²

A similar problem was evident in Russia's Ukrainian neighbour to the southeast. Putin's self-justifying speech on the eve of the invasion listed features of the devalorization of Ukrainian capital: 'Sectors including machine building, instrument engineering, electronics, ship and aircraft building have been undermined or destroyed altogether.' Putin listed several output-gap victims:

> In 2021, the Black Sea Shipyard in Nikolayev went out of business. Its first docks date back to Catherine the Great. Antonov, the famous manufacturer, has not made a single commercial aircraft since 2016, while Yuzhmash, a factory specialising in missile and space equipment, is nearly bankrupt. The Kremenchug Steel Plant is in a similar situation. This sad list goes on and on.⁵³

The neoliberals and neoconservatives setting the economic and security agenda for the US and NATO begin with a geopolitical fait accompli: Western determination to exploit Putin's interventionist wages for their own global reset of Western-Eurasia relations. With US President Biden terming Putin a 'war criminal' subject to trial, and Secretary of Defense Lloyd Austin declaring, 'We want to see Russia weakened to the degree that it can't do the kinds of things that it has done in invading Ukraine', Washington spent 2022 further arming Ukraine but also amping up the militarist rhetoric to the point that a negotiated settlement of the war was swept off the table. Indeed, it is difficult to see multilateral processes that could end the war with the potential for Russian re-assimilation highly unlikely in the short and even medium term. As the war becomes increasingly intractable the risks rise radically. As the American foreign policy 'realist' thinker, John Mearsheimer, remarked in mid-2022:

> … each side has powerful incentives to find ways to prevail and, more important, to avoid losing. In practice, this means that the United States might join the fighting either if it is desperate to win or to prevent Ukraine from losing, while Russia might use nuclear weapons if it is desperate to win or faces imminent defeat, which would be likely if U.S. forces were drawn into the fighting.⁵⁴

Multilateral advocates are conceding that the best hope for drawing together the imperial and sub-imperial powers is not in the United Nations, or the more compact and selective Security Council. They are putting more hope in the G20, hosted in November 2022 in Bali by Indonesian President Jokowi Widodo, who has already put important efforts into trying to mediate between Russian and Ukraine. A similar effort by Turkish leader Recep Tayyip Erdoğan failed. But with Ukraine's nuclear energy reactors themselves increasingly threatened as collateral damage, the risk factor also included the triggering of Chernobyl-scale accidents, underscoring the failures of multilateral diplomacy.

The Ukraine war and the response from the US and other NATO countries has led to a further fracturing of multilateralism and the inter-state system. Given the sanctity of property rights in the West, no one could have anticipated how quickly Russia's rights to overseas property would be annihilated by the West's sanctions campaign as part of its 'hybrid war' (with some parallels to be drawn with other boycotts against Iran, Venezuela, Cuba, and others). All the built-in protections that multilateral capitalism had promised and seemingly won – especially with secure financial havens and contractual trade relationships – in defence of global capital and the world's richest individuals were simply negated by US Treasury orders in alliance with other Western powers.

The resulting geo-financial battle would excite anger in numerous commentators across the Global South. Brazil's most active representative at the IMF and BRICS New Development Bank during the 2010s was the Lula-aligned Paulo Nogueira Batista. In mid-2022 he remarked:

> The US has abused the role of its currency and financial institutions by transforming them into weapons of economic wars … the current economic measures against Russia are unprecedented in scale, involving among many other sanctions a freeze of financial assets of about $300 billion, amounting to around half of Russia's international reserves, including dollar and also euro holdings. In Russian official circles, discussion has begun on what is being called the R5 project, taking a cue from the coincidence that the five BRICS currencies begin with the letter R.[55]

Was this a genuine move to *economic* unity within the BRICS, instead of just political posturing? In a period of world economic prosperity, low underlying inflation and rising raw-material commodity super-cycle pricing – not the volatility of the chaotic 2020-22 mini-boom – a BRICS financial network might well have had traction. But with the OECD forecasters estimating world GDP growth down to 3 per cent in 2022 – a 1.5 per cent cut from pre-invasion projects – and even lower in 2023, and with inflation still running at decades-long highs across the West in 2022, economic resilience was in short supply. Pessimism from the global turmoil was in order: 'If the war escalates or becomes more protracted, the outlook would worsen, particularly for low-income countries and Europe.'[56]

In such a scenario, might a gap open for the BRICS to march through, bearing an alternate multilateral agenda to the geopolitical turmoil? According to Marxist economist Michael Roberts, 'Putin may think Russia can be an imperialist power, but the economic reality is that Russia is just a large peripheral economy outside the US-led imperialist bloc like Brazil, China, India, South Africa, Turkey, Egypt etc. – if with a larger military than most'.[57] China *does* have more scope to advance rapidly from a regional to a world – even an inter-imperial – power. But Beijing and Moscow have the most to lose if their gambles fail, as has happened so often in the past.

MULTILATERAL BARRIERS AND FANTASIES

Will a new post-multilateral, pluralistic order emerge from the recent frustrations and chaos in the main global institutions of health, climate, and economics discussed above? And will a new power balancing help resolve the potentially catastrophic dangers that continued rising into mid-2022? Let us conclude by considering several standpoints established by the challengers, from within the BRICS bloc, to the current practices of multilateralism in a February 2022 joint statement by Putin and Xi in Bejiing, at the outset of the Winter Olympic Games.[58] There they pointed to the importance of a more collaborative expansion of Chinese and Russian capital into their hinterlands, neighbouring states and contested spaces:

> The sides are seeking to advance their work to link the development plans for the Eurasian Economic Union and the Belt and Road Initiative … The sides agreed to continue consistently intensifying practical cooperation for the sustainable development of the Arctic … The sides reaffirm their strong mutual support for the protection of their core interests, state sovereignty and territorial integrity, and oppose interference by external forces in their internal affairs. The Russian side reaffirms its support for the One-China principle, confirms that Taiwan is an inalienable part of China, and opposes any forms of independence of Taiwan.

A second standpoint, in relation to climate change, is to continue collaborating within a Western-dominated multilateralism already fatally compromised by refusals to challenge corporate prerogatives, and opposition to trade barriers that could potentially emerge from bilateral climate sanctions or opposition to Arctic oil drilling:

Jointly celebrating the 30th anniversary of the adoption of the UNFCCC, they reaffirm their commitment to this Convention as well as to the goals, principles and provisions of the Paris Agreement ... The sides oppose setting up new barriers in international trade under the pretext of fighting climate change.

The UNFCCC has been the most decisive multilateral site for China, Russia, other BRICS, and similar fossil-dependent states to agree to Western demands that there be no binding processes on greenhouse gas emissions reductions. This included acceptance of such crucial issues as: no reparations for climate-related 'loss and damage'; no counting of military-related (or shipping or air) emissions; no insistence on fossil fuel firms leaving 'unburnable carbon' resources as stranded assets; the confirmation of carbon markets and offsets so as to privatize the world's atmosphere; and the confirmation of IP rights to delimit the spread of solar, wind, and other vital technologies to those importers willing to pay the market price. At the 2021 Glasgow negotiations, collaboration between the US, India, and China was essential in order to weaken proposed language regarding coal extraction and combustion.

A third position of the China-Russia statements relates to mutual support for the imperial powers' *rhetorical* agenda of ever-more liberalized world trade. Since the 1994 Marrakesh negotiations expanded the WTO, this was a vital site of collaborative contributions to strengthening global corporate power:

The sides support and defend the multilateral trade system based on the central role of the WTO, take an active part in the WTO reform, opposing unilateral approaches and protectionism. The sides are ready to strengthen dialogue between partners and coordinate positions on trade and economic issues of common concern, contribute to ensuring the sustainable and stable operation of global and regional value chains, promote a more open, inclusive, transparent, non-discriminatory system of international trade and economic rules.

Reality has departed, not infrequently, from this rhetoric. From the mid-2010s there was a shift to much more antagonistic cooperation due to Washington's growing geopolitical hostility to the expansive agendas of both China and Russia. As the US pushed NATO eastward in Europe and Obama introduced a military 'pivot' to Asia that also threatened China's trade routes, bilateral trade and commercial harassments have become common.

Finally, with global multilateralism at a standstill within the United Nations from its own institutional impotence and inter-state fissures, Xi and Putin's statement agreed that there would need to be collaboration directly between the imperial/sub-imperial powers in a special-purpose forum:

> The sides support the G20 format as an important forum for discussing international economic cooperation issues and anti-crisis response measures, jointly promote the invigorated spirit of solidarity and cooperation within the G20, support the leading role of the association in such areas as the international fight against epidemics, world economic recovery, inclusive sustainable development, improving the global economic governance system in a fair and rational manner to collectively address global challenges.

In the areas of concern listed, the 'leading role' in the provisioning of 'global public goods' in G20 multilateralism was just as likely to disappoint. Xi himself explained his own country's approach at the World Economic Forum in 2017: 'We must remain committed to developing global free trade and investment, promote trade and investment liberalisation.'[59]

If the corporate-dominated multilateralism already in place was at a crossroads, such strategic thinking meant the leadership of the BRICS bloc was hardly venturing to take a different path. The dysfunctionality at the core of the governance of the capitalist inter-state system – witnessed in vaccine apartheid, climate wars, and geopolitical turmoil – suggests that socialist strategies must return to a stage of contestation over local and national power rather than retain fantasies of negotiated multilateral solutions, especially with the likes of Xi, Putin, BRICS, and their assorted allies.

NOTES

1 For Vijay Prashad, the word 'mutual' reoccurring in the communique harked back to the 'the Asian-African Conference held in Bandung, Indonesia, in 1955, which led to the formation of the Non-Aligned Movement in 1961. The Samarkand Spirit mirrors, for a different period, the Bandung Spirit with an emphasis on sovereignty and equality.' With Iran joining, 'India's leadership in the SCO and the possibility of Türkiye's entry into the organization show that the SCO is increasingly becoming an instrument for Eurasian integration'. Yet more enthusiastic was Pepe Escobar: 'The increasing Russia-China-Iran interpolation – the three top drivers of Eurasia integration – scares the hell out of the usual suspects, who may be starting to grasp how the SCO represents, in the long run, a serious challenge to their geoeconomic game … Even India under Modi is having second thoughts about relying on western blocs, where New Delhi is at best a neo-colonized "partner".' Vijay Prashad, 'Will

"Samarkand Spirit" revive the word "mutual" in world affairs?', *Asia Times,* 22 September 2022; Pepe Escobar, '"Samarkand Spirit" to be driven by 'responsible powers' Russia and China,' *The Cradle,* available at: thecradle.co. The exceptionally detrimental socio-economic-ecological aspects of such 'sovereignty' for subordinate countries in the world's heartland, including climate catastrophe, sharper inequality, over-indebtedness, and worsening over-production generally go unremarked upon.

2 Paige McGlauflin, 'The world's 10 biggest pharmaceutical companies raked in over $700 billion in revenue in 2021', *Fortune,* 16 August 2022.

3 In the second quarter of 2022 alone, ExxonMobil recorded profits of $18 billion (up nearly four times from the same period in 2021), with $11.5 billion at Chevron and $10 billion at Shell. The Norwegian oil company Equinor's first-quarter 2022 profits were $18 billion, up from $4 billion in the same quarter in 2021. Paris-based TotalEnergies recorded $17.4 billion in early 2022, more than double that of 2021. Oliver Milman, 'Largest oil and gas producers made close to $100bn in first quarter of 2022', *The Guardian,* 13 May 2022.

4 Even extending to the two Shanghai-based multilateral development banks, the BRICS New Development Bank and Asian Infrastructure Investment Bank, which prioritized New York credit-rating agency approval over Moscow's own role as co-founder of both. Press Trust of India, 'BRICS Bank Follows AIIB And Puts Transactions in Russia On Hold', *NDTV,* 4 March, available at: www.ndtv.com.

5 Notwithstanding the brief interruption, when due to Covid-19 there was an episode of fiscal generosity in 2020-21.

6 World Economic Forum, 'The Great Reset', 2020, available at: www.weforum.org/great-reset.

7 World Economic Forum, *Global Risks Report,* 2022, available at: www.weforum.org/reports/global-risks-report-2022.

8 Vladimir Putin, 'Address to participants and guests of the 10th Moscow Conference on International Security', Moscow, 16 August 2022, available at: en.kremlin.ru/events/president/news/69166.

9 Ismail Lagardien, 'What Putin really wants is the return of an empire', *Business Day,* 2 August 2022, available at: www.businesslive.co.za.

10 Putin continued, 'modern Ukraine was entirely created by Russia or, to be more precise, by Bolshevik, Communist Russia. This process started practically right after the 1917 revolution, and Lenin and his associates did it in a way that was extremely harsh on Russia – by separating, severing what is historically Russian land.' See: 'Russia ready to show what true de-communization means for Ukraine – Putin', *TASS,* 21 February 2022, available at: www.tass.com.

11 The leading force behind the restoration of corporate profitability was Chinese capital, notwithstanding Covid-related supply chain disruptions and lockdowns, and a worsening internal crisis within property market, construction, and associated financial capital (leading to vigorous protests by household debtors), as well as the state's disciplining of Big Data corporations and financiers (by banning cryptocurrencies and tightening exchange controls). The 2021 revenue share of corporations based in greater China (i.e., including Taiwan and Hong Kong) compared to the rest of the Fortune 500 was 31 per cent, exceeding that of US-based firms for the first time. But profits made on the global stage did not translate into ambitions to change the rules.

Chinese leaders often spoke of world crises, but at least at this stage were apparently uninterested in taking any leadership roles in multilateralism. See: *Fortune,* Global 500, August 2022, available at: www.fortune.com.

12   Ana Garcia, Miguel Borba, and Patrick Bond, 'Western Imperialism and the Role of Sub-imperialism in the Global South', *New Politics,* 18(2), 2021, available at: www.newpol.org.

13   Rarely mentioned was that two such initiatives – the 2014 Contingent Reserve Arrangement (CRA) alternative to the IMF and an oft-mentioned BRICS credit ratings agency – had simply failed to materialize over the past decade. The missing CRA was a glaring gap for South Africa, when in August 2020 the IMF made a $4.3 billion Covid loan that locked in the most brutal austerity conditions ever experienced, for years to come.

14   At a time in March 2022 that the rate of full adult vaccination across Africa was still in single digits, one health scholar concluded, 'Vaccine apartheid has contributed to the death of nearly 5.2 million people and enabled emergence of five variants of concern in the very countries that requested the TRIPS waiver.' See: James Pfeiffer, 'A global day of action to end vaccine apartheid', *GlobalHealth,* Washington University, St. Louis, 10 March 2022, available at: globalhealth.washington.edu.

15   From a self-interested standpoint, the Gates Foundation had invested $300 million to develop a vaccine, including a $40 million stake in CureVac which 'delivered profits in tens of millions of dollars' according to *India Today* in 2021, and moreover his 'involvement in the partnership between the University Oxford and AstraZeneca prevented the vaccine from having an open distribution model'. See: *India Today,* 'Bill Gates believes Covid 19 vaccine tech should not be given to India, what he said and why he said it', 3 May 2021, available at: www.indiatoday.in.

16   Vishwas Satgar, 'Epidemiological neoliberalism in South Africa', in Greg Albo, Leo Panitch, and Colin Leys, eds, *Socialist Register 2022: New Polarizations, Old Contradictions,* London: Merlin Press, 2021.

17   *The Economist,* 'Coronavirus excess deaths', 22 May 2022.

18   Russia's excess deaths were recorded at 1.23 million (even higher than the US' 1.18 million), and its rate was the world's highest (851/100,000) according to *The Economist.* Brazil was close behind with 780,000 excess deaths (351/100,000), with Mexico next at 660,000 (520/100,000). See: Soutik Biswas, 'Why India's real Covid toll may never be known', *BBC News,* 5 May 2022.

19   Waasila Jassat, Lovelyn Ozougwu, Shehnaz Munshi, Caroline Mudara, Caroline Vika, and Tracy Arendse, 'The intersection of age, sex, race and socio-economic status in COVID-19 hospital admissions and deaths in South Africa', *South African Journal of Science,* 118(5/6), 2022.

20   During apartheid, this was the country that pioneered heart transplants (at a public hospital), *for the benefit of white patients,* so its scientific capacities in healthcare were not in doubt. But the oft-demanded National Health Insurance (NHI, 'single-payer', or 'Medicare for All' in US jargon, i.e., similar to Canada's financing system) was avoided by the ruling party, even though its own policy papers had endorsed NHI since 2007. See: Cebelihle Bhengu, 'Ramaphosa laughing at Malema's threats to nationalise hospitals is everything', *TimesLive,* 19 March 2020, available at: www.timeslive.co.za.

21 Macrotrends, 'South Africa Life Expectancy', 2022, available at: www.macrotrends.net/countries/ZAF/south-africa/life-expectancy.
22 Sharon Lerner and Lee Fang 'Factory owners around the world stand ready to manufacture Covid-19 vaccines', *The Intercept,* 29 April 2022.
23 Ravi Kanth, 'DG allegedly defies WTO rules, espouses controversial JSIs at MC12', *SUNS South North Development Monitor 9594,* 14 June 2022, available at: www.twn.my/title2/wto.info/2022/ti220615.htm; Ravi Kanth, 'DG's alleged "pressure tactics" to push through decisions at MC12', *SUNS South North Development Monitor 9592,* 10 June 2022, available at: www.twn.my/title2/wto.info/2022/ti220610.htm.
24 Andy Bounds, 'WTO agrees partial patent waiver for Covid-19 vaccines', *Financial Times,* 17 June 2022.
25 Fatima Hassan, 'A New and Weak WTO Deal on TRIPS is Not Fit for Purpose', *Think Global Health,* 1 July 2022, available at: www.thinkglobalhealth.org.
26 She continued, 'The agreement only grants a limited flexibility on one provision; excludes all forms of IP except patents; excludes treatments and tests; and requires far more intrusive monitoring and reporting than the existing rules (among other excessive restrictions), resulting in a 'TRIPS-plus' agreement rather than a real waiver. The final text on this issue even states that 'developing countries with existing capacity to manufacture Covid-19 vaccines are encouraged to make a binding commitment not to avail themselves of this agreement'. 'Disgracefully, the outcome on vaccines will probably not save a single life from Covid, and the agriculture outcomes will not address the fundamental problems causing food insecurity. On each of the issues – flexibilities from harmful WTO rules on IP and agriculture – developing countries did not achieve their main outcome, and instead were left trying to mitigate the damage of developed countries' demands to extend the free rides for Big Tech and Big Fish. The WTO failed to deliver what the world needed in each and every arena.' Deborah James, 'The WTO after the 12th Ministerial Conference', *CounterPunch,* 27 June 2022.
27 Maayan Hoffman, 'Sputnik vaccine efficacy data published in Lancet are "statistically impossible"', *Health Policy Watch,* 13 July 2022, available at: healthpolicy-watch.news.
28 Eunice Stolz, 'Russia's Sputnik V Covid-19 vaccine turned down over HIV concerns', *Mail & Guardian,* 18 October 2021.
29 Pauline Kairu, 'Africa dream of drug self-reliance given reality check', *The East African,* 18 August 2022, available at: www.theeastafrican.co.ke.
30 Benjamin Mueller and Rebecca Robbins, 'Where a Vast Global Vaccination Program Went Wrong', *New York Times,* 2 August 2021.
31 Libby Brooks, 'Hundreds of global civil society representatives walk out of Cop26 in protest', *The Guardian,* 12 November 2021.
32 Greta Thunberg, Tweet, 13 November 2021, available at: www.twitter.com/gretathunberg/status/1459612735294029834.
33 United Nations Framework Convention on Climate Change, 'Glasgow Climate Pact', New York, 13 November 2021, available at: unfccc.int/documents/310475.
34 Jess Shankleman and Akshat Rathi, 'India's Last-Minute Coal Defense at COP26 Hid Role of China, U.S.', *Bloomberg,* 14 November 2021.
35 Bill McKibben, 'With Climate Agreement, Obama guts Progressive Values', *Grist,* 19 December 2009, available at: grist.org.

36 Patrick Bond, 'The case for a people's smart sanctions campaign against Trump's America', *The Conversation,* 19 January 2017.
37 Peter du Toit, 'R131bn from rich countries will help Eskom speed up new power projects, De Ruyter says', *News24,* 3 November 2021.
38 Patrick Bond, 'Global North climate reparations to prevent Southern fossil fuel conflict', *CADTM,* 19 August 2021, available at: www.cadtm.org.
39 Climate Justice Charter Movement, 'Make ending coal, gas and oil investment a condition for financial support to South Africa', Change.org, 20 February 2022.
40 Jonathan Canard, 'Cancel Eskom's odious debt to the World Bank', CADTM, 3 September 2019, available at: www.cadtm.org.
41 Tiara Walters, 'Russia's 500 billion-barrel bombshell in Earth's last unmined frontier', *Daily Maverick,* 18 November 2021, available at: www.dailymaverick.co.za.
42 Tiara Walters, 'As 'ice curtain' descends, Ukraine speaks out about Antarctic war shocks', *Daily Maverick,* 26 May 2022, available at: www.dailymaverick.co.za.
43 Siphamondli Zondi, 'Russia invites BRICS to St. Petersburg international economic forum in June', *SABC News,* 28 May 2022.
44 Indigenous Environmental Network, 'Statement Re Proposed Inflation Reduction Act', Bemidji, Minnesota, August 2022, available at: www.ienearth.org.
45 After initially condemning the invasion at the UN, even demanding immediate retraction of Moscow's troops, the South African position suddenly changed in early March, to neutrality, coincidentally when a $700,000 donation from a manganese mining house set up by Russian multi-billionaire Viktor Vekselberg was made to Ramaphosa's ruling African National Congress, which otherwise recorded no other contributions that quarter. See: Jan Gerber, 'ANC received R10m from Russian oligarch, Chancellor House-owned company', *News24,* 31 May 2022.
46 *SABC News,* 'President Cyril Ramaphosa and German Chancellor Olaf Scholz media briefing in Pretoria', 24 May 2022.
47 Patrick Bond, 'Lessons from the assassination of Fikile Ntshangase', *CADTM,* 21 October 2021, available at: www.cadtm.org.
48 The CBAM aims to halt 'leakage' from the internal EU emissions reduction strategy insofar as imported greenhouse gases would logically result from the outsourcing of production, as corporations search for less expensive industrial and raw-material inputs. Economies with relatively high shares of greenhouse gas inputs into their energy systems, and in turn embedded in their exports, will then face higher tariffs on goods headed to Europe, and eventually also the UK, US, and other Western economies which will adopt their version of a CBAM. In the EU, the tariff levels will be tied to the bloc's Emissions Trading Scheme, which revealed its exceptional price volatility in early March 2022 after the Ukraine invasion, by crashing 40 per cent, from near $100 to $60 per ton. And research was emerging that this rate should be thirty times higher to more closely approximate a realistic 'social cost of carbon' that takes into account all the damage expected in coming decades as feedback loops kick in. See: University College London, 'Economic cost of climate change could be six times higher than previously thought', London, 6 September 2021, available at: www.ucl.ac.uk.
49 Patrick Bond, 'China's role in amplifying Southern Africa's extreme uneven development', *CADTM,* 30 June 2021, available at: www.cadtm.org.

50 World Bank, *Rebalancing Act,* Washington, DC, December 2021, available at: https://documents1.worldbank.org/curated/en/099730001072271154/pdf/P17579700654ca02f0a3ba07ea043314196.pdf.
51 David Harvey, *The New Imperialism,* Oxford: Oxford University Press, pp.185-86.
52 IMF, 'Russian Federation: 2020 Article IV Consultation', Washington, DC, February 2021, available at: www.imf.org/en/Publications/CR/Issues/2021/02/08/Russian-Federation-2020-Article-IV-Consultation-Press-Release-Staff-Report-50068.
53 Vladimir Putin, 'Speech', 21 February, 2022, available at: www.theprint.in/world/modern-ukraine-entirely-created-by-russia-read-full-text-of-vladimir-putins-speech/843801.
54 John Mearsheimer, 'Playing With Fire in Ukraine', *Foreign Affairs,* 17 August 2022.
55 Paulo Nogueira Batista Jr., 'BRICS financial cooperation – a force for fairness', *CGTN,* 24 June 2022, available at: news.cgtn.com.
56 OECD, 'Editorial: The price of war', *OECD Economic Outlook*, 2022(1), June 2022, available at: www.oecd-ilibrary.org.
57 Michael Roberts, 'Russia under Putin', *The Next Recession,* 15 August 2022.
58 Russian Federation and the People's Republic of China, 'Joint Statement on the International Relations Entering a New Era and the Global Sustainable Development', Beijing, 4 February 2022, available at: http://en.kremlin.ru/supplement/5770. The points below are drawn from this text.
59 Xi Jinping, 'Opening plenary address', World Economic Forum, Davos, 17 January 2017, available at: www.weforum.org.

THE 'CORPORATE GOVERNANCE' MYTH

STEPHEN F. DIAMOND

Capitalism relies as heavily on ideology to maintain its dominance as it does physical power. For the past seventy years a cornerstone of capital's ideological framework has been the view that the corporation must be managed so that it creates value for shareholders to the exclusion of any concern for other potential constituencies. Thus, it came as a surprise to many on the left and right when the Business Roundtable, a leading US-based business advocacy group made up of some of the most important CEOs from finance and industry, announced in 2019 that in addition to shareholders, corporations had a wider responsibility to 'stakeholders', including employees, customers, and communities.[1] This commitment from the 'commanding heights' of capital triggered a new global debate about the purpose and social impact of the corporation. The debate emerged in tandem with the rise of substantial pools of capital devoted to so-called 'ESG', an investment strategy that allocates funds based on an assessment of environmental, social, and governance metrics. In addition, there have been new efforts to use legislation to alter corporate governance in favour of a stakeholder approach. Corporations in several states, including California, Illinois, and New York, are under political and legislative pressure to diversify their boards of directors by including more women as well as members of under-represented communities. At the national level, Senator Elizabeth Warren has introduced the Accountable Capitalism Act, which would mandate a more significant role in corporate governance for stakeholders, including board representation for employees.[2]

Instead of heralding a new post-neoliberal era, however, this apparent momentum towards an alternative to the shareholder wealth maximization norm only highlights the impasse that exists in law and theory about the structure and purpose of the corporation. Both 'stakeholder' and 'shareholder value' advocates maintain that the corporation can serve their agenda. Ironically, this impasse is due, in large part, to a view shared by both camps about how the corporation, capitalism's central institution, is structured and operates – in other words, how it is 'governed'. According to this century-old view, first crystallized in the New Deal era, the 'separation of ownership and control' in the modern corporation can lead to an outcome that is either 'efficient' (the right-wing 'shareholder value' view) or 'progressive' (the predominantly left-wing 'stakeholder' view).[3] The field of corporate law and governance remains wholly occupied by this 'separation thesis', as broken into these competing camps. As a result of this intellectual monopoly, no genuine alternatives to the dominant legal and theoretical framework that shapes our understanding of how capitalism governs itself have emerged.

I argue here, however, that the foundational concept shared by the left and right – 'corporate governance' – is itself an ideological construct, more myth than reality. Its advocates largely draw a veil over what is actually occurring inside the corporation and in inter-corporate relationships. I explain that, instead of a structural divide between outside investors and inside managers, a relatively coherent and dominant class of investors and share-owning senior executives jointly run modern corporations in order to carry out key capitalist processes, namely *capital accumulation* and the *valorization* of capitalist profits. To be coherent, any discussion of 'corporate governance' must place that centralized ownership structure and that concomitant animating purpose of the corporation at the heart of its analysis.

I apply this alternative approach here to help break apart the current intellectual and political impasse. First, I place in historical context the development of the two major, if illegitimate, offspring of the founder of modern corporate governance theory, the New Deal-era legal scholar Adolph Berle. Second, I describe the capitalist mandates of accumulation and valorization that, in turn, drive the governance of the corporation by real capitalists. Third, I chart the emergence of the 'actual capitalist class' from the early twentieth to the early twenty-first century. Finally, I conclude by pointing to some of the broader political and intellectual implications of this reframing of corporate governance theory.

BERLE'S EPIGONES

Both the dominant shareholder value school, also known as 'agency' theory, as well as the alternative minority 'stakeholder' view, trace their lineage to the collaboration between legal scholar, and later, architect of the New Deal, Adolf A. Berle and the economist Gardiner C. Means. Berle and Means' ground-breaking empirical work and innovative theoretical approach, published in their iconic 1932 text *The Modern Corporation and Private Property*, appeared to settle the question of whether a new managerial class had displaced capitalist control of large public corporations. Berle and Means told a rich story of political usurpation, in which the rise of a managerial class portended a potential dark turn for democratic life. However, their late-twentieth century agency school adherents (who now dominate every major American economics department and law and business school) ignored this wider context, and maintained narrowly that the 'separation' of ownership and control in the corporation was a rational evolution of the corporate form.[4]

Their bastardization of Berle and Means enabled a metaphor of 'separation' to emerge as a form of capitalist ideology. In the eyes of these orthodox thinkers, the alleged 'separation' resulted in a centralization of authority in the corporation's board of directors that created efficiencies, i.e., greater profitability, thus enabling the corporation to exploit larger and more complex investment opportunities. They deftly recast the Berle-Means socio-political dynamic as simply a problem of potential conflict between shareholder 'principals' and their managerial 'agents'. Shareholders risk incurring so-called 'agency costs' for the delegation of authority to the board as its agent. These arise because of the potential for 'shirking' at some level by corporate insiders. However, such costs can be minimized, agency theorists contend, by contract-based monitoring mechanisms that emerge from 'private ordering' supplemented by the surrounding markets for corporate control and executive talent, occasional judicial gap-filling and, where helpful, default fiduciary or statutory provisions made available by courts and legislatures.[5] In fact, I argue here that because the original concept of a separation of 'ownership' from 'the control' itself is incorrect, there is little or no basis to use a 'principal-agent' metaphor in assessing the relationship among key elements or layers of the corporate power structure at all.

The minority stakeholder approach to corporate governance also accepts the separation thesis. It largely builds its case, however, on the critical, but long neglected and misunderstood, 'pluralist' dimension of the Berle and Means argument. Stakeholders assert that because of their dominant scale and scope, corporations should be viewed as powerful *political* institutions not just as objects of mere economic interest.[6] Instead of a narrow rational calculus of 'net present value' by directors and executives (which Berle and Means called 'the control' and which today are widely known simply as 'managers') aimed at maximizing the value of a firm's equity, modern corporate managers must, and should, negotiate among a complex array of constituencies that include shareholders, employees, creditors, and the surrounding community. A corporate manager who ignores this pluralistic 'political' environment risks destruction of firm value. It is within this tendency that one finds the strongest support today for what have become known as 'corporate social responsibility' (CSR) obligations and investment strategies that promote ESG norms. Corporations are viewed by this school as largely fixed, stable centres of social and economic power that must (objectively, for success) and should (a normative side of the argument) take on what is, in essence, a political function akin to traditional democratic institutions like legislatures or administrative agencies. The skills of a 'post-capitalist' bureaucrat, therefore, are arguably required to lead today's large corporate structures.

When thought of as political institutions, corporations must then exercise their power 'legitimately' to minimize the risk of dysfunctional social and political conflict. Socio-political 'conflict' emerges because a failure to internalize costs through appropriate governance mechanisms can lead those who are, instead, asked to bear those costs to protest. Examples might include the longstanding debate over pollution, the lack of labour rights in China, or the mining of 'conflict diamonds' under horrific conditions in Central Africa. All of these can be seen as 'negative externalities'.[7] Arguably, only a political approach allows the firm to internalize those costs that should properly be borne by the firm. The legitimacy of firm governance can only be generated then, the argument goes, if the mechanisms that control the corporation, such as the board and senior management, are themselves reflective of, and answerable to, the constituencies that make up, or are impacted by, the corporation. Thus, if the corporation legitimately represents and serves its stakeholders it can serve as part of a pluralist bulwark against concentrations of power, both private and public.[8]

It is, thus, the stakeholder school that holds closest to the idea of the corporation as an *agora*, a new centre for social and political decision-making.[9] Seen as such, it is understandable that many modern stakeholder advocates want to 'democratize' the corporate entity. This is taking on extreme forms today as some in this milieu attempt to replace traditional business structures entirely with 'decentralized autonomous organizations', widely known as DAOs, to carry out tasks via 'smart contracts' (essentially tightly focused algorithms) on distributed computer networks. This was not quite what Berle and Means had in mind, even if one could credibly claim they held a similar normative preference. Their best hope was to rein in the new 'princes of industry', not to dethrone them. But the fatalistic limit of Berle and Means dooms the analysis of even the more radical wings of the stakeholder school as well. There is no place for genuine democratic decision-making in an institution designed for other, namely capitalist, purposes. And, as I will explain, the myth of a 'democratic' or 'progressive' capitalism that captivates so many within the stakeholder camp is not enough to overcome this problem.[10]

REAL CAPITALISTS OWN *AND* CONTROL

The illusory 'managerial revolution'

Freeing us from the conceptual monopoly held by the Berle-Means paradigm requires, first, a reconsideration of its origins and evolution, in other words, of its 'original meaning'. Berle and Means' core idea of a 'separation' of ownership from control was deeply flawed or, at best, comprehensible only as, and when, used by the authors in the very particular historical and ideological context in which they were working. Earlier Progressive-era thinkers were important influences on Berle, particularly Louis Brandeis whom Berle knew personally through his father. Brandeis's famous 1914 articles on the role of investment bankers in forming large new corporate structures were widely read and certainly influenced the young Berle.[11] The emergence of powerful investment banks in the transition from small 'sole proprietor' capitalism at the *fin de siècle* led to the first wave of criticism of centralized corporate power. For Brandeis and the young Berle, this meant a preference for competition, trust-busting, and a kind of 'small is beautiful' ideological orientation.[12]

The techniques used by the newly dominant *corporate* capitalists to maintain their control of ever larger firms were subject to ruthless and detailed criticism by Berle in a series of law journal articles that he collected and published in 1928 as *Studies in the Law of Corporation Finance*.[13] He focused his concern on the fact that these capitalists both owned shares *and* controlled the management of the firms they operated. The full implications of the emerging tensions between that group and the everyday small retail shareholder were just coming into focus as the stock market mania of the 1920s unfolded. Only with the publication of *The Modern Corporation* in 1932 did Berle make the more dramatic argument that those tensions had evolved into a rupture in the nature of private property itself.

Arguably, the singular theoretical contribution that Berle makes with *Corporation Finance* was to recognize a shift in the nature of capitalist operations that laid the groundwork for the deeper claims of *The Modern Corporation*. Namely, Berle notes that with the rise of the new massive 'quasi-public' firms such as United States Steel, Standard Oil, Goodyear Rubber, and the Union Pacific Railroad Company, power was no longer exercised in a personal manner by 'a closely knit body of stockholders, generally located near the business and able to stroll down to the plant or call at the office at will'.[14] Instead,

[t]oday, with the growth of American business, the concentration into large financial units, and the increased liberality of incorporation statutes, the center of interest has shifted. The problems now revolve about *financial relationships* between the various participants in the corporate enterprise.[15]

The personal domination of a single natural person or small localized group of persons over a business's operations was now expressed through these new arms-length 'financial' relationships. In *Corporation Finance* Berle wrote about the 'controlling power' and the 'controlling influence' but not always, or simply, about 'managers', much less managers who controlled but did not own (a key category of the typology found in *The Modern Corporation*). Instead, it was clear from his analysis of the impact of potentially manipulative financial techniques such as the issuance of no-par stock,[16] or new methods of concentrating corporate power such as non-voting stock, that he was concerned about a *subset of owners* who were able to exercise control out of proportion to their ownership stake:

> [T]he system of corporation finance is based on the thesis that a small, dominant, management group will control the business operations of any corporation of reasonable size; although the substantial property interests have been contributed in large measure by non-management security holders .... one group with a relatively small beneficial interest, controlling large amounts of property beneficially owned by others.[17]

Thus, he promoted expanded 'fiduciary duties' in the new corporate context, clearly foreshadowing the legal obligations a dominant or controlling stockholder today owes to minority stockholders or the fiduciary obligation of all directors to the entire body of stockholders.[18] At this stage his 'thesis' is evolutionary, not revolutionary, although he concludes that 'this is a power over private property probably exceeding any which has been asserted in modern civilization'.[19]

It is with the publication of *The Modern Corporation* four years after *Corporation Finance*, likely influenced by the 1929 crash and the unfolding Great Depression and bolstered by the empirical work of his economist partner Means, that Berle concludes that something truly revolutionary has taken place with the shift of power inside the corporation to a new *non-owning* managerial class. As the authors concluded about the nature of the modern corporate form: 'This dissolution of the atom of property destroys the very foundation on which the economic order of the past three centuries has rested.'[20] Instead of individually owned and controlled 'private' property we have a new system where 'those who control the destinies of the typical modern corporation' no longer own enough shares to worry about their, and their fellow shareholders', financial interests. 'The explosion of the atom of property *destroys the basis of the old assumption that the quest for profits* will spur the owner of industrial property to its effective use.'[21]

It cannot be overemphasized how important Berle's point about 'the quest for profits' is. If the profit motive, in his eyes, has given way to something else (e.g., managerial entrenchment) then capitalism itself has really come to an end. 'The basic premise of all "technocratic" and corporatist thought,' Arthur Lipow noted in his study of Edward Bellamy, 'from Veblen, who was one of Bellamy's heirs, to Burnham and the neo-corporatists such as Berle, is that as the result of the separation of ownership from actual control, those who run the corporation, the managers, are free of the "profit motive"' thus enabling this 'elite without commercial motives to serve society through full production of superior products'.[22]

This conclusion is far reaching and has largely escaped the attention of prior work on corporate governance. Thus, Berle would now describe his research as indicating 'a major shift in civilization' towards a post-capitalist 'industrial feudalism'.[23] It was this development that led Berle to now call these corporations 'quasi-public' because they were, in fact, a new kind of social institution. ATT, for example with a centralized management team overseeing billions in assets, 450,000 employees and more than 500,000 shareholders, was, in his eyes, by 1930 'perhaps the most advanced development of the corporate system'. Thus, the problem of 'finance' described in *Corporation Finance* would give way to the problem of 'government' (both in the sense of intra-corporate governance and of state intervention) in *The Modern Corporation*. It was at this point that the modern myth of 'corporate governance' was born. As Berle's biographer Jordan Schwarz recognized,

> It was a powerful thesis: American capitalism headed toward an oligarchical concentration of economic power unless Washington's regulation of the marketplace protected a liberal economy from a dictatorship of unscrupulous corporate interests. Congress would have to regulate corporations with laws consistent with financial practices.[24]

Powerful and risky: absent the emergence of a new kind of (non-capitalist, of course) 'statesman' to manage this system in the broad balanced interest of society Berle feared that something 'tantamount to a revolution' might occur.[25]

How are capitalist firms governed?

However, Berle was wrong, both logically and empirically.[26] He never provided an explanation for precisely why or how a rational capitalist who, *ab initio*, both owns *and* controls, would sacrifice such a position, or, rather, could engineer its literal dissolution. Certainly, a successful entrepreneur might be offered a high enough price to sell all or part of their interest, as, for example, Andrew Carnegie did to the investor group organized by J.P. Morgan to form the giant conglomerate known as U.S. Steel. But in doing so, ownership and control would and did move together to the new group which, collectively, would then own and control the new entity. The new corporate trusts did represent a significant financial and legal innovation consistent with the evolutionary conclusions reached in *Corporation Finance* but not supportive of the revolutionary pronouncement about a kind of post-capitalist era made in *The Modern Corporation*. As Berle notes in the former, the use of non-voting stock and other similar mechanisms do not do away with the idea of a unity of capitalist ownership and control, they only enhance it. Non-voting stock issued to new dispersed and passive investors reinforces the centralized power of the *shareholding* and profit seeking 'controlling group', it does not dissolve it.[27]

Not surprisingly, then, the problem of consolidation of ownership with control continues to this day in a similar form. Thus, dual- or triple-class stock that restricts voting rights of outside investors have appeared more frequently in the technology sector and beyond. One prominent social media company went public in 2017 with non-voting stock, the first time such an offering had been allowed on a major stock exchange in recent decades. Founders like Mark Zuckerberg at Facebook (now Meta) or Sergey Brin and Larry Page at Google (now Alphabet) wish to *retain* control together with ownership, rather than allow their power to slip away, in a manner never quite explained by managerialism's advocates, into the hands of a new layer of bureaucratic non-owning managers. The goal in the current environment is not to fend off a managerial class uprising but to avoid the rise of activists within the dispersed shareholder base coalescing into a competing power centre of potential owners. Thus, firms that go public with multiple class share structures in place are more able to prevent the emergence of competitive threats to the current owners' control of the business entity.

Attempts to use that centralized power for personal non-profit goals as is implied by managerial theory are rare and subject to judicial sanction. In a leading Delaware case, where most large US public corporations are chartered, the giant auction website company eBay successfully defeated such an effort by the idealistic founders of the online site craigslist.com. As the court held:

> Having chosen a for-profit corporate form, the craigslist directors are bound by the fiduciary duties and standards that accompany that form. Those standards include acting to promote the value of the corporation for the benefit of its stockholders …. I cannot accept as valid … a corporate policy that … seeks *not* to maximize the economic value of a for-profit Delaware corporation for the benefit of its stockholders.[28]

In another example, Etsy, an online marketer of handmade goods, including many from the developing world, was one of the first so-called 'Certified B Corporations' to go public. The B Corp. certification allegedly committed the firm to social responsibility. In its 2015 IPO prospectus Etsy claimed it was 'building a human, authentic and community-centric global and local marketplace'.[29] But when Etsy ran into financial difficulties just two years after its IPO, it dropped the B Corp. commitment, fired its founder CEO, and laid off 8 per cent of its workforce. Its stock price quickly recovered.

Instead of two fiercely contending forces ('shareholders' v. 'managers'), as Berle and Means, and now their epigones, argue are such a fundamental characteristic of the large public corporation, I maintain that a relatively coherent centralized class of capitalists occupy the three paradigmatic institutional layers that make up the superstructure of the corporation, namely:

- Large shareholding 'institutional' investors (i.e., 'financial capitalists');
- The board of directors (made up of representatives of both financial and industrial capital) who are also almost always themselves shareholders; and
- Senior shareholding executives led by the chief executive officer ('CEO') (i.e., the firm's 'industrial capitalist(s)').

Further, instead of being locked in a ceaseless conflict resembling that of Laocoön and the serpents, as the Berle-Means school contends, the occupants of these roles, largely *cooperate* in the execution of the common primary 'capitalist' mandates: *valorization* and *capital accumulation*.

I focus attention on these two key components of capitalism – valorization and accumulation – to highlight their role in shaping modern debates about corporate finance and governance. These are specialized terms that summarily express the core activities of a capitalist economy.[30] 'Valorization' refers to the increase in surplus value – the source of capitalist profits, interest, and rent – often measured at the end of a certain period (a quarter or fiscal year). Valorization should be understood, however, as a continuous process, as the means of production (labour, raw materials, machinery) are purchased and deployed to produce 'commodities' whose presumed 'value' must then be 'realized' or validated through exchange in the market and which are then redeployed, now as 'use values', in a new round of, usually or hopefully, *expanded* production. As a result of this ongoing 'valorization process', money capital is 'accumulated' to enable a new round of expanded production and thus, in turn again, to realize larger profits if possible.

Accumulation can both support and undermine the valorization process. Primarily, of course, accumulation is a positive driver of the valorization process – to compete successfully, capitalists *must* expand production. In other words, they must accumulate money capital via exchange of commodities from the first cycle to invest in varying combinations of new technology, more machines, and more workers to complete the valorization cycle successfully. Inevitably, they intensify productivity in order to do so. Both expansion and intensification are means of accumulation. Intensification has, in the modern era of science, taken on great importance, but it is also a source of risk because of the potential it has to undermine the nominal value of financial capital previously invested to purchase currently employed machinery and processes. This potential risk, in turn, weighs heavily on the valorization process because financial instruments sold to support that process are highly sensitive to changes in the pace of capital accumulation. Bourgeois theories, such as the 'efficient markets hypothesis', are efforts to capture and measure this sensitivity so that a crude form of 'planning' or allocating capital effectively can take place.

Of course, concisely explaining these concepts in print is one thing; carrying them out successfully in the real world of flesh and blood workers, technology, and competition is quite another. To pursue these twin goals of valorization and accumulation, therefore, the occupants of all three layers of the corporate structure *share* amongst themselves authority such that within each layer one can find a unity of ownership with control, not an antithesis. Thus, *contra* the view of leading agency school figures like the Nobel prize winning economist Eugene Fama and his co-author Michael Jensen, there is *no* meaningfully clear 'separation of decision and risk-bearing functions ... in large corporations ....'[31] Both investors and executives desire the same thing: surplus value that can be accumulated in the form of expanded production of yet more surplus value.

Each institutional layer has appropriately distinct ownership interests and management rights, of course. Investors typically own the bulk of the firms' financial assets, its stock and debt instruments, but these always come with legally enforceable governance rights sufficient to ensure participation in the exercise of 'strategic decision making'. Characterizing them as 'outsiders' or as mere 'owners' misses this key point. One frequently finds the most financially powerful and concentrated elements of the ownership-control unity within this now quite large institutional investor layer. Warren Buffett's conglomerate Berkshire Hathaway, a large private equity buyout group like KKR or Blackstone, and the giant pension fund CalPERS, would all make suitable ideal types. Each manages hundreds of billions of dollars. These large asset managers, of course, are more easily able to diversify their holdings across firms in pursuit of an investment strategy that tailors their risk profile so that their returns are not dependent solely on the outcome at a particular firm. These 'outside' investors, far from being passive, as they are often characterized, are actively assessing the capitalist economy, as a whole, in a search for opportunities to maximize their returns from the *general* process of accumulation and valorization across individual firms. They trade off day to day influence over those processes at a particular firm against the value they gain by investing across the spectrum of capitalist firms.

Boards of directors, on the other hand, have historically been made up of either a smaller core group of owners (at start-up companies, for example, or at investment firms such as asset managers and hedge funds) or, more commonly today, hired agents of those owners who are rewarded with cash fees generated out of the firms' profits as well as stock or options, whose value is dependent on the firm's profit rate. Board members are compelled to act as fiduciaries to the extent they represent a distinct layer of outside owners. Their financial reward in the form of fees or stock is closely tied to their success in enabling capital accumulation and valorization as reflected, typically but not necessarily exclusively, in the firm's stock price.

Finally, CEOs, if not founder-owners themselves, are hired sub-agents of the board who also are obligated as fiduciaries and are compensated out of a firm's profits directly through cash payments and/or equity linked compensation such as stock or options. While they may seem to simply be acting at the behest of the board and large outside investors, quite often their equity position when combined with their direct operational knowledge of the particular entity and/or industry makes them, as I describe below in the case of Tim Cook at Apple, the dominant element within this structure. Together, boards and CEOs, inevitably, have more direct day to day control of the productive assets of a particular capitalist firm than financial investors.

The occupants at all three levels, however, share characteristics that enable them, collectively, to carry out the fundamental goals of the corporation, which is simply a legal form for executing those goals. Together, these three elements (investors, boards, and executives) hold the complete bundle of rights needed to carry out the purpose of the corporation: *sustaining the valorization and capital accumulation process*. And it is their shared commitment to that process, reinforced by their financial claims and legal rights, that holds these three elements together as a socio-economic milieu or class. 'The capitalists,' as Marx wrote, 'like hostile brothers, divide among themselves the loot of other people's labour which they have appropriated ....'[32]

The power to direct the activity of a corporation is within the hands of individual(s) and entities that *both own* a claim to a share of the firm's profits *and possess* (either individually or collectively) the legal rights to *control* the firm. In other words, *contra* Berle and Means, real capitalists both own *and* control. When the firm is understood as being owned and operated by a relatively coherent class of financial and industrial capitalists, it becomes clear that debates about shareholder, director, or CEO 'primacy' are either irrelevant or, at best, a second order concern.

This is a conclusion that is at odds with the view of those now raising an alarm at the apparent singular dominance of large institutional investors like BlackRock and Vanguard, with one research team even tagging them as 'the new titans of Wall Street'.[33] The key mistake made by these authors is that they discount the importance of the separate roles played within capitalism by what Marx called the 'money capitalist', on the one hand, and the 'industrial' or 'functioning' capitalist, on the other. When highlighting the 'specter of the giant three'[34] or the 'problem of twelve'[35] in their examination of the growing centralization of assets in a small number of investment firms these authors highlight an important new development in capitalism but ignore the persistent fundamental categories that explain more fully the nature of the system. These asset managers' power is heavily diluted by the complex internal decision-making structures that characterize these entities. Those scholars that highlight their rise fail almost entirely to account for the importance of the *industrial* capitalist, concentrating so heavily on the new forms that *financial* capital has taken. Both types of capitalists, however, have ownership *and* control rights in the firm. Occupants of both positions in the system of capitalist production and reproduction are entitled to membership in the capitalist class.

These authors most likely make this mistake because they labour in the wake of the widespread adoption of the Berle-Means paradigm. The major figures who helped solidify the dominance of this paradigm, including James Burnham, John Kenneth Galbraith, Henry Manne as well as Berle in later work, had as one of their major goals, in essence, the erasure of the very concept of the industrial capitalist in favour of their newly discovered 'managers'.[36] These managers were said by some to be a newly discovered third social class, in addition to workers and capitalists. These managers were allegedly evolving into leaders of a new American 'economic republic',[37] which was thought to be, even hoped to be, a form of non-Statist collectivism that could, indeed had to, compete globally with its rising statist counterpart, the Soviet Union.[38] Thus, Berle wrote that the role of 'the institutionalized corporation' 'was not purely economic' … it 'developed a vast, non-Statist organization of men and finance, an organization which increasingly raises problems of power'.[39] In the worldview of Berle and Keynes and Galbraith, both the money capitalist and the industrial capitalist were being phased out of existence. Keynes wrote, famously, of the 'euthanasia of the rentier' to describe what he thought of as the increasingly irrelevant role of the money capitalist.[40] Berle, together with Means, mis-stated the history of early-twentieth century corporate capitalism to eliminate the industrial capitalist from the picture.

THE ACTUAL CAPITALIST CLASS

It is the failure, then, to pay attention to the actual structure of the modern capitalist class that is responsible for the impasse that corporate governance theory has reached. The right to ownership and control held by that class emerged through long, and often conflict-laden, historical experience with the evolving demands of capital accumulation and valorization. As part of that historical experience those rights were designed and, in various ways, 'allocated' among the three institutional layers, largely through contracts, but also by statutory language that can be understood as a form of default built upon the many years of contractual experience. In that process the modern conception and design of those institutions themselves emerged. Those three layers comprise in the modern era (roughly, from *post-bellum* America forward) what can be called owners of 'capital',[41] and the occupants of those layers make up the broader 'capital*ist* class'. Every natural person who takes a seat within any of those layers will, therefore, find themselves obligated to pursue the mandate of the capitalist system: the creation and appropriation of value, the management of the valorization of that value, and the defence of the corporate entity's role in that process. The mandate comes from the overarching power of the laws of competition and exchange that drive this continuous process – in other words, from current economic reality. Thus, it is not a choice; and attempts to breach the mandate in favour of purely personal goals, or some undefined broader social purpose, are met with swift punishment, either financially or legally.⁴² If, for example, ESG goals are consistent with that process – which can be the case – they may be advocated by investors and executed by boards and CEOs. If not, they are going to be met with swift resistance by those capitalists as well as their representatives in courts and legislative bodies.

One classic historical example often used to illustrate the alleged separation of ownership and control is the sale of Carnegie Steel to public investors engineered by J.P. Morgan. Berle and Means, in fact, cite the steel industry as an example of 'management control', the fifth, and most extreme, category in their typology where 'ownership is so widely distributed that no individual or small group has even a minority interest large enough to dominate the affairs of the company'.⁴³ Yet, in fact, not only was this not true at the formation of the U.S. Steel conglomerate, the merged group into which Carnegie Steel was folded in 1901, it was not true thirty years later when Berle and Means conducted their research. Their own book lists the names of the members of the boards of directors of both firms, several of whom (4 out of 13) were, still in the early 1930s, 'Carnegie men', that is, major stockholders of the predecessor entity who had managed to hold on to sufficient shares in, and to lead, the new firm in such a manner that they retained control of its strategic decision making three decades later. Another board member at the time of *The Modern Corporation* was J.P. Morgan, Jr., the son of the architect of the original U.S. Steel structure. Others on the board have been categorized as part of the Morgan camp. Economist Robert Gordon thus easily concluded that the entity was under 'a strong and continuing influence' by the Morgan bankers, a group which owned *and* controlled, well into the 1930s.⁴⁴ Ferdinand Lundberg made a similar point about AT&T, Berle and Means' quintessential example of 'management control', in his *America's 60 Families*:

> J.P. Morgan and Company would, of course, deny that it controls A.T.&T., whose advertising stresses that no individual owns so much as one per cent of its stock. Working control, however, resides in a small Wall Street group, whose own stock is buttressed by shares under the control of brokers, although held 'for account of others'. Undisputed control – a consequence of the extensive public dispersal of more than half the company's shares – is exercised by the board of directors, and it is obviously a Morgan board …. The twenty largest stockholders held 4.6 per cent of stock, but – there was no one among the myriad small stockholders strong enough to dispute their sway.⁴⁵

This ability of a minority investor to be a dominating capitalist force – both owning and controlling – continues to this day. Nonetheless, in a similar fashion to Berle and Means, decades later, Mark Roe argued that in the modern era General Motors offered a striking example of *management* control. In the opening pages of his 1994 book, *Strong Managers, Weak Owners: The Political Roots of American Corporate Finance*,[46] Roe repeats an anecdote about two representatives of pension funds with large but far from majority shareholdings in GM who complain to GM leadership about the company's failing business model in the late 1980s. They were summarily 'rebuffed', Roe notes, thus in his eyes confirming the Berle-Means thesis about managerial power in the large public corporation.[47] Yet, as Roe finally concedes in passing some 200 pages later, GM's CEO retired soon after the pension funds' concerns surfaced as 'his strategy for GM … had suffered punishing blows' according to *The Wall Street Journal*.[48] His immediate successor was ousted summarily within a year and a half under pressure from those same pension funds.

Roe provides no clear explanation for the inconsistency in his argument. GM executives may have been rude to the anonymous fund managers, their bosses, but they were not exercising autonomous power. Those same fund managers were capable of helping organize a sufficient number of stockholders to pressure one CEO into retirement, fire his replacement, and change the company's strategic direction. Similar campaigns to oust non-controlling CEOs took place across industrial America in the early 1990s.[49] While many of those executives may have resembled Berle's apocryphal managers, that did not mean there were no owning and controlling capitalists exercising real power. At General Motors those pension funds, together with a relatively small number of other institutional investors, had assumed the position previously occupied by the Du Pont family, which had long controlled GM through its large, though minority, stock position. A similar shift had taken place at numerous other corporations. The Du Ponts sold; institutional investors bought. Control and ownership moved together from one element of the capitalist class to another – first in the hands of a large family, then into the hands of a small number of large pools of capital such as pension funds and mutual funds.

By way of contrast to Berle and Roe, i.e., advocates for the standard 'separation thesis' model, the German socialist economist Rudolf Hilferding clearly understood the actual impact of the newly emerging 'joint stock companies' of the early twentieth century:

With the development of the joint-stock system there emerges a distinctive financial technique, the aim of which is to ensure control over the largest possible amount of outside capital with the smallest possible amount of one's own capital. This technique has reached its peak of perfection in the financing of the American railway system ....[50]

He concludes that this leads to a new oligarchical power rooted in a combination of ownership and control:

In fact the corporations – especially the most important, profitable and pioneering ones – are governed by an oligarchy, or by a single big capitalist (or a bank) who are, in reality, vitally interested in their operations and quite independent of the mass of small shareholders. Furthermore, the managers who are at the top of the industrial bureaucracy have a stake in the enterprise, not only because of the bonuses they earn, but, still more important, because of their generally substantial shareholdings.[51]

Unlike the liberals Berle and Roe, Hilferding was a student of Marx and developed his view of the new corporate and financial stage of capitalism emerging at the *fin de siècle* through intense political warfare inside the German socialist movement. His *Finance Capital* was, arguably, the most important study of capitalism since Marx. As it turns out, Hilferding's major intellectual opponent in that battle, the reformist socialist Eduard Bernstein, is the real intellectual father of the modern, if misguided, 'separation thesis' held now over several generations by scholars like Berle, Manne, and Galbraith, and down to today's agency and stakeholder theorists. Bernstein viewed the new joint stock companies as forms that enabled a democratization of capitalism from within to emerge, in part, via widespread stock ownership. To Bernstein,

[T]he increasing platoons ... of shareholders ... represent a force with a powerful influence on the economic life of society. The share restores those interim stages in the social scale which, as heads of production, had been obliterated from industry by the concentration of businesses.[52]

This presaged the view held today, primarily by stakeholder advocates, that the corporation can itself be the locus of democratic life.

Capital had other ideas. A new form of capitalist class emerged by the end of the nineteenth century, and new forms of corporate 'governance' were being designed that would enable that class to oversee a new stage in the history of capitalism itself. An apparent form of 'ownership' was created to attract outside capital, but this only helped enable the continuing dominance of the capitalist class made up of shareholding executives, directors, and key elements among the non-managing shareholders and other investors. The central advantage of the corporate form was that it enabled control and mobility at the very same time – as founding owners stepped back into a 'mere' director or shareholder role, they could use both newly gained time and diversified, liquid, and fungible capital to reach out and found new firms or exercise influence across the economy through the capital markets and other governance mechanisms such as multiple directorships. Hence, the Du Ponts were able to expand from chemicals to the emerging car industry in the early twentieth century and take a substantial position in General Motors, which they held until the early 1960s, at least. The structures that emerged in the late-nineteenth and early-twentieth centuries, while understandably derided by figures like Berle and Louis Brandeis as manipulative and deceptive, were, in fact, powerful innovations that greatly strengthened the hold of the capitalist class over the capital accumulation and valorization process. As Hilferding described it:

> The expansion of the capitalist enterprise which has been converted into a corporation, freed from the bonds of individual property, can now conform simply with the demands of technology. The introduction of new machinery, the assimilation of related branches of production, the exploitation of patents, now takes place only from the standpoint of their technical and economic suitability. The preoccupation with raising the necessary capital, which plays a major role in the privately owned enterprise, limiting its power of expansion and diminishing *its* readiness for battle, now recedes into the background. Business opportunities can be exploited more effectively, more thoroughly, and more quickly, and this is an important consideration when periods of prosperity become shorter.[53]

A class of capitalists occupy positions as pure investors, as well as shareholding executives and directors, and thereby make up the 'controlling group' that exercises, collectively, *strategic* decision-making over the direction and functions of the firm. A focus on 'strategic' decision-making is a core feature of the British 'Warwick School', in whose path I situate my approach to the nature of firm governance. This classification is fundamentally distinct from the neoliberal agency school which poses the firm in a permanent, if contractually constrained, binary conflict between shareholder and managers.

Thus, as two key figures associated with the Warwick School noted:

> the power to make strategic decisions can be equated with the power to control a firm, where control implies the ability to determine broad corporate objectives. Put another way, it may be argued that the power to make strategic decisions is the power to plan the overall direction of production in the firm. This includes the power broadly to determine a firm's geographical orientation, its relationship with rivals, with governments, and with its labour force.[54]

A third leading figure in that school, Christos Pitelis, summarized the school's view of the relevant aspect of their theory of the firm as follows:

> As controlling group I define the group that can determine strategic decisions of the firms, despite resistance from others …. The controlling group consists of large-scale shareholders and big level managers. It follows that the rest of the shareholders, including those who take the operational decisions of the firms (small level managers) are not controlling.[55]

And later, in his book-length treatment of the issue of corporate control, Pitelis concluded that 'the modern corporation of today is controlled by a group of big shareholders and high-level managers (capitalists) who exercise this control *via* only partial ownership'.[56] This system of *control with partial ownership* evolved, Pitelis argues, from a system where rational founders who owned firms outright expanded by selling some shares without surrendering control. This reverses the causality typically found in those who work within a model that combines alleged 'managerial' dominance with widely dispersed and passive share ownership.

It is within that controlling milieu or among those individuals or entities, almost always a very small group, that the critical judgments about the path of the firm are made – whether to change course in a significant manner or, perhaps, whether to give up the ship altogether as opposed to merely trimming the sails. The sharing or allocation of the original, *ab initio*, unity of authority of the firm amongst those layers can be thought of as existing on a continuum. Take as an example, a paradigmatic *industrial* capitalist like Tim Cook, the engineer of Apple's global supply chain under Apple founder Steve Jobs who rose to the CEO position upon Jobs' death. Cook has substantially more influence on the strategic direction of Apple than, perhaps, Safra Catz, the CEO of Oracle, where a dominant living founder like Larry Ellison still acts as board chair and Chief Technology

Officer. Thus, one portrait of Cook notes that his 'transformation of Apple's operations and deep understanding of every aspect of the business was pivotal to the success of the company's dramatic comeback'. This detailed description of Cook's overhaul of the guts of Apple's manufacturing and distribution systems is reminiscent of how iconic industrial capitalists like Andrew Carnegie and Henry Ford mastered the details of their respective firms' operational processes in order to maximize profits.[57] Thus, Cook has been able to withstand challenges to his control because he is CEO; and because he is CEO, he also owns, arguably, the largest single personal share of Apple's common stock. He both owns and leads the controlling group of shareholders at Apple.[58]

If, however, Apple were to run aground because Cook made serious strategic mistakes, there exists, within the quiver of arrows held in reserve by the company's largest *financial* capitalists, sufficient power to intervene and force Cook to change course or, perhaps, leave altogether. One might say, then, that large institutional investors with significant holdings in a particular firm, such as large asset managers, have a residual option to intervene at the margin when a firm faces critical turning points. This does not mean that they cannot, and do not, voice their opinions on strategic questions facing the firm on a regular basis, however. While such firms are traditionally viewed by managerial theorists as simply passively echoing managerial decisions (including, for example, voting with management on key decisions like re-election of the board of directors, a central example in Berle and Means' book), in fact, these savvy and powerful institutional investors can and do deploy a sophisticated engagement tool set with respect to their portfolio firms, once again eliding the binary distinction between risk and decision making that neoliberal agency theorists allege is so fundamental.[59]

Apple's Dividend Policy: A Case in Point

A striking example of how this relationship works in practice played out at Apple several years ago as the company amassed enormous sums of cash generated by its worldwide profits and its cross-border tax avoidance strategy.[60] Facially it appeared to be the kind of conflict that embodied the Berle-Means paradigm with beleaguered and widely dispersed shareholders denied access to cash payouts of accumulated surplus value by an empire-building centralized management team. In the face of this apparently unused pile of cash just sitting in the bank, the veteran corporate raider Carl Icahn took a minority but significant stake in Apple shares and loudly claimed that he was pressuring Apple to return cash to its shareholders. Icahn filed a proposal with Apple to increase its stock buyback program by a sizeable $50 billion.[61]

Arguably, at first glance, this looked like a classic example of a battle between powerful 'entrenched' inside *agents* (Cook and the Apple board) and weak outside *principals* (widely dispersed shareholders welcoming their white knight, activist Icahn) consistent with the story long told by Berle-Means influenced theorists, that outside investors must fight hard to defend their position against managerial dominance. Despite the publicity attached to Icahn's investment, however, his behaviour is more easily understood as that of an opportunistic non-controlling shareholder free-riding on strategic decision-making by those who both owned and controlled the company.[62] That 'controlling group', as the Warwick School would describe it, led by Tim Cook, was pursuing the inevitable logic of valorization and capital accumulation by reinvesting some of its profits, defending their value to shareholders by avoiding taxes and returning a portion of cash in the form of stock buybacks and dividend payments. Rather than policing management empire-building, Icahn was, in the eyes of that dominant control group, merely engaged in 'financial engineering' that interfered with a long term innovation strategy that required careful balancing between reinvestment of firm profits in research and development, on the one hand, and returning unneeded cash to shareholders in a tax efficient manner, on the other.[63] At the time, Apple was facing growing competition in its core product groups and needed to find a way to refresh its lineup.[64] As one industry expert expressed Apple's situation in the face of Icahn's offensive:

> This kind of financial engineering isn't in the long-term interest of Apple's shareholders ... They're still a tremendously valuable company, but stock price boosts from financial engineering shouldn't distract from the fact that their business model doesn't look as solid and dominant as it did four years ago.[65]

New York City's Comptroller, trustee for a coalition of public sector pension funds managing $149 billion in assets including $1.3 billion of Apple shares, echoed this concern for innovation in a letter to fellow Apple shareholders:

> As Mr. Icahn himself notes ... the majority of Apple's revenues come from two products, the iPhone and iPad, first released in 2007 and 2012, respectively. While Apple's impressive track record for innovation bodes well for the future, it would be short-sighted and foolish to deprive the company of a sufficient cash cushion to weather unwelcome setbacks and seize new opportunities, including major acquisitions. In last week's

interview with the *WSJ*, Tim Cook said, 'We have no problem spending 10 figures for the right company'.[66]

In fact, the real centre of control at Apple, Tim Cook, backed by a substantial number of other long-term institutional investors, had already instituted Apple's first post-Steve Jobs stock buyback and dividend program the year *before* Icahn publicly announced his position in the company.

Once clear opposition among institutional investors surfaced, Icahn withdrew his proposal. Icahn dumped his Apple shares in early 2016, two and a half-years after buying in to the company, clearing a $2 billion profit. The argument some had made that he was engaged in short term stock manipulation rather than voicing deeper concerns among shareholders about the direction of the company under Cook took on greater salience.[67] Apple has continued its policy of returning some cash to shareholders to the present day, years after Icahn sold his shares, yet has also continued innovating successfully enough to have become the first American company valued at more than a trillion dollars.[68] In other words, there is substantial evidence that Apple followed a balanced policy of retaining sufficient cash to valorize its profits successfully and otherwise return unneeded cash to its shareholders. This is a result that is consistent with a view that capitalist firms follow the demands of accumulation rather than succumb to the demands of an illusory managerial class or an anarchic array of dispersed non-controlling shareholders.

'CORPORATE GOVERNANCE' DEMYSTIFIED

If it is a myth to think that real controlling owners ever disappeared, much less capitalism itself, it is equally a myth to think that the corporation is, in any meaningful sense, 'governed' or 'governable' at all. It was very important for Berle and Means to use political metaphors because of the distinctive purpose that underlay their particular project – a project motivated by both the normative views of the authors themselves and the exceptional historical situation in which they worked, namely, during a deep crisis of legitimacy for the American system. Berle and Means were working within a distinct intellectual and political tradition that had its precedents in the reformist movement that grew out of the socialist movement, led by figures like Bellamy, Bernstein, and Brandeis. From the very first pages of their classic work Berle and Means make clear they are dealing with the 'corporate *system*' – not just the corporate form – because the corporation had become a 'major *social* institution', not simply an efficient or convenient means of carrying on economic activity.[69] The corporation, they wrote:

is coming more and more to be the industrial unit with which American economic, social, *and* political life must deal. The implications of this fact challenge many of the basic assumptions of current thought.[70]

This reflects the 'socialism from above' perspective explored most notably by Hal Draper in a series of articles in the 1960s.[71] Draper makes clear that Berle, among others, was groping for a way to convey that the socio-economic system was evolving well beyond the confines of capitalism, namely, towards

a new social order which is neither capitalist nor socialist, but which is based on the control of both economy and government by an elite bureaucracy – forming a new exploitive ruling class – which runs the fused economic-political structure not for the private-profit gains of any individual or groups but for its own collective aggrandizement in power, prestige, and revenue, by administrative planning-from-above.[72]

This new Berlean intellectual tendency very much wanted to see the emerging managerial layers of the increasingly complex and large corporation as a possible source of socially responsible leadership of the new, and to some, terrifying, industrial economy.

Once we strip away that (understandable) ideological concern, however, an objective view of the corporation eliminates any notion that it can or does function as an *agora*, as a substitute for political life itself, which the Berle-Means viewpoint implied and which the modern stakeholder approach still champions.[73] In fact, what we think of today as 'corporate governance' is an amalgam of two sometimes overlapping but distinct developments: first, the inevitable process of conflict resolution that must take place among and between the layers of the corporate power structure as the capitalists – financial and industrial – who reside there engage in the complex and unpredictable capital accumulation and valorization process; and, second, the effort by wider society to impinge on the exercise of authority by that power structure through various mechanisms of 'social control'. It is within the latter that one can situate many of today's CSR or ESG initiatives, particularly those led by organized labour, as efforts by society to impinge upon the rule of capital.

What, then, are the implications of placing the fundamental dynamic of capitalism at the centre of our analysis of corporate theory? It upsets the traditional dominant approach to corporate governance, an approach held in common by both the agency and the stakeholder schools of thought.

Consider once more Mark Roe's influential *Strong Managers, Weak Owners*, one of several major modern works written in the tradition of Berle and Means. Roe's *idee fixe* is the decline of General Motors in the late 1980s and early 1990s. At that point in time, it *appeared* to Roe that 'finance' – i.e., GM's apparently widely dispersed shareholders – was unable to generate sufficient strength to impact what is portrayed as a headstrong and destructive CEO backed by entrenched largely non-owning managers. Roe presents this acute situation as a metaphor for the entire modern history of western, or at least Anglo-American, capitalism. He then asks how this condition came to pass, how was it that finance had ended up in such a feckless and weak position relative to the *apparent* power of the ascendant managerial class. That mistaken presumption then serves to undergird his historical argument about the alleged political effort to weaken financial 'owners' in the wake of the Great Depression. As noted above, however, the financial capitalists that owned substantial stakes in GM were more than able to exert their strategic decision-making power when needed to oust the GM CEO. In contrast to, for example, the longstanding tenure of CEOs like Apple's Tim Cook, GM's CEO had no substantial ownership position sufficient to resist this pressure.

It is fair to say that the kind of thinking that Roe and others engage in has served as the 'great myth' of the modern corporate governance framework that dominates academia and the broader policy debate about corporate power. Whether it is conservative legal scholar Stephen Bainbridge, who advocates what he calls a 'director primacy' model of corporate governance, or his somewhat more liberal nemesis Lucian Bebchuk, who makes the case for 'increasing shareholder power', both, in essence, concede the Roe point of view: managers are strong in Bainbridge's view and justly so, while for Bebchuk financial 'owners' should be restored to their proper role in the governance framework of the corporation. Of course, Roe was, more or less consciously, simply restating the original Berle-Means myth as 'fragmented ownership, a shift in power to the CEO, and suppression of large owners'.[74] And in doing so, he and those who accept that myth cannot make sense of what happened to American capitalism in the late 1980s or early 1990s, or in fact during any period since the late nineteenth century.

These authors also seem blissfully unaware of the lack of originality in their argument.[75] It is not just that they have ended up repeating the Berle shareholder 'atomization' myth, but they are also seemingly unaware that Berle himself was simply, if with a new empirical patina, re-telling a myth created within the German social democracy at the turn of the century in response to the emergence of the then-new era of corporate capitalism.

The key to understanding this historical origin is noting the use, by Berle and others, particularly in the stakeholder school, of political metaphors – references to corporate democracy, the town hall, shareholders' franchise, etc. – as if a capitalist institution, the firm, can be subjected to governance at all. This represented an effort to inject some form of a legitimating culture inside a capitalist system that had largely left behind the era of small property holders which formed the foundation of early democratic theory. Thus, Eduard Bernstein first articulated such a 'political' or 'populist' approach to a fundamentally economic problem as modern corporate capitalism was emerging in late-nineteenth and early-twentieth century Germany.[76] His aim was to undercut the potential power of an increasingly militant new industrial working class by claiming that widespread share ownership was a strong indicator of the need for a gradual, not revolutionary, democratization of capitalism from within capitalist institutions themselves.

Berle's work came to prominence at a similar inflection point in the history of capitalism, the 1930s, when big capital once again feared the revolutionary potential of a new working-class uprising seen most clearly in the rise of the Congress of Industrial Organizations (CIO), which threatened not only Henry Ford's control of *his* company, but the entire capitalist system. As C.L.R. James wrote of this important social movement:

> It was no instrument for collective bargaining and getting out the vote for the Democratic Party. It was the first attempt of a section of the American workers to change the system as they saw it into something which would solve what they considered to be their rights, their interests, and their human needs.[77]

Capitalism in the 1930s was desperately in need of a new legitimating ideology which, in part, the Berle-Means theory of managerial power provided. Similarly, in the wake of industrial decline in the early 1970s there was a wave of working-class revolt. Neoliberal theory emerged then, led by figures like Milton Friedman, to justify the destruction of worker incomes by the combination of globalization and technological change, now claiming in a manner reminiscent of Bernstein that widespread share ownership in a competitive capital market could generate a socially legitimate allocation of capital. We see this approach still at work today in the now open class conflict emerging at giant firms like Amazon and Starbucks. The fear of this new social tension is likely driving the willingness of groups like the Business Roundtable to search for its own form of a legitimating ideology when it jumps on the new 'stakeholder capitalism' bandwagon. But no increase in the 'diversity' of corporate boards or sharper supervision of firms' 'agency' costs by courts is going to result in dramatic improvements in the lives of baristas or warehouse workers.

What Bernstein and Berle share with their modern counterparts like Friedman, Posner, and Roe, then, is the mistaken view that the corporation is, in any sense, 'governed' at all. In fact, corporations are not governed. They are ruled by capitalists in order that capitalists can rule society. And these rulers are a sophisticated class of controlling stockholders whose only 'purpose' is to carry out the laws of the capitalist economic system – capital accumulation and valorization – whatever the wider social consequences of that mandate may be.

NOTES

1   'Statetment on the Purpose of a Corporation', Business Roundtable, 19 August 2019, www.businessroundtable.org.
2   *Accountable Capitalism Act*, S.3348,115th Cong. (2018).
3   Adolf A. Berle and Gardiner C. Means, *The Modern Corporation and Private Property*, New Brunswick: Transaction Publishers, 1991 [1932], p. 5; Michael C. Jensen and William H. Meckling, 'Theory of the Firm: Managerial Behavior, Agency Costs and Ownership Structure', *Journal of Financial Economics* 3(4) 1976, pp. 305-360; Gérard Duménil and Dominique Lévy, *Managerial Capitalism: Ownership, Management and The Coming New Mode of Production*, London: Pluto Press, 2018, pp. 58-9, 216.
4   While the story I tell here is predominantly one rooted in the Anglo-American capitalist world, it has taken on wider significance in the wake of the thirty-year post-Cold War effort to mold the global economy to the requirements of that world.
5   Jensen and Meckling, 'Theory of the Firm'; Richard A. Posner, *Economic Analysis of Law*, Boston: Little, Brown and Company, 2nd edition, 1977, pp. 289-314.
6   Adolf A. Berle, *The 20th Century Capitalist Revolution*, New York: Harcourt, Brace and Company, 1954, p. 5; Dalia Tsuk, 'From Pluralism to Individualism: Berle and Means and 20th-Century American Legal Thought', *Law & Social Inquiry* 30(1), 2005, pp. 179, 181.
7   Ronald H. Coase, 'The Problem of Social Cost', *Journal of Law and Economics* 3, 1960, pp. 1-44.
8   'Law and economics' adherents would respond by saying that there is a Coasean solution to any such externalities in the form of assigning appropriate property rights and then allowing trade to take place. Perhaps one way to dissolve the tension between these two camps is to argue that if externalities are pervasive, a governance solution in the form of stakeholders might be transaction cost efficient.
9   The *agora* was an open space considered the 'center of public activity' in ancient Greek city-states where 'all the citizens could assemble'. It was used for multiple purposes including markets, religious ceremonies, military activities, and theatrical performances. Buildings that housed activities essential to the carrying on of democratic life, including courts and civic offices, surrounded the space. Mabel L. Lang, *The Athenian Citizen: Democracy In The Athenian Agora*, 2d edition, Athens:

American School of Classical Studies at Athens, 2004, p. 5. Socrates carried on his famous conversations in the Athenian *agora*. Debra Nails, *Agora, Academy, and the Conduct of Philosophy*, Philosophical Studies Series Vol. 63, Dordrecht: Kluwer Academic Publishers, 1995, p. 205.

10 This is not to argue that democracy, *tout court*, is incompatible with capitalism. Clearly some democratic institutions and forms flourish within some (if not most) capitalist societies. But we are talking here about democracy *inside* the quintessential modern capitalist institution, the corporation.

11 Jessica Wang, 'Neo-Brandeisianism and the New Deal: Adolf A. Berle, Jr., William O. Douglas, and the Problem of Corporate Finance in the 1930s', *Seattle University Law Review*, 33(4), 2010, pp. 1221-1246, 1231.

12 Later, in the depths of the Depression, Berle would break sharply from the 'Brandeisians' and opt for a state driven crisis response that pointed clearly to his emerging post-capitalist ideological orientation. See Jordan A. Schwarz, *Liberal: Adolf A. Berle and the Vision of an American Era,* New York: The Free Press, 1987, p. 104.

13 Adolf A. Berle, Jr., *Studies in the Law of Corporation Finance*, Buffalo, NY: William S. Hein & Co. Inc., 1995/1928.

14 Berle, *Corporation Finance*, p. v.

15 Berle, *Corporation Finance*, p. v. (emphasis added).

16 No-par stock carries no value on the face of its certificate or in the corporate charter. This denies third party creditors any reassurance that the entity is financially stable. This was more controversial in the early twentieth century than it is today when disclosure requirements provide more information to third parties.

17 Berle, *Corporation Finance*, p. 190.

18 Berle, *Corporation Finance*, pp. 62-63.

19 Berle, *Corporation Finance*, p. 190.

20 Berle and Means, *The Modern Corporation*, p. 8. Marx famously noted near the end of Volume One of *Capital*: 'The centralization of the means of production and socialization of labour reach a point at which they become incompatible with their capitalist integument. This integument is burst asunder. The knell of capitalist private property sounds. The expropriators are expropriated.' Karl Marx, *Capital: A Critique of Political Economy*, Volume One, trans. Ben Fowkes, New York: Vintage Books, 1977 [1867], p. 929. Of course, as I suggest below, Marx's conception of the capitalist dynamic was fundamentally different than that held by Berle and his epigones.

21 Berle and Means, *The Modern Corporation*, p. 8. (emphasis added).

22 Arthur Lipow, *Authoritarian Socialism: Edward Bellamy and the Nationalist Movement*, Berkeley: University of California Press, 1982, p. 89.

23 Schwarz, *Liberal*, p. 56.

24 Schwarz, *Liberal*, p. 56.

25 Schwarz, *Liberal*, p. 56.

26 The relevant empirical work can be found in W.L. Crum, 'On the Alleged Concentration of Economic Power', *American Economic Review*, 24(1) 1934, pp. 69-83; Paul Sweezy, 'The Illusion of the "Managerial Revolution"', 6 *Science and Society* 6(1) 1942, pp. 1-23; Clifford G. Holderness, 'The Myth of Diffuse Ownership in the United States', *The Review of Financial Studies*, 22(4) 2007, pp. 1377-1408; Clifford G. Holderness, Randall S. Kroszner, and Dennis P. Sheehan, 'Were the Good Old Days That Good? Changes in Managerial Stock Ownership Since the Great Depression',

Journal of Finance 54 (2) 1999, pp. 435-469; Clifford G. Holderness, 'A Survey of Blockholders and Corporate Control', *FRBNY Economic Policy Review* 9(1) pp. 51-64, 2003; Alex Edmans and Clifford G. Holderness, 'Blockholders: A Survey of Theory and Evidence' in Benjamin Hermalin and Michael Weisback, eds., *The Handbook of the Economics of Corporate Governance*, Vol. 1, Amsterdam: North-Holland (Elsevier), 2017, pp. 541-636; but see Brian Cheffins and Steven Bank, 'Is Berle and Means Really a Myth?' *The Business History Review* 83(3) 2009 pp. 443-474, 463.

27 Berle, *Corporation Finance*, pp. 41-2.
28 *eBay Domestic Holdings, Inc. v. Newmark*, 16 A.3d 1, 89 (Del. Ch. Ct. 2010). (Emphasis in original.)
29 Etsy, *Final Prospectus*, 15 April 2015, p. 1.
30 Detailed explanations can be found in Marx, *Capital* at pp. 293-306 and pp. 707 ff; Jacques Camatte, *Capital and Community*, New York: Prism Key Press, 2011; David Norman Smith, 'Sharing, Not Selling: Marx Against Value', *Continental Thought & Theory* 1 (4), 2017, pp. 653-695; and David Norman Smith, *Authorities, Deities, and Commodities: Classical Sociology and the Problem of Domination*, Department of Sociology, University of Wisconsin-Madison, Ph.D. dissertation, 1988, (on file with author), pp. 979 ff.
31 Eugene F. Fama and Michael C. Jensen, 'Separation of Ownership and Control', *Journal of Law and Economics* 26(2), 1983, pp. 301-325.
32 Karl Marx, *Theories of Surplus Value*, Part II, London: Lawrence & Wishart, 1969, p. 29.
33 Lucian Bebchuk and Scott Hirst, 'The Specter of the Giant Three', *Boston University Law Review* 99(3), 2019, pp. 721-741; John C. Coates, 'The Future of Corporate Governance Part I: The Problem of Twelve,' Harvard Law School Discussion Paper No. 1001, April 2019; Jill Fisch, Assaf Hamdani and Steven Davidoff Solomon, 'The New Titans of Wall Street: A Theoretical Framework for Passive Investors', *University of Pennsylvania Law Review*, 168(1), 2019, pp. 17-72; Edward B. Rock and Marcel Kahan, 'Index Funds and Corporate Governance: Let Shareholders be Shareholders', NYU Law and Economics Research Paper No. 18-39, 4 April 2019.
34 Bebchuk and Hirst, 'Specter of the Giant Three'.
35 Coates, 'The Problem of Twelve'.
36 Adolf A. Berle, *Power Without Property: A New Development in American Political Economy*, New York: Harcourt, Brace and Company, 1959; 'Modern Functions of the Corporate System', *Columbia Law Review*, 62(3), 1962, pp. 433-449; and *American Economic Republic* (1963); James Burnham, *The Managerial Revolution: What is Happening in the World Now*, New York: The John Day Company, Inc., 1941; John Kenneth Galbraith, *The New Industrial State*, Boston: Houghton Mifflin Company, 1967; Henry Manne, 'The "Higher Criticism" of the Modern Corporation', *Columbia Law Review*, 62(3), 1962 pp. 399-432.
37 Berle, *American Economic Republic*; and 'Foreword', in Edward S. Mason, ed., *The Corporation in Modern Society*, Cambridge: Harvard University Press, 1959, at pp. ix-xv.
38 Hal Draper rightly critiqued this as a form of 'socialism from above'. Hal Draper, 'Neo-corporatists and neo-reformers', *New Politics* 1(1), 1961, pp. 87-106.
39 Berle, 'Foreword', p. ix.
40 John Maynard Keynes, *The General Theory of Employment Interest and Money*, New York: Harcourt, Brace and Company, 1936, p. 376.

41 'Capital' is no longer well or widely understood. Thomas Piketty's wildly popular book, *Capital in The Twenty-First Century*, Cambridge: Harvard University Press, 2014, certainly put the concept back into wider social discourse. Unfortunately, Piketty adopts the economic convention (in the course of making an unconventional and important argument about inequality) that defines capital, simply, as an income-producing asset ('land, real estate, financial instruments, industrial equipment, etc.' that generate 'rent, dividends, interest, profits, capital gains, royalties, and other incomes', Piketty, *Capital,* 19). The position taken here is consistent with the long tradition started by Marx, based on a definition of capital as a *social relationship* through which capitalists, who occupy the three institutional layers in the corporation, carry out valorization and accumulation by appropriating value created via exchange in the market by the use of labor power they acquire from workers. Managing technological progress and the increasing productivity of capitalism is central to understanding how the capitalist system works.

42 This should *not* be interpreted to mean that efforts to build support for such a broader social purpose are wasted. Such efforts, led for the most part by non-controlling shareholders and outside non-shareholding activists, can raise broader social awareness of the pathological nature of capitalism and, on rare occasions, to actual compromises by the system itself in favor of progressive reforms.

43 Berle and Means, *The Modern Corporation*, p. 78.

44 Robert Aaron Gordon, *Business Leadership in the Large Corporation*, Berkeley: University of California Press, 1961, p. 207.

45 Ferdinand Lundberg, *America's 60 Families*, New York: The Vanguard Press, 1937, pp. 42-3.

46 Mark Roe, *Strong Managers, Weak Owners: The Political Roots of American Corporate Finance*, Princeton, NJ: Princeton University Press, 1994.

47 Roe, *Strong Managers, Weak Owners,* p. xiii.

48 Roe, *Strong Managers, Weak Owners,* pp. 223-4; Stephen Miller, 'GM Chief Tried to Transform Auto Maker But Couldn't Halt Its Decline', *Wall Street Journal*, 1 December 2007.

49 Micheline Maynard, *Collision Course: Inside the Battle for General Motors*, New York: Carol Publishing Group, 1995, pp. 6-7.

50 Rudolf Hilferding, *Finance Capital: A study of the Latest Phase of Capitalist Development*, London: Routledge & Kegan Paul, 1981, p. 119.

51 Hilferding, *Finance Capital*, p. 121.

52 Eduard Bernstein, *Preconditions of Socialism,* trans. Henry Tudor, Cambridge: Cambridge University Press, 1993, pp. 65-6; William Smaldone, *Rudolf Hilferding: The Tragedy of a German Social Democrat,* Dekalb, IL: Northern Illinois University Press, 1998, 48; and 'For Rudolf Hilferding, Socialism Was About Freedom', *Jacobin,* 12 October 2020.

53 Hilferding, *Finance Capital*, p. 123.

54 Keith Cowling and Roger Sugden, 'The Essence of the Modern Corporation: Markets, Strategic Decision-making and the Theory of the Firm', *The Manchester School* 66(1), 1998, pp. 59-86, 64; see also Maurice Zeitlin, 'Corporate Ownership and Control: The Large Corporations and the Capitalist Class', *American Journal of Sociology* 79(5), 1974, pp. 1073-1119.

55 Christos N. Pitelis, 'Corporate Control, Social Choice and Capital Accumulation: An Asymmetrical Choice Approach', *Review of Radical Political Economics* 18(3), 1986, pp. 85-100, 97.
56 Christos N. Pitelis, *Corporate Capital: Control, Ownership, Savings and Crisis*, Cambridge: Cambridge University Press, 1987, p. 4.
57 Leander Kahney, *Tim Cook: The Genius Who Took Apple to the Next Level*, New York: Penguin, 2019.
58 While asset managers nominally own far more stock in Apple than Cook, no single natural person owns nearly as much as Cook with the exception of longstanding board member and veteran of the Steve Jobs' era, Arthur Levinson. Firms like Vanguard and Blackrock are merely intermediaries collectively managing shares on behalf of thousands of smallholding individuals and yet other asset managers. And the ownership of those firms themselves is held among a larger number of outside investors. Thus, Cook stands at least *primus inter pares* in the Apple boardroom and at annual shareholders' meetings.
59 BlackRock, *2019 Investment Stewardship Annual Report*, August 2019; Carol Loomis, 'BlackRock: The $4.3 trillion force', *Fortune*, 7 July 2014; Fisch, Hamdani and Solomon, 'The New Titans', p. 43ff.
60 Josh Hoxie, 'Apple Avoided $40 Billion in Taxes. Now It Wants a Gold Star?', *Fortune*, 18 January 2018.
61 Carl Icahn, 'Open Letter to Tim Cook', May 18, 2015, available at carlicahn.com/carl-icahn-issues-open-letter-to-tim-cook.
62 See 'Apple Announces Plans to Initiate Dividend and Share Repurchase Program', *Agence France-Presse*, 19 March 2012; Won-Youn Oh and Seoyeon Park, Apple: Corporate Governance and Stock Buyback, Haskayne School of Business, University of Calgary, Case #W14736, Ivey Publishing, 27 March 2015. The latter noted that 'even before Icahn's proposal, Apple was engaged in a major stock buyback program'.
63 Among the opponents of Icahn's intervention were a coalition of large public pension funds who publicly backed Cook as well as the influential proxy advisory firm, ISS, which recommended that institutional investors oppose Icahn's proposal.
64 Oh and Park, *Apple*, p. 8.
65 Aaron Pressman, 'Icahn's Plans for Apple Unlikely to Help Long-Term Shareholders', Yahoo! Finance, 19 August 2013.
66 Scott M. Stringer, Letter to Apple Shareowners, Proxy Solicitation filed with SEC by Apple, Form PX14A6G, 10 February 2014, www.sec.gov/Archives/edgar/data/320193/000121465914001019/m210141px14a6g.htm.
67 William Lazonick, Matt Hopkins, and Ken Jacobson, 'Carl Icahn's $2 billion Apple stake was a prime example of investment inequality,' *MarketWatch*, 7 June 2016.
68 In fact, it soon became clear that the shortsighted Icahn had left a lot of money on the table by ignoring Apple's long-term investment strategy. Chuck Jones, 'Carl Icahn Sold Apple Too Soon & It Cost Him $3.7B', *Forbes*, 10 November 2017. Rob Davies, 'Apple becomes world's first trillion-dollar company', *Guardian*, 2 August 2018. Davies noting that, 'Apple's astounding recent performance has left rivals in the competitive technology sector trailing in its wake.' Apple has maintained its valuation even in the wake of the Covid-19 crisis, reaching a valuation of more than $1.6 trillion as of July 28, 2020.
69 Berle and Means, *The Modern Corporation*, p. 2 (emphasis added).

70 Berle and Means, *The Modern Corporation*, p. 44.
71 Hal Draper, 'Neo-corporatists'; Hal Draper, 'The New Social-Democratic Reformism', *New Politics* 2(2), 1963, 100-116; Hal Draper, 'The Mind of Clark Kerr', *New Politics* 3(4), 1964, pp. 51-61; Hal Draper, 'The Two Souls of Socialism', *New Politics* 5(1), 1966, pp. 57-84.
72 Draper, 'Neo-corporatists', p. 87-8.
73 See Merrick Dodd, 'For Whom Are Corporate Managers Trustees?', *Harvard Law Review* 45(7), 1932, pp. 1145-1163; Charles R.T. O'Kelley, 'Merrick Dodd and the Great Depression: A Few Historical Corrections', *Seattle University Law Review* 42(2), 2019, pp. 513-533; Lipow, *Authoritarian Socialism*.
74 Roe, *Strong Managers, Weak Owners*, p. 7.
75 The one exception to this characterization is Duménil and Lévy in their *Managerial Capitalism* who claim that Bernstein 'had a much more realistic assessment of the future of capitalism' (p. 185) than Marx, Engels, Kautsky, Luxemburg, and, for good measure, Lenin. Notably, their book fails to mention the important work of Hilferding.
76 Bernstein, *Preconditions*.
77 C.L.R. James, *American Civilization*, Cambridge: Blackwell Publishers, 1993, p. 173.

BATTLING THE BEHEMOTH: AMAZON AND THE RISE OF AMERICA'S NEW WORKING CLASS

CHARMAINE CHUA AND SPENCER COX

On an early April afternoon in 2022, Christian Smalls popped a bottle of champagne outside the National Labor Relations Board (NLRB) offices in Brooklyn to celebrate an unprecedented victory. Less than two years before, Smalls had been fired from JFK8, a Staten Island Amazon fulfillment centre, when he led a walkout in protest of unsafe working conditions at the start of the pandemic. Now, despite rampant retaliation from Amazon, whose union-busting tactics included arresting Smalls twice for 'trespassing', firing workers, forcing them to attend 'required trainings', and more, JFK8 had just become the first Amazon warehouse in history to win formal recognition of their union. 'We want to thank Jeff Bezos for going to space,' Smalls now-famously quipped, 'because when he was up there, we was signing people up.' The upset, journalist Alex Press noted, was a historic event for which 'there are few parallels in the US labor movement's post-Reagan history'.[1]

In the aftermath of the victory, publications and pundits from the liberal mainstream to the left sought to understand how workers pulled it off. Journalists attributed workers' success to factors ranging from cultural conjunctures to hard work: some argued that the success was owed to a generational stirring of young people newly awakened to class struggle; others identified the charisma of Smalls himself, the conjunctures of a tight labour market and a 'cultural moment' of record-high support for unions, and the success of tactics such as horizontal organizing and 'hardscrabble' worker-to-worker organizing.[2] Missing from these analyses, however, have been efforts to place this apparent resurgence of working-class struggle in its proper context: that is, in relation to processes of capitalist restructuring in the deindustrialized US core that have led to a turbulent process of class recomposition, and which will shape the possibilities for structural change in the future. The victory of a small group of twenty core organizers over a company with $470 billion in sales in 2022 was significant not only for its David and Goliath dimensions, but also for what it revealed about the demographic and geographic composition of America's new working class.

If the left has been fascinated by Amazon's role in coalescing a certain revival of working class protagonism, perhaps most significantly, this is a working class separated from production proper: Amazon workers produce nothing, but deliver everything. Furthermore, unlike the stereotype of a white working class as the face of organized labour, the faces of America's contemporary proletariat are Black, brown, and white, immigrant and women. JFK8's victory was also a struggle waged far from the familiar leftist rallying points of Wall Street and Washington Square Park, in a suburb often dubbed the 'forgotten borough'. The warehouse is fortified by miles-long fencing topped by barbed wire. Situated in one of the hundreds of industrial retail factories concentrating and socializing workers in the hinterlands of America's urban clusters, many workers commute between 90 minutes to three hours to get to work. In the context of the long crisis, during which surplus populations have faced both increasing housing scarcity and decreasing availability of secure waged work, Amazon warehouse workers are the fastest-growing sector of the working class. Their racially diverse and geographically exurban class location is not ancillary but central to the Amazon Labor Union's successful mobilization.

In this essay, we argue that a fuller understanding of Amazon workers' shift to become the focal point of the labour movement requires placing the meteoric expansion of Amazon.com within the long crisis of the last half-century. As a technology company that has combined both e-commerce operations and digital services into a single corporate entity, Amazon is emblematic of structural transformations central to the remaking of global capitalism – namely, the dramatic shift in the logics of accumulation toward accelerating the circulation of commodity capital through globe-spanning 'just-in-time' supply chains. By situating Amazon as a force driving class decomposition, we also seek to understand how capital is recomposing a new working class in the United States.[3] Situating the rise of Amazon within processes of capitalist restructuring since the political economic upheavals of the 1970s, we demonstrate how the ascendance of the neoliberal hegemonic bloc facilitated Amazon's pursuit of surplus profits, fundamentally reworking the dynamics of capital accumulation. We analyze how Amazon has reshaped the geography of class in US cities, recomposing urban class structure. Concentrated in gentrified urban cores, Amazon's rise has been driven by a dramatic transformation in retail and logistics as high-salaried, college-educated consumers have moved their purchasing online and driven a surge in e-commerce sales. Serving this customer base are Amazon's warehouses in the suburban and exurban hinterlands of American cities – the spaces where the majority of the US working class now resides. These fundamental transformations in the retail and logistics sectors have been a key force driving racial and ethnic segmentation and working-class atomization, which Amazon in turn exploits in its labour recruitment and warehouse locational strategy. Examining the contradictions produced by Amazon's efforts to monopolize the logistics industry allows us to assess the systemic cracks that make the building of a revolutionary class consciousness within the warehouse both possible and necessary.

THE 'NEW ECONOMY' AND AMAZON'S BIRTH

On September 7, 2001, Amazon CEO Jeff Bezos stood before a crowd on Wall Street wearing an exuberant if smug grin as he rang the bell to open the day's trading on the NASDAQ stock exchange. It was the close of the decade of the long boom, a period of continuous economic expansion in the American economy fueled by the rise of Internet-based firms. Embodying a certain optimism about the 'dot-com' bubble that would soon burst for most internet companies save a precious few that included his own, Bezos had become the face of the 'New Economy' – the name given to the political economic restructuring in the United States that commenced in the 1970s, reorienting industrial and occupational structure away from industrial manufacturing toward finance, high-technology, and services. The bourgeois celebration of this period of transformation – its optimism implicit in the term – heralded American economic rebirth, even though this was a conclusion far from given based on the country's sharp decline two decades prior.

Amazon's rise embodied radical shifts in the US economy. Launched as a commercial venture in 1994 after a long period of crisis and structural transformation in the US economy, Amazon's success emerged from the rise of the 'New Economy' a decade after the presidency of Ronald Reagan marked a rocky transition to neoliberalism and the effort to reassert American economic competitiveness and global pre-eminence. At its core, neoliberal economic policy sought to weaken union power and expand the non-union workforce, strengthen financial capital and reassert the centrality of the dollar as the international means of payment along with dollar-denominated financial assets, and undertake a massive expansion in spending on defence-backed information and communication technology industries, positioning the US as a global pioneer in emerging high-tech industries.[4]

Picking up on these shifts, Amazon transformed a network of technologies previously invested in pie-in-the-sky, futuristic defence projects into commercial commodities capable of attracting investments from more risk-averse financial capital. Having noted the rise of the internet and the growing power of retailers such as Walmart, Jeff Bezos left New York high finance in a bid to take advantage of the commercial opportunities the internet could afford. Choosing Washington state in 1994 as its initial location due to the density of skilled technical employees at Boeing and Microsoft, and to Washington's 'pro-business' anti-income tax environment, Amazon emerged amidst the froth of surplus capital seeking investment in 'New Economy' firms. With an 'angel investment' of $245,000 secured from his parents, Bezos tapped into the capital-rich venture capital network burgeoning in Silicon Valley, securing $8 million in first round funding from famed venture capital firm Kleiner Perkins Caulfield and Byers.

Like other emerging dotcom and internet firms, Amazon.com struggled to turn a profit. It faced stiff competition in the book market from incumbent retailers whose relationship with suppliers, market size, and established networks of distribution provided a cost advantage. In search of a viable market strategy, Bezos began by modeling Amazon.com after Walmart, which in the decade prior had achieved immense success as merchant capital operating in the retail space.[5] Walmart's strategy had been twofold: it secured surplus rents in the retail sector, while playing a decisive role in stitching together what it recognized as increasingly globalized production networks.[6] In so doing, Walmart diminished the power of large monopoly manufacturers. Its command of massive retail spaces allowed the company to leverage its access to a growing market, which it then used to compel manufacturers to sell to the company at significantly reduced rates. This strategy put downward pressure on the profit margins of industrial manufacturers while expanding the retailer's slice of the final sales price. As manufacturing firms sought to increase their own profit margins by taking advantage of lower labour costs overseas in Mexico and the Pacific Rim, competition accelerated and further drove down consumer prices, contributing to Walmart's market share. Walmart itself often operated as both industrial and merchant capitalist: it established relations with independent Chinese manufacturers to produce commodities that undercut firms with less financial and operational capacity to redirect production overseas. By leveraging its growing customer base, Walmart could then undercut competitors to secure market share for their own products with higher profit margins per unit sold.

Bezos realized that if he was to lower prices, capture markets, and exercise pricing power over large manufacturers, he would need to dramatically expand his consumer base. The Amazon vision of online retail was thereby born: anyone with an internet connection was a potential customer. Buoyed by venture investors willing to wait for this 'revolutionary' idea to bear future rewards, Bezos recognized that he had to 'get big fast' to achieve necessary economies of scale. Strategically, he leveraged abundant investment capital to buttress a predatory pricing strategy that undercut competitors and built Amazon's market share.

Amazon's model of 'get big fast' crystallized new strategies by entrepreneurial and financial capital that also sought to forsake immediate profitability in favour of scale in the belief that new business models could fundamentally restructure existing industries. For other firms, however, this strategy often failed, with restructured incumbent firms often outcompeting new entrants in retaining market share. According to Morgan Stanley's index of 199 internet firms in 1999 – the year that Amazon expanded its sales from books to consumer electronics, software, toys, and much more – Amazon's market capitalization topped $450 billion and its total annual sales totaled $21 billion. *Net profits,* however, remained deep in the red, totaling a net loss of $6.2 billion.[7]

Yet at this formative stage, the fact that Amazon was a loss-making enterprise was framed not as a challenge to its long-term growth but rather its precondition. Whereas large manufacturing firms committed to manufacturing networks that often had excess capacity still returned profits to institutional investors rather than seeking to expand their market share through large infrastructural investments, in the 1990s venture capital boom, dotcom companies such as Amazon served as outlets for surplus capital in financial markets, which sought to establish competitive advantages through ever-larger efforts to extend market share (often with little success despite burning through billions of dollars). In this respect, Amazon's logistics activities are not so different from other tech and especially platform companies. Many have had something of a common strategy of taking short-term losses in order to pursue long-term market domination, control internet infrastructure, and turn user access into a rent-bearing asset.[8] Unlike other platform companies, however, Amazon's ambition was not limited to controlling internet infrastructure. The Amazon gambit was also to fundamentally transform the retail industry – notably, the entirety of the global supply chains involved in producing, transporting, and warehousing its goods.

What distinguished Amazon from other dotcom start-ups was its prescient recognition of the changing spatialities of consumer markets coupled with an innovative strategy to exploit them. Prior to the Great Recession of

2008, Amazon remained a niche retailer. The US National Retail Federation ranked it twenty-fifth on its list of largest retail companies, while retail giants Walmart and Target held first and third place. Amazon's strategy, however, was different. Walmart's fixed capital infrastructure focused on capturing rapidly growing working-class suburban and exurban markets with a strong focus on the Sunbelt. In contrast, Amazon sought to capture urbanizing, college-educated, professional, managerial, and 'creative' worker consumption – a demographic whose high rates of internet usage and lack of proximity to suburban box stores produced a distinct market niche for Amazon to fill, with its box-store prices and wide selection. To deliver the goods to customer doors, Amazon processed orders through its million-square-foot-plus 'fulfillment centres': enormous, custom-produced warehouses that store millions of commodities on vast rows of shelves where 'pickers' with handheld scanners find, process, and then ship customer orders.

Walmart warehouses still operate today as highly efficient cross-dock facilities, where inbound goods are processed, shipments are disaggregated based on final store destination, and then shipped rapidly to shop shelves that serve as both storage and display. In contrast, Amazon's warehousing model not only drastically expands warehouse capacities, but reconceives the relations between warehouse, store, and factory. In fact, the way that Amazon warehouses restructure supply chains well exceed the vernacular conception of a 'warehouse', commonly understood as a repository into which goods are stored and then transported elsewhere. Instead, Amazon warehouses have been a vanguard of the global economic restructuring often termed the 'logistics revolution'. By rapidly expanding its warehouse footprint and bringing goods as close as possible to their final destination at the consumer's doorstep, Amazon sells 'just-in-time' consumer delivery as a service, turning warehouses into what we call 'retail factories'. And in doing so, Amazon directly – and radically – integrates formerly distinct spheres of production, transportation, and consumption into a single e-commerce system aimed at the long-term consolidation and transformation of the retail industry into a vast logistical enterprise.[9]

FROM RETAIL INDUSTRY TO LOGISTICS NETWORK

Through the reorganization of low-productivity retail work into technologically intensive, industrially organized production, Amazon fulfillment centres both *reorganized* and *centralized* retail labour, enfolding the retail sector into a massive global logistics network that changed the relation between the production and circulation of an unprecedented volume of goods. Whereas retail workers were once dispersed across a broad range of retail stores in a variety of warehouse, driving, and customer-centric roles, Amazon acts as a centripetal force. It draws workers into the factory form for the picking, packing, sorting, and delivery of commodities, combining formerly disparate service and logistics activities into one centralized process.

Just as the factory line in mass production industries replaced specialized, skilled workers with the despotic orderliness of continuous workflow and degraded work, the Amazon fulfillment centre revolutionizes the labour process. Involving thousands of employees in each fulfillment centre, these vast retail factories rely on a complex technical division of labour, high levels of labour process routinization, automation, extreme data surveillance and management, and brutally intensive work regimes to increase the *relative* rate of exploitation compared to other retailers in the sector. Through a drastic increase in the relative rate of exploitation, Amazon can offer additional services – delivery to customer doors – at close to the same prices of what is offered by traditional big-box store retailers.[10] In a classic sense, through 'new combinations', Amazon has driven a process of creative destruction in the retail industry, attacking the heart of profits of traditional 'brick and mortar' retailers while securing both increased market share and, in the long-run, a competitive advantage capable of securing surplus profits relative to the market average.

Crucial to Amazon's success was its geographical strategy, which sought to exploit tax-hungry metropolitan and suburban municipalities struggling to find new sources of revenue and employment in the aftermath of the long downturn. Prior to 2012, Amazon's fulfillment centre model exploited favorable e-commerce tax structures. As long as a retailer maintained no infrastructure within a state, a state could not charge sales tax on items sold online to state residents. Seizing this loophole, Amazon located its fulfillment centres in states with low population densities (and smaller consumer markets) such as Kentucky, Nevada, and Kansas, but which had strong radial road networks connected to larger urban markets such as Chicago, Los Angeles, and New York, leveraging subcontracted relationships with United Parcel Service, the United States Postal Service, and FedEx to execute package delivery within two-week time frames for the majority of consumers.

In its early years, Amazon's main hubs were in the growing logistics complex of eastern Pennsylvania, within the nation's largest inland logistics centre in Kentucky, and in Nevada, Kansas, Tennessee, Arizona, and South Carolina. However, as states desperately sought to increase local sales tax bases to compensate for declining tax receipts amidst the Great Recession, they saw lifting the e-commerce loophole and charging a sales tax on e-commerce companies as an easy fix. Political support for this legislative move was often easy to find – large traditional retailers, competing with the increasing popularity of e-commerce, were all too happy to see the playing field levelled in their favour. Sensing a shift in the winds, Amazon pivoted.

In a risky move, Amazon shifted its strategy from two-week delivery times to a model focused on expanding its 'Prime' membership base. Amazon Prime pioneered in 2005, a first-of-its-kind subscription program that charged a $79 annual fee to members in exchange for two-day delivery. Prior to this launch, the prospect that consumers would willingly pay an annual charge for expedited shipping seemed an 'indulgent luxury' to most in the retail industry.[11] Betting on a market strategy to increase this membership base was a risky proposition: the Prime membership program is so expensive to run that today it still *costs* Amazon money based on the increased costs for two-day delivery. In 2005, Amazon's net shipping costs (the cost of outbound shipping subtracted from shipping revenues) were negative by 239 million dollars. By 2010, shipping costs were at $1.38 billion, and in 2021, they were at a whopping $75.1 billion. Finding that Prime members purchased significantly more products on Amazon.com than non-members, often citing faster delivery as the reason for increased everyday consumption, Amazon bet that lowering delivery times on online orders would ensnare even more consumers into the Amazon e-commerce ecosystem. 'Our *judgment*,' Bezos declared in his 2005 Letter to Shareholders in the first year Prime launched, 'is that relentlessly returning efficiency improvements and scale economies to customers in the form of lower prices creates a virtuous cycle that leads over the long term to a much larger dollar amount of free cash flow, and thereby to a much more valuable Amazon.com'.[12] This was a grandiose vision. In the crucial 'last mile' of delivery, the fact that most e-commerce consumers were concentrated in urban centres meant that packages travelled relatively short distances from the warehouse to their destination. Labour and operating costs could be reduced with more items boxed together into single shipments and a higher volume of packages in each truckload.

At the time, however, Amazon had still not figured out how it could capture value and turn a profit through the e-commerce retail trade. The cost of shipping individual items straight to customer doors increased costs significantly, and a reliance on last-mile delivery intermediaries such as FedEx and UPS cut into margins. Having sought for nearly a decade, between Amazon's founding in 1997 and its launch of Prime in 2005, to demonstrate the benefits of e-commerce models to no avail, Amazon's once unparalleled access to capital markets dwindled as e-commerce remained only a niche within the retail sector. In the early aughts, few consumers deemed online purchasing a better alternative to the immediacy of driving to a brick-and-mortar store. Fewer in the logistics and retail industry, and even fewer investors in the stock market, believed Amazon could sufficiently devise a logistics model that could turn a long-term profit. Indeed, as far as Amazon *Logistics* is concerned, the company is still in the red in 2022.

FULFILL, SORT, DELIVER, SWALLOW

But Amazon is not just a retailer, and there lies the lynchpin of its expansion strategy: Amazon Web Services (AWS), its cloud computing arm, represents Amazon's major profitable breakthrough. As a first mover and holder of substantial market share in commercial computing and data storage, AWS generated immense profits on high margins nearly immediately when it launched in 2006 to offer IT infrastructure and web services to businesses in what would come to be known as 'cloud computing'. Leveraging profits generated from AWS, Amazon could cross-subsidize its logistics operation, re-investing AWS revenue into expensive efforts to increase its warehouse footprint while cutting prices, despite the fact that each sale in its retail arm operated at a loss. Still, if AWS profits were not sufficient to drive the expansion of the company as a whole, they made Amazon a safer bet for Wall Street. In the years after the Great Recession, as the Federal Reserve's quantitative easing program fuelled private investment by buying debt and pushing asset prices further along the risk spectrum, Amazon tapped into financial markets and secured debt at historically low interest rates to make strategic investments.

This ready availability of cheap capital was crucial to Amazon's geographical expansion. To generate the shorter delivery times key to the growth of its Prime member base, Amazon sought to relocate and expand its fulfillment centres from a few concentrated hubs to the suburban and exurban periphery of every mid-sized and large city in the country. Such an expansion strategy drew on the geographies of labour and land that had been rendered surplus in the aftermath of deindustrialization: Amazon understood that its growth could rely on taking advantage of low land costs, proximity to urban markets, and, crucially, the large supplies of under-employed suburban and exurban labour necessary to staff its retail factories. That is, Amazon could draw on the surplus populations being pushed out from city centres, as the very urban revitalization programs that led to an influx of tech workers into major urban areas also led to gentrification and rising rents.[13] Amazon offered this displaced working class just slightly better than average retail wages and health benefits, enabling it to soak up suburban and exurban reserve armies of the underemployed. *As well*, Amazon could source workers from the competing regional complexes that employed large swathes of people in the service industries – big box stores, chain restaurants, and deregulated third-party logistics centres – which offered lower wages and inconsistent, part-time work with no benefits.[14]

Between 2012-15, Amazon nearly tripled its fulfillment footprint. In a fragmented and balkanized suburban environment produced by the fragmentation of city governments into suburban municipalities in the 1990s, Amazon used post-incorporation suburbs' job- and tax-hungry bases to its advantage, creating regional competitions between suburban and exurban cities eager to buttress residential tax bases with any additional industrial and commercial tax base they could get.[15] From 2012-21, Amazon secured more than $1 billion in tax breaks through deals ranging from commercial tax increment financing deals, tax easements in exchange for job creation, or municipal-funded infrastructure expansions. Suburban and exurban cities such as Shakopee, Minnesota ($5,766,414), Etna, Ohio ($17,543,000), and Lakeland, Florida ($4,500,000) channelled revenues they could have put towards rehabilitating crippled social infrastructure into subsidizing Amazon jobs.[16] These deals were, in a sense, nothing new. State and regional economic development agencies – typically insulated, anti-democratic institutions led by consortia of lobbyists and boosters – have long engaged in regional job competitions to attract employers through tax subsidies and other schemes that exchange the social wage for corporate welfare.

Amazon's robbery of working-class suburban and exurban municipalities went largely unnoticed by media elites; that is, until Amazon attempted to replicate the strategy on a grand and public scale in its 'HQ2 bid' for a second headquarters alongside Seattle. The deep irony of its expansion, however, is that as Amazon produced e-commerce warehouse jobs in one suburb, that suburb's employment gains were met with a net loss of retail jobs in other regional suburbs: one Target sales representative exchanged for one Amazon warehouse worker. Though Amazon rearranged the geographies of employment, the often-invoked claim that it is a 'job creator' is a ruse. Amazon's arrival into a regional market led to the loss of retail jobs, as big box stores and malls crumbled and went bankrupt even as it re-concentrated those employment losses into its retail factories. The result is a net balance – or even loss – of employment gains in any given metropolitan region.[17] In a 2016 report, for example, the Institute for Local Self-Reliance found that Amazon has eliminated about 149,000 more jobs in retail than it has created in its warehouses.[18] Nationally, this pattern of an expanding logistics sector and shrinking brick-and-mortar stores shows how Amazon is not just a paradigmatic example of the structural transformations engendered by the logisticalization of retail, but has also upended longstanding relationships between commerce and place, and patterns of employment more generally: as Kyle Loewen shows, from 2009 to 2019, there was a staggering 91 per cent increase in warehousing and storage employment in the US and a 51 per cent increase in courier and messenger employment, while retail jobs only increased by 7.5 per cent.[19]

AMAZON ASCENDANT

By 2014, Amazon's experiment was starting to bear fruit. Both e-commerce market share and total revenue grew tremendously, which Amazon furiously reinvested into fixed capital, expanding its warehouse footprint across the US and the world. Despite this investment, delivery costs per package continued to *increase*. Even though AWS was generating significant profits, Amazon filed negative net income in seven out of the twelve quarterly earnings reports between 4Q 2012 and 4Q 2015. In an effort to gain greater control over shipping operations and costs, Amazon started to move downstream in the last-mile delivery process, scaling up two experiments in trimming its logistics costs.

The first was its regional sortation network, a system of facilities closely located to fulfillment operations that processed and palletized items to be sent to USPS for final delivery to the broader metropolitan market. Secondly, perpetually underfunded and on the rocks, USPS signed a sweetheart deal with Amazon on shipping rates, offering substantial cost savings compared to UPS or FedEx and expanding USPS shipments on Sundays. This process boosted throughput for USPS but barely increased its margins, forcing USPS to further cut wages, benefits, and full-time work for its unionized workforce. UPS met with a similar fate. Boosted throughput made UPS believe a long-term relationship with Amazon would buttress its fulfillment network, naively believing that Amazon would never emerge to compete in its bread-and-butter parcel delivery network. This bet, it would turn out, vastly underestimated both Bezos's ambition and the profound reshaping of delivery networks that Amazon's expansion made possible.

Amazon's sortation model changed the geography of last mile delivery across North America. With its network of fulfillment, sortation, and delivery centres, Amazon could quickly locate items in fulfillment centres increasingly stored near a consumer, move it to a regional sortation centre to be organized by postal code, then deliver it on 'next day' delivery routes. This provided Amazon with a strategy for expansion into the parcel delivery sector. Last mile routes are most profitable in urban cores where residential density and purchasing power are at their highest. Beginning in 2014, Amazon cleverly and steadily started to separate the most profitable last mile urban routes with the lowest per-mile delivery costs for its own delivery centres, while leaving the less profitable rural and sprawling suburban and exurban routes for USPS and UPS.

This was a long-term strategy to build a continent-spanning logistics infrastructure that encompassed warehouses and last-mile delivery, fanning out from city centres to adjacent hinterlands. As fulfillment and sortation centres require large warehouse footprints, Amazon increasingly concentrated these facilities in new working-class suburbs where cheap land and labour were readily available. The delivery stations that process packages and organize them by delivery route are, in contrast, significantly smaller warehouses that leverage a mix of subcontracted delivery drivers (typically in Amazon-branded vans) and Amazon Flex drivers to deliver to doors. To dominate the market in last-mile delivery, Amazon strategically located these delivery stations in industrial neighborhoods in either close proximity to, or directly within, neighborhoods of concentrated urban poverty.[20] Amazon's seizure of control over the last mile allows it to offer marked price advantages over its competitors. Whereas UPS and USPS depend on highly paid unionized delivery drivers, Amazon's delivery labour force is largely subcontracted, temped-out, or paid hourly wages that pale in comparison to union jobs. Despite UPS's initial strategic position that Amazon could never match their infrastructural capacities, in less than a decade Amazon had built one of the most robust and encompassing logistics networks across North America.

By locating a greater percentage of packages near urban consumers and capturing the most profitable last-mile delivery routes, Amazon both reduced its delivery costs and drastically expanded its market share, offering increasingly reliable and shorter delivery times and even managing to cut free two-day delivery to a single-day for Prime members. By 2019, Amazon's competitive advantage in e-commerce had led to increasing market shares in both e-commerce and retail and enabled it to further its monopsony bargaining power, emerging as a 'platform' monopoly that combined the data gathering mastery of large tech firms like Google, the bargaining power of Walmart over suppliers of commodities, and a competitive advantage in the logistics of last-mile shipping.[21] Leveraging both its online and logistics network platform, Amazon secures favourable pricing partnerships with third-party sellers desperate to access Amazon's Prime consumer base, capturing large percentages of the value from each sale. With more eyeballs on its site and unsurpassed data-tracking capacities, Amazon is able to leverage consumer data to launch its own product line in high-demand areas and undercut third-party suppliers. All the while, Amazon maintains control over its web search functions, allowing it to increase its capacity to secure highly profitable advertising revenue, including leveraging its control over its platform web page to prioritize pay-to-play vendors.

By 2018, Amazon's twenty-year profit problems finally began to turn around. Its margins and net income transformed the company into a veritable cash cow, securing its position as one of the world's most valuable firms by market capitalization. Amazon has leveraged its monopsony power to acquire competitors strategically – notable examples being Whole Foods and Diapers.com – and undercut competitors when necessary. Moreover, Amazon has selectively invested in companies that enable it to assemble a network of technologies – machine vision, advanced robotics, smart cities, self-driving electric cars, and others – that reinforce Bezos's original mission to become a merchant behemoth with dominating market power in logistics and e-commerce. Today, Amazon has moved far from its origin as a venture firm dependent on finance capital, to a firm funded by debt-fuelled expansion aimed at gaining overwhelming market power.

Yet, it would be a mistake to conclude that the political project emerging from this analysis is to oppose Amazon as a unique evil, or even to oppose 'big business' more generally. Our aim is not to suggest, as a wealth of books and articles about Amazon do, that 'the market' might be restored to some mythical proper functioning once the ills of monopolistic power have been thwarted. Rather, what Amazon congeals in its vampiric quest for market domination is a tendency inherent in the current phase of capitalism, with its prominent positioning of merchant capitals like Amazon. Amazon has become the paradigmatic example of the corporate features of such firms: intensifying global labour arbitrage by putting downward pressure on profit rates for small US manufacturers; suppressing the domestic wage rate in manufacturing nations of the Global South by exercising monopsony power over third-party retailers; displacing local brick and mortar stores; siphoning municipal revenues into corporate tax subsidies rather than the social wage; swallowing competing delivery service providers; and centralizing the logistical coordination of a vast global supply chain network in order to exercise market domination over the end-to-end supply chain. How can we do battle with the Amazon behemoth?

FROM CLASS DECOMPOSITION TO CLASS RECOMPOSITION

Our task, as socialists, is always to seek out and nourish the seeds of revolution in any conjuncture. Today, a crucial challenge is to identify the contradictions that the Amazon model produces and to locate emerging opportunities for working-class struggles.

Amazon's warehouse model not only reorganized the geographies of supply chain management, and the logistics industry as a whole, but also drew its labour force from the surplus populations increasingly displaced from metropolitan centres. As the long downturn produced both a decaying, industrialized suburbia and a decline in employment, the post-industrial reinvention of cities brought about 'urban renewal programs' that prioritized private real estate accumulation over public housing or a jobs guarantee, inviting an influx of the 'creative class' into the finance, real estate, and insurance sectors that would underpin the tech boom of the 1990s. Amazon took full advantage of these geographies of displacement to feed its voracious appetite for surplus labour. Outside of every city, in the flat plains of proletarian hinterlands and in pockets of urban disinvestment, Amazon workplaces rely on the twin geographies of deindustrialization and dispossession to recruit warehouse labour, disproportionately workers and immigrants of colour, to perform the gruelling work of unloading, packing, sorting, and loading goods with intense demands to meet 'rates' and fulfill the growing appetite for 'just-in-time' delivery.[22]

The majority of left analysis on Amazon's evolution have rightly studied the impacts of its expanding empire on workers, many probing the nightmarish working conditions that involve peeing in bottles, draconian pick 'rates', and other dehumanizing forms of labour exploitation. Yet the contradictions of this mass immiseration also produce, in the daily grind of making a living, class conflict and struggle. Although producing more value within Amazon's vast empire simultaneously devalues the workers who produce it, it is crucial to grasp the scope and scale with which Amazon concentrates and socializes thousands of workers from diverse racial, gender, cultural, and political backgrounds in each retail factory. Amazon's increased market power, while a legitimate threat to many small businesses, is not necessarily a negative organizing terrain for workers. If the structural reorganization of the US economy in the 1980s drove a spatial transformation in the organization of production and distribution, the 'new' fixed capital investments of supply chains and logistics networks are now socializing the working class across the social atomization of race, class, and gender into mature spaces of production and increasingly sedimented working-class – often suburban – neighborhoods.[23] Thus, as Kim Moody has argued, rather than viewing the dissolution of working-class power as a permanent feature of deindustrialized economies, a new terrain of class formation is solidifying in the United States as a result of fixed capital investment into new geographical space.[24]

In the metropolitan suburban and exurban periphery of American cities nationwide, Amazon is at the heart of new spaces of working-class socialization. As of 2021, Amazon has over 264 major fulfillment centres, with each containing one- to three-thousand full-time workers during non-peak seasons, and more than double this labour force during seasonal 'peaks' around Christmas and its self-created July Prime Day celebration. Amazon's retail factories *alone* make up a shocking 13.2 per cent of blue-collar workplaces (including mining, construction, manufacturing, and trade/transport sectors), with a thousand or more non-supervisory employees.[25] In each city, Amazon's labour force is a microcosm of the region's predominantly service sector working class. Each facility combines a multi-ethnic mix of recent immigrants: Latino, Asian, and African. It mixes into singular workplaces white and Black workers; evangelical, Muslim, queer and trans workers; and, similar to other service sector work, often tilts more toward women than men. The social problems these workers face are no different than those of working-class and poor people in the hinterlands of American cities: soaring housing costs, defunded public schools, car dependence, low-wage jobs, unaffordable healthcare, and families exhausted from overwork and experiencing a crisis in the ability to care for their children, elderly or sick relatives, and themselves. Amazon workers, in other words, are the face of America's new working class.

One should, of course, not be over-optimistic about the prospects of a sudden turn to political activism. Just as Amazon socializes the suburban working class, its retail factories are the embodiment of managerial domination and working-class individualization. Far from unique to Amazon, these dynamics are emblematic of low-wage work in the United States today. It is not just a *physical* toll Amazon exerts on its workers; rather, Amazon actively implements management techniques that engender an atmosphere of intra-class competition through the manipulation of emotional affect. A consequence is that legitimate working-class resentment and anger manifests in either brutal self-exploitation in a zero-sum competition or, increasingly, in individual rather than collective acts of resistance. In either case, Amazon workers unable to cope with their brutal working conditions frequently quit – in droves.

LESSONS FROM THE TRENCHES OF AMAZON ORGANIZING

The only means of challenging the brutal working conditions and political self-isolation of employers like Amazon is to build power through solidarity and care on the shop floor, often through acts that often must overcome ethnic and racial segmentation to forge a new multi-racial, multi-ethnic working class 'for itself'. We can draw several lessons from years of organizing together with – and in Spencer's case, as – Amazon workers in Amazonians United.

First, building revolutionary class consciousness in this current phase of capitalism requires an organizing strategy attuned to the logics of profitability and geography that structure Amazon's distribution network. The designers of logistics emphasize the ways in which capitalist supply chains require flexible networks with multiple 'fault-tolerant' redundancies to make effective disruption at any one point formidable. Yet, even as Amazon reshapes the geographies and temporalities of how goods are warehoused, packed, and shipped, it is inflexible in one aspect: the goods have to be delivered *somewhere,* to consumers concentrated in the gentrified urban cores of major cities. Capital seeks mobility, but logistics is necessarily a place-based industry with nodes that cannot be offshored. Amazon's over five-hundred distribution facilities are most concentrated in clusters around major metropolitan regions. Because wealthier counties represent both a higher share of Prime subscribers and high real estate costs, Amazon invests in warehouses located in exurban districts with cheaper rents and land costs, but with proximity to urban delivery zones.

The geographical re-composition of the US working class into peripheries such as Staten Island, New York and Bessemer, Alabama becomes an extraordinary opportunity to organize workers in facilities that cannot be so easily shifted elsewhere. A work stoppage at a single facility, however, will not create a dent in Amazon's vast distributional network unless workers organize regionally, rather than unionizing (as at Bessemer) site-by-site. This means that models of shopfloor organizing that draw their insights from the era of industrial organizing, where stopping production in a single mass production factory could create massive reverberations throughout the system, have to be rethought when logistical mobility between distribution nodes sets different conditions of possibility for worker militancy. As Amazonians United has demonstrated, however, multi-site work stoppages, such as a recent walkout at two Chicago-area delivery stations, can demonstrate solidarity across warehouses, interrupt Amazon's delivery lines, delay the 'just-in-time' model, and effectively win concessions.[26]

A second lesson is that worker-to-worker organizing is also anti-racist struggle. In North America, the suburbs are often where racialized and underemployed surplus populations, displaced from city centres, have moved, and have thus become the recruitment targets for warehouse work. Organizing at the intersection of race and class requires moving into the suburbs, beyond the metropolitan urban centres where community organizing and social justice non-profit organizations centre their work. Fostering working-class protagonism is one of the most effective tactics for transformational racial justice. Building bridges across ethnic, racial, and gender divides within the workplace is the conscious act of workplace organizers, and historically has been the major thrust for producing solidarity across racial groups within the US working class.[27]

William Z. Foster, the US communist and revolutionary strategist, wrote about this explicitly in his now-landmark treatise on the tactics of labour organizing, *Organizing Methods in the Steel Industry*, arguing that organizers need to keep one foot in the broader economic terrain, and the other specially attuned to the specific oppression of different ethnic and racialized groups; a strategy that proved decisive in the industrial organizing campaigns that had to overcome deep internal ethnic and racial divides in the US working class.[28] When people learn through direct experience that a worker's leverage is their labour power, the collective action required to carry out a walkout or slowdown builds solidarity across groups, and shows workers that solidarity is key to making material changes in their self-interest. As Jonathan Bailey, an organizer and worker with Amazonian's United New York City puts it, 'It's different when you feel it: the first time that you stand up to your boss with your coworkers. Even if it's a small thing, like we are not going to accept you stealing sixty seconds from our break time, that feeling changes you.' When it becomes abundantly clear through lived experience that getting what you want is impossible without respecting the humanity of those who you need in order to get it, people acquire the impetus to change.

A third lesson follows from Amazon's strategy to hire precarious workers whose lives intersect with multiple forms of inequality rarely limited to the workplace itself. Labour organizers need to connect shopfloor concerns to the issues of working-class people in the cities and communities in which they live. In Shakopee, Minnesota, for example, the rising cost of housing relative to wages drove the Awood Center, which organizes the majority Somali immigrant women Amazon workforce, to make a broad demand for Amazon to invest in new housing solutions. Scott County, where Shakopee is located, has boomed, producing jobs at a far faster pace than available housing. Organizing Amazon workers therefore also means being engaged with the need to increase the affordable housing stock, including allocation of land from corporate real estate to housing needs.

Workers also face immediate issues around transit. In suburban warehouses around the country, public transit to and from urban and suburban working-class neighborhoods to suburban and exurban industrial parks remains underdeveloped. Intra-suburban bus routes are rare, with significant mass transit investment instead operating within a radial network format that connects workers to downtown, even though such downtowns increasingly operate as spaces for professional and managerial occupations.

Accordingly, what should be fifteen- to thirty-minute trips instead take two to three hours. These transit issues are also global, intersecting in some cases with issues of border mobility. In Otay Mesa, just outside the US-Mexico border, Amazon's 3.3 million square foot fulfillment centre, SAN3 employs a significant workforce that lives across the border and commutes on foot from Tijuana, Mexico. Many workers paid 'raiteros' of $3 to $5 for the two-mile ride to the Amazon warehouse. But recently, workers organized carpools to get themselves to work, then marched on the boss and delivered a petition to management signed by more than 600 workers demanding – and winning – free transportation from the border. Building power around social reproductive issues, such as social housing and public transit, as urgent community needs simultaneously builds working-class power and identity in the warehouse.

Finally, union organizing cannot escape making gender justice a priority. In the logistics industry, the workforce is often composed of more women, trans, and nonbinary people than men; concerns around gendered reproductive labour, from childcare to domestic abuse, are frequent topics on the shopfloor. When Amazon recently shifted work schedules to a crushing overnight 'megacycle' shift that begins at 1:30 AM and ends at noon, the restructured schedules made childcare, sending kids to school, and picking up a second morning shift impossible for women. Recognizing this, Amazonians United placed mothers and caregivers at the centre of their demands: calling on Amazon to accommodate shifts for single parents with young children, and having the union's solidarity fund prioritize caretakers and mothers facing hardship.

Amazon's just-in-time delivery system grants workers immense power. The labour of Amazon workers powers the conduits that connect corporate global supply chains to the doors of American consumers. Even small collective disruptions by workers can cause temporary and localized crises that also ripple across the logistics network. Unions in struggle help workers learn the potential sources and magnitude of their power in concerted and collective action. By fighting both for issues connected to workers' experience at work *as well as* the issues facing workers in suburban spaces, Amazon workers can leverage solidarity developed at work to struggle for the broader working class.

It is no coincidence that the first successful unions within Amazon warehouses are Amazonians United and the Amazon Laborers Union, two independent unions that deployed tactics of shop floor, worker-led organization. Too often, existing service sector unions replace worker action on the shop floor with political campaigns attempting to leverage political power. Any successful unionism today must build power, and class – even revolutionary – consciousness through shopfloor struggles, without relying on legal recognition from the NLRB.

In the current economic and political impasse, it is in the interstices of the urban fringes and exurban zones that too often slip the attention of the left that new horizons for struggle are emerging. This is a politics not directed 'at and for the class' in the older styles of business unionism, but rather a participatory class struggle unionism 'of the class'. In the vast logistical networks of Amazon, the worker-led organizing by minority solidarity unions such as Amazonians United and the Amazon Laborers Union are seeking to challenge the Amazon behemoth. There is much for the North American left to learn from these struggles to build autonomous working-class organizations rooted in the everyday lives of workers.

NOTES

We would like to thank Kyle Loewen for commenting on an early draft of this paper.

1. Alex Press, 'A Stunning New Chapter Begins for Amazon Warehouse Workers', *Jacobin*, 4 April 2022.
2. See for instance: Harold Meyerson 'A Generational Worker Revolt Hits Its Stride', *The American Prospect*, 1 April 2022; Jodi Kantor and Karen Weise, 'How Two Best Friends Beat Amazon', *The New York Times*, 2 April 2022; Jamelle Bouie, 'Amazon Tried One of the Oldest Tricks in the Book, and It Backfired', *The New York Times*, 5 April 2022; Eric Blanc with Angelika Maldonado, 'Here's How We Beat Amazon', *Jacobin*, 4 April 2022; Luis Feliz Leon, 'Amazon Workers on Staten Island Clinch a Historic Victory', *Labor Notes*, 1 April 2022; and Kim Kelly, 'How did Amazon workers go against a rich corporation and win? Look back 100 years', *NBC*, 4 April 2022.
3. We define class decomposition as the destruction of previous social relations of production and reproduction that lead to the dissolution of existing class structure, and the dissolution of accompanying class political organizations that ideologically and materially help a class make sense of their world and how to act within it.
4. Robert Brenner, *The Economics of Global Turbulence: The Advanced Capitalist Economies From Long Boom to Long Downturn, 1945-2005*, London: Verso, 2006, pp. 166-67; Mike Davis, *Prisoners of the American Dream*, London: Verso Books, 1986; Barry Bluestone and Bennett Harrison, *The Deindustrialization of America*, New York: Basic Books, 1984.
5. While we do not have the space to elaborate fully in this essay, we refer to merchant capital as more than retail but rather as firms overseeing the coordination of vast subcontracted global supply chains. The 'new' merchant capitalists began to seek alternative sources of profit during the long slowdown in economic growth since the 1990s, where firms formerly invested in manufacturing capital began to experiment with expanding investments in distribution so as to coordinate global production networks. While much attention has been paid to financialization, merchant capital

became a second vanguard sector of economic restructuring. By leveraging their ability to make new markets – e-commerce consumers primed for 'just-in-time' delivery in Amazon's case – merchant capitalists are able to negotiate a higher rate of profit for themselves rather than for competing capitalists.

6   Richard Applebaum and Nelson Lichtenstein, 'A New World of Retail Supremacy: Supply Chains and Workers' Chains in the Age of Wal-Mart', *International Labor and Working Class History*, 70(1), 2006, pp. 106-25.

7   Brian McCullough, 'A revealing look at the dot-com bubble of 2000 – and how it shapes our lives today', *Ted Ideas*, 4 December 2018, available at: ideas.ted.com.

8   Brett Christophers, *Rentier Capitalism: Who Owns the Economy, and Who Pays for it?* London: Verso, 2020.

9   See W. Bruce Allen, 'The Logistics Revolution and Transportation', *The Annals of the American Academy of Political and Social Science*, 553(1), pp. 106 -16; Deborah Cowen, *The Deadly Life of Logistics: Mapping Violence in Global Trade,* Minneapolis: University of Minnesota Press, 2014; Alberto Toscano, 'Lineaments of the Logistical State', *Viewpoint Magazine*, 4, October 2014; and Charmaine Chua, 'Logistics', in Beverly Skeggs, Sarah Farris, and Alberto Toscano, eds, *The Sage Handbook of Marxism*, London: Sage, p. 1442-57.

10 For an in-depth examination of the exploitation entailed in the labor process in Amazon warehouses, see Alessandro Delfanti, *The Warehouse Workers and Robots at Amazon,* London: Pluto Press, 2021.

11 Jason Del Rey, 'The making of Amazon Prime, the internet's most successful and devastating membership program', *Vox*, 3 May 2019.

12 Jeff Bezos, 'Letter to Shareholders', 2005, available at: ir.aboutamazon.com/annual-reports-proxies-and-shareholder-letters.

13 Here, we draw inspiration from Ruth Wilson Gilmore's influential analysis of the four categories of surplus that explain the prison-building boom in the 1970s and '80s. Ruth Wilson Gilmore, *Golden Gulag: Prisons, Surplus, Crisis, and Opposition in Globalizing California,* Los Angeles: University of California Press, 2007.

14 It is important to note in this sense that the oft-invoked refrain mobilized against unionization in its warehouses – that Amazon is a major job provider – rationalizes an expansion strategy grounded not in a commitment to 'good wages' and 'worker welfare', as Amazon claims, but in monopoly capture aimed at strangling its competition.

15 In the early 1990s, anti-tax leaning, disproportionately white suburban homeowners organized to increase their political power, choosing to incorporate as suburban cities in the late 1980s and early 1990s. Suburban municipal incorporation was initially informed by reactionary racism in response to increasing neighborhood integration, where white homeowners saw incorporation as a way to enable greater control over zoning and growth, particularly seeking to curtail new multi-family development. However, one of the consequences of suburban incorporation was that working-class residential exurbs soon found themselves in tax holes for already under-funded social services.

16 Thomas Cafcas and Greg LeRoy, *Will Amazon Fool Us Twice? Why State and Local Governments Should Stop Subsidizing the Online Giant's Growing Distribution Network*, Washington DC: Good Jobs First Report, December 2016.

17 Janelle Jones and Ben Zipperer, 'Unfulfilled Promises', Washington DC: Economy

Policy Institute Report, 1 February 2018.
18 Stacy Mitchell and Olivia LaVecchia, 'Amazon's Stranglehold: How the Company's Tightening Grip is Stifling Competition, Eroding Jobs, and Threatening Communities', *Institute for Local Self-Reliance,* November 2016.
19 Kyle Loewen, forthcoming dissertation, with figures drawn from the U.S. Census Bureau's Current Population Survey. In addition, Loewen adds: 'Extending this range from 2009 to 2020 to include the initial effects of the pandemic, these numbers are starker with a 109 per cent growth in warehousing and storage and a 74 per cent increase in courier and messenger work, compared to a 2 per cent growth in retail employment.'
20 Kaveh Waddell, 'When Amazon Expands, These Communities Pay the Price', *Consumer Reports,* December 2021.
21 Nick Srnicek, *Platform Capitalism*, Cambridge: Polity Press, 2017. A detailed examination of Amazon's market power can be found in Lina Kahn, 'Amazon's Antitrust Paradox,' *The Yale Law Journal*, 126(3), pp. 564-907. Kahn's report on Amazon launched her political career, where she is currently Biden's doyen on antitrust policy. Yet to the dismay of lawyers everywhere, a good legal argument for demonstrating monopoly power is relatively worthless without the political power to rewrite laws.
22 Ellen Reese, 'Gender, Race, and Amazon Warehouse Labor in the United States' in Jake Alimahomed-Wilson and Ellen Reese, eds, *The Cost of Free Shipping: Amazon in the Global Economy*, Pluto Press 2020, pp. 102-15.
23 Regarding industrial maturation in the United States, the share of national employment in 'mature' firms aged five years or more today includes more than 90 per cent of all employees, with 48 per cent growth in the amount of workers in firms with 500 or more employees. In retail alone, 36 per cent of workers in 1978 worked in large firms compared to 62 per cent in 2019.
24 Moody's argument is posited against the argument of theorists such as Joshua Clover or the 'Endnotes' collaborative, who argue that the fundamental mechanics of class formation have broken down in post-industrial societies as factory labour disaggregated and relocated. Instead, Moody adopts the position here that the post-World War II 'working class' has been fundamentally reworked by capitalist restructuring, but the maturation of the initial period of capitalist restructuring has laid down fixed capital that has re-socialized workers into new spaces, leading to inchoate forms of class development still in formation. Kim Moody, 'Organize. Strike. Organize', *Jacobin*, 22 May 2018.
25 Bureau of Labor Statistics, 'Number of business establishments'. 'Blue-collar' industries total only 2000 establishments of such size, a number equivalent to the total number in education and health services, which remain some of the most concentrated spaces of work in the New Economy.
26 Jeff Shuhrke, 'Capping Off a Year of Labor Action at Amazon, Warehouse Workers Walk Off the Job in Illinois', *In These Times,* 22 December 2021.
27 Todd Gilpin, *The Long Deep Grudge: A Story of Big Capital, Radical Labor, and Class War in the American Heartland,* Chicago: Haymarket Books, 2020.
28 William Z. Foster, *Organizing Methods in the Steel Industry*, 1936, available at: www.marxists.org/archive/foster. Notably, the core organizers of the Amazon Labor Union led reading groups of Foster's text in the lead up to their election.

THE ILLUSIONS OF 'STAKEHOLDER CAPITALISM': THE CASE OF UNILEVER

KYLE BAILEY

It was the best of times, it was the worst of times, it was the age of wisdom, it was the age of foolishness, it was the epoch of belief, it was the epoch of incredulity ... we were all going direct to Heaven, we were all going direct the other way ...

– Charles Dickens, A Tale of Two Cities

Despite the failings of capitalism occupying centre stage in political debate since the 2007–08 global financial crisis, the liberal consensus continues to ignore the stark choice between democratic socialism and far-right authoritarian barbarism facing humanity. Instead, mainstream political parties have doubled down on an agenda of 'reinventing capitalism'. The most prominent form this has taken is 'stakeholder capitalism' – a project to cleanse the system of its apparently incidental defects through a widening of the governance of corporations via the inclusion of 'community interests' and more social diversity (especially in senior executive and board mandates and positions). Seeking to justify this shift to free-market conservatives, Larry Fink, chairman of BlackRock – the world's largest asset manager and Wall Street's 'sustainable darling', writes in his most recent annual letter to CEOs, titled 'The Power of Capitalism', that:

> Stakeholder capitalism is not about politics. It is not a social or ideological agenda. It is not 'woke'. *It is capitalism* ... the fair pursuit of profit is still what animates markets ... [and] a company must create value for and be valued by its full range of stakeholders in order to deliver long-term value for its shareholders.[1]

The last few years have seen an embrace of this stakeholding ethos, particularly in the Atlantic heartland of global capitalism. While campaigning to take the reins of the imperial presidency from Donald Trump, Joe Biden proposed to 'put an end to the era of shareholder capitalism – the idea that the only responsibility a corporation has is to its shareholders'.[2] This declaration echoed the US Business Roundtable's 2019 statement redefining the purpose of a corporation as promoting 'an economy that serves all Americans' and not just shareholders.[3] Similarly, Mark Carney, United Nations (UN) special envoy for climate finance and COP26 advisor to Boris Johnson, after a long career at Goldman Sachs and as governor of the central banks of Canada and Britain, proclaims that 'capitalism is part of the solution' to climate change.[4] The founder of the World Economic Forum (WEF), Klaus Schwab, argues that 'the pandemic has hastened the shift toward a stakeholder model of corporate capitalism' and calls for world leaders to 'move on from neoliberalism in the post-COVID era'.[5] And Paul Polman, the former CEO of Unilever and Chairman of the International Chamber of Commerce (ICC), declares that 'the current [capitalist] model, which is basically shareholder primacy ... is a failed model'.[6]

This emerging movement amongst influential sections of the corporate elites highlights how the unfolding crisis of neoliberal globalization has inspired bold declarations of a new phase of capitalist development centred on a new capitalist model for corporate governance.[7] Alongside the much vaunted 'return of the state' since 2008, this 'post-neoliberal' zeitgeist has had multinational corporations (MNCs), politicians, management consultants, and academics queuing up to embrace a nominally more 'cooperative', 'people-centred', and 'sustainable' multi-stakeholder capitalism.

But is the imperative to move on from neoliberalism and shareholder-value maximization what really accounts for this embrace of 'stakeholder capitalism' within the upper echelons of the corporate class? This essay argues that rather than foreshadowing the radical promise of a post-industrial 'Green New Deal' or a return to the 'old' post-war welfare state, the primary impact of the various discourses of stakeholding is to neutralize, co-opt, and deflect ongoing popular-democratic struggles to reduce the environmental and social harms wrought by corporations into a hegemonic project of making society and nature safe for capital accumulation. Nowhere is this better illustrated among large MNCs than in the case of Unilever, which has arguably gone furthest down the strategic path of ostensibly aligning profit-making with ecological and social 'purpose'.

LEGITIMIZING CAPITALIST POWER

Since the global financial crisis, a contradictory and conflictual political terrain has taken shape, one which reveals the stark disjuncture between the potential for radical change evoked by capitalist crisis and the severe limits imposed upon that potential by the structural power arrayed on the side of MNCs. In this context, a legitimation *deficit* has been steadily rising since the 'lock-in' of neoliberal reforms during the 'long 1990s'. From the Bush administration's disastrous post-9/11 military interventions on, a steady series of mass protests against social inequalities have erupted, now intertwined with more than a decade of economic turmoil extending from the financial crisis to the current global Covid pandemic. The tally of 'morbid symptoms' is lengthy and suggestive of a wider legitimation *crisis*: growing economic inequality and social exclusion; decades of austerity eroding public infrastructure; the rise of political leaders disdainful of globalization; the climate emergency being daily revealed in extreme weather events; the return of 'stagflation'; and the catastrophic spread of war and the nuclear arms race, centred on the strategic expansion of North Atlantic Treaty Organization (NATO) into multiple fronts across Eurasia. The initial post-Cold War zeitgeist of perpetual progress under the banner of free markets and private property has vanished.

Despite these political and economic tensions, the absence of an organizationally coherent and widely supported working-class politics has meant that 'post-neoliberal' possibilities have remained limited, distorted, and co-opted by the socio-institutional dominance of corporate capitalism. Capitalist states are, moreover, always hostile to political agendas intended to compensate for the overall failure of the market and are biased toward incremental policy adjustments designed to paper over specific 'market failures'. In this respect, the counterparts to policy incrementalism are the exceptional policy measures and authoritarian state interventions that have proven essential to preserving the conditions for 'free markets' in a context where the ideological discrediting of neoliberalism is widespread and the long-term consequences of market-expanding policies impossible to ignore. In today's 'post-neoliberal' zeitgeist, economic constraints on state intervention have been relaxed precisely because governments have made credible political commitments that 'nothing will fundamentally change' and advances by the labour movement and more radical 'post-neoliberal' alternatives will be contained or crushed as necessary.

In the corporate realm, neoliberal ideology remains institutionalized in corporate management strategies for 'shareholder-value' creation. Creating value, in this sense, is premised on maximizing financial performance as registered in corporate profitability and the prices of company shares on stock markets, which are regarded as indexes of societal welfare. But here, too, the fractures in the legitimacy of the corporate governance consensus are evident, with increasing appeals to philanthropy, support for public spaces, and corporate social responsibility (CSR).

In this moment of political and corporate disjunctures, forged by the contradictory imperatives of accumulation and legitimation facing global neoliberalism, the project of 'stakeholder capitalism' has emerged to sustain an ideological *illusion*: that corporate capitalism really *can* change its spots and prioritize the interests of people and planet above those of profit and class interest.

A tale of two capitalisms

Already in 2009, the WEF's 'Global Redesign Initiative' was calling for the unfolding global financial crisis to be resolved by constructing 'a new stakeholder paradigm of international governance analogous to that embodied in the stakeholder theory of corporate governance on which the [WEF] itself was founded'.[8] Schwab and others sought to position 'stakeholder capitalism' as an ideological 'third way', between 'shareholder capitalism' and 'state capitalism', where corporations create 'long-term' value for their various 'stakeholders' instead of maximizing shareholder value at their expense.[9] As Joel Bakan comments:

> Creative capitalism, inclusive capitalism, conscious capitalism, connected capitalism, social capitalism, green capitalism – these were the new kinds of buzzwords that came to the fore … The key idea, whatever rhetoric it was wrapped in, was that corporations had changed fundamentally, that while [CSR] and sustainability had previously been located on the fringes of corporate concerns – a bit of philanthropy here, some environmental measures there – now they became entrenched at the core of companies' ethos and operating principles.[10]

Alongside becoming a routine fixture at meetings of the WEF, G20, OECD, UN, and other international bodies, this promotion of an ostensibly more socially and environmentally conscious variant of capitalism has emerged as the rallying cry for an ever-expanding industry of management theorists and consultancies urging the US and other economies to dispense with 'the tyranny of quarterly capitalism'. Foremost among them are Michael Porter and Mark Kramer of the Harvard Business School, who in 2011 proposed the concept of 'creating shared value' (CSV) as a more strategic alternative to

CSR. Reflecting the new stakeholding ethos, Porter and Kramer argue that CSV has the potential to 'reinvent capitalism' by overcoming the dualistic separation of 'business' and 'society' within the firm:

> The capitalist system is under siege ... Companies are widely perceived to be prospering at the expense of the broader community. Even worse, the more business has begun to embrace corporate responsibility, the more it has been blamed for society's failures ... Business is caught in a vicious circle.
>
> Companies must take the lead in bringing business and society back together ... The solution lies in the principle of shared value, which involves creating economic value in a way that *also* creates value for society by addressing its needs and challenges ... A growing number of companies known for their hard-nosed approach to business – such as GE, Google, IBM, Intel, Johnson & Johnson, Nestlé, Unilever, and Wal-Mart – have already embarked on important efforts to create shared value by reconceiving the intersection between society and corporate performance ...

For Porter and Kramer, remaking the 'purpose of the corporation' as 'creating shared value, not just profit per se' would 'drive the next wave of innovation ... in the global economy'. There was little, it seemed, that shared value could not accomplish from 'reshap[ing] capitalism and its relationship to society' to offering the 'best chance to legitimize business again'.[11]

In 2011, Dominic Barton – then the UK-based Global Managing Director of McKinsey and later becoming the 'long-term' economic strategist to the Trudeau government in Canada – proposed 'three essential elements' to 'fight the tyranny of short-termism'.[12] Ongoing collaboration between Barton and Mark Wiseman – the President and CEO of the Canada Pension Plan Investment Board (CPPIB) created in 1997 to reorient the Canadian Pension Plan toward financial markets and operation as a 'sovereign wealth fund' – led to the formation of Focusing Capital on the Long-Term (FCLT) in 2013.[13] Three years later, McKinsey and the CPPIB joined with BlackRock, Dow Chemical, and Tata to found FCLT Global, which decries the problems of 'quarterly capitalism' and seeks to 'change the investment strategies and approaches of the players who form the cornerstone of our capitalist system: the big asset owners'. With Wiseman (as Chairman), Barton and Fink, as well as Unilever's Polman among its original board members, FCLT Global has since grown to encompass over sixty corporate participants.[14]

Allied with FCLT Global has been the Coalition for Inclusive Capitalism, established in 2014 with an original working group including Polman, Barton, and Fink. Its first conference was co-hosted by the City of London with support from both the Ford and Rockefeller foundations in 2014, and included companies accounting for over $30-trillion in investable assets – one third of the global total, and speeches by Carney, Christine Lagarde, Bill Clinton, Lawrence Summers, Arianna Huffington, and the Prince of Wales (now King Charles III).[15] In their statement introducing the conference, Polman and Lynn Forester de Rothschild wrote that,

> Capitalism has often proved dysfunctional in important ways ... If these costs cannot be controlled, support for capitalism may wane – and with it, humanity's best hope for prosperity ... We see this in movements such as Earth Day and Occupy Wall Street ...
>
> Addressing the failures of modern capitalism will require strong leadership and extensive cooperation between businesses, governments, and NGOs ... [W]e are convening key global leaders in London ... to establish tangible steps that firms can take to begin ... rebuilding public confidence in capitalism. Such an effort can bear fruit, as Unilever's own actions demonstrate ... [Yet] transformational change will come only from businesses and others acting together.[16]

The limits to capitalist valuation

These efforts to reposition BlackRock and other leading institutional investors as enlightened opponents of 'quarterly capitalism', alongside encouraging 'non-financial' MNCs such as Unilever to internalize competitiveness-relevant environmental, social, and governance (ESG) factors[17] within their core business models, have garnered some significant approval from institutionalist critics of free market 'dogma'. Will Hutton, for example, has argued that 'British capitalism is in trouble'. The political right has found a 'new villain' in 'stakeholder capitalism', as '[t]oo many companies are following woke Unilever and sacrificing profit and performance for lofty talk of pursuing sustainability and social purpose'. But for Hutton,

> [Such] thinking is fossilised in the 1980s ... Companies shape and are shaped by the society of which they are part and this includes the evolving preferences of shareholders ... Founded in the 1880s, Unilever's purpose was 'to make cleanliness commonplace and lessen the load for women'. Today's investors want it to continue with an updated purpose – making 'sustainable living commonplace'... Unilever, and the growing number of companies like it, are only responding to their shareholders' priorities.

Purposed brands, as Unilever's own data shows, outperform their non-purposed rivals. And that means profit.[18]

Others are more cautious than Hutton in their praise of Unilever. One well-known policy advocate of 'stakeholder capitalism', Mariana Mazzucato, has argued that the conception of this promoted by Unilever, Fink, and others, is based on a 'conceptual sleight of hand'. More 'radical reforms', and a more substantial challenge to shareholder interests, she insists, are necessary 'to transform capitalism in the interests of people and planet'.[19] But Mazzucato's conception of value as being 'co-created by producers and consumers, workers and managers, inventors and administrators, regulators and investors' continues to obstruct an adequate explanation of *why* this is the case. The problem is that the apparent 'betrayal' of the *concept* of 'stakeholder capitalism' identified by Mazzucato is merely symptomatic of the *material* centrality of the profit motive within capitalism. By understating the political obstacles to 'co-creating' more egalitarian distributional bargains and democratic modes of governance within a class-divided society where production remains dominated by private profit, Mazzucato and other reform-oriented proponents of 'stakeholder capitalism' still gloss over the contradictory aspects of the concept itself and the political conflicts necessary to make inroads into corporate property rights and challenge the primacy of profit-making within the firm. Insofar as these calls for a reformed capitalism eschew wider processes of class mobilization and large-scale state transformation, as opposed to simply raising the proportion of government spending vis-à-vis market-led investment, such perspectives invite co-optation by influential sections of the corporate elites (as Mazzucato herself appears to recognize).

Starkly put, any radical agenda seeking transformative structural change through a decisive break from neoliberalism will be compelled to reckon with the materiality of *capitalism*, conceived as a historically specific form of social relations and mode of production with its own logic of reproduction tied to the requirements of profit-oriented and market-mediated exchange, class exploitation, and balance of forces, as well as the form and functions of the capitalist state. In this regard, the discourses and practices of actually existing 'stakeholder capitalism' – which amount to a political project for ensuring capitalism's survival in an era of multidimensional crisis – invariably internalize the fundamental tensions, antagonisms, and contradictions of the capital relation as delimited by Marxist value theory.

In the first volume of *Capital*, Marx specified the essential contradiction between the use-value and exchange-value moments of the commodity form, through which value is crystallized as the alienated form of social wealth produced by labour under capitalism. From the perspective of value, commodities must be both produced and consumed. But while their purchase as use-values presupposes the abundant natural and social wealth of the commons, this abundance exists in constant tension with the socially induced scarcity of ongoing primitive accumulation and enclosure, privatized accumulation of exchange-value, and capitalist exploitation without which commodities would not be produced.[20] These exchange- and use-value moments of the commodity form are manifested in a variety of structural contradictions inherent to the capital relation, including those spanning labour power (abstract labour/extraction of value versus concrete labour/skills), wages (cost of production versus source of demand), money (exchangeable currency/interest bearing capital versus medium of exchange), productive capital (abstract value in motion/realized profits versus concrete fixed capital/managerial control), and the state ('ideal collective capitalist' versus factor of cohesion in a class-divided society).[21] Until wealth is no longer counted solely as value, the domination of use by exchange will entail the systematic distortion, devaluation, and destruction of the former by the latter, while attempts to integrate the universal conditions of humanity and nature within the logic of capitalist reproduction will invariably prioritize the interests of capital at the expense of people and planet.

There is, then, no capitalist route to transcending the dualism between 'business' and 'society'. Indeed, in an era of a protracted legitimation crisis where the neoliberal ideology of 'free markets'/shareholder value-maximization has been delegitimized but the continued strength of capital and persisting weakness of labour remain the material anchor of class and institutional power, the domination of use value by exchange has reached paradoxical new heights. Just as the 'freeing' of markets has all along required 'strong' states to underwrite the conditions for neoliberal policy regimes championing liberalization, 'deregulation', and privatization, so too the 'activist' role for corporations entailed by the roll-back of the Keynesian welfare state, the smashing of the labour movement, and the broad shift from trade union-driven 'producer' to NGO-driven 'consumer' politics has only heightened since 2008. It is the intensification of the contradictions associated with state-mediated market liberalization, market-enabling state intervention, and state- and corporate-sponsored NGO-ization which has led the capitalist class to embrace 'stakeholder capitalism'. Stakeholding emerges as an ideological formation and managerial practice congruent with efforts by the corporations to manage the 'systemic risks' birthed by their own existence. The case of Unilever is a prime example of this endeavour.

UNILEVER: PROFITING AS PURPOSE

Originally formed by the 1929 merger of British soap manufacturer Lever Brothers and the Dutch Margarine Union at the tail end of the 'roaring twenties' business expansion, Unilever is one of the oldest, largest, and most internationalized European MNCs. At the time of its founding, the Anglo–Dutch giant was probably *the* largest European company, having come into being as the combined corporate offspring of colonialism and capitalism traversing two empires.[22] Today, Unilever remains the world's largest tea company and producer of ice cream, with the firm's statistics revealing that it purchases a sizable percentage of the world volume of key agricultural crops, including frozen spinach (28 per cent), black tea (12 per cent), frozen peas (12 per cent), palm oil (4 per cent), and tomatoes (7 per cent).[23] Unilever ranks in the top tier of firms manufacturing the vast bulk of consumer goods that end up in shopping baskets, alongside the likes of Procter & Gamble (P&G), Nestlé, Mondelēz, Colgate-Palmolive, Coca-Cola, PepsiCo., Mars, Danone, Associated British Foods, General Mills, and Kellogg's.[24]

In contrast to the assumption of 'political neutrality' which pervades the company histories written by mainstream business historians, or the pluralist conception of corporate business as one competing interest group lobbying a 'neutral' state apparatus,[25] it is clear that the capacity of capitalist states to govern is structurally dependent on Unilever and other large capitalist corporations. It is the latter which form the vectors of capital accumulation and the corporate organization of the world economy. Unilever has figured prominently within the principal policy-planning departments through which capitalist states seek to organize competing capitals into a class force and sustain capital accumulation as a whole. Since its founding, the company has played an integral role within the Atlanticist economic and political alliances, led by the US, underpinning the exercise of capitalist class power and the spread of capitalism globally.[26] In particular, given its longstanding place at the centre of the world market and practices of neo-colonialism, Unilever has come to play a distinctive role in pioneering ideologies and strategies of corporate legitimation designed to prevent the creation of more egalitarian and sustainable polities and policy regimes that might encroach on private property rights and profit-making. The strategy of 'stakeholder capitalism', that emerged in the 1990s and became more pronounced since the crisis after 2008, is the latest iteration.

From post-war atlantic order to neoliberal globalization

Unilever was one of the few European-based MNCs that entered the early post-war period relatively intact, 'with over a hundred factories in Continental Europe alone, of which more than forty were in West Germany'.²⁷ But the company's various business lines also faced threats of disruption from European protectionism, inter-state rivalry over markets, and communist and national liberation movements. These threats included the nationalization of its massive eastern European Schicht subsidiary by the Soviet Union in 1945 and the closing down of its large Chinese investments after the 1949 revolution. Similar risks were facing both its Indian and Indonesian businesses and the United Africa Company (UAC), which was Unilever's largest subsidiary and dominated the West African *économie de traite* in Nigeria, Ghana, and Sierra Leone.²⁸ In response to this system-wide politicization of its activities, Unilever was unavoidably drawn onto the terrain of inter-state politics, and overtly supporting US-led Atlanticism and neo-colonialism through the construction of new bilateral linkages, the Bretton Woods system, NATO, and European integration. The firm's managerial cadre acted as a nodal point of economic-corporate mediation between the main Anglo-Saxon and West German ruling-class networks through its major role in groupings such as the Anglo-German Fellowship of the 1930s, the ICC, European League for Economic Co-operation (ELEC), Bilderberg Group, Atlantic Institute for International Affairs, UK-German Königswinter conference, and the *Foundation Européenne de la Culture*.²⁹

During the 1970s crisis of post-war 'embedded liberalism', the viability of national class compromises and distributional bargains centred on full employment in Fordist mass production, mass consumerism, and the Keynesian welfare state was overturned. After incurring a 'decade of lost growth' amidst 'stagflation', renewed labour militancy in the core capitalist countries, and growing calls from the liberation movements demanding a 'New International Economic Order', Unilever threw its weight behind the emerging neoliberal counter-revolutions in the US and Britain, the reorientation of European 'coordinated' capitalisms towards 'international competitiveness', and the structural adjustment policies of the IMF. In this new context of neoliberal discipline and finance-led industrial restructuring to restore corporate profitability, Unilever embraced a strategy premised on maximizing shareholder value for itself and more broadly. Indeed, its personnel not only participated in but took on major leadership roles in organizations that advanced neoliberal restructuring across various sites and scales, including Keith Joseph's Centre for Policy Studies in the UK, the Trilateral Commission (TC) which emerged from the Bilderberg conferences, the confederations of British and Netherlands industry, the European Round Table of Industrialists (ERT) of which Unilever was a founding member, and the Union of Industrial and Employers' Confederations of

Europe (UNICE).³⁰

Notably, Unilever emerged as a major supporter of trade liberalization and global market integration. During the Clinton administration, Unilever remained steadfastly committed to a new round of 'free trade' agreements, liberalizing reform of Europe's Common Agricultural Policy (CAP), and closer US–EU cooperation to prise open southern markets at the WTO. In doing so, it drew on powerful advisory directors to cement leading roles on these and other international business associations.³¹

But when faced with a growing 'anti-globalization' backlash amidst the shift to NGO-driven 'consumer' politics after the 1992 Rio Earth Summit, capitalist states sought to address the growing legitimacy deficit of major corporations by articulating an alternate social vision of globalization with a 'human face'. Through global partnerships for CSR and 'sustainable development', governments and multilateral institutions experimented with incorporating MNCs and NGOs within flexible and networked forms of multi-stakeholder 'global governance' consistent with an emerging 'post-Fordist' economy.³² Ditching its traditional low profile, Unilever joined the ICC/World Business Council for Sustainable Development (WBCSD) campaign to consolidate a 'global partnership' with the UN,³³ leading to its first forays into 'stakeholder capitalism' through the Unilever Sustainable Agriculture Programme (1995), Unilever–WWF Marine Stewardship Council (1996), UN Global Compact (launched at the WEF's 1999 Davos meeting by Kofi Annan), Hindustan Unilever's Project Shakti program for women in rural India (2001), Roundtables for Sustainable Palm Oil and Responsible Soy (2004-06), and the unveiling of a new 'Vitality' mission and corporate logo to be displayed on all its products for the first time (2004-10).³⁴

False dawn: the Unilever sustainable living plan

Following the crisis of 2008-10, the imposition of another decade of austerity helped to delegitimize the 'post-political' neoliberal consensus epitomized by Clintonism in the US and 'Third Way' social democracy in Europe. The ensuing economic and political anxieties, centred on US decline and rivalry with China (and Russia), have been coupled with climate change shifting from one policy problem among many into a full-fledged ecological emergency.³⁵ Although it had initially emerged in response to the 'anti-globalization' backlash during the 'long 1990s', the 'new corporation' movement came of age only after 2008, when faced with the potentially explosive tensions between the requirements of global capital accumulation and national political legitimation in the evolving multidimensional crisis.³⁶

When Joel Bakan queried participants at the WEF's 2020 Davos meeting 'who among corporate leaders best exemplifies this ideal [of the new corporation], most people [pointed] to former Unilever chief Paul Polman'. Polman spent 27 years at P&G's European subsidiary before becoming the first outsider to lead Unilever from 2009-19.[37] One of the first CEOs to champion 'stakeholder capitalism', Polman catapulted Unilever to cult status within the wider 'movement' and amassed a vast array of positions at the top table of neoliberal 'global governance'. He sat on the WEF's International Business Council, represented big business on the UN High Level Panel which devised the Sustainable Development Goals (2012), chaired the WBCSD (2012-17) and ICC (2018-20, honorary chairman from 2020-22), served as vice-chair of the UN Global Compact (2018-present), and was nominated to the Rockefeller Foundation's board of trustees in 2019.[38] After stepping down as Unilever CEO in 2019, Polman started the 'Imagine' consultancy with various ex-Unilever people including Jeff Seabright, who worked at the US State Department, USAID, and directed the Clinton White House's Task Force on Climate Change before joining Coca-Cola and subsequently becoming Unilever's Chief Sustainability Officer.

On his first day as Unilever CEO in January 2009, Polman informed the markets that the company would oppose financial 'short-termism' by no longer publishing quarterly guidance or reports for shareholders.[39] Instead, it would serve 'people and planet' by championing the needs of stakeholders, including suppliers, creditors, governments, sustainability-conscious consumers, smallholder farmers, and climate change activists. Polman's flagship project, the Unilever Sustainable Living Plan (USLP), was formally unveiled in 2010.[40] Envisioned as a core business strategy for doubling the size of its business while integrating 'responsibility' and 'sustainability' into all company operations, from sourcing to consumer use and disposal, the USLP placed three ostensibly non-financial objectives at the heart of Unilever's business strategy: (1) helping one billion people improve their health and well-being; (2) halving the environmental footprint of making and using its products; and (3) enhancing the livelihoods of those in its value chain.[41]

Under the guise of transcending the business/society dualism within the firm as it saw it, Unilever abolished its autonomous CSR department and 'elevated' responsibility for the USLP across all senior management.[42] The company's group of external environmental advisors (founded in 1995) was also recast as a USLP Advisory Council chaired by its Chief Sustainability Officer.[43] Mission statements were developed for all core product brands seeking to convey their socially or environmentally beneficial purpose[44] and the company brokered or participated in literally hundreds (if not thousands) of public–private and business–NGO partnerships.⁴⁵ To support the USLP's 'improving health & wellbeing' goal, for example, the Unilever Foundation at the WEF's 2012 annual meeting announced global partnerships with Oxfam, Population Services International (PSI), Save the Children, UNICEF, and the UN World Food Programme in conjunction with leading brands such as Lifebuoy, Domestos, Pureit, Knorr, and Walls.⁴⁶

Just as Unilever's 'shared value' initiatives exploit market opportunities arising from chronic hunger, malnutrition, and poverty in the Global South, so too the 'improving nutrition' pillar of the USLP's 'improved health and well-being' goal seeks to profit from the social crisis of 'overnutrition' manifested in obesity and 'lifestyle-related' illnesses (such as diabetes) in the Global North. This includes the ongoing marketization of climate and social justice 'activism'. For example, Unilever plays a supersized role in asserting corporate influence over the vegan movement by entrenching 'the shift of political power away from traditional farms and local markets towards biotech companies and multinationals' that are emerging as the dominant providers of 'climate-friendly', non-meat consumer products.⁴⁷

The four pillars of Unilever's 'reducing environmental impact' goal, in turn, seek to manage exposure to ecological 'risks' emanating from its enormous greenhouse gas (GHG) emissions footprint, water use, waste and packaging, and raw materials across the product lifecycle. Within the logic of this goal, the firm's contributions to causing the climate crisis are recast as opportunities for lowering operational costs, increasing energy resilience, securing raw materials, reducing exposure to environmental taxes and regulation, and improving its attractiveness to investors who are increasingly considering 'climate-related financial risks'.⁴⁸ Unilever has also sought to financialize the basic tenets of its sustainability plan by issuing its first-ever Green Sustainability Bond rooted in these principles in 2014.⁴⁹

In terms of raw materials sourcing for many of Unilever's key products, commodity-driven deforestation linked to palm oil and soy monocultural plantations, cattle rearing, and timber harvesting for paper and pulp is estimated to contribute 15 per cent of GHG emissions globally. Unilever implausibly claims, however, to be 'protecting our forests' by eliminating deforestation from its agricultural supply chains and supporting myriad 'voluntary' private sector 'net zero' pledges, 'sustainable sourcing' certification, the New York Declaration on Forests, UN Sustainable Development Goals, and the Paris Agreement. To further its valuation of 'natural capital' and anticipate future carbon taxes, the company also implemented a 40-euro price on carbon for internal investment decisions.⁵⁰

The contradictory nature of Unilever's sustainability goals can also be seen with respect to water, where scarcity threatens the supply and cost of agricultural commodities, energy production, and household consumption. Unilever's Home Care and Beauty & Personal Care divisions, however, boast that its product categories account 'for more than 90 per cent of the water used in people's homes, from washing dishes to washing hair, skin and clothes'.[51] Beyond the household, rising temperatures, more frequent droughts, and unpredictable rainfall patterns associated with climate change are precipitating worsening conditions for farmers. Unilever has responded by attempting to impose a Sustainable Agriculture Code and Responsible Sourcing Policy on its suppliers in the name of boosting yields, implementing 'climate smart' agriculture, and 'modernizing' farming practices in the water-scarce countries producing its most water-intensive crops (particularly the tomatoes used as inputs for Knorr products).[52]

In its capacity as the world's largest tea company – purchasing some 10-12 per cent of the world's black tea annually – Unilever also claims to be planting a million trees to address the contribution of deforestation to water shortages and droughts. Yet, this planting occurs only insofar as such events negatively impact tea production on its Tanzanian and Kenyan plantations and in the southwest Mau Forest in the Rift Valley.[53]

Unilever is the world's largest producer of ice cream and, as another example its 'green' strategy, has committed to accelerating the roll-out of freezer cabinets that use more 'climate-friendly' natural (hydrocarbon) refrigerants. This target, in turn, forms part of a broader aim to make the manufacturing, distribution, and retailing of its products 'carbon positive' by 2030 through investments in 'clean' technologies, growing energy efficiency, renewable energy sources, and innovation and efficiency in transportation.[54]

To implement its USLP target of halving the waste associated with the disposal of its products by 2020 (as compared to 2010 levels), Unilever claimed to be breaking with the linear 'take-make-dispose' model of consumption and 'accelerating the transition towards a circular economy for plastic'. However, as of 2021 the company (then a 'principal partner' for the UN COP26 climate summit in Glasgow) ranked third on the list of the world's top five corporate plastic polluters, which manufacture the bulk of the plastic packaging waste that litters the streets, countryside, and pollutes the seas.[55]

These examples all illustrate the contradictory logic at the heart of Unilever's revised corporate strategy – its claims of 'stakeholder capitalism' as an ecological alternative that sustains profitable accumulation of capital. Polman captured the company's new operating ethos in 2014 when he stated, without irony, that Unilever is 'the world's biggest NGO … The only difference is, we're making money so we are sustainable'.[56] More recently, Hanneke Faber, president of Unilever Europe, has claimed that 'the future of branding is activism'. Drawing on Ben & Jerry's, now cast as Unilever's 'most purposeful, activist brand', she contends that 'brand builders need to take a stance, to create movements, to evangelize and even sacrifice'.[57] Yet while some specific manufacturing efficiencies and cost-cutting have undoubtedly been achieved by reducing carbon emissions, water, and waste 'per consumer' in areas under its direct control, the overall environmental impact at Unilever has only increased since the introduction of the USLP in 2010.[58] Indeed, a decade on, Polman's successor, Alan Jope, tried to deflect this uncomfortable truth by arguing that turnover growth of 18 per cent was 'higher than our GHG emissions have grown, which is an indication of decoupling'.[59]

Faced with a slowing trend rate of annual organic sales growth since 2012 amidst intensified competition in the consumer goods sector, Unilever has sought to balance heightened investor pressure to raise profitability against its legitimation claims to be genuinely responsive to social and environmental 'stakeholders'. Following a failed hostile takeover bid by Kraft Heinz in 2017, the company underwent a renewed wave of internal restructuring designed to 'reassure' investors that it could continue to generate 'lucrative returns' as an independent entity. The reassurance came in the form of a multi-billion-pound rewards package for shareholders encompassing share buybacks and a raised dividend, increased profit margin targets, cost cutting across the organization, the sell-off of its historic margarine and spreads division, plans to increase its financial leverage ratio to two times core earnings, and a review of the dual nationality of its legal and corporate structure.[60]

When a 2018 proposal to consolidate Unilever's 'unwieldy' Anglo-Dutch legal structure into a simpler, less institutionally 'rigid', and more 'flexible' holding company incorporated in the Netherlands was rejected by UK-based shareholders, Polman was ousted. The new board, led by Jope, instead proposed in June 2020 that it be reconstituted as a single firm headquartered in London.[61] As Unilever's share price soared by nearly 8 per cent – making it for a time the largest FTSE 100-listed company – the relocation plan met with near-unanimous approval from both Dutch and UK-based shareholders, and was finalized relatively quickly under the EU's cross-border mergers regime by November 2020.[62] The result has been a leaner and meaner organizational structure that will only intensify the firm's role in generating the social and ecological crises which its multi-stakeholder/ESG strategies unjustifiably claim to be resolving. Amidst the uncertainty generated by the coronavirus pandemic, Unilever has once again begun re-centring its corporate strategy on its most profitable and fastest growing 'core' assets (especially in home care) while divesting from those now rendered increasingly 'peripheral' by changing conditions of competitive accumulation (particularly in foods and refreshments).[63]

Since becoming Unilever CEO in January 2019, Jope has by and large continued along the same broad trajectory laid out by Polman. For example, he has launched Unilever's Climate Transition Action Plan (put to a shareholder vote in 2021) and further consolidated the company's sustainability and business strategies into the 'Unilever Compass'. The latter is steeped in the 'stakeholder capitalism' discourse and supposedly offers a 'new, fully integrated corporate strategy' encompassing 15 multi-year priorities that 'is underpinned by the same rigour as the USLP, and will be more holistic, inclusive, and far-reaching than ever before'. Jope capped all this off with his appointment as WBCSD vice-chair in 2020, already having served on its executive committee since the previous year.[64]

Yet, as the USLP reached its tenth and final year in 2020, his remarks at an event celebrating its achievements on 6 May clearly indicated that Unilever's decade-long journey to 'make sustainable living commonplace' had – despite all the talk of saving the planet – been almost entirely circuitous, ending up pretty much where it began:

> The pressures on the planet are getting worse, and social inequality has reached a critical point, being made even more severe by the devastating pandemic we're living through ... As the Unilever Sustainable Living Plan journey concludes, we will take everything we've learned and build on it ... And while we don't really know what the world will look like post-Covid-19, I am convinced that there will be no future unless we double down on our commitments to look after people and the planet ... Before the Covid-19 crisis, it was already clear that the current capitalist model is in need of repair. Globalisation and capitalism are good for a business like ours, but globalisation and capitalism at the expense of people and the planet are not. It's therefore up to businesses like us, working with partners – NGOs, government organisations, academics, suppliers, customers – to drive a new model of capitalism, and build a better future.[65]

STAKEHOLDING CAPITALISM AS SUSTAINABILITY?

Unilever's Sustainable Living Plan is emblematic of 'stakeholder capitalism', with its claims to integrate social responsibility and sustainability into all company operations. But it is less a genuine alternative to shareholder-value maximization than an alternative strategy for realizing it via corporate governance reforms that rebalance and legitimize global capitalism. The long march of CSR through the corporate strategy of Unilever and the coordinative organizations of corporate capital has 'elevated' it from the margins of stockholder meetings to the boardroom in the guise of 'stakeholder capitalism'. But this has only further intensified the contradictory logic at the heart of modern corporate governance, in firms like Unilever but also corporate capitalism as a whole, between the competitive imperatives to maximize firm profitability while also addressing the societal objectives of 'stakeholders' in ecological sustainability and social justice.

The strategy of 'competitiveness through sustainability' is only possible to the extent that firm competitiveness remains unhindered. Bakan makes this point very well, observing that, given their legal obligation to act in the financial 'best interest' of shareholders, corporations 'can only do as much good as will help them do well'. This socio-legal structuring of the corporate form thereby presents 'a profound constraint in terms of what kinds and amounts of good they are likely to do' and effectively licences them 'to do "bad" when there's no business case for doing good'.[66] As Unilever itself has experienced, failure to meet this test can expect retaliation from both the shareholding and managerial fractions of the corporation and the wider capitalist class.

Indeed, the embrace of 'multi-stakeholder' partnerships by MNCs is far less a movement toward some notion of 'responsible capitalism' and much more an effort to socialize the growing costs and risks of private investment and infrastructure inside the state. Polman, Fink, the ICC, WBCSD, and other leading corporate advocates of 'multi-stakeholder' capitalism advance an interpretation of CSR and sustainability as evolutionary outgrowths of market imperatives. That is, 'competition through sustainability' is a rational business response to changing socio-ecological constraints and market opportunities conferring 'eco-efficiencies', cost savings, and competitive advantages. Yet, the exceptional nature of scenarios where profitability also serves social purpose implies that any conceivable economic or socio-environmental benefits will be more than overshadowed by the total costs of company CSR and sustainability programs.[67] Stakeholder capitalism is primarily, then, a political and ideological process of long-term financial and productive outlays for internal initiatives and external partnerships that typically fail to generate profit in the short term.[68] Outlays on corporate sustainability and responsibility are necessarily constrained by market disciplines, as the Unilever case demonstrates, even while legitimating and protecting the interests of particular firms and the wider interests of corporate capital as a whole.[69]

The 'shareholder' and 'stakeholder' strategies for corporate governance therefore should not be seen as two opposed forms of capitalism; rather, they are integrally related features of corporate restructuring. As the analyst of the European business elite Eelke Heemskerk concludes, 'CSR conveys the message that there is more to corporate governance than a focus on profits. Yet it does so without attacking the basic premise of shareholder supremacy.' Instead, in current corporate strategy, 'the argument is that investing in stakeholder relations and acting socially responsibly will, in the long run, add to the profitability of firms'.[70] By endowing nominally 'economic' and 'private' entities such as Unilever and other MNCs with a sense of 'public' purpose and 'civic' identity, 'stakeholder capitalism' shields the grotesque inequalities, exploitation, and environmental damage at the heart of capitalist accumulation by representing them as necessary pathways to 'long-term', socially 'responsible', and ecologically 'sustainable' corporate practices. The claim that MNCs act as 'good' corporate citizens not only blurs the discursive boundary between the public and private spheres of capitalist states; it fundamentally strengthens the material differentiation between the economic and the political constitutive of capitalist social relations.[71]

The displacement of class conflict into disputes over 'stakeholding', or more recently into issues over the 'diversity and representativeness of boards', is far removed from a transition to an alternative, ecologically sustainable model of development. The left cannot settle for a 'multi-stakeholder' variant of capitalism, or even see this as one of the 'structural reforms' that need to be part of union demands or a wider political program. We are far beyond that. Rescuing humanity and the planet from the systemic social and ecological harms being wrought by the major corporations today necessitates posing worker-centred, eco-socialist alternatives to capitalist exploitation and social irresponsibility.[72]

NOTES

This essay is dedicated to the memory of Leo Panitch – teacher, supervisor, friend, and comrade. The epitome of a socialist intellectual, stolen from us by the pandemic.

1   Larry Fink, 'Letter to CEOs: The Power of Capitalism', BlackRock website. Fink's ascent to become the 'undisputed king of Wall Street' speaks to the 'massive shift' towards concentrated share ownership which has accompanied the rise of the 'Big Three' asset managers – BlackRock, Vanguard, and State Street – since 2008. See: Jan Fichtner, Eelke M. Heemskerk, and Javier Garcia-Bernardo, 'Hidden power of the Big Three? Passive index funds, re-concentration of corporate ownership, and new financial risk', *Business and Politics*, 19(2), June 2017, pp. 298–326; Stephen Maher and Scott Aquanno, this volume.

2   Joe Biden, 'Joe Biden Speech Transcript on Economic Recovery Plan', Rev, 9 July 2020, available at: www.rev.com/blog/transcripts. See also: Dawn Lim and Gregory Zuckerman, 'BlackRock Emerges as Wall Street Player in Biden Administration', *Wall Street Journal*, 1 December 2020.
3   Business Roundtable, 'Business Roundtable Redefines the Purpose of a Corporation to Promote "An Economy That Serves All Americans"', Business Roundtable, 19 August 2019.
4   Channel 4 News, 'Can capitalism combat climate change? Bank of England says business can benefit from saving planet', YouTube, 31 July 2019.
5   Klaus Schwab, 'We must move on from neoliberalism in the post-COVID era', World Economic Forum web blog, 12 October 2020, available at: www.weforum.org/agenda.
6   Vivian Hunt, Paul Polman, and Diane Brady, 'Stakeholder capitalism: A conversation with Vivian Hunt and Paul Polman', *McKinsey Podcast*, 6 May 2021. Schwab, Fink, and Carney sit on the WEF's foundation board alongside Al Gore, Kristalina Georgieva, Christine Lagarde, Ngozi Okonjo-Iweala, Chrystia Freeland, and the CEOs of Nestlé, Salesforce, Siemens, AXA, Accenture, Bain & Company, and the Carlyle Group.
7   Sam Gindin, 'Premature Declarations of Austerity's Death', *The Bullet*, 16 November 2021, available at: www.socialistproject.ca.
8   World Economic Forum, *Everybody's Business: Strengthening International Cooperation in a More Interdependent World – Report of the Global Redesign Initiative*, Geneva: World Economic Forum, 2010, p. 29.
9   Schwab, 'We must move on from neoliberalism'.
10 Joel Bakan, 'Charming Psychopaths: The Modern Corporation – An Interview with Joel Bakan', in Nick Buxton, ed., *State of Power 2020: The Corporation*, Amsterdam: Transnational Institute, 2020.
11 Michael E. Porter and Mark R. Kramer, 'Creating Shared Value', *Harvard Business Review*, January–February 2011, pp. 62–77.
12 'First, business and finance must jettison their short-term orientation and revamp incentives and structures in order to focus their organizations on the long term. Second, executives must infuse their organizations with the perspective that serving the interests of all major stakeholders – employees, suppliers, customers, creditors, communities, the environment – is not at odds with the goal of maximizing corporate value; on the contrary, it's essential to achieving that goal. Third, public companies must cure the ills stemming from dispersed and disengaged ownership by bolstering boards' ability to govern like owners.' See: Dominic Barton, 'Capitalism for the Long Term', *Harvard Business Review*, March 2011, pp. 85–91.
13 Dominic Barton and Mark Wiseman, 'Focusing Capital on the Long Term', *Harvard Business Review*, January–February 2014, pp. 44–51. See also: James K. Rowe and Alexis Shotwell, 'Canada's 'Vampire' Pension Plan', *The Bullet*, 22 August 2019, available at: www.socialistproject.ca.
14 In 2018, Wiseman left CPPIB to join his wife at BlackRock, where he became Global Head of Active Equities and Chairman of BlackRock Alternative Investors.
15 Chrystia Freeland, 'It's Not Just George Soros Anymore: What does it mean when the capitalist vanguard starts talking about inequality?', *Politico*, 8 June 2014; Diana Carney and Chrystia Freeland, eds, *Making Capitalism More Inclusive: Selected Speeches and Essays*

from Participants at the Conference on Inclusive Capitalism, London: Coalition for Inclusive Capitalism, 2014.

16 Paul Polman and Lynn Forester de Rothschild, 'The Capitalist Threat to Capitalism', *Project Syndicate*, 23 May 2014.

17 Whereas 'socially responsible investing' (SRI) foregrounds the moral case for divesting from 'unethical' industries, ESG emphasizes enhancing firm profitability by including non-financial factors within financial decision-making. The term was coined in 2004 after Kofi Annan invited the CEOs of 50 major financial firms to participate in a UN Global Compact initiative. See: UN Global Compact Financial Sector Initiative, 'Who Cares Wins: Connecting Financial Markets to a Changing World', Washington DC: Work Bank Group, 2017; Georg Kell, 'The Remarkable Rise Of ESG', *Forbes Magazine*, 11 July 2018.

18 Will Hutton, '"Woke" capitalism is the new villain of the right. It's also the only way forward', *The Guardian*, 30 January 2022.

19 Mariana Mazzucato, 'Larry Fink's Capitalist Shell Game', *Project Syndicate*, 11 February 2022. See also: Mariana Mazzucato and Stephanie Flanders, 'A Mission-Oriented Approach to Stakeholder Capitalism', *Aspen Ideas*, 23 February 2021; Mariana Mazzucato, *The Value of Everything: Making and Taking in the Global Economy*, London: Allen Lane, 2018.

20 Alfredo Saad-Filho, 'Value, Capital and Exploitation', in Alfredo Saad-Filho, ed., *Anti-Capitalism: A Marxist Introduction*, London: Pluto Press, 2003; John Bellamy Foster, Brett Clark, and Richard York, *The Ecological Rift: Capitalism's War on the Earth*, New York: Monthly Review Press, 2011.

21 Bob Jessop, *The Future of the Capitalist State*, Cambridge: Polity Press, 2002, pp. 19–21.

22 See, for example: Walter Rodney, *How Europe Underdeveloped Africa*, Cape Town: Pambazuka Press, 2012 [1972], Ch. 5; Jules Marchal, *Lord Leverhulme's Ghosts: Colonial Exploitation in the Congo*, London: Verso, 2017; Counter Information Services, *Unilever's World: CIS Anti Report No. 11*, Nottingham: Russell Press, 1975; Charles Wilson, *The History of Unilever: Volume One*, London: Cassell and Company, 1954.

23 Unilever, *Growing for the Future: Unilever and Sustainable Agriculture*, Rotterdam: Unilever NV, 2005, p. 8.

24 With over 550 subsidiaries and 400+ brands (ranging from food and beverages to home and personal care) selling to 2.5 billion consumers in 190 countries, Unilever in 2017 amassed a turnover of €53.7 billion. The company also has a unique position in 'emerging' markets, from which it derives 58 per cent of its €30.8 billion in total sales. To this end, Unilever boasts the world's second largest marketing budget (surpassed only by its major US rival P&G). See: Stefan Van Rompaey, 'Coca-Cola is world's biggest brand, Unilever strongest manufacturer', *Retail Detail*, 21 May 2019.

25 Geoffrey Jones, *Renewing Unilever: Transformation and Tradition*, Oxford: Oxford University Press, 2005.

26 On Marxist state and international relations theory see: Leo Panitch and Sam Gindin, *The Making of Global Capitalism: The Political Economy of American Empire*, London: Verso, 2012.

27 Charles Wilson, *The History of Unilever: Volume Three, Challenge and Response in the Post-War Industrial Revolution, 1945–1965*, London: Continuum, 1968, p. 8.

28 David K. Fieldhouse, *Unilever Overseas: The Anatomy of a Multinational, 1895–1965*, London: Croom Helm, 1979; Fieldhouse, *Merchant Capital and Economic Decolonization: The United Africa Company 1929–1987*, London: Clarendon Press, 1994; Anne Phillips, *The Enigma of Colonialism: British Policy in West Africa*, London: James Currey, 1989.

29 For example, Bilderberg was set up by Joseph Retinger, Unilever chairman Paul Rijkens, and Prince Bernhard of the Netherlands in the social milieu of the Allied exile governments in London. Unilever's advisory directors during this period included Jan Beyen (former President of the Bank of International Settlements and leader of the Dutch delegation to Bretton Woods, Dutch foreign minister, and author of the 'Beyen Plan' for a European common market – which decoupled economic from geopolitical integration through acceptance of NATO); Frank Roberts (Ernest Bevin's principal private secretary and UK ambassador to Yugoslavia, NATO, the USSR, and West Germany before representing Unilever at the Atlantic Institute, International Chamber of Commerce, and Trilateral Commission), and two IMF managing directors (H. Johannes Witteveen and Pierre-Paul Schweitzer).

30 Norman Strauss, a Unilever marketing executive, became a key advisor to the Centre for Policy Studies before being seconded from Unilever in 1979 by Keith Joseph to work in No. 10 Downing Street. Lord Peter Bauer – a neoliberal development economist, friend of Friedrich von Hayek, and Mont Pelerin Society member – was employed as a personal consultant to Unilever's Special Committee already in 1960.

31 These included the ERT, UNICE, TC, and WEF. For instance, Niall FitzGerald, Unilever's chairman from 1996–2004, chaired the WEF's International Business Council and sat on its Foundation Board from 2002–11. Unilever chairman Floris Maljers proposed the idea for the influential EU Competitiveness Advisory Group, while the head of Unilever France, François Perigot, was President of UNICE from 1988–98. See: Belén Balanyá, Ann Doherty, Olivier Hoedeman, Adam Ma'anit, and Erik Wesselius, *Europe Inc.: Regional and Global Restructuring and the Rise of Corporate Power*, London: Pluto Press, 2003, p. 33. Notable Unilever advisory directors during this period included George Mitchell (US Senate Majority Leader), Leon Brittan, Lynda Chalker, Romano Prodi, Onno Ruding, Karl Otto Pöhl, David Simon (BP), Jeroen van der Veer (Shell), Derek Birkin (Rio Tinto Zinc), Hilmar Kopper (Deutsche Bank), Bertrand Collomb (Lafarge), James W. Kinnear (Texaco), Claudio X Gonzalez (Kimberly-Clark de Mexico), and Narayana Murthy (Infosys).

32 Susanne Soederberg, *Global Governance in Question: Empire, Class and the New Common Sense in Managing North–South Relations*, London: Pluto Press, 2006.

33 Dominic Kelly, 'The International Chamber of Commerce', *New Political Economy*, 10(2), 2005, pp. 260–71; Adil Najam, 'World Business Council for Sustainable Development: the greening of business or a greenwash?' in Helge Ole Bergesen, Georg Parmann, and Oystein B. Thommessen, eds, *Yearbook of International Cooperation on Environment and Development 1999–2000*, London: Routledge, 1999, pp. 65–77.

34 Perry Anderson describes Annan as the 'academically dim son of a manager for Unilever in colonial Ghana'. See his 'Our Man: The Inglorious Career of Kofi Annan', *London Review of Books*, 29(9), 10 May 2007.

35 Martijn Konings, ed., *The Great Credit Crash*, London: Verso, 2010.

36 Leo Panitch and Sam Gindin, 'Trumping the Empire', in Leo Panitch and Greg Albo, eds, *Socialist Register 2019: A World Turned Upside Down*, London: Merlin Press, 2019.

37 Joel Bakan, *The New Corporation: How 'Good' Corporations are Bad for democracy*, New York: Vintage Books, 2020, p. 19. On the uneven internationalization of European MNCs under the dominance of American capital see: Panitch and Gindin, *The Making of Global Capitalism*.
38 In 2011, the Global Compact – which includes the ICC general secretary among its board members – sponsored 'an unprecedented working group co-chaired by UN Secretary-General, Ban Ki-moon, and [Polman]… to develop a framework to support more large-scale transformative partnerships between the UN and the private sector'. See: David Grayson and Jane Nelson, *Corporate Responsibility Coalitions: The Past, Present, and Future of Alliances for Sustainable Capitalism*, Stanford: Stanford University Press, 2013, p. 100.
39 Andy Boynton and Margareta Barchan, 'Unilever's Paul Polman: CEOs Can't Be "Slaves" to Shareholders', *Forbes*, 20 July 2015.
40 The USLP launch panel was moderated by Jonathan Dimbleby and featured 'intellectual architects' of the 'sustainability revolution' such as John Elkington (who coined the 'triple bottom line') and Jonathan Porritt (co-founder of the Prince of Wales's Business & Environment Programme and inaugural chair of Tony Blair's UK Sustainable Development Commission). See: Porritt, *Capitalism as if the World Matters*, London: Earthscan, 2005; Elkington, *Cannibals with Forks: The Triple Bottom Line of 21st Century Business*. Oxford: Capstone, 1999.
41 The USLP's three broad goals branch out into nine 'pillars' – covering health & hygiene, nutrition, greenhouse gases, water use, waste & packaging, sustainable sourcing, workplace fairness, opportunities for women, and inclusive business – and over 50 specific targets. See: Bartlett, 'Unilever's New Global Strategy', p. 3.
42 Bartlett, 'Unilever's New Global Strategy', pp. 4–5.
43 As of 2019, its members included Porritt (who had participated since 1996), Prof. Val Curtis (London School of Hygiene & Tropical Medicine), Christiana Figueres (former UNFCCC executive secretary), Katja Iversen (CEO of Women Deliver), Bill McDonough (the 'father of the circular economy'), Ricken Patel (Avaaz.org founder), Kavita Prakash-Mani (WWF markets), and Prof. John Ruggie (Harvard Kennedy School and intellectual architect of the Global Compact. See: Unilever, 'Our Sustainability Governance', available at: www.unilever.com.
44 Unilever, 'Our Brands', available at: www.unilever.com/brands.
45 Kyle Bailey, 'Stakeholder Capitalism Against Democracy: Relegitimising Global Neoliberalism', *Journal of Australian Political Economy*, 86, 2020, pp. 85–121.
46 'Unilever launches Global Foundation', Unilever global website, 27 January 2012.
47 Martin Cohen and Frédéric Leroy, 'The dark side of plant-based food', *The Conversation*, 10 December 2019. See also: Matthew Glover, 'Unilever, McDonalds & KFC Are Not the Enemy', Veganuary UK website, June 2018; Ben Selwyn, 'The Two Souls of Veganism', *The Bullet*, 21 January 2020, available at: www.socialistproject.ca.
48 Unilever, 'Reducing environmental impact by half', available at: www.unilever.com/sustainable-living/reducing-environmental-impact.
49 This £250 million 2% fixed rate bond was the first green bond issued in the sterling market and by a FMCG company. See: 'Unilever issues first ever green sustainability bond', available at: www.unilever.com/news/press-releases.

50 Unilever, 'Reducing environmental impact'.
51 Unilever, 'Reducing environmental impact'.
52 'Unilever's Sustainable Agriculture Code', UN One Planet network website, available at: www.oneplanetnetwork.org.
53 Unilever, 'Reducing environmental impact'.
54 Unilever, 'Reducing environmental impact'.
55 Greenpeace Southeast Asia, 'COP26 sponsor Unilever rises in the ranks to be the world's third worst plastic polluter according to 2021 Brand Audit', Greenpeace website, 25 October 2021, available at: www.greenpeace.org.
56 'The Surprising and Sensible Remarks of Unilever CEO Paul Polman', Center for Global Development blog, 18 February 2014, available at: www.cgdev.org.
57 Christian Sarkar, '"The Future of Branding is Activism" – An Interview with Unilever's Hanneke Faber', *Marketing Journal*, 10 February 2019. See also Kyle Bailey, 'Ben and Jerry's, Unilever, and Global Capitalist Apartheid', *The Bullet*, 22 July 2021, available at www.socialistproject.ca.
58 In 2019, Unilever's greenhouse gas impact 'per consumer' was around 6 per cent higher than in 2010, while its overall footprint of approximately 60 million metric tons of carbon dioxide equivalent was 15 per cent more than in 2010. In 2018, its water impact per consumer increased by roughly 1 per cent compared to 2010, leading the firm to admit that it remains 'a long way short' of halving its water impact. See: Unilever, 'Reducing environmental impact'.
59 Anmar Frangoul, 'Unilever lays out plans for $1 billion investment in climate and nature fund', *CNBC News*, 15 June 2020.
60 'Unilever to reward shareholders after restructuring plan, denies splitting speculation', *CNBC News*, 6 April 2017.
61 The original relocation proposal was supported by the Dutch Prime Minister, Mark Rutte – himself a former Unilever executive. See: Mehreen Khan, 'Unilever decision forces Dutch government to review controversial tax break', *Financial Times*, 5 October 2018; Zoe Wood, 'Unilever picks London as its home over Rotterdam', *The Guardian*, 11 June 2020.
62 Zoe Wood, 'Unilever surge makes it most valuable FTSE company at £121bn', *The Guardian*, 23 July 2020; Judith Evans, Attracta Mooney, and Arash Massoudi, 'Unilever back in political spotlight over UK return', *Financial Times*, 11 June 2020.
63 Notably, as younger consumers have increasingly ditched homogenous black tea for coffee and upmarket herbal teas promising 'wellness', Unilever revealed a month after announcing its London relocation plan that it would begin de-merging its historic tea business – including brands such as Lipton and Brooke Bond (the manufacturer of PG Tips). See: Nils Pratley, 'BT will hope to turn Huawei pain into gain by calling in favours', *The Guardian*, 30 January 2020.
64 Jope is also chair of UNICEF's Generation Unlimited, vice co-chair of the Consumer Goods Forum, a member of the WEF's International Business Council executive committee, and of the B20 International Advocacy Caucus (alongside the likes of Tony Blair, Klaus Schwab, Elon Musk, Mark Carney, and Michael Bloomberg).
65 'Unilever celebrates 10 years of the Sustainable Living Plan', available at: www.unilever.com/news/press-and-media/press-releases.
66 Bakan, 'Charming Psychopaths'.

67 David F. Murphy and Jem Bendell, 'Partners in Time? Business, NGOs and Sustainable Development', *UNRISD Discussion Paper No. 109*, United Nations Research Institute for Social Development, August 1999, p. 38.
68 David L. Levy, 'Environmental Management as Political Sustainability', *Organization & Environment*, 10(2), June 1997, pp. 126–47.
69 Such 'best practices', championed by Unilever, are already being generalized across the capitalist system. See, for instance, Anglo-American's 'Sustainable Mining Plan'.
70 Eelke M. Heemskerk, *Decline of the Corporate Community: Network Dynamics of the Dutch Business Elite*, Amsterdam: Amsterdam University Press, 2007, p. 144.
71 Ellen Meiksins Wood, *Democracy Against Capitalism*, London: Verso, 1995; Wood, *Empire of Capital*, London: Verso, 2003; Kyle Bailey, 'The Empire of "Global Civil Society": Corporations, NGOs, and International Development', in Debra Chapman, Tania Ruiz-Chapman, and Peter Eglin, eds, *The Global Citizenship Nexus: Critical Studies*, New York: Routledge, 2020.
72 See, for instance, David Whyte, '"Death to the Corporation": A Modest Proposal', in Leo Panitch and Greg Albo, eds, *Socialist Register 2019: A World Turned Upside Down*, New York: Monthly Review Press, 2019.

TRANSNATIONAL CAPITAL AND REGULATING AFRICAN EXTRACTIVES: ZIMBABWE'S BLOOD DIAMONDS

RICHARD SAUNDERS

In the 2000s, voluntary schemes for the regulation of the global extractive industries emerged prominently in response to rising public criticism and activism which highlighted the role of the sector in fuelling violent political conflict, fostering corruption, and promoting multiple overlapping development distortions. Critical advocacy campaigns by domestic social movements and international NGOs brought to global attention notorious cases of abuse perpetrated by transnational oil, gas, and mining companies. African cases of extractives' destructive impacts featured prominently, from the Niger Delta to the diamond fields of Sierra Leone and Angola and beyond. The corrective to this situation, the extractive industries argued, in conjunction with western governments and Southern commodity-trading states, was the establishment of voluntary self-regulatory mechanisms.

These initiatives, convened and led by private sector interests and including multi-stakeholder membership, emerged as a defining feature of the international regulation of extractives in the early 2000s. They would play a key role in redefining regulatory standards for the production, trade, and financing of extractives, with their influence extending to a wide range of natural resource sectors including forestry management and palm oil production, as well as issues of biodiversity.[1] Voluntary schemes soon displaced state regulatory codes, laws, and other mechanisms which had defined state-capital relations across the Global South. The simultaneous and combined transnationalization and privatization of extractives regulation would drive a dramatic shift in global mining regulation away from the priorities of publicly-defined extractives strategies in host countries, towards the privileging of transnational capital's interests.[2] The latter included the development of codes around transactional 'transparency', 'fair-dealing' practices, and 'ethical' standards that could be deployed by dominant Western players for gatekeeping purposes in gaining access to resources in increasingly competitive global mining markets. As one early critic noted, such schemes amounted to the establishment of a 'new transnational legal order' under the leadership of the dominant fractions of transnational capital.[3]

In Africa, important questions were raised around the substance, direction, and impact of the new emerging order before the end of their first decade. Accumulating evidence suggested that freshly minted multi-stakeholder initiatives were assisting African political-economic elites in their efforts to consolidate rent-seeking by closer integration into global value chains. Compliance with market-led ethical standards both buoyed the flow of African minerals into international commodities markets and strengthened, rather than disrupted, opportunities for local elites to divert mineral rents into parallel realms of private accumulation: ethical cleansing, elite predation, and accumulation compacts between capital and local states were seamlessly linked. A critical factor in this dispensation was the structural privileging of government and industry interests in the funding, management, and technically-grounded activities within the extractives regulatory schemes – and the corresponding marginalization of the voices and priorities of their tripartite partners, civil society, and social movements. Codified standards influenced by the priorities of governments and leading industry actors set low bars for transactional compliance and became difficult to renovate in keeping with a changing production and trading terrain. By the 2010s the growing gap between the interests and effective power of governments and industry, on the one hand, and civil society, on the other, emerged as a primary target of renewed civil society activism in Africa around resource governance. Struggles by civil society activists to reform various transnational schemes by loosening the entrenched power of governments and mining capital remained a defining feature of popular engagement with transnational extractives regulation into the 2020s.

The African experience of voluntary regulatory schemes in the 2000s points to the need for a close assessment of these initiatives and a critical reappraisal by progressive social forces of how to engage them. Important unresolved questions revolve around the viability of effective local participation and popular resource governance practices under these schemes, and the capacity of progressive African social movements for sustaining a meaningful critical role within the structural constraints of transnational regulation. While recognizing that different institutional architectures among private-public regulatory schemes have created different opportunities for popular actors to engage effectively in strengthening regulatory outcomes, this essay draws on the case of Zimbabwe's diamond sector and its emergence in the 2000s as a focal point of intense power struggles within the Kimberley Process Certification Scheme (KP), the international voluntary agreement established in 2003 with the aim of eliminating the burgeoning trade in conflict diamonds centred in West and Central Africa. The case of Zimbabwe's diamonds evoked both early hopes of the KP's capacity to discipline and contain the violent and politically corrosive looting of critical public resources, and later realizations that the body forcefully served to consolidate and institutionalize predatory rent-seeking and market power. Drawing on the experiences of the KP in Zimbabwe, it is argued that the specific convergence of interests among African states and elites, global mining capital, and multilateral political actors in international voluntary regulatory bodies has raised new threats to the mobilization of critical resource governance strategies by African social movements and progressive forces.

A 'NEW' ORDER EMERGES

In the 2000s, a hallmark of global mining capital's approach to resource governance was the inclusion of notions of public participation, tripartism, and transparency in new private-public regulatory conventions. The foregrounding of international benchmarks around transparency and transactional best practices was politically and financially supported by governments in the West and South, international financial institutions, and multilateral development agencies including agencies of the United Nations, and public and private donors from mining countries in the West. The common strategy informing these schemes – the orientation of regulatory principles around the transactional 'best practices' as defined by the leading extractives industry players – deeply influenced the centre of gravity of domestic policy debates and popular advocacy in Africa and across mineral-rich countries in the Global South. In many ways the 'new normal' of international resource governance schemes would continue to shape the contours of policy contestations around extractives' management into the 2020s.

While formally multi-stakeholder in membership and internal governance, the new initiatives which emerged in the 2000s were dominated from the outset by industry and government, with significant support from bilateral and multilateral donors. An important benchmark in this process was the Extractive Industries Transparency Initiative (EITI), established in 2003, which quickly rose to prominence as perhaps the most far-reaching of these schemes. Bolstered by strong financial and political support from the IFIs, governments and industry, by the 2020s the EITI stood as the global extractive sectors most well-established voluntary regulatory scheme, with a permanent secretariat funded by bilateral and multilateral donors and industry, and a membership including 55 country governments, leading transnational extractives players, and a wide range of civil society actors including more than 50 organizations from Africa.[4] Its initial goals of developing standards and rules aimed at enhancing transparency around minerals payments and revenue distribution, however, would increasingly be called into question by social movement critics and progressives, who pointed to the EITI's industry-friendly displacement effect on progressive strategies for resource governance.[5]

A similar tripartite approach involving voluntary self-regulation stood behind the formation of the KP, formally launched in 2003 with the main aim of preventing the flow of 'blood diamonds' (or more commonly, 'conflict diamonds') into the global diamond trade.[6] The KP came in direct response to a campaign by resource governance and human rights NGOs which revealed the role of the diamond trade in fuelling and sustaining organized political violence, including notably the civil conflicts in Sierra Leone, Liberia, and Angola in the 1990s.[7] A 2000 report suggested that this was a predominantly African problem, with African countries accounting for the bulk of conflict diamonds, then estimated to make up 15 per cent of the total global trade.[8] Under the political stewardship of diamond-exporting governments, and in collaboration with the global diamond industry and civil society actors who had been prominent in conflict diamonds campaigns, the KP was established to formulate rules and oversight mechanisms to ensure the legitimate chain of custody in the extraction, handling, and export of rough diamonds (stones which have not been processed by means of cutting and polishing). Wide international support came in the form of endorsement of the KP by resolutions of the UN General Assembly and UN Security Council,[9] by the G8, the World Bank and other international financial institutions. Although a voluntary entity rather than a legally binding treaty, the KP's effective reach was wide, because international diamond markets aligned with the KP were barred from accepting rough diamonds from non-member states. For most diamond exporting countries, therefore, participation in the KP was effectively mandatory. It was also legally enforceable at the national level: the KP's minimum compliance criteria obliged member governments to enact legislation bringing their diamond production, security controls, trading statistics, and related measures into alignment with KP standards. To carry out its priority tasks, including the monitoring of members for compliance, tracking of production statistics, and establishment of standards for diamond valuation and taxation, the KP established a set of tripartite Working Groups. Compliant countries were permitted to issue KP certificates, certifying their stones were conflict-free and met minimum KP protocols for security, documentation, and statistical record keeping; non-compliant countries faced the threat of suspension as approved diamond exporters.[10]

By the 2010s the KP claimed to have prevented 99.8 per cent of the world's conflict diamonds from entering the legal global trade.[11] However, this assertion was soon hotly contested from within the KP, as civil society members, grouped in the Civil Society Coalition (CSC), pointed to a rising wave of diamond related violence in a number of member countries in Africa and Latin America. Ensuing debates would reveal critical conceptual and administrative shortcomings embedded in the KP at the time of its founding. One problem stemmed from the KP's original definition of 'conflict diamonds'. In 2003, this definition entailed stones extracted in the context of organized violence perpetrated by anti-government rebels, a definition which fits closely with the situations in Sierra Leone and Angola that had preceded the KP's establishment. Yet in the 2000s, the CSC and others argued, recurring instances of organized and extreme violence were in evidence. Much of this violence was perpetrated by governments themselves, not rebel forces. But because 'legitimate authorities' were the source of diamond-related conflict, the stones extracted did not fit the criteria of 'conflict' established by the KP and were therefore deemed to be in compliance with the scheme's protocols. A CSC campaign to revise the definition of conflict diamonds to fit the changed conditions of the 2000s was consistently resisted and blocked by the KP. This pointed to a second weakness within the scheme: the decision-making convention established in the KP Core Document, which required consensus-based decision-making on critical issues. In practice, this convention enabled a handful of reform-averse governments to block changes to the KP's operating principles and practices; by extension, it also ensured that dissenting member governments could delay or defer the disciplining of non-compliant countries, effectively erasing the threat of sanctions for even egregious cases of compliance violations.[12] By the 2010s, groups of allied governments formed within the KP to blunt efforts at internal KP reforms and derail efforts to sanction non-compliant countries.

Africa's extractives sector was a critical terrain for KP interventions starting in the early 2000s, with the KP focusing much of its efforts over the past two decades on 'regularizing' diamond extraction on the continent. The global positioning of Africa as a key anchor in extractives value chains – and consequently, as the site of intense competition among established global mining players like Canada, Australia, and South Africa, and emerging

Southern powerhouses including China, Brazil, and India – helped to catalyze pressure by Western governments, allied global mining capital and commodity markets for the accession of African mineral producers to such regulatory standards. It is a scenario currently being replayed in light of rising global concerns with renewable energy transition, in which Africa's world-class reserves of critical minerals like cobalt, copper, lithium, and nickel, among others, feature prominently; the Democratic Republic of the Congo alone accounts for 66 per cent of the global supply of cobalt, critical in the manufacture of EV batteries and other green energy technologies. The drive to lock in access to reliable mineral value chains has placed African mining countries at the heart of intense competition among global extractives firms, mineral traders, and manufacturers linked to renewable energy markets.

At the same time, African governments were relatively receptive to new regulatory mechanisms that both promised to facilitate new investment and offered opportunities for local elite participation in the global commodities boom. Pressures to align with standards of transactional transparency were weighed against the costs of exclusion, including the deep discounting of parallel market exports and the threat of financial sanctions leveraged through the withholding of Official Development Assistance and other donor aid. African governments' widespread accession to the new extractives regulatory dispensation was codified in the African Mining Vision (AMV), a broad strategy for African mining established in 2009 and endorsed by 54 heads of state.[13] Developed with important technical inputs from the United Nations Economic Commission for Africa,[14] the AMV closely reproduced two key pillars of the emerging international voluntary extractives regime. It both affirmed the role of national governments in leading the coordination of mining's expansion and the local embedding of regulatory standards, and unambiguously endorsed those rules' adherence to a new extractivist approach which saw economic growth as being heavily leveraged on local participation in global commodity markets.[15] Under the AMV, the expansion of Africa's extractive industries would include the integration of local players and interests – for example, artisanal and small-scale miners, and local manufacturers and mine suppliers – through the state-led nurturing of productive linkages. For some critics of African extractive industries, the foregrounding of African states' roles represented a transformational step forward.[16] However the AMV's underlying assumption was that these advances at the local level would depend importantly on the broader stabilization and growth of national mining sectors, which in turn rested on the establishment of attractive investment conditions. Those conditions included now-familiar norms involving state-capital transactional transparency, such as taxation and contracting rules aligned with new transnational standards. As a result, some saw the transformational thrust of the AMV's blueprint as endangered from the outset by the realities of the global commodity markets to which it was moored. Slow progress in implementing the AMV's recommendations at the national level appeared to confirm this view.[17]

The AMV's 'home-grown' approach was, unsurprisingly, enthusiastically supported by the global mining players and received significant political support from international financial institutions and multilateral development agencies. But the AMV's parallel appeal to actors in civil society and local mining sectors would pose further challenges, notably in growing campaigns for strengthened resource governance in the 2000s. Leading African civil society organizations working on extractives firmly embraced the AMV's principles and recommendations, including for example, the Alternative Mining Indaba, a network of progressive labour groups, community-based organizations, and NGOs. For resource governance activists, the enforcement of standards around transactional transparency and other monitoring innovations were seen as enabling challenges to systemic transgressions by state agencies, foreign miners, and mineral trading networks. In reality, innovations of this kind in the AMV, like those in other private voluntary regulatory initiatives, were disappointingly slow to materialize and low in impact. More important, perhaps, was the disarming effect these initiatives had on local policy debates, and particularly on interventions from critical actors and popular constituencies. For nearly two decades, the benchmarks of 'inclusive', 'participatory', 'ethical', and 'equitable' extractives regulation in Africa would be dominated by frameworks largely designed by the extractives industries themselves, in collaboration with national elites in mining countries. The profoundly negative consequences of this systematic inclusion/demobilization of popular constituencies under the regulatory regimes of the 2000s would become most apparent at the country level, where the power of transnational mining capital and state elites converged to enforce that order's often violent – and rarely transparent – mode of accumulation.

NEW FACETS OF OLD POWER: THE KP IN ZIMBABWE

The case of Zimbabwe's alluvial diamonds stands as a sobering example of how the convergent interests of global mining capital and national elites in the KP's country-level interventions blunted the scheme's capacity to enforce greater transparency and reduce violent conflict in diamond mining and facilitated the consolidation and legitimization of elite and transnational accumulation strategies. Mediated through the KP, Zimbabwe's emerging diamond sector was transformed from a network of small-scale mining linked to parallel markets into a formalized sector of government-linked commercial miners operating with international legitimacy. In this transition, efforts by civil society to bring greater transparency to the public management of diamond resources and strengthen domestic participation and sharing in the resulting revenues were derailed by administrative and political manoeuvres within the KP. At the same time, the Zimbabwe state's aggressive harassment of mining community representatives and local civil society critics, often with the tacit consent if not active support of Zimbabwe's political allies within the KP, further eroded the foundations of a viable resource governance for diamonds. As a result, the KP's intervention would underscore the unmatched regulatory power of domestic elites and international market allies within the KP, call into question the scheme's willingness and capacity to critically supervise the global trade, and threaten the legitimacy and purpose of the KP itself. Given the eventual resounding defeat of civil society activism within the KP, the Zimbabwe case also raised difficult questions about the viability of civil society participation in the scheme and the alternative strategies available to popular movements seeking to contest and transform practices within global diamond value chains.

Marange, Zimbabwe: diamonds in a field of conflicts

In 2006, an internationally significant deposit of alluvial diamonds in Marange District in eastern Zimbabwe was revealed by the UK-registered company which had recently taken control of the disused claim.[18] Like most alluvial deposits, the Marange strike was relatively accessible and could be exploited, initially at least, without the need for capital intensive mechanization or the use of foreign-dominated technology. While it offered opportunities for domestic-led production, it also meant the resource was initially more difficult to secure and monitor. While the value of the diamond strike was initially unclear, evidence of vast potential revenues soon emerged from the informal, mostly unsupervised artisanal mining first encouraged by the government in 2006. By 2010, up to 20 per cent of the global rough diamond trade was estimated to come from the Marange fields, much of it via parallel markets,[19] with one industry expert predicting annual exports of about $2 billion and others suggesting a likely 20-year mining cycle.[20] While these forecasts would later prove to be overly optimistic, industry consensus was that Marange represented a globally significant and lucrative diamond resource.

Within Zimbabwe, the promise of diamond revenues came in the midst of a spiralling political and economic crisis – a context which would play a large role in shaping the state's initial response to the new opportunity. The early 2000s were marked by a fiscal and political crisis of the state punctuated by the first waves of economic fallout from fast-track land resettlement and the crash of commercial agriculture, compounded by rapid deindustrialization, donor boycotts, and worsening foreign exchange shortages. By 2006 the ruling Zimbabwe African National Union – Patriotic Front (ZANU-PF) government of President Robert Mugabe faced a surging challenge from the Movement for Democratic Change (MDC), the main opposition party led by Morgan Tsvangirai. Indigenization of foreign-owned businesses and the wider economic participation of Zimbabweans soon became ideological pillars of ZANU-PF's governing platform in defence against MDC critiques of ZANU-PF corruption, militarization, and maladministration. It was in this context that in 2006 ZANU-PF officials publicly invited popular occupation of the Marange diamond fields, displacing the UK commercial mining company which legally held the claim and 'reclaiming' the resource for the people. Within weeks, more than twenty thousand informal small-scale miners – including informal diggers, organized gangs, local residents and individuals from around the country, and international parallel market traders – descended on Marange.

The resulting chaos of what became known as the 'free-for-all' phase of diamond mining generated myriad contradictory outcomes: widespread access to surface diamond deposits by impoverished individuals mediated by patterns of extreme violence and sexual assault; rapid accumulation of wealth in local hands alongside dismal revenue flows to state coffers; and government promises of local development and investment followed by uncompensated displacement, extensive environmental degradation, and a decline in social infrastructure commitments. Weakening the state's monitoring and supervisory presence in Marange by encouraging informal extraction, the Zimbabwe government thereby ensured that its parastatal mining and minerals marketing entities were marginalized from the main action.[21] Allegations soon emerged of elite and security agencies' involvement in the burgeoning parallel trade in rough diamonds. By early 2007, the large-scale intervention of police forces in the diamond fields confirmed early reports of security force and elite collusion in the underground trade. Rather than eliminating informal mining, national security agencies appeared to have captured it with the aim of systematizing and controlling diamond extraction for elite benefit. In 2008, with a closely contested election in which the MDC prevailed and a dramatically worsening macroeconomic climate, ZANU-PF moved to lock in control of Marange's diamond wealth, declaring the area a national security zone and shrouding production from close inspection. A tidal wave of violence was unleashed by state security agencies later that year with the aim of consolidating control over Marange. This resulted in the deaths of more than 200 miners and local residents amid reports of widespread gross human rights abuses.[22] First reported by local researchers, the diamond massacres soon sparked an international outcry over the world's latest case of 'blood diamonds'.[23] Marange quickly emerged as an urgent focus of attention for the KP.

The KP in Zimbabwe: 2006-2011

Zimbabwe had joined the KP in 2003, after which it began the process of aligning its national regulatory standards with those of the scheme, thereby enabling diamond exports from an established Australian-owned mine. A KP country review mission to the recently opened Marange fields was made in 2007 at the height of the 'free-for-all' phase of mining, when informalized mining was widespread and international smuggling networks were already rampant and documented. Astonishingly, the 2007 KP monitoring team gave Marange and Zimbabwe a clean bill of health. KP CSC members, reviewing the mission visit and its unexpected positive verdict, found that the mission team under the leadership of an official from the ZANU-PF-allied Russian government had been shepherded for the duration of its visit by Zimbabwe government officials, and prevented from obtaining independent testimony from witnesses of abuse or visiting the Marange diamond fields to inspect local conditions. This manipulation of the KP's review mission raised questions about the precedent being set in Zimbabwe for KP monitoring. So, when reports of large-scale killings and human rights abuses by state security agencies in Marange in 2008 came to light in early 2009, there was intense debate within the KP about how to respond. The Zimbabwe government refuted reports of state-led violence and breakdowns in security in the handling of diamonds, and resisted pressure from within the KP for a new revision mission. But in the face of new CSC reports from Marange and rising industry concerns, Harare agreed to a review visit in mid-year organized under the chairmanship of Namibia – another supportive ZANU-PF ally. The new mission heard testimony of extreme violence waged by state security forces on local miners and communities, noted the 'securitization' of the diamond fields by the national military, and uncovered serious shortfalls in protocols to safeguard the legitimate chain of custody in the handling of Marange diamonds.[24] The evidence was compelling and unambiguous, and suggested that Marange's diamonds were non-compliant with KP standards in several key areas and should be sanctioned from accessing global markets.

The 2009 mission report provoked a new round of conflict within the

KP, deepening the fault lines between the CSC, some industry members, and governments on the one hand, and the Zimbabwe government and its political allies, including then-KP Chair Namibia, on the other. Using the Chair's administrative authority, Namibia fought to suppress the 2009 report's details and recommendations, including the suggestion that Zimbabwe should be suspended by the KP Plenary in Namibia later that year. At the meeting, civil society witnesses from Marange were barred from participating and traditional leaders from Marange were pressured to disavow reports of state abuses. But despite these irregular interventions allowed by the Chair, threats posed to diamond retail markets and the prospect of further CSC advocacy campaigns pushed the Plenary to impose a qualified suspension of Zimbabwe's diamond exports. A Joint Work Plan was agreed to steer the country into compliance, supervised by a KP-appointed South African Monitor, and it was agreed that Marange miners could resume exports once they demonstrated compliance.[25] In principle, Zimbabwe's diamond exports remained blocked until November 2011. In reality, the Zimbabwe government and its KP allies concertedly whittled away the restrictions, while opening multiple alternative channels for diamond exports even if these had not been approved by the KP Plenary.

While Zimbabwe's 2009 suspension was initially celebrated by CSC progressives, the strict limitations of the victory soon became clear. While the most serious human rights abuses of 2008 ended, there was no accountability for the perpetrators, admission by the state of its culpability, or compensation for victims, and no agreed mechanisms within the KP for addressing these issues. Meanwhile, ZANU-PF's response to the terms of the Joint Work Plan would lead to new abuses in Marange. The government's strategic shift away from informal mining and towards the contracting of mechanized commercial miners in Marange – a move to align the country with the KP's preferred model of extraction – led directly to the large-scale displacement of local communities. There were forced relocations of villages and homesteads without compensation, and unmet promises of community investment by the new companies. Persistent harassment and threats of violence against people living near the diamond fields were perpetrated by government and mining companies alike.[26] The government's lack of transparency around diamond revenues and diamond exports records, a recurring complaint of the CSC and KP officials during the 'free-for-all' phase, continued, and indeed likely *worsened* and became more entrenched during the formalization period.

Formalization, compliance, consolidation: the ethics of elite pacts

The paradox of Zimbabwe's formalization period is that the country successfully moved into compliance with KP norms while systematizing destructive forms of elite rent-seeking, engaging in highly suspect diamond trading practices, and continuing to use state-sponsored violence as a leveraging tool over miners and their communities. The contradictions of the Zimbabwe case pointed to profound weaknesses in the KP's administrative and political structures, which generated highly uneven relations of power both within the KP and at the national level of its country members. At both scales, the standing, capacity, and voice of the CSC, popular organizations, and social movements were attacked, marginalized, and otherwise undermined. The priorities of diamond trading markets and local elites were privileged and buttressed. In many ways, formalization provided states, elites, and industry a licence for the codification of their interests and power in the process of bringing a country into KP compliance – and legitimacy.

The problem of member countries' state institutional integrity represented a key challenge in this regard. The Zimbabwe case reflected a wider problem within the KP. In the 2000s the ZANU-PF leadership had deliberately weakened state bureaucratic autonomy and professionalism, leading to the uneven capture of state institutions by competing factions of the ruling party and the rise of ministerial diktat as a form of bureaucratic administration.[27] The state's restructuring from above, which included its creeping militarization, created opportunities for the institutionalization of rent-seeking by factions of elites.[28] In the extractives sector this was reflected in the expanding economic participation of state and ruling party-based elites through the shedding of public mining holdings into private hands via untendered asset sales, hazily constructed joint ventures and arrays of shell companies held offshore, a pattern widely reproduced and documented in a range of other economic sectors.[29] This trend was compounded by ZANU-PF-MDC power sharing arrangements during the Government of National Unity (2009-2013), when cohabitation saw control over ministries allocated on a party basis. The fragmentation and selective capture of state institutions played out with devastating effect in the mining sector, where Obert Mpofu, the ZANU-PF mining minister, undertook the secretive licensing of hand-picked new operators in Marange in 2009 and after. In overseeing the entry of new commercial operators, he ignored the entreaties of his ministry's professional staff, unhindered by established licensing protocols, and undertook no public consultation – irregular prejudicial practices later confirmed by a parliamentary investigation headed by a ZANU-PF Member of Parliament.[30] Mpofu's criteria for the selection of new diamond miners skewed heavily towards the ruling party and allied national security agencies, including the Zimbabwe National Army and the Zimbabwe Republic Police.³¹ As senior security agency officials weighed in heavily on diamond decision-making, ministries with a direct interest in diamonds management, notably the MDC-controlled Ministry of Finance and the Zimbabwe Revenue Authority, were kept at arm's length.³² The architecture for systemic, institutionalized rent-seeking was therefore established under the umbrella of the KP.

The consequences were predictable and widely reported. Inconsistent and dubious diamond revenue flows to the state treasury, secret contracts and prejudicial taxation deals with ruling party allies, the obscured role of anonymous shell companies registered offshore, and the continuation of a vigorous illicit trade in Marange stones: all were well-documented in reports available to the KP.³³ While the 2009 ban on exports and continuing international sanctions on Zimbabwe provided government and exporters cover for shrouding their diamond dealings and encouraging parallel market trading, the lifting of the export ban in 2011 led to further uncovering of questionable state practices. Further revelations emerged of the government's unusually generous tax concessions in licensing contracts to its business partners. There was weak oversight, and state representation on the boards of joint venture diamond companies was entirely absent. The state only loosely enforced reporting rules for diamond exports, and tolerated comparatively weak commitments to local development by mining companies.³⁴ These anomalies stood behind a series of inexplicable revenue shortfalls in the 2010s, amid new allegations of significant transfer pricing fixes and officials' involvement in a parallel trade.³⁵ A 2012 investigation by a leading CSC member documented organized networks of smuggling, transfer pricing, tax evasion, and other non-compliant criminal activity attached to the formal mining and marketing operations put in place under ZANU-PF, and wryly observed,

> While the government has won praise from some quarters for 'regularizing' operations in Marange by bringing in new joint venture partners, there continues to be an entirely unrecorded, parallel trade of diamonds that is not only known to, but condoned by, those senior government officials.³⁶

KP fallouts: the end of the tripartite myth

Within the KP, the disappointing economic and development consequences of ZANU-PF's unfolding compliance strategy, and the continuing threat of rights abuses, became the subject of intense debate. In important ways,

Zimbabwe became a litmus test for the viability of the KP's established monitoring mechanisms, and more broadly, for the sustainability of the KP as a tripartite body and its legitimacy as a guarantor of a diamond's conflict-free status. A 2010 discussion paper prepared by the CSC for the KP highlighted critical points of dysfunction and the need for organizational reform.[37] Drawing on the case of Zimbabwe and other 'anomalies' of KP compliance, the coalition cited the need to restructure the KP's funding and monitoring procedures with the aim of enhancing consistency, transparency, and accountability. It recommended that the considerable power of member governments – not infrequently the source of violations of KP standards – should be reconsidered and more closely calibrated with that of other tripartite members. It also held that the independence of the KP's Working Group on Monitoring, a key component of compliance monitoring, should be guaranteed through financial and political support, and strengthened with the inclusion of independent, politically autonomous expertise. The CSC report further called for the KP's formal recognition of the need to redefine the key term 'conflict diamonds' to include stones extracted under conditions of human rights abuses – a point, the report noted, which had been considered by the KP's founding members in early drafts of the scheme's Core Document.[38]

The CSC's report, both as a discussion document and a manifesto for reform, came amid heightened tensions surrounding the circumstances of the KP's role in Zimbabwe. They would together define the limits of the KP tripartite model and confirm the increasingly dysfunctional, uneven balance of power with the scheme.

In a further encroachment on the KP's monitoring norms, new reports of diamond violence in Zimbabwe in 2010 nevertheless were accompanied by irregular recommendations from the KP-appointed Zimbabwe Monitor for the lifting of sanctions on some Marange commercial operators, despite serious unaddressed security violations.[39] But renewed civil society advocacy around Zimbabwe was confronted by increasingly aggressive push-back by the Zimbabwe government. Mining Minister Mpofu repeatedly attacked CSC campaigners inside and outside the KP who pushed for continuing sanctions, deploying resource nationalist rhetoric to bully critics as unpatriotic saboteurs.[40] It was a strategy assisted by KP industry members with the implicit backing of the World Diamond Council. International donors also provided incentives for the softening of criticism by CSC members. Competition among civil society organizations for donor funding and government recognition frequently parlayed into greater tolerance for compromise with industry within the KP, and helped to stoke divisions among civil society organizations, and within mining communities themselves. Organizations which eschewed the 'normalization' of elite predation, community displacement, and other consequences of the emerging new model of diamond mining found themselves increasingly in disfavour with funders, isolated under government's divide-and-rule approach to civil society, excluded from national debates, hampered in information gathering, and rendered more vulnerable to harassment by the diamond mining companies. For example, the Chiadzwa Community Development Trust, a local community organization formed in Marange to challenge the inequitable and heavy-handed relocation of residents from diamond mining areas, was harassed and marginalized in local government's management of relocations, while counter-organizations patronized by state authorities were recognized as community representatives.[41] Similar government tactics and intra-civil society divisions were mirrored within the KP. In mid 2010, the arrest by Zimbabwean security police of a prominent Zimbabwe CSC member implicated the KP Monitor himself as a contributing actor, further fuelling tensions within the body. The activist was only released following negotiations led by the KP's World Diamond Council industry grouping that resulted in the further relaxation of sanctions on Zimbabwe. There were allegations of hostage-taking aimed at obtaining market access, facilitated by the mediation of industry interests within the KP.[42] At the same time, the CSC's reform thrust was deflected by the KP, which pointedly offered little to guarantee better protection of CSC members from member states' threats. The creation of a 'Local Focal Point' for CSC members in Zimbabwe, ostensibly to strengthen protections for such actors and activists, resulted in further pressures on local CSC members to align with the government's perspectives on compliance measures.[43]

By 2011, exasperated by the KP's lack of adherence to its own principles and its hostility to civil society voices, the CSC walked out of the KP's mid-year meeting. It subsequently boycotted the annual Plenary in November 2011, at which the green light was given for the lifting of remaining export restrictions on Marange's stones. It was the beginning of the end of the KP's pretence of being a functionally multi-stakeholder body. Founding CSC members led by Global Witness withdrew permanently from the body, unwilling to condone and legitimize its continuing irregularities.[44] Several leading CSC members would follow. For Ian Smillie, a prominent founding member of the KP who had resigned in protest in 2009, the shredding of the KP's regulatory mission was the work of 'governments and the others that are currently active behind the scenes', for whom 'business and politics trump human rights and the very purpose of the Kimberley Process; …

trump good management; … trump common sense and decency; and trump the long-term interest of the entire diamond industry'.[45] South Africa, the new KP Chair in 2013, weakly attempted to salvage the situation by promising to foreground the human rights concerns of the CSC within the body's monitoring. But hostile governments blocked further progress and the CSC's reform push quickly faded. A further benchmark of the CSC's rupture with the KP came in 2016, when Dubai and the United Arab Emirates became KP Chair against the firm objections of the CSC.[46] In the face of promised but unrealized reforms by the incoming Chair, a full CSC boycott of Dubai's chairmanship took place and further CSC resignations ensued. The KP offered the concession of a three-year cycle of reform led by an Ad Hoc Committee on Review and Reform to address CSC concerns; the cycle ended with no progress and continued resistance to change by a small group of states including Zimbabwe.[47] IMPACT, a founding KP CSC member from Canada, issued a devastating assessment as it left the scheme in 2017:

> *The so-called KP family has proved to be dysfunctional.* After three years of excruciating negotiations on reform, the KP has said this week: *We agree that we don't agree on anything substantial.* The Civil Society Coalition is sure that many among you will not even agree to that … While many of you will return to your capitals in triumph or victory for having obstructed widening the KP remit, we will return to our communities who suffer from torture, sexual abuse and killings at the hands of private and public security forces …[48]

IMPACT warned of the collateral damage to the diamond industry itself arising from its efforts to block meaningful reform:

> Dear colleagues in government and in industry. Money laundering, synthetics, human rights violations, illicit trade, formalization of artisanal miners – you risk being overtaken by these emerging issues if you keep clinging on to the idea of the KP from 2003. That KP is obsolete. Your failure to reform has made it so.[49]

By the early 2020s, there was little evidence that this wakeup call had been heard by industry or governments in the KP. A new CSC report pointed to the key contradiction at the KP's heart, arguing that 'the lack of consensus in addressing problems like diamond-related violence may also reflect prevailing commercial dynamics in the global diamond supply chain that can incentivize states to maintain the current status quo ... (f)or some, bad ethics makes for good business'.⁵⁰ As one CSC member surmised, the KP was 'first and foremost a government-dominated body serving to protect national diamond-sector interests'.⁵¹ The most capacitated CSC members responded to the collapse of tripartism by leaving the body. By 2022 the rump of the CSC was comprised almost entirely of Africa-based organizations, many of which were vulnerable to government pressure and faced greater technical resource shortages than the CSC's former Western NGO members.⁵²

Confirming the decisive shift in power in the 2010s and underscoring the weakened position of the remaining CSC members, the KP increasingly tolerated attacks on its African CSC members, which became more frequent and often more aggressive.⁵³ The ground for this harassment of KP activists at the national level, which had been seeded by Zimbabwe in the midst of its KP crisis in 2009-2012, was repeatedly reaped by other KP government members in subsequent years. A touchstone of the disciplining behaviour of governments and donors was the KP's post-2011 consensus on Marange: those who rejected the decisions of the primary global body certifying acceptable practice could be dismissed as harbouring alternative agendas and dealt with via political means. The chilling effect on vigorous investigation of rights abuses and other aspects of non-compliance was palpable. In Zimbabwe, the highly contentious 2015 restructuring of Marange production through the establishment of a single state diamond mining company and the subsequent shrouded reincorporation of favoured players, proceeded with little fanfare and even less concern within the KP⁵⁴ – even while local organizations continued to report criminal activity, state-mediated violence, and illegal market trade into the late 2010s.⁵⁵ Then-President Mugabe's infamous quip in 2016, that as much as $15 billion in diamond revenues had gone missing and therefore something needed to be done, stood more as a political meme than as a point of serious concern and reflection within the KP. Six years later, Zimbabwe was set to assume the KP Chair for the first time.

The Zimbabwe case raises important questions about the limits of creative progressive activism at the local and international levels within bodies like the KP, and particularly the difficulties faced in efforts to shift the focus of regulatory schemes from issues of market security towards challenges of participation, equity, and social and economic benefits. It also points to the effective marginalization, fragmentation, and silencing of progressive resource governance campaigns at the national level, and the tacit consolidation of elite-industry compacts built around the privatization of access to extractive resources. Despite several years of concerted Zimbabwean and international civil society activism within the KP calling for stronger inclusive resource governance, greater mining transparency, and fairer redistribution of diamond mining revenues and production opportunities, the KP-compliant model of diamond mining which emerged in the 2010s succeeded in achieving a key goal of the scheme's dominant interests: the formalization of local political and military elite power, exercised in collaboration with leading corporate players in the global diamond trade.

This toxic convergence of local elite, state, business, and donor interests around a regulatory model which had few teeth and less inclination to address the systemic challenges of the trade underscored the dominant power embedded within the voluntary scheme and the extreme vulnerability – and limited effectiveness – of popular organizations within it. Yet new reform efforts by social movements and NGOs outside the KP, including a 'KP+' strategy mooted by some former CSC members, proved challenging to initiate given the recent negative experiences within the scheme. Twenty years after its establishment and a decade following the first exodus of key civil society players – and the beginning of the collapse of its claim to multi-stakeholder legitimacy – the KP remained the only global regulatory scheme for certifying the ethical provenance of rough diamonds.

CHALLENGING THE NEW NORMAL

Two decades of African struggles around international extractives governance provide sobering lessons for African activists and social movements. In the 2000s, the repackaging and ethical cleansing of transnational mining capital's power converged with the reassertion of national elites' role within international regulatory schemes to produce a formidable alliance of industry and state actors defending a consolidated market-oriented extractives status quo. An important consequence was the accumulation of limitations on civil society constituencies and social movement actors both within and outside of recent multi-stakeholder initiatives. This growing power gap between tripartite partners was especially stark in Africa. Since the early 2000s, growing evidence of capacity weaknesses and political and institutional vulnerabilities posed critical questions for resource governance constituencies around the terms of engagement with extractives sector regulatory bodies, and the need for alternative strategies for contesting the power of global extractives capital. For the left, there is a need to understand and respond to the disempowering features of regulatory schemes, and to develop strategies for contesting their normalization of extractives capital's power and the formalization of elite anti-developmental rent-seeking. Debates around the KP are instructive.

Liberal reform agendas in the 2010s and 2020s continued to place faith in the KP's model of voluntary tripartite regulation. Analysts argued that the political shortcomings of the KP as seen in Marange and other contested cases of officially 'compliant' producers could be addressed by strengthening stakeholder participation or tinkering with the legal framework of the KP's Core Document.[56] Others held that on the face of the evidence, and in spite of its episodic shortcomings, the KP remained relatively effective in achieving its main objective of removing conflict diamonds from the global trade by bringing together diamond industry, state, and civil society actors for defined ends.[57] Some deflected the problem of KP weaknesses onto the public, pointing to the KP's consumer education campaigns as a critical weak link. The implication was that *if only the public was better informed* the KP would be pressured into a more aggressive stance on issues of human rights violations, its operational definition of 'conflict diamonds', and questions of state non-compliance and penalties, a position shared by some in the KP's World Diamond Council industry grouping.[58]

It is now clear that these optimistic assessments failed to take stock of the resounding failure of attempts at democratic reform within the KP over a period spanning more than a decade. The decisive defeat of the most recent 'reform cycle' in 2017-19 underscored the affirmation of diamond industry and state power within the body, the marginalization of civil society partners, and the KP's rejection of repeated attempts to render the global diamond trade more transparent, accountable, and conflict-free. The entrenched structural unevenness at the heart of the KP, cemented in an industry-elite compact around administrative and political power, and catalyzed by common interests in legitimized accumulation, remain unaddressed in liberal research and media accounts. For some contributors, the matter of the KP's organizational capture by member governments was flipped on its head, with the KP's relative *incapacities* to enforce its mandate raising questions about why states would bother to invest political energy in the scheme in the first place.[59] In these assessments, a curious analytical disconnect emerged between well-documented KP compliance violations at country level and the evidence about the direct beneficiaries of such practices within the KP's membership. An acknowledgement of modes of accumulation wrapped in elite rent-seeking practices were nowhere to be found. A failure to identify the core structural origins of the KP's regulatory weaknesses meant that the recommended fixes for the KP – a greater resolve to be more inclusive, a softening of the body's rigid definition of conflict minerals, and so forth – would fall short in addressing the disabling, systemic political weaknesses baked into the foundations of the scheme at its outset.

Left assessments have more clearly acknowledged the KP's structural

Achilles' Heel. Yet at the country level, the links between structural critiques of the KP and local strategies for improving development outcomes were less clear, and recommended strategies often unconvincing. For example, some underscored the KP's anti-small-scale miner biases, as reflected in industry and government portrayals of small-scale diamond operators as violent, criminal, and corrosive of development. But while embracing a 'livelihoods' approach, such critiques nonetheless struggled to advance an alternative which incorporated popular interests beyond the narrower realm of small-scale miners and their communities.[60] National constituencies with concurrent claims to the socialization of mineral revenues were less adequately accounted for, not least local mining labour and service sectors, both of which saw state-led formalization and domestication of mining as a path to employment expansion, stronger productive linkages, higher state revenues, and a stronger institutional basis for supporting small scale livelihoods.[61] The focus of some KP critiques on small scale miners' autonomy and its disruption by industry discourses around formalization and market security, missed the need for greater structural inclusion of civil society at the local level, involving *formalization of a different kind* that specifically incorporated national popular constituencies and local mining communities, and facilitated the sharing of benefits among them. A critical point of strategic tension was left unresolved: how to both acknowledge and challenge, engage and resist, a well-established regulatory order that proved equally adept at consolidating elite power and absorbing and demobilizing social movements. Current debates which focus on new forms of collective and public ownership of natural resources and strategic extractive industries provide an important venue for the exploration and mobilization of new popular strategies.

Evidence from international voluntary regulatory initiatives outside of the mineral sector may provide important lessons for African resource governance social movements, mining communities and other popular local interests as they explore more effective strategies for engaging global mineral value chains to ensure greater local benefits and accountability. Recent research at the global level underscores the potential for significant beneficial impacts emerging from the participation of most-affected local interests – including small-scale miners, mining communities, mineworkers and tax justice social activists – in key stages of international regulatory schemes' formulation, establishment and implementation.[62] The active and equitable inclusion of local workers and agriculturalists in the norm production, monitoring and enforcement of regulatory standards in the forestry, garment-making, and other industries has been critical to the success of those sectors' voluntary regulatory schemes in delivering stronger protections for workers' rights, environmental standards, local livelihoods, and other social benefits.

For African extractives-governance social movements, these notable cases of producer-centred governance schemes suggest a rethink of their engagement with bodies like the KP, and correspondingly, a recalibration of popular interests' cooperation with local states and the international mining industry. By these means, the key aims, processes and outcomes of international regulatory schemes might be pulled into closer alignment with the priority needs of African miners and host countries: improved accountability and transparency in the management of mineral value chains, to be sure, but also strengthened local participation, local equitable redistribution of economic and social benefits, and local co-management of the evolving global terrain of extractive industries regulation. Recent waves of resource nationalism in a number of African countries suggest there is a strong appetite for a new approach to resource governance from below. The challenge now for progressive African social movements is to imagine, identify, and build the political and social coalitions that will be an essential ingredient in any popular gains on the front of extractives regulation on the continent and at global level.

NOTES

1   See: D. Brinks, J. Dehm, K. Engle, and K. Taylor, *Power, Participation, and Private Regulatory Initiatives: Human Rights Under Supply Chain Capitalism*, Philadelphia: University of Pennsylvania Press, 2021.
2   Bonnie Campbell, ed., *Mining in Africa: Regulation and Development*, London: Pluto Press, 2009.
3   David Szablowski, *Transnational Law and Local Struggles: Mining, Communities and the World Bank*, Portland: Hart Publishing, 2007.
4   The EITI's current membership registry is available online at www.eiti.org.
5   See for example, A. Zalik and A. Osuoka, 'Beyond transparency: A consideration of extraction's full costs', *The Extractive Industries and Society*, 7(3), 2020, pp. 781-85; and D. Szablowski and B. Campbell, 'Struggles over extractive governance: Power, discourse, violence, and legality', *The Extractive Industries and Society*, 6(3), 2019, pp. 635-41.
6   For accounts of the KP's origins and establishment see: Franziska Bieri, *From Blood Diamonds to the Kimberley Process: How NGOs Cleaned Up the Global Diamond Industry*, Farnham: Ashgate, 2010; and, Ian Smillie, *Blood on the Stone: Greed, Corruption and War in the Global Diamond Trade*, London: Anthem Press, 2010. More recent comparative assessments of the KP in practice include: Nathan Munier, *The Political Economy of the Kimberley Process*, Cambridge: Cambridge University Press, 2020; and Nigel Davidson, *The Lion that Didn't Roar: Can the Kimberley Process Stop the Blood Diamonds Trade?*, Canberra: ANU Press, 2016.

7   In the period leading to the KP's establishment, more than a dozen reports on diamond-fuelled conflict and industry indifference were issued between January 2000 and October 2002. See: Smillie, *Blood on the Stone*.
8   Ian Smillie, 'The heart of the matter: Sierra Leone, diamonds and human security', Ottawa: Partnership Africa Canada, January 2000. In the 2000s, African producers typically contributed more than 60 per cent of the world's annual diamond supply.
9   UN General Assembly Resolution 55/56, December 2000; UN Security Council Resolution 1459, January 2003.
10 Kimberley Process Certification Scheme, 'Core Document', 2003, available at: www.kimberleyprocess.com/en/kpcs-core-document.
11 Kimberley Process Certification Scheme, 'What is the Kimberley Process', available at: www.kimberleyprocess.com.
12 The 'consensus' convention gave effective veto power to each of the KP's 54 member states. See: Munier, *Political Economy of the Kimberley Process*, pp. 5-6.
13 African Union, 'African Mining Vision', Addis Ababa: African Union, February 2009.
14 See the seminal report which figured prominently in the framing of the AMV: United Nations Economic Commission for Africa, *Minerals and Africa's Development: The International Study Group Report on Africa's Mineral Regimes*, Addis Ababa: UNECA, 2011.
15 A. Bohne and I. Thiam, eds, 'The Africa Mining Vision: Can Business as Usual be Visionary? Perspectives from Four Regions', Materialien, No.23, Berlin, Rosa Luxemburg Stiftung, 2018.
16 Y. Graham, 'Escaping the Winner's Curse: The Africa Mining Vision and some challenges of the international trade and investment regime', 2013, available at: warwick.ac.uk/fac/soc/law/research/clusters/international/devconf/participants/papers/graham_-_escaping_the_winners_curse.pdf
17 Eight years after the AMV's establishment, only one country, Lesotho, had fully implemented an AMV Country Mining Vision in alignment with the initiative. See: Oxfam, 'From Aspiration to Reality: Unpacking the African Mining Vision', *Oxfam Briefing Paper*, March 2017, available at: www-cdn.oxfam.org/s3fs-public/bp-africa-mining-vision-090317-en.pdf.
18 For a comprehensive account of the first decade of diamond mining and political contestation in Marange see: Richard Saunders and Tinashe Nyamunda, eds., *Facets of Power: Politics, Profits and People in the Making of Zimbabwe's Blood Diamonds*, Johannesburg/Harare: Wits/Weaver, 2016.
19 Chaim Even-Zohar, 'Presentation on Marange Diamonds to the 2010 Kimberley Process Certification Scheme Intersessional Meeting', Tel Aviv, 22 June 2010.
20 'Marange diamond output could reach 40 million carats', *Mining Review*, 1 September 2010.
21 Richard Saunders, 'Geologies of Power: Blood Diamonds, Security Politics and Zimbabwe's Troubled Transition', *Journal of Contemporary African Studies*, 32(3), 2014, pp. 378-94.
22 Human Rights Watch, 'Diamonds in the Rough: Human rights abuses in the Marange diamond fields of Zimbabwe', New York, 2009.
23 Centre for Research & Development, 'A Preliminary Report of the Atrocities Committed by the Police and Army in Mutare and Chiadzwa under "Operation

24 Hakudzokwi" (you will not return) in 2008, Mutare, Zimbabwe', Mutare: CERD, Zimbabwe, 2009.
24 Kimberley Process Certification Scheme, Review Mission to Zimbabwe, 'Final Report, June 30–July 4, 2009', available at: graphics8.nytimes.com/packages/pdf/world/ZimFinaldraft020909.pdf
25 Kimberley Process Certification Scheme, 'Joint Work Plan', adopted by Plenary, Swakopmund, Namibia, 5 November 2009.
26 Melanie Chiponda and Richard Saunders, 'Holding Ground: Community, Companies and Resistance in Chiadzwa', in R. Saunders and T. Nyamunda, eds, *Facets of Power: Politics, Profits and People in the Making of Zimbabwe's Blood Diamonds*, Johannesburg/Harare: Wits/Weaver, 2016.
27 R. Saunders and A. Caramento, 'An Extractive Developmental State in Southern Africa? The cases of Zambia and Zimbabwe', *Third World Quarterly* 39(6), 2018, pp. 1166-90.
28 Saunders, 'Geologies of Power'.
29 Martin Dawson and Tim Kelsall, 'Anti-developmental patrimonialism in Zimbabwe', *Journal of Contemporary African Studies*, 30(1), 2012, pp. 49-66.
30 Parliament of Zimbabwe, Committee on Mines and Energy, 'First Report on Diamond Mining (with Special Reference to Marange Diamond Fields) 2009–2013', Presented to Parliament June 2013.
31 Global Witness, 'An Inside Job – Zimbabwe: The State, the Security Forces, and a Decade of Disappearing Diamonds', London, 2017, available at: www.globalwitness.org.
32 R. Saunders, 'The Politics of Resource Bargaining, Social Relations and Institutional Development in Zimbabwe Since Independence', in K. Hujo, ed., *The Politics of Domestic Resource Mobilization for Social Development*, Basingstoke: Palgrave Macmillan and UNRISD, 2020.
33 See: Partnership Africa Canada, 'Reap What You Sow: Greed and corruption in Zimbabwe's Marange Diamond Fields', Ottawa, 2012, available at: impacttransform.org; and, Global Witness, 'Diamonds: A good deal for Zimbabwe?', London, 2012, available at: www.globalwitness.org.
34 O. Nyamucherera and M. Sibanda, 'Tracing Progress Towards Revenue Transparency and Revenue Sharing in the Zimbabwe Extractives Sector 2013-2019: Zimbabwe Case Study', Publish What You Pay, March 2020, available at: www.pwyp.org.
35 Richard Saunders, 'High-Value Minerals and Resource Bargaining in a Time of Crisis: A Case Study on the Diamond Fields of Marange, Zimbabwe', *UNRISD Working Paper 2018-1*, Geneva, UNRISD, January 2018..
36 Partnership Africa Canada, 'Reap What You Sow', p.6.
37 Ian Smillie, 'Paddles for Kimberley: An agenda for reform', Partnership Africa Canada, Ottawa, June 2010, available at: impacttransform.org.
38 KP, 'Core Document', 2003. In the KP's founding Core Document 'conflict diamonds' were narrowly defined as those which fuel rebel violence against a legal government.
39 A. Chikane, 'Kimberley Process Certification Scheme, Second Fact Finding Mission Report', report by KP Monitor for Marange, Zimbabwe, 24-28 May 2010, available at: www.swradioafrica.com. The report's recommendations were all the more

remarkable given Chikane's role in the detention of civil society diamond campaigner Farai Maguwu.

40 Partnership Africa Canada, 'Reap What You Sow', 2012.
41 Chiponda and Saunders, 'Holding Ground'.
42 Farai Maguwu was detained a total of six weeks on trumped-up charges which were later dropped after negotiations for his release and the relaxation of sanctions were concluded. See: Farai Maguwu, 'The Kimberley Process and the Continuation of "Conflict Diamonds"', in, D. Brinks et al., *Power, Participation, and Private Regulatory Initiatives*.
43 See: F. Maguwu, 'The Kimberley Process', and Shamiso Mtisi, 'Enforcer or Enabler? Rethinking the Kimberley Process in the Shadow of Marange', in R. Saunders and T. Nyamunda, eds, *Facets of Power*.
44 'Global Witness leaves Kimberley Process, calls for diamond trade to be held accountable', *Global Witness*, 2 December 2011, available at: www.globalwitness.org.
45 'Ian Smillie addresses human rights, diamonds and the Kimberley Process', *Rapaport News*, 10 September, 2010.
46 Partnership Africa Canada, 'Civil Society Boycotts Conflict Diamonds Certification Scheme,' Press Statement, 17 November 2015. Dubai's record of dubious accounting at its diamond exchange and its unguarded hostility towards issues of human rights raised by the CSC were well-documented.
47 International Peace Information Service, 'Focus on Kimberley Process after failed reform cycle', IPIS Briefing November 2019, available at: ipisresearch.be.
48 Emphasis in original. KP CSC, 'Closing Speech,' KPSC Plenary, New Delhi, 22 November 2019, available at: www.kpcivilsociety.org/wp-content/uploads/2019/11/20191122_KP-CSC-Closing-Speech2019.pdf.
49 IMPACT, 'Remarks from IMPACT, Kimberley Process Plenary', Brisbane Australia, 14 December 2017, available at: impacttransform.org.
50 Kimberley Process Civil Society Coalition, 'Real Care is Rare: An on-the-ground perspective on blood diamonds and the fifth "C"', KP CSC D/2019/4320/13, September 2019, available at: www.kpcivilsociety.org.
51 KP CSC, 'Closing Speech,' KPCS Plenary, 22 November 2019.
52 In 2022 only one of the KP CSC's thirteen members was not based in Africa – the Belgium-based International Peace Information Service.
53 'False Consumer Confidence in Diamonds: Decline of Credibility in the Kimberley Process', *IMPACT*, December 2017, available at: impacttransform.org.
54 The Zimbabwe Consolidated Diamond Company, whose legal basis remained unclear for an extended period, forcibly consolidated the six mining companies then operating in Marange. See: Global Witness, 'An Inside Job', 2017.
55 Centre for Research and Development in Zimbabwe, 'Government controlled diamond mining in Marange masking resource leakages and human rights abuse', 28 January 2020, available at: kubatana.net/2020/01/28/government-controlled-diamond-mining-in-marange-masking-resource-leakages-and-human-rights-abuse.
56 A. Winetroub, 'A Diamond Scheme is Forever Lost: The Kimberley Process's Deteriorating Tripartite Structure and its Consequences for the Scheme's Survival', *Indiana Journal of Global Legal Studies*, 20(2), 2013, pp. 1425-44; M. Murdoch, 'Polishing Up the Diamond Trade: How to revitalize the Kimberley Process', *Journal of Corporation Law* 46(2), 2020-21, pp. 464-81.

57 S. Borsky and A.M. Leiter, 'International trade in rough diamonds and the Kimberley Process Certification Scheme', *World Development*, 152, 2022; Davidson, *The Lion that Didn't Roar*.
58 A.P. Santiago, 'Guaranteeing Conflict Free Diamonds: From compliance to norm expansion under the Kimberley Process Certification Scheme', *South African Journal of International Affairs*, 21(3), 2014, pp. 413-29; Kimberley Process Civil Society Coalition, 'Real Care is Rare', 2019.
59 Munier, *Political Economy of the Kimberley Process*.
60 S. Spiegel, 'Contested diamond certification: Reconfiguring global and national interests in Zimbabwe's Marange fields', *Geoforum*, 59, 2015, pp. 258–67.
61 ZELA, ZIMCODD, ZCC and AFRODAD, 'Inequalities in Mining Communities in Zimbabwe', Harare, Norwegian Church Aid, September 2020, available at: zimcodd.org/sdm_downloads/inequalities-in-mining-communities-in-zimbabwe-september-2021.
62 Brinks et al., *Power, Participation, and Private Regulatory Initiatives*.

FROM '996' TO 'LYING FLAT': CHINA'S REGIME OF ACCUMULATION

MINQI LI

Since the global economic crisis in 2008-09, China has emerged as the driving engine of global capitalist economy. According to World Bank data, China accounted for 47 per cent of global economic growth (measured by market exchange rate), 32 per cent of global exports growth, 29 per cent of global imports growth, 66 per cent of global manufacturing value added growth, and 44 per cent of global manufacturing exports growth for the period 2011-20.[1] Measured by market exchange rates, China now accounts for 17 per cent of global economic output, and is set to overtake the United States to become the world's largest economy in the coming years.

It is well known that China's rapid economic growth over the past several decades has been made possible by the intensive exploitation of a large cheap labour force. Until recently, China's economic growth had been mainly led by the manufacturing sector. The manufacturing sector continues to play an important role in the Chinese economy, and manufacturing exports account for about 90 per cent of China's total exports. However, in recent years, a growing proportion of China's employment growth has been driven by various new service industries made possible by platform technologies. In addition, the Chinese government has pursued strategies of industrial upgrading to transform the Chinese economy into one led by high valueadded leading technologies.

Despite these transformations, both the new service industries and the emerging high-tech sector continue to depend on intensive exploitation and overworking of workers to make profits. In Huawei and other hightech companies, workers are expected to follow the '996' working-schedule (working 12 hours daily, from nine o'clock in the morning to nine in the evening, six days a week), which amounts to a 72-hour working week.

China's intensive mode of exploitation as well as rising costs of living (especially surging housing prices) have greatly reduced both the time and financial resources available for young people. In response, many Chinese young people have adopted the attitude of 'lying flat' (refusing to marry, have children, or participate in the pursuit of unnecessary consumption). This has contributed to a drastic decline of China's fertility rate. If this trend is not reversed, it will lead to the massive decline of China's young and physically capable labour force, and China's rapid economic growth, which is based on population growth as well as the shift from rural to urban employment, will soon come to an end. Moreover, as the bargaining power of the working class thereby improves, the demise of China's current regime of accumulation could pave the way for a new era of social transformation.

'NEW PATTERNS OF EMPLOYMENT'

Before the global economic crisis of 2008-09, China's economic growth was largely led by the export-oriented manufacturing sector. Since then, the various service industries have played a more important role in driving China's economic growth.

According to China's National Bureau of Statistics, the share of secondary industries (including mining, manufacturing, utilities, and construction) in China's GDP declined from 47 per cent in 2010 to 38 per cent in 2020. During the same period, the share of tertiary (or service) industries increased from 44 per cent to 55 per cent. From 2010 to 2020, while total employment in the secondary industries declined from 218 million to 215 million, total employment in the tertiary industries increased from 263 million to 358 million.[2]

Within service industries, employment growth has been led by the so-called 'new patterns of employment' made possible by platform technologies. According to China's National Information Center under the National Development and Reform Commission, 'new patterns of employment' include various forms of new employment that have been made possible by artificial intelligence, 'big data', cloud computing, and digital technologies. Under these new patterns of employment, workers often do not enter into legally binding employment contracts with their actual employers. Instead, workers perform tasks requested by customers directly through network platforms set up by their actual employers.[3]

What the Chinese government refers to as the 'new patterns of employment' is very similar to what is understood as the 'gig economy' in the Western literature. According to an article published by the Davos World Economic Forum, 'the gig economy uses digital platforms to connect freelancers with customers to provide short-term services or asset-sharing'.[4] In China, some of the most popular activities associated with 'new patterns of employment' include platform-ordered fast delivery, domestic services, after-school education, ride-sharing and bicycle-sharing, virtual medical care, virtual skills improvement, personal finance platforms, and rental sharing platforms.[5] According to Chinese government estimates, as of 2020, 84 million workers were employed in the platform sectors, and more broadly defined 'flexible employment' reached about 200 million.[6]

According to information from *Our World in Data*, in 2017, an average worker in Mexico worked 2,255 hours, an average worker in China worked 2,174 hours, an average worker in Vietnam worked 2,170 hours, an average worker in India worked 2,117 hours, an average worker in the United States worked 1,757 hours, an average worker in Japan worked 1,738 hours, an average worker in Canada worked 1,696 hours, an average worker in the United Kingdom worked 1,670 hours, an average worker in France worked 1,514 hours, and an average worker in Germany worked 1,354 hours.[7] Thus according to these figures, Chinese workers' annual working hours are clearly higher than the working hours in the developed capitalists economies, but seem comparable to the long hours in several other low- or middle-income countries. However, other research suggests that the actual working time of Chinese workers is likely to be much longer than what is reported by *Our World in Data*.

A survey conducted in 2010 found that an average factory worker in the Pearl River Delta worked 57 hours a week, while one in the Yangzi River Delta worked 55 hours a week. The Pearl River Delta (where Guangzhou and Shenzhen are located) and Yangzi River Delta (where Shanghai is located) are two areas where manufacturing exporters are concentrated.[8] Many workers worked under hazardous or dangerous conditions. According to official data, China has 975,000 confirmed cases of occupational diseases (pneumoconiosis accounts for about 90 per cent of the confirmed cases). Researchers believe that the actual number of cases is likely much higher. It is estimated that about 200 million Chinese workers are regularly exposed to hazardous work environments.[9] In the early 2000s, there were more than one million major work safety incidents each year and more than 100,000 workers died each year due to work-related incidents. Since then, China has managed to improve work safety conditions. Nevertheless, in 2020, about 38,000 major work safety incidents occurred, and 27,000 workers died as a result.[10]

While the Chinese manufacturing enterprises have been notorious for their sweatshop-style exploitation, most factory workers are at least covered by some form of social insurance program. By comparison, as the new service industries based on platform technologies grow rapidly, workers who work under the 'new patterns of employment' often do not have any labour insurance coverage.

According to a recent interview of Mr. Zheng Gongcheng, President of China's Association of Social Security Studies and a member of the Standing Committee of the National People's Congress, only about 15 per cent of the workers under the 'new patterns of employment' have entered into formal labour contracts with their employers, and most are not covered by pension insurance or medical insurance.[11]

Even for those workers who nominally have some form of insurance, the legal process to receive benefits is often prohibitively costly and time-consuming. *The Workers' Daily* (the newspaper of China's official labour union, the ACFTU) reported a case in which a fast delivery worker was injured in a traffic accident during work. After two labour dispute arbitrations and three court hearings, he still could not have his actual employer identified as the employer legally responsible for his injury.[12]

In China's mainstream literature, 'new patterns of employment' are supposed to provide workers with more 'flexibility' in their working schedule, allowing them to seek an ideal balance between income and 'leisure'.[13] In reality, in order to earn a minimum income that allows for a decent living standard in China's urban environment, workers under the 'new patterns of employment' often have to work incredibly long hours. In China's so-called 'first-line cities' (such as Beijing, Shanghai, Guangzhou, and Shenzhen), takeout-dining delivery workers often have to work 15 hours a day, constantly shuttling in busy traffic.[14] Similarly, a *Didi* (China's equivalent to Uber) driver explains that he and his driver friends rarely work less than 12 hours a day, and it is a 'luxury' for him to take more than three days off in a month.[15]

'CHERISH YOUR LIFE, STAY AWAY FROM HUAWEI'

Realizing that the Chinese economy cannot rely upon the exploitation of cheap labour force forever, in recent years, the Chinese government has used industrial policies to promote the growth of various high-tech economic sectors.

In 2015, the Chinese government announced a national industrial policy known as 'Made in China 2025' intended to transform China from a 'world factory' based on exploitation of cheap labour into a new technology-intensive powerhouse. The Chinese government considers aerospace, biotech, information technology, smart manufacturing, robotics manufacturing, advanced rail, electric vehicles, biomedicine, and pharmaceuticals to be the leading industries that will receive strong government support.[16]

In China's Fourteenth Five-Year Plan, presented in 2021, the development of the semi-conductor industry and chip-manufacturing technology is considered to be a key component of the 'nation-strengthening strategy'.[17] Huawei Technologies Company is considered to be the 'industry champion' in China's semi-conductor and telecommunication equipment industry.[18]

Huawei was founded by Ren Zhengfei in 1987.[19] In 2012, it overtook Ericsson to become the world's largest telecommunication equipment producer and in 2018, it overtook Apple to become the world's second largest smart phone manufacturer.[20] Huawei reports that in 2021 the company had an operating revenue of 100 billion dollars, a net profit of 18 billion dollars, and net assets (equity) of 65 billion dollars.[21] This implies a net profit margin of 18 per cent and a rate of return on equity of 28 per cent. Huawei is ranked number 44 in *Fortune*'s list of the world's 500 largest companies.[22]

Huawei claims itself to be a '100 per cent employee-owned company'. According to Huawei's shareholding structure, Huawei's founder, Ren Zhengfei, holds one per cent of the total shares and the other 99 per cent are held by Huawei's 'labour union' committee. However, the so-called 'labour union' committee is controlled by Ren Zhengfei's protégés. Huawei's shareholder meetings usually have the participation of only two people, one is Ren Zhengfei himself and the other person nominally representing the 'labour union' committee. Moreover, the company's charter allows Ren Zhengfei to have veto power over any important decision and appoints Ren Zhengfei to be the sole representative of the Huawei Investment and Holding Company at the Huawei Technology Company (the latter is the subsidiary 100 per cent owned by the former). These arrangements allow Ren Zhengfei and his family members to have full control over Huawei while pretending to be dedicated managers of an 'employee-owned' company.[23]

As of December 2021, Huawei employed about 200,000 staff and workers, including 110,000 working on research and development.[24] Huawei does not report its employees' salaries, but it is generally believed that the average income of Huawei employees is several times the Chinese urban worker's average income, and substantially higher than the average annual income for employees in other high-tech companies. One Huawei employee recently revealed that the average annual income for Huawei's senior employees is about 700,000 yuan (about 105,000 US dollars), and for junior employees is about 300,000 yuan (about 45,000 US dollars).[25] By comparison, the average annual wage for workers in China's urban 'non-private' sector was about 97,000 yuan (about 14,550 US dollars), and the average annual wage for the workers in the urban private sector was about 58,000 yuan (about 8,700 US dollars) in 2020.[26]

With such high salaries (by Chinese standards), Huawei has managed to attract some of the highest-quality engineers and technical workers. The company inculcates its employees with 'wolf-like culture', demanding unconditional sacrifice and unlimited loyalty. Employees are 'encouraged' to sign 'commitment-to-struggle agreements' with the company. By agreeing to 'struggle' for the cause of the company, an employee is committed to taking no more than five days off in a year and giving up maternity leave 'voluntarily'.[27]

Huawei is one of several leading technology companies in China that practices the so-called 996 work schedule. A former product manager at Huawei complained that the 996 schedule completely took over his personal life. He had no time for family, leisure, or even sleep. He lost interest in anything after work. Even though the 996 schedule is Huawei's 'official' policy, the former employee explained that, in practice, many had to work till eleven in the evening every day, effectively working 14 hours per day.[28]

Because of the enormous and inhumane stress imposed on Huawei employees, many have suffered from physical or mental breakdowns. Since 2006, there have been at least thirty-eight cases of 'unnatural deaths' of Huawei employees. Among the causes of these fatalities were sudden death at work and suicide. Some Huawei employees express a sense of self-ridicule in the oft-repeated saying, 'Cherish your life, stay away from Huawei'.[29]

The frequent reports of unnatural deaths suggest that Huawei's 'wolf-like' culture and 996 working-schedule have been physically as well as mentally damaging to the employees, dramatically reducing workers' productive lives. Rather than responding to employees' physical and mental crisis by abandoning its model of super-exploitation, Huawei has tried to dump employees it considers to have lost the capacity to 'struggle', even if they have worked for the company for many years. In 2017, Huawei took measures to 'clear' all project maintenance workers that were older than thirty-four, while all research and development employees older than 40 were forced to resign or retire early.[30]

The 996 work-schedule – and the model of super-exploitation built upon it – are not limited to Huawei, but prevalent among China's high-tech enterprises.[31] According to the World Health Organization, long working hours tend to cause deaths from heart disease and stroke. A study sponsored by the WHO concludes that working fifty-five or more hours per week is associated with an estimated 35 per cent higher risk of stroke and a 17 per cent higher risk of dying from ischemic heart disease, compared to working 35-40 hours a week.[32] In China, there has been no official estimate of the annual deaths caused by long working hours. However, according to China's National Center of Cardiovascular Diseases, each year there are more than 500,000 cases of sudden death caused by cardiovascular diseases in China.[33] This statistic suggests that hundreds or thousands of Chinese workers may have died each year due to excessively long working hours imposed by the super-exploitative regime of accumulation.

'LYING FLAT' – A NEW STRATEGY OF RESISTANCE?

Hundreds of millions of workers in China's manufacturing and service industries have to work excessively long hours, often under hazardous or dangerous conditions. Even the relatively 'privileged' workers in high-tech enterprises must struggle to survive the 996 working-schedule that tests the limits of their physical and mental endurance. It is fair to say, therefore, that the Chinese accumulation regime has in no small part been based on the super-exploitation of a large cheap labour force.

Why have Chinese workers tolerated such intense exploitation up to this point? One plausible answer is that the Chinese economy has managed to provide rapidly rising levels of material consumption to large sections of the working class. According to the *China Statistical Yearbook*, the average nominal wage of the urban, non-private sector increased from about 37,000 yuan in 2010 to 97,000 yuan to 2020, with an average annual growth rate of 10.1 per cent. Using the official consumer price index, the average real wage in the urban non-private sector grew at an average annual rate of 7.4 per cent between 2010 and 2020. During the same period, the average nominal wage in the urban private sector increased from about 21,000 yuan to 58,000 yuan, with an average annual growth rate of 10.7 per cent. Corrected for inflation, the urban private sector's real average wage grew at an average annual rate of 8 per cent.[34]

With an annual real wage growth rate of 7-8 per cent, the average Chinese urban worker's material consumption level approximately doubles every 9-10 years. This growth rate gives workers some reasonable hope that, within one generation, the living standards of themselves and their families can be materially transformed, and their children can look forward to a brighter future.

Moreover, there is still a large urban-rural divide in term of living standards in China. In 2020, disposable income per person in rural areas was about 17,000 yuan, while disposable income per person in urban areas was about 44,000 yuan. This massive urban-rural divide implies that, as a worker moves from a rural area to an urban area, theoretically the worker could expect an approximate doubling of his or her income. From 2010 to

2020, China's rural employment declined from 414 million to 288 million, as urban employment increased from 347 million to 463 million.[35] Thus, more than 100 million workers have moved from rural areas to urban areas during the past decade. Millions of migrant workers newly arrived in the urban labour market might consider it worthwhile to spend several years under harsh working conditions in exchange for a potential doubling of their material living standard.

However, wage growth for Chinese workers is now beginning to be overtaken by various living costs that are not fully captured by the official price index. A major financial burden for Chinese urban households is related to mortgage payments for housing. According to a report by the China News Network, about 30 per cent of urban residents between 18 and 44 years old require more than 40 per cent of their income to service their mortgage payments.[36] Yet housing prices are not part of the official consumer price index, because they are treated not as consumption but as part of household 'investment'.[37]

According to new research published by the Beike Research Institute, about 45 per cent of China's urban youth (between 18 and 35 years old) lives in self-owned housing units (usually flats) while the rest rents housing. However, housing ownership is often seen as a prerequisite for young people to enter into a serious relationship, and for marriage to be considered. Only about 19 per cent of female respondents in the survey would accept renting as a long-term residential option. Additionally, in recent years, as housing prices rise, rental costs have increased accordingly. In China's top-line cities, such as Beijing, Shanghai, and Shenzhen, average rental costs have exceeded 30 per cent of the annual income of a typical young white-collar worker.[38]

Figure 1 shows the number of square metres of urban housing that could be purchased with an urban worker's average wage based on the national average housing price (assuming the entire annual wage is spent on the purchase of housing). The figure helps to illustrate the real purchasing power of urban workers' wages measured against urban housing prices.

In 2000, the average wage in the urban non-private sector could purchase 4.8 square metres of urban housing, and the average wage in the urban private sector could purchase 3.2 square metres (one square metre is approximately 11 square feet). In 2014, the average wage in the urban non-private sector could purchase 9.5 square metres of urban housing, and the average wage in the urban private sector could purchase 6.1 square metres. Thus, between 2000 and 2014, the real purchasing power of the Chinese workers' wages increased substantially in terms of area of housing that can be purchased.

Figure 1. Area of Housing That Can Be Purchased by Average Wage in China, 2000-2020

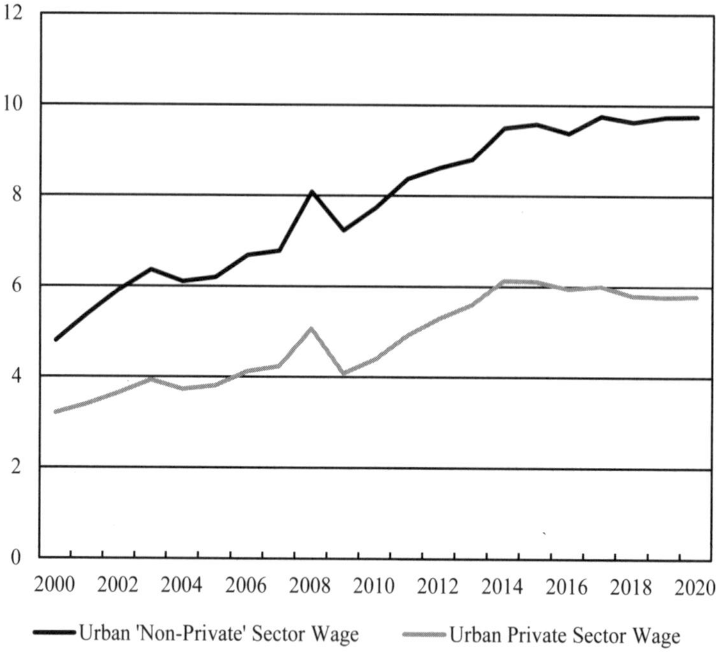

⬛ Urban 'Non-Private' Sector Wage ── Urban Private Sector Wage

Source: *Statistical Yearbook of China.*[39]

However, since 2014 Chinese workers' real purchasing power in terms of housing has stagnated. By 2020, the average wage in the urban non-private sector could purchase 9.8 square metres of urban housing (a marginal improvement compared to 2014), and the average wage in the urban private sector could purchase 5.8 square metres (a small decline compared to 2014). If urban housing has always been unaffordable for the majority of the urban working class, before 2014 the workers could at least hope rising wages would eventually close the gap between affordability and what is needed for a decent living standard in the not-very-distant future. With workers' wages struggling to keep up with surging housing prices since 2014, a decent urban living has become a distant dream for a majority of Chinese workers.

In addition to housing, the costs of other necessary items (such as education and health care) absorb a large portion of the incomes of urban workers.[40] According to the recently published *China Fertility Cost Report*, the cumulative cost of raising an urban child in China from 0 to 17 years old is about 630,000 yuan. This is more than six times an average worker's wage in the urban non-private sector, or eleven times an average worker's wage in the urban private sector. China's cumulative fertility cost per child is about seven times per capita GDP. By comparison, cumulative fertility cost per child is about two times per capita GDP in Australia and Singapore, three times per capita GDP in Sweden, and four times per capita GDP in the US and Japan. In relative terms, China is among the most expensive places in the world to raise a child.[41]

As a decent life in China's urban environment becomes increasingly unaffordable and many workers reach their physical and mental limits under China's super-exploitative accumulation regime, a new generation of young people has begun to realize it is pointless to try to improve their living conditions by working 'hard'. In this context, in 2021, a new phrase became popular on China's social media: '*Tang Ping*' or 'lying flat'.

Like many other social media phrases 'lying flat' has been loosely defined and may mean many different things to different people. According to a report by Radio France International, lying flat is used by many Chinese young people as a strategy of life. It can be summarized as five 'no's' – 'do not buy house, do not buy cars, do not marry, do not have children, do not consume (unnecessarily)'. For some, it is seen as a form of resistance against China's existing economic and social regime – 'just maintain the minimum subsistence, and not turn (ourselves) into machines to make money or slaves to be exploited by the capitalists'.[42]

It remains to be seen if lying flat will become a general movement of resistance. However, in one area, young people in China have already lain 'flat' and this may steadily undermine the foundation of China's current regime of accumulation.

SHORTAGE OF YOUNG PEOPLE

In recent years, the Chinese population's birth rate has declined precipitously. Figure 2 compares China's annual marriage registration and live births from 2000 to 2020.

China's annual marriage registrations peaked in 2013 at 13.5 million. By 2020, annual marriage registrations fell to 8.1 million, a decline of 40 per cent from the peak level. In 2010, there were about 16 million live births in China. In 2011, the Chinese government began to relax the one-child policy.[43] The following year, the number of live births surged to nearly 20 million. However, the surge in the birth rate proved short-lived. In 2015, the Chinese government officially allowed all married couples to have second children, and the next year, the number of live births recovered to about 19 million. Since then, China's birth rate has declined sharply and probably irreversibly. In 2020, there were only 12 million live births in the country, a decline of 8 million compared to the peak level in 2012.

Figure 2. Marriage Registrations and Live Births in China, 2000-2020

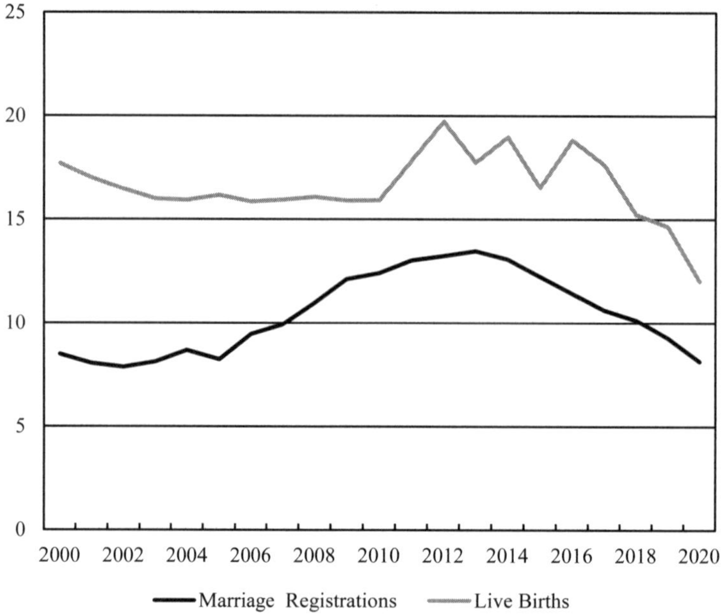

Source: *Statistical Yearbook of China*.

The United Nations projects that, under the 'low fertility' scenario, China's prime working-age population (adults 25-59 years old) will fall from 765 million in 2020 to 580 million in 2050, a decline of 24 per cent. The prime working-age population largely determines the size of a country's total labour force. Within the prime working-age population, those who are 25-34 years old are expected to decline from 227 million in 2020 to 157 million in 2050, or by 31 per cent.[44] Given that China's super-exploitative accumulation regime heavily depends on a young and healthy labour force that can physically endure the extremely stressful long working hours, the coming shortage of young people will raise deep contradictions, and even possibly spell the end of China's current regime of accumulation.

The United Nations 'low fertility' scenario assumes a total fertility rate of 1.3 (that is, the total number of births a woman is expected to give through her entire life). Yet other estimates suggest that China's total fertility rate has already declined to 1.1.[45] Thus, China's young labour force could decline even more rapidly than is projected by the United Nations.

Could the Chinese government take measures to reverse the decline of China's birth rate? According to the *China Fertility Cost Report*, many countries have attempted to use economic incentives to revive the birth rate, but none have succeeded to any significant degree. The report estimates that, if the Chinese government adopted cash subsidies and other economic incentives amounting to 5 per cent of GDP, China could perhaps stabilize its birth rate.[46] The recommended policies, if implemented, are likely to require a massive increase in taxes on China's wealthy capitalists. However, China's total individual income tax revenue was only 1.1 per cent of GDP in 2020.[47] Thus, most of the economic incentives recommended by the *China Fertility Cost Report* (for the purpose of reducing child-raising costs and raising birth rate) have very little chance of being implemented.

China could attempt to offset the decline of the labour force by increasing investment to boost labour productivity. However, China already has the highest investment ratio to GDP among the world's major economies, and has suffered from declining rates of return in recent years. Using the incremental capital-output ratio (the ratio of investment share of GDP over economic growth rate) as an indicator of investment efficiency, it can be shown that, in 2000, each yuan of economic growth required 3.2 yuan of investment; in 2010, each yuan of economic growth required 4.4 yuan of investment; and in 2019, each yuan of economic growth required 7.3 yuan of investment. Thus more and more investment has been required to sustain a given amount of economic growth. In 2020, China's gross capital formation (that is, total investment) accounted for 43 per cent of GDP. Because of the Covid-19 crisis, China's economic growth rate in 2020 declined to 2.3 per cent, and the incremental capital-output ratio surged to 18.7.[48]

China's declining investment efficiency can also be illustrated by the falling profit rate in China's industrial sector. Figure 3 compares the profit rate of China's private industrial enterprises with the profit rate of the US manufacturing corporate sector.

In most years, the profit rate of China's private industrial enterprises stayed substantially above the profit rate of the US manufacturing corporate sector. This is consistent with the observation that China's regime of accumulation has been based on the super-exploitation of a cheap labour force. However, the profit rate of China's private industrial enterprises peaked in 2011 at 28 per cent. By 2020, China's profit rate fell to 14 per cent or one-half of the peak level.

A recent research paper by the Lowy Institute argues that because of the decline in the size of the labour force and falling rate of return on investment, China's economic growth will begin to slow down sharply. China's economic growth rate is projected to fall to about 2 per cent by 2040, as a result of which its per capita GDP would remain below one-half the US level.[49]

Figure 3. Industrial Profit Rates: China and the US, 2000-2020

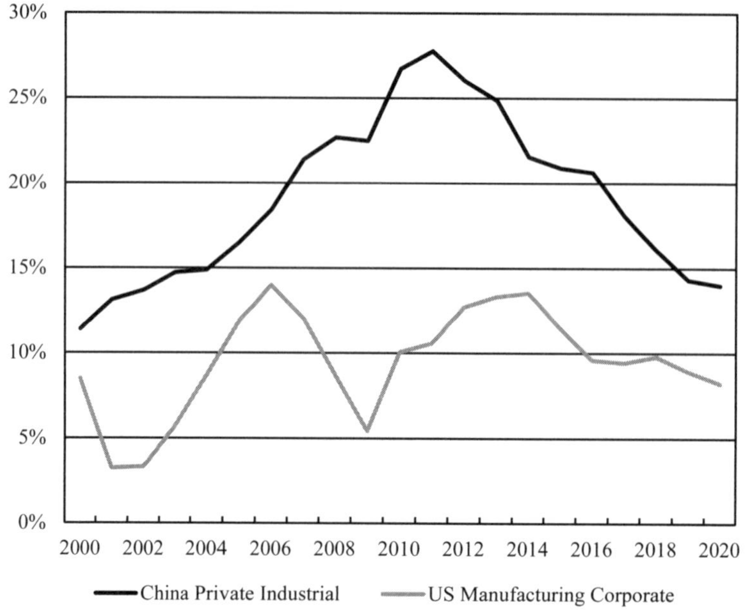

Source: The profit rate of China's private industrial enterprises is calculated using data from *Statistical Yearbook of China*; the profit rate of the US manufacturing corporate business sector is calculated using data from the Bureau of Economic Analysis.[50]

If the growth rate of per capita GDP in China slows to 2 per cent, it will take almost four decades for average living standards to double. If one takes into account income inequality, and the fact that the official price index may understate real inflation for working people, a 2 per cent growth rate of per capita GDP could very well translate into stagnating material consumption levels for most working-class families. In that case, there would be very little incentive for Chinese workers to tolerate excessively long working hours, as they would no longer anticipate a rapid rise of material consumption (what 'lying flat' is already revealing).

On the other hand, China's rural labour force has been declining. China's current rural employment is about 280 million. Over the past ten years, it has declined at an average pace of 13 million per year. If this pace is sustained, it will take just about twenty years before China's remaining rural labour force becomes nearly depleted. As China's rural surplus labour force approaches depletion, there will no longer be a reserve army of millions of workers who are willing to accept harsh working conditions in exchange for higher living standards if they move into urban areas.

Urban workers, moreover, will no longer be threatened by a massive reserve of cheap labour in rural areas ready to migrate and compete for employment by accepting lower wages and harsher working conditions. In such a scenario, urban workers might well be emboldened to demand higher wages and better working conditions. If Chinese capitalists are unable to meet the demands of urban workers because of falling profit rates, the conflict may open the space for a more dramatic transformation, or a remaking of the growth model that has propelled China to the centre of the world market.[51]

THE DEMISE OF CHINA'S ACCUMULATION REGIME?

For many years, China's economic prosperity has been based on manufacturing exports made possible by the intensive exploitation of a large cheap labour force. However, in recent years, employment in manufacturing has declined, and a growing proportion of China's employment takes place in various new service industries made possible by platform technologies. Moreover, the Chinese government has pursued strategies of industrial upgrading to transform the economy into one led by leading high value-added technologies.

Both the new service industries and the high-tech sector continue to depend on intensive exploitation and overworking of workers to make profits. In Huawei and other high-tech companies, workers have to work according to the 996 working-schedule, which is equivalent to 72-hour working week. If one assumes that an average Huawei worker works 50 weeks a year, a 72-hour working week would translate into an annual working time of 3,600 hours. Such incredibly long working hours greatly exceed not only the typical annual working hours in developed Western capitalist economies (about 1,400 to 1,800 hours), but also the annual working hours that generally prevail in other East Asian economies.

Intensive exploitation and overworking have greatly increased the reproduction costs for Chinese urban workers. A new generation of young people in China has responded by pursuing a strategy of life known as 'lying flat', refusing to marry, have children, or participate in the pursuit of unnecessary consumption. As more young people have adopted this attitude, China's fertility rate has declined precipitously. The decline of the labour force not only threatens China's prospects for economic growth, but also helps to increase working-class bargaining power as the surplus rural labour force approaches depletion. In this sense, China's current regime of accumulation could be brought down by the general attitude of 'lying flat' among a shrinking labour force.

China is not the only country threatened by the prospect of a declining labour force. In Western Europe and North America, there has been a long tradition of international migration that has helped to alleviate labour shortages, although the growth of foreign migrant workers could bring about other social contradictions. In East Asia, there has not been a tradition of employing foreign migrant workers on large scales. Due to cultural and linguistic barriers (for example, only a small fraction of the population can speak English fluently), it is unlikely for international migration to play a significant role in alleviating labour force shortages in the East Asian context.

Within East Asia, China, Japan, and South Korea are all confronted by the challenge of declining fertility and labour force shortages. According to United Nations estimates and projections, Japan's prime working-age population (the population that is between 25 and 59 years old) peaked in 1995 at about 62 million and is projected to fall to 54 million by 2025.[52] That is, Japan's labour force is expected to decline by 13 per cent thirty years after its peak. By comparison, China's prime working-age population is believed to have peaked in 2020 at 765 million and is projected to decline to 569 million by 2050, representing a decline of 26 per cent thirty years after the peak. Therefore, China is projected to experience a labour force crisis significantly worse than Japan's.

South Korea's prime working-age population peaked in 2015 at 28 million and is projected to fall to 19 million by 2045, representing a decline of 32 per cent thirty years after the peak.[53] It would be interesting to see how South Korean capitalism confronts such a drastic decline in its labour force, and whether South Korea's existing economic and political systems can survive in the coming decades.

Since the 1990s, Japan has experienced economic stagnation but has otherwise remained mostly stable in political and social terms. Japanese capitalists have responded to the economic stagnation by successfully accelerating labour productivity growth and substituting overseas investment for domestic investment.[54]

As is explained in the previous section, although China's labour productivity continues to grow, this has been made possible by excessive investment that has led to a rapid decline of rates on return. This is a trend that is unlikely to be sustainable. Eventually, the decline of the profit rate will lead to an investment crisis, and the growth of labour productivity would slow down sharply as a result.

While China's investment in foreign assets has grown rapidly in recent years, much of China's overseas investment has resulted in assets with relatively low rates of return (such as US Treasury bonds), and only a very small fraction of China's total overseas investment has taken place in Africa, Latin America, and Southeast Asia to exploit cheap labour and resources in those areas. As a result, even though China has accumulated net international assets of more than 2 trillion dollars, China's net investment income from abroad has been consistently in negative territory (that is, China pays more to foreign capitalists in China than it receives from investment abroad). By comparison, Japan regularly receives more than 150 billion dollars of net investment income from abroad each year, an income that accounts for more than 3 per cent of Japan's GDP.[55]

In the future, as China's economic growth decelerates sharply, Chinese workers will no longer be rewarded by the prospect of rapid increase in material consumption that has in the past persuaded many to accept excessively long working hours. Moreover, as the rural surplus labour force approaches depletion, capitalists may no longer be able to effectively 'discipline' urban workers using the threat of lay-off. This would encourage workers to demand shorter working hours and better working conditions. If workers are neither motivated by the prospect of rising material consumption, nor 'disciplined' by the threat of a large reserve of cheap labour, there is little reason for them to continue accepting physically as well as mentally intolerable working hours. At some point, a general breakdown of labour discipline throughout the Chinese economy cannot be ruled out.

At the Nineteenth National Congress of the Chinese Communist Party, General Secretary Xi Jinping promised that, by 2050, the Chinese Communist Party would lead the Chinese people into a new era of prosperity with 'comprehensive socialist modernization', which suggests that China will by then become one of the leading developed countries in the world.[56] Thus, much of the legitimacy of China's current political system rests upon the expectation that the Chinese Communist Party will continue to deliver rapid economic growth in the coming years, and that living standards will match those in developed countries by the mid-twenty-first century.

When Japan's labour force peaked in 1995, Japan's per capita GDP was about 81 per cent of US per capita GDP. When South Korea's labour forced peaked in 2015, South Korea's per capita GDP was about 66 per cent of US per capita GDP. By comparison, when China's labour force peaked in 2020, China's per capita GDP was only about 27 per cent of US per capita GDP.[57]

According to the Lowy Institute, as China's labour force declines, China's per capita GDP is unlikely to exceed one-half the US level by the mid-twenty-first century. If China's future economic growth decelerates sharply before China becomes 'developed', this could deal a fatal blow to the legitimacy of China's current political regime. If political legitimacy falters and capitalists could no longer enforce labour discipline, it is difficult to see how China's existing regime of accumulation could survive.

NOTES

1. World Bank, *World Development Indicators*, 2022, available at: databank.worldbank.org/source/world-development-indicators#.
2. National Bureau of Statistics, People's Republic of China, *Statistical Yearbook of China*, Beijing: National Bureau of Statistics, 2021.
3. National Information Center of National Development and Reform Commission, People's Republic of China. '*Wenjiuye Beijingxia de Xinjiuye Xingtai Fazhan Yanjiu*' (A Study of the Development of New Patterns of Employment against the Background of Employment Stabilization), 8 March 2022, available at: www.ndrc.gov.cn.
4. Emma Charlton, 'What Is the Gig economy and What's the Deal for Gig Workers?', World Economic Forum Jobs Reset Summit, Geneva, Switzerland, 26 May 2021, available at: www.weforum.org.
5. Yingjia Caifu Wang (Winner Wealth Website), 'Gongxiang Jingji Shige Hangye Douyou Naxie' (What Are the Ten Sectors of Sharing Economy?), 8 October 2020, available at: www.yjcf360.com.
6. Zhongguo Zhengfu Wang (The Chinese Government Website), 'Woguo Jiang Duojucuo Jiaqiang Xinjiuye Xingtai Laodongzhe Quanyi Baozhang' (Our Country Will Adopt Multiple Measures to Improve the Protection of Rights and Benefits of Workers under New Patterns of Employment0, 8 July 2021, available at: www.gov.cn.
7. Charlie Giattino, Esteban Ortiz-Ospina, and Max Roser, 'Working Hours', *Our World in Data*, last revised December 2020, available at: ourworldindata.org/working-hours.
8. Liu Linping, Yong Xin, and Shu Fenfen, 'Laodong Quanyi de Diqu Chayi – Jiyu dui Zhusanjiao he Changsanjiao Diqu Wailaigong de Wenjuan Diaocha' (Regional Differences in Labour Rights and Benefits – A Questionnaire Survey of Migrant Workers in Pearl River Delta and Yangzi River Delta), The Chinese University of Hong Kong, Service Centre for China Studies, August 2011, available at: ww2.usc.cuhk.edu.hk.
9. *Zhongguo Xinwen Wang* (China News Network), 'Zhongguo Leiji Baogao Zhiyebing 97.5 Wanli, Shiji Fabing Renshu Genggao' (China Reports 975,000 Cumulative Cases of Occupational Diseases, But the Actual Number of Cases Are Higher), 30 July 2019, available at: www.chinanews.com.cn.
10. Ministry of Emergency Management, People's Republic of China, '2020 Nian Quanguo Shengchan Anquan Shigu Siwang Renshu Jiangzhi 2.74 Wanyu Ren' (In 2020, Nationwide Deaths Due to Production Safety Incidents Fell to More Than 27,400), 29 January 2021, available at: www.mem.gov.cn.
11. *Nanfang Dushi Bao* (Southern Metropolitan Newspaper), 'Weilai Chengshi Yonggong Qicheng Wei Linghuo Yonggong, Yanglao Gongshang Baoxian Yao Quanfugai' (In the Future 70 per cent of Urban Employment Will Be Flexible Employment, Need to Aim for Full Coverage of Pension and Injury Insurance), 6 March 2022, available at: m.mp.oeeee.com.
12. *Gongren Ribao* (The Workers' Daily), 'Xin Jiuye Xingtai Laodongzhe Shuliang Dafu Zengzhang, Laodong Guanxi Rendingnan Deng Wenti Shangdai Jiejue' (Workers under the New Patterns of Employment Have Grown Substantially, the Difficult Issue

of Identifying Employment Relationship Remains to Be Solved), 29 October 2021, available at: www.jxzfw.gov.cn.
13   National Information Center, 'A Study of the Development of New Patterns of Employment', 8 March 2022.
14   Tengxun Wang (Tengxun Network), 'Yixian Chengshi de Waimaiyuan Zaoshang 8 Dian Kaishi Paodan, Gongzuo Dao Wanshang 11 Dian, Zhiyan Xinku' (Takeout Delivery Worker in First-Line Cities Begins Taking Orders at 8am and Work Till 11pm, Bluntly Complains Being Exhausted), 25 April 2020, available at: new.qq.com/omn.
15   *Chejiahao* (Automobile Home), 'Didi Siji: 996 Suanshenme? Wo Meitian Zuishao Kai 12 Xiaoshi' (Didi Driver: 996 Is Nothing, I Drive At Least 12 Hours Every Day), 19 April 2019, available at: chejiahao.autohome.com.cn.
16   Scott Kennedy, 'Made in China 2025', Center for Strategic and International Studies, 1 June 2015, available at: www.csis.org.
17   Zhongguo Zhengfu Wang (The Chinese Government Website), 'Zhonghua Renmin Gongheguo Guomin Jingji he Shehui Fazhan Di Shisige Wunian Guihua he 2035 Nian Yuanjing Mubiao Gangyao' (Fourteenth Five-Year Planning of National Economic and Social Development of the People's Republic of China and Outline of Prospective Objectives in 2035), 13 March 2021, available at: www.gov.cn.
18   Jeffrey Melnik, 'China's "National Champions": Alibaba, Tencent, and Huawei', *Education About Asia*, 24:2, 2019, pp. 28-33, available at: www.asianstudies.org.
19   Nathaniel Ahrens, *China's Competitiveness: Case Study Huawei*, Washington: Center for Strategic and International Studies, 2013.
20   Samuel Gibbs, 'Huawei Beats Apple to Become Second-Largest Smartphone Maker', *The Guardian*, 1 August 2018.
21   Huawei Investment and Holding Company Limited, 'Huawei Touzi Konggu Youxian Gongsi 2021 Nian Niandu Baogao' (2021 Annual Report of Huawei Investment and Holding Company Limited), 31 March 2022.
22   *Fortune*, 'Global 500', 7 February 2022.
23   *Jiemian Xinwen* (Interface News), 'Huawei Guquan Sheji Jiemi: Ren Zhengfei Ruhe Yong 1% Guquan Kongzhi Gongsi' (Revealing the Secret of Huawei's Share Structure Design: How Ren Zhengfei Uses 1% Share-Holding to Control the Company), 19 September 2017, available at: www.jiemian.com.
24   Huawei, '2021 Annual Report', 31 March 2022.
25   *Wangyi* (Networking Easily), 'Huawei Zhenshi Xinzi Shi Duoshao? Huawei Yuangong: Huawei Xinzi Shi Zhendi Buxing' (How Much Is the Actual Salary at Huawei? Huawei Employee: Huawei's Salary Is Actually Not That Great), 19 November 2021, available at: www.163.com.
26   National Bureau of Statistics, *Statistical Yearbook of China*, 2021. In China's official employment and wage statistics, the so-called urban 'non-private' sector includes not only the general government and state-owned enterprises, but also foreign-invested enterprises and the urban private sector refers to the sector of domestic private enterprises.
27   *New Tang Dynasty Television*, 'Langxing yu Nuhua – Toushi Huawei Qiye Wenhua' (Wolf-Like or Enslavement – Perspective on Huawei's Business Culture), 29 January 2019, available at: www.ntdtv.com.

28 Xiao Bang, 'Former Huawei Employee Speaks Out on Shenzhen's "996" Culture as Chinese City Enforces Paid Leave', *ABC News Australia*, 1 January 2021.
29 *New Tang Dynasty Television*, 'Wolf-Like or Enslavement'.
30 'Wolf-Like or Enslavement'.
31 Xiao Bang, 'Former Huawei Employee Speaks Out', 1 January 2021.
32 World Health Organization, 'Long Working Hours Increasing Deaths from Heart Disease and Stroke', 17 May 2021, available at: www.who.int.
33 National Center of Cardiovascular Diseases of National Medical Care and Health Committee, People's Republic of China, *Report of Cardiovascular Diseases in China 2018*, Beijing: China Encyclopedia Press, available at: https://www.nccd.org.cn.
34 National Bureau of Statistics, *Statistical Yearbook of China*, 2021.
35 National Bureau of Statistics, *Statistical Yearbook of China*, 2021.
36 *Zhongguo Xinwen Wang* (China News Network), 'Sancheng Shoufang Qingnian Zhufang Zhichu Zhan Shouru 40% Yishang' (Three-Tenths of Interviewed Young People Spend More Than 40% of Their Income on Housing), 27 April 2021, available at: www.chinanews.com.cn.
37 *Zhongguo Xinwen Wang* (China News Network), 'Tongjiju Huiying Fangjia Weihe Bu Jiru CPI: Busuan Xiaofei Suan Touzi' (Statistical Bureau Explains Why Housing Price Is Not Included in CPI: It Counts as Investment Rather Than Consumption), 31 August 2007, www.chinanews.com.cn.
38 Beike Yanjiu Yuan (Beike Research Institute), *2021 Xin Qingnian Juzhu Xiaofei Baogao* (2021 Report on Residential Consumption of New Youth), 10 May 2021, available at: pg.jrj.com.cn.
39 National Bureau of Statistics, *Statistical Yearbook of China*, 2021. Area of housing that can be purchased is calculated using average annual wage divided by national average housing price, which is derived by dividing the total sales revenue of marketable residential housing by the total volume of sales. For example, in 2020, the total sales revenue of marketable residential housing is 15.46 trillion yuan and the total volume sales is 1.549 billion square metres; it follows that the national average housing price is 9,980 yuan. In 2020, the urban 'non-private' sector's average wage is 97,379 yuan which theoretically can purchase 9.76 square metres if the entire annual wage is used for housing purchase.
40 In recent years, China's education and health care systems have become partially privatized. According to information provided by China's Ministry of Education, there are 183,500 private schools in China, accounting for 35 per cent of the total number of schools in China. Privately owned kindergartens account for 62 per cent of the total number of kindergartens in China. See *Souhu*, 'Zhongguo You Duoshao Suo Youeryuan, Xiaoxue, Zhongxue? Jiaoyubu Liang Jiadi' (How Many Kindergartens, Elementary Schools, and Middle Schools Does China Have? The Ministry of Education Reveals the Balance), 24 July 2019, available at: www.sohu.com. According to information provided by China's National Medical and Healthcare Committee, there are 23,700 private hospitals, accounting for 67 per cent of the total number of hospitals in China. The average size of private hospitals tends to be smaller and public hospitals continue to dominate in terms of employment and hospital beds (public hospitals account for 71 per cent of total hospital beds and 78 per cent of total employment in hospitals). See: Wang Ershi, 'Yiwen Dudong Zhongguo Minying

41 *Yuwa Renkou Yanjiu* (Yuwa Population Research), 'Zhongguo Shengyu Chengben Baogao' (China Fertility Cost Report), February 2022, available at: download.caixin.com.

Yiyuan' (This Article Helps You to Understand China's Private Hospitals), *Zhongguo Yiliao* (China Medical Website), 22 November 2021, available at: med.china.com.cn.

42 Radio France International Chinese Edition, 'Tangping Zhuyi Weixian Ma' (Is Lying-Flat-Ism Dangerous?), 1 June 2021, available at: https://www.rfi.fr/cn.

43 *Tengxun Wang* (Tengxun Network), 'Quanguo 31 Shengfen Junyi Fangkai Shuangdu Jiating Sheng Ertai Zhengce' (31 Provinces throughout the Country Have All Adopted the Policy Allowing Families in Which Both Parents Were the Single Child to Have Second Children), 26 November 2020, available at: https://news.qq.com.

44 Population Division, United Nations Department of Economic and Social Affairs, *World Populations Prospects*, 2019, available at: population.un.org.

45 Yuwa Population Research, 'China Fertility Cost Report', February 2022.

46 Yuwa Population Research, 'China Fertility Cost Report', February 2022.

47 National Bureau of Statistics, *Statistical Yearbook of China*, 2021.

48 National Bureau of Statistics, *Statistical Yearbook of China*, 2021.

49 Roland Rajah and Alyssa Leng, 'Revising Down the Rise of China', *Lowy Institute*, 15 March 2022, available at: www.lowyinstitute.org.

50 Bureau of Economic Analysis, Government of the United States, National Income and Product Accounts and Fixed Assets Tables, available at: apps.bea.gov. Profit rate is defined as the ratio of before-tax profit over net stock of fixed assets.

51 Indeed, according to Yu Chunsen, in China's high-tech factories connected to global supply chains, the precarious migrant factory workers are already forming a new class that identify themselves as a group with common interests and are willing to take collective actions, a class that may be dangerous for both the capitalists and the government. See: Yu Chunsen, 'All Workers are Precarious: The "Dangerous Class" in China's Labour Regime', in Leo Panitch and Greg Albo, eds., *Socialist Register 2020: Beyond Market Dystopia*, London, Merlin Press: 2019, pp. 143-60.

52 United Nations, *World Populations Prospects*, 2019.

53 United Nations, *World Populations Prospects*, 2019.

54 Charles Goodhart and Manoj Pradhan, *The Great Demographic Reversal: Aging Societies, Waning Inequality, and An Inflation Revival*, London: Palgrave Macmillan, 2020, pp. 129-48.

55 Minqi Li, 'The Capitalist World System and Economic Imperialism in East Asia', in Z. Cope and I. Ness, eds., *The Oxford Handbook of Economic Imperialism*, New York: Oxford University Press, 2022, pp. 455-74.

56 Xi Jinping, 'Juesheng Quanmian Jiancheng Xiaokang Shehui, Duoqu Xinshidai Zhongguo Tese Shehui Zhuyi Weida Shengli' (Win the Decisive Victory in the Comprehensive Building of A Society of Moderate Prosperity, Win the Great Victory of Socialism with Chinese Characteristics in the New Era), Report at the 19th National Congress of the Communist Party of China, 27 October 2017, available at: www.gov.cn.

57 World Bank, *World Development Indicators*, 2022. Per capita GDP is measured by Purchasing Power Parity.

INFRASTRUCTURAL CAPITALISM: HIGH-SPEED RAIL AND CLASS CONFLICT IN CHINA

PUN NGAI AND CHEN PEIER

In his analysis of 'the production of space', David Harvey argues that 'capital represents itself in the form of a physical landscape created in its own image'.[1] For the 'infrastructural capitalism' that dominates China today, its own image can be found in the state-led, mega-scale construction of high-speed rail (HSR), attempting to reach into every corner of the country and even beyond.[2] In terms of its operational mileage and speed, China's HSR network ranks first in the world. Transportation networks mark one of the 'hallmarks of the geography of capitalism'. In China, the HSR network also represents a novel scale 'spatial fix' in the form of a state-led development model attempting to contain the crisis dynamics of overaccumulation that emerged with the Great Recession of 2008 and economic developments of the last decade.[3]

Capital alone, however, cannot create such a national spectacle, built at an impressive pace, to realise the 'Chinese Dream'.[4] A project as ambitious as China's infrastructural capitalism depends upon mobilizing a dual logic of power, namely the logic of capital and the logic of territorial power. Harvey's conceptualization of these two logics is useful for the analysis of mega-scale infrastructural constructions initiated by the Chinese government as a strategic response to overaccumulation. For Harvey, territorial logic means 'the political, diplomatic, economic and military strategies deployed by the state apparatus in its own interest',[5] within a bounded territory, to 'mobilize its human and natural resources'[6] for the purpose of capitalistic expansion as well as crisis alleviation (notably in the neoliberal period). The capital logic, in contrast, 'focuses on the way in which money flows across and through space and over borders in the search for endless accumulation', to command the regime of capital accumulation.[7] These two logics are closely interwoven, but Harvey has recently argued that there is an increasing trend for the capital logic to override the territorial logic in China.[8]

The contention that the state acts as a territorial 'power container' while capital is 'non-territorial' has been subject to critiques. Some have argued, for example, that Harvey's binary logic oversimplifies the complex interplay of capital and territorial logics of power. The capitalist logic depends upon the support of the territorial (or geopolitical) logic.[9] Indeed, 'territorial logics of power can also be terrifying mobile'.[10] In China, the logic of territorial power, as materialized in the political technologies of the state, has been central to attempts to resolve the economic slowdown over the last two decades, with its visible registers in the overcapacity in domestic production and stagnant consumption. But to deal with this economic crisis within a bounded nation-state the Chinese state has also, paradoxically, rescaled its territorial practices, extending them into its Asian neighbours and beyond, partly to secure natural resources for domestic production and partly to expand and secure access to overseas export markets. These actions manifest themselves in emerging international geo-economic rivalries over control of markets and political leadership. As such, the two logics – of territory and of capital – are intertwining and mutually constituting each other, despite their potential conflicts and tensions, in China's infrastructural capitalism.[11]

We borrow the concept of 'infrastructure' from anthropological studies and political science.[12] We develop infrastructural capitalism, however, as a political concept grounded in Marxism, to understand the current configuration of China's capitalism and its particular intertwining of the political logics of territory and capitalism. The building of infrastructure already follows the logic of capital in driving its expansion and filling the landscape with the built environment necessary for accumulation. Two interrelated themes can also be identified in the specific infrastructural powers of territory and labour.

Territorial infrastructural power refers to the state's tactical power to serve capitalistic expansion through building infrastructure for the 'general interest of capital' and for the social reproduction of capitalist social relations. China's development of infrastructural capitalism was not, we contend, an alternative model for global capitalism but at best a reaction to the impasse of neoliberal policy entailing a reconfiguration in political technologies of power.[13] Two dominant tendencies of this process have been identified. First, some Chinese state enterprises and leading private capitalists have gradually achieved a monopolistic status and a dominance in global production networks. This includes firms operating both domestically and internationally in strategic industries such as rail infrastructure, technology, and e-commerce.[14] Second, the strategic infrastructure bases established, including HSR networks, have played an important role in resolving China's various forms of crisis and sustaining a measure of economic cohesion on a national scale while accentuating uneven geographical development. The infrastructural bases are, in turn, foundational to the monopolizing process of capital and the internationalization of Chinese state and leading private capital, further deepening the process of state-initiated infrastructural development.[15]

The concept of infrastructural power, as we develop it, can also be 'turned upside down' to shift our focus to the infrastructural power of the working class.[16] The organizational agency and power of workers directly impacts the spatial fixes underpinning the conflictual geographies of capitalism and labour.[17] If the working class is constrained by its place in the social structures of infrastructural capitalism, for example, it also exerts its own infrastructural power for collective actions in workplaces and politically through strikes and protests that enter into the infrastructural development process.[18] In short, China's infrastructural capitalism has had the unintended consequence of opening up a field for various forms of class struggle to emerge.

The intensification of infrastructural development in China has become an incubator for various forms of class conflicts in China, and these axes of contentious politics merit highlighting as they impinge on HSR projects.[19] First, infrastructural development is reliant on processes of accumulation by dispossession.[20] Over the last three decades, land disputes over dispossession and corrupt administrative processes have been central to many conflicts, with dispossessed peasants often forming the base of the new working class and in the vanguard of labour protests. Second, although the World Bank has remarked that the debt levels for financing high-speed rail in China meet international debt standards,[21] a high level of government debt has accumulated in financing infrastructural development that could pose problems for future economic stability, especially as the debt is likely to be amplified in the coming period as China continues to rely on similar modes of development.[22] Third, infrastructure construction has consistently created labour abuses through labour subcontracting and wage theft. Recurring construction worker protests have been an integral feature of infrastructural capitalism in China.[23] Finally, infrastructure projects are central to accelerating the circulation of capital, and the employment of the transport and logistics workers that are constitutive of the infrastructural power base of labour. The labour processes of these workers connect them, in turn, to the vast majority of manufacturing and service workers, with the potential to undergird the formation of a new working-class politics.

With the transition from the diversified investment of product commodities by private capital in the early reform period of competitive capitalism to the tremendous investments in grand infrastructure projects by the Chinese state and private capitals in this period of monopolization, a new terrain of class conflicts has formed.[24] This requires investigating how the dual logics of capital and territorial power intersect with the infrastructural capitalism of China, forming the social contradictions and class conflicts bubbling just below the surface. The contemporary form of China's capitalism cannot just be analyzed from the standpoint of 'power from above', but also needs to account for the active making of the Chinese working class in the struggles over infrastructural capitalism. To support our claims, we look at how the dual logic of power works in the high-speed rail network in China, following on discussions of 'variegated capitalism', notably, the role of embedded institutional processes such as strategic state planning, public investments, corporate restructuring, and labour relations in generating class conflicts.[25]

GOVERNING THE HIGH-SPEED RAIL INFRASTRUCTURE

'China's high-speed railway network ranks first in the world in terms of operational mileage, scale of railways under construction, number of trains in service, and operational speed,' according to Liang Dong, deputy director of the planning division of China Railway Economic and Planning Research Institute.[26] HSR development could never achieve this speed and scale without the full support of the Chinese state. Although China's railway had experienced a six-fold speed increase on major lines between 1997 and 2008, it was with the opening of the Beijing-Tianjin intercity rail on 1 August 2008, with its highest speed of 350 km/h, that China celebrated its true entry into the HSR era.[27] In 2013, reaching a total mileage of 10,463 km, China become the world's largest operator of HSR.

This tremendous growth of the HSR network can be understood as a strategic response to the global financial crisis in 2008. It was estimated that 40 per cent of the government stimulus fund went directly to transportation infrastructure, and one of the biggest beneficiaries was the HSR. This government stimulus package, coupled with the 12th Five-Year Plan – the explicit manifestation of the operation of a dual logic of state infrastructural power – together foregrounded China's long-term infrastructural development strategy.[28] Despite the massive liabilities – 5.49 trillion yuan – shouldered by the China Railway Corporation, the state still advanced infrastructural investment in HSR construction as the core goal of economic growth and security in the context of a Sino-American trade war and the Covid-19 economic recession.[29] Indeed, the China Railway Corporation later announced that the HSR network would reach 70,000 km by 2035 under its railway expansion strategy.[30]

More than merely an economic project, HSR construction is also seen as a political project to realize the 'great rejuvenation of the Chinese nation' and construct a unified 'community of shared future'. The logic of territorial power in China operates amidst a web of complications related to the state-socialist legacy as well as market rationality. As we will see, the state has played three key roles in relation to infrastructure development: powerful strategic planning, corporate restructuring, and public finance and investment.

Firstly, the state has played a powerful role in strategic planning. A key milestone in China's high-speed rail development was the design and implementation of 'The Medium to Long Term Railway Development Plan' (MLTRP) in 2004. Approved by the State Council and jointly issued by the Ministry of Railways and National Development and Reform Commission, the MLTRP was the first attempt to propose a HSR network with a target of 12,000 km of high-speed lines to form four horizontal and four vertical corridors by 2020.[31] Aimed at stimulating the economy following the 2008 global downturn, the Chinese government announced it was going to accelerate the HSR programs. Accordingly, additional projects – nine regional intercity networks – were proposed, and the 2020 development target was expanded to 16,000 km. Further ambitious revision to the MLTRP came in 2016 when the HSR network structure was expanded to eight horizontal and eight vertical corridors based on the former skeleton with an estimated total length of HSR lines over 38,000 km by 2025. This continuous and consistent plan has consolidated the strategic position of HSR as an economic engine in a time of crisis and for long-term development. The MLTRP demonstrates the territorial power of the state not only in that it provides a clear and consistent framework for firm-level strategy and operations, but also that it signals continuous commitment and support from all layers of the government, as well as other social entities linked to the state, for the HSR. Indeed, HSR-advancing technologies are developed within a technology innovation ecosystem comprising state-funded universities, research institutes, and other related manufacturing SOEs.[32] A series of state-governed cooperation agreements and state-funded HSR-related R&D projects were mobilized to ensure participation and cooperation among the different components of this system.

Secondly, the state has facilitated corporate restructuring. Bold measures in organizational restructuring were enacted by removing the obstacles for corporate institutional reform so as to fulfil the logic of capital monopolization under the auspices of the state. Two major phases of organizational restructuring of railway transportation took place: the 2013 reform and the 2019 restructuring. The 2013 reform served to separate the conventional government administration from business operations, which was the first step towards their operation on a commercial basis, while the 2019 restructuring aimed at setting up a more commercially oriented enterprise system to facilitate investment by state capital in HSR, as well as capitalizing and privatizing state assets on a shareholding basis. In these two phases of reforms, state control over the rail sector has not been weakened as expected; instead, a monopolistic railway industry dominated by state-owned enterprises has gradually been developed for capital valorization, with state-backed competitive advantages in both domestic and foreign markets.

Holding the highest authority over China's railways by combining administrative power with commercial activities, the Ministry of Railways has long been criticized as 'the last fortress of China's planned economy'.[33] However, triggered by the Wenzhou accident, rampant corruption and the huge debt burden,[34] it was not until March 2013 that the Ministry of Railways was finally split into the National Railway Administration (NRA), which performs administrative functions, and the China Railway Corporation, which carries out business functions.[35] With a registered capital of 1.04 trillion yuan, the China Railway was restructured from its traditional organization as a 'people-owned state enterprise' and became directly administered by the central government.[36] This separation, however, did not change its strong planned-economy structure, and its privileged allocation of resources. In addition, as a mega-scale SOE, it not only comprised 16 administrative departments and seven directly administered railway bureaus as well as three specialty companies, but also two million employees who were transferred from the Ministry of Railways. No one would deny that the China Railway serves as a mini-Ministry of Railways.[37]

To further its corporate restructuring and deepen the market-orientation of its operations, China Railway embarked on its second step in its transformation from a 'people-owned' state enterprise to a wholly 'state-owned limited corporation'.[38] With China Railway acting as sole investor, the 18 regional rail bureaus and their subordinated non-transportation enterprises registered as limited companies, which further expanded their business scope to cover real estate development, logistics, tourism, and finance. China Railway itself was formally renamed in 2019 as the China State Railway Group Co., Ltd., the last step in its corporate structural reform. At this time, China Railway's registered capital increased to 1.7 trillion yuan, with around 2 million employees. As the world's largest railway company, China Railway achieved a monopoly over the rail industry.

Finally, a mega-scale project like HSR construction would be impossible without massive state financial support. It is commonly noted that the timeline for the HSR to be profitable could be extremely long, and thus market logic would lead fewer capitalist societies to invest such a large amount of capital in rail development. In China, the state took the lead in providing unprecedented support to address HSR financing issues – covering not only investments, but also bank financing, bonds and loans, mergers, and financial controls. Funding mainly came from three sources.[39] First, state budget allocations and direct loans from state-owned banks were an important source. Between 2007 and 2017, the annual state budget for investment ranged from 12 to 22 per cent allocated to investment in fixed assets in railway transportation. Similarly, bank loans with low interest rates and unspecified repayment periods characterized half of the capital investment in HSR projects.[40] Second, revenue that the Railway Construction Fund extracted from HSR lines was mainly used for nationally planned large- and medium-sized railway construction projects.[41] Third, Railway Construction Bonds supported by the central government were issued to finance railway construction. These three sources of funding endorsed by the Chinese state guaranteed the financial availability of the HSR projects.

Few countries could overcome the economic and political barriers to develop HSR on such a giant scale. Besides the central state-financed networks, local governments were also mobilized to finance HSR's local lines. Local governments were also enthusiastic about rail construction, as they viewed it as a chance to boost their local economy.[42] Local governments' infrastructure spending therefore accelerated significantly, with less concern over how to repay debt.[43]

LABOUR INFRASTRUCTURAL POWER AND WORKERS' RESISTANCE

We have already seen how the two logics of power were central to the building of a world-leading high-speed rail network. Yet the deepening of China's infrastructural capitalism entailed social-spatial contradictions and class conflicts, embodied in uneven infrastructure development, on the one hand, and corporate restructuring and labour reform, on the other. These two increasingly intertwined processes, in turn, engendered spatial injustices and class-based labour conflicts. It is these class-based conflicts, targeted at the government and state-owned enterprises, that enabled workers engaged in the spatialized production network[44] to interrupt the circulation of capital and challenge the legitimacy of the state through individual and collective actions. Such struggles constitute what can be called labour infrastructure power.[45]

The analysis of the concept of labour infrastructure power takes place on two levels – structural and social – in illustrating how the Chinese working class affects the accumulation of capital. Structurally, given the key role of the Chinese state in guaranteeing infrastructure projects as well as in sustaining the capitalist regime, all economic struggles over class exploitation which emerge from China's infrastructural capitalism are automatically turned into political struggles. Socially, a wide range of the Chinese working class, including peasants and migrant workers, has engaged in heightened class struggles that are grassroots and mass-based.

Despite the surface success of the corporate restructuring initiated by the state, as it did not result in mass unemployment, this process nevertheless intensified capital-labour contradictions and caused widespread resistance. Multiple forms of infrastructural power that derived from these labour conflicts are illustrated by worker grievances generated in the labour process, and their collective actions against authoritarian management and exploitation.

Workers' grievances

The corporate restructuring of China Railway resulted in a significant change in capital-labour relations: the end of permanent employment and the abolition of the privileged status of workers in state-owned enterprises. This change brought about the rise of a labour subcontracting system to structure labour relationships with China Railway. Many subcontracted workers were employed to replace regular workers, resulting in a serious deterioration of working and living conditions. Workers' legal rights, such as contracts and wages, were violated, while managerial discipline over workers through regulations and deductions was intensified. As such, worker grievances revolved around low wages, deductions, and an unfair subcontracting system.

Unsurprisingly, the issue of low wages was of utmost importance, leading to the most complaints and triggering collective action. As noted, along with the corporate restructuring in 2013 and 2019, pay methods were changed and tied to a capitalist logic. The eighteen regional limited corporations and subsidies under China Railway lowered the pay level, thereby increasing their profit. The pay method based on a per-trip basis was changed to a per-hour basis, directly resulting in a relative reduction in train drivers' wages. Based on this new payment system, the drivers found that:

> If you do not work overtime, you cannot earn enough money to support your family. For example, your basic monthly salary is around five to six thousand yuan. But adding the overtime compensation, the salary will

increase to eight to nine thousand yuan. For the money, no one will refuse to work overtime.[46]

What followed was a chronically intensive workload with high risks of occupational disease suffered by the workers.

Workers' strong sense of dissatisfaction and anger also accumulated from increasing managerial discipline, especially as exercised through various forms of pay deductions. A performance assessment system enforced by a graded fine system was imposed to manage and control workers.[47] In effect, the assessment was arbitrary: management not only set the quantity of fines each month, but also had the final say in determining whether workers committed violations or not. Much worse, fines collected from workers were used as bonuses for management. This placed these two parties in an oppositional position, and a distinct class line was drawn.

An unfair subcontracting system, jointly used by the state and capital, resulted in second-class status for dispatched workers – with lower wages and lack of employee benefits such as annual leave and housing allowance – compared to regular workers in the same positions.[48] HSR infrastructure facilitates the flow of dispatched workers, including peasant-workers and urban poor, as cheap labouring bodies for the use of capital, but it also results in a strong sense of unfairness related to deepening economic inequality among workers. As a petition co-signed by the dispatched workers from Nanchang Group noted:

> There is a wage polarization between the regular workers and us. Why? Just because we are dispatched workers even though we are doing the same work ... We demand a fair chance to transform to be regular workers. It is our responsibility to strive for our legitimate rights and interests.[49]

Grievances and anger over the socio-economic injustices created by the HSR development has initiated an awakening. Workers have gradually realised that they have been deprived by the state and capital of the 'qualification' to take the HSR train to a destination of promised prosperity. In this high-speed infrastructural capitalism, they are 'left behind'. As a response, widespread resistance has emerged.

Workers' resistance

The class struggles embedded in the expanded spatiality of HSR lines has united workers to stage collective actions in resistance against state and capital. In January 2011, railway drivers protested following the announcement of the new per-hour payment system.⁵⁰ When several temporarily elected workers' representatives were invited to negotiate with management, more than 170 railway drivers spontaneously gathered outside, and three demands were highlighted: a continuation on a per-trip basis rather than a per-hour basis; providing overtime compensation according to the Labour Law of the People's Republic of China; and a prohibition on management constantly monitoring workers via CCTV. The railway drivers signed this petition and turned in their driver's licences, initiating a two-day work stoppage. This strike paralyzed the traffic system, as more than ten trains were heavily delayed or cancelled. As a result of this protest, workers' solidarity was advanced:

> It is necessary to unite your co-workers. Sometimes you may not make it on your own. But teamwork works. We can act collectively in opposition to management. To be simple, if everyone asks for leave at the same time, the locomotive depot will be in disorder.

These railway drivers were clearly conscious of their shared class interests, and sensitive to the collective nature of the labour process in this spontaneously collective action. In turn, collective resistance stood out as an effective way to affect the labour process under infrastructure capitalism.

Together with these collective actions initiated by the railway drivers, a surge in the number of labour disputes also occurred between dispatched workers and China Railway, as the latter was requested to deal with its excessive number of dispatched workers by February 2016.⁵¹ The intersection of long-term accumulating unfairness around low wages and deteriorating working conditions, alongside the fear of being dismissed, drove dispatched workers to act collectively against the exploitative subcontracting system and advance their demand to be regular employees. It was reported that in February 2016, dozens of dispatched workers from Nanchang Group held mass gatherings outside the company's offices and chanted the slogan – 'I am working for this company, but I am not an employee of it' and 'I want to be a regular employee'.⁵² Since then, along with spreading petitions on the Internet, massive gatherings of dispatched workers have taken place outside company offices in several cities – first in Xi'an, then in Harbin and Shenyang – where hundreds of workers took collective actions to demand: 'equal work, equal pay'.⁵³

Recent years have also witnessed an increase in labour disputes as a result of dispatched workers turning to the labour arbitration system to air grievances and seek economic justice. In the three years from 2020 to 2022, nearly 2,000 court cases were recorded on China Judgements Online.[54] Most of the cases were related to employment contracts and social insurance compensation. The discontented dispatched workers often filed cases directly with the railway groups instead of the agency companies to claim their legal employment rights and benefits, such as pensions and other insurance. These collective cases were always split into individual ones when they went to court. Although the claims could only be handled individually by the courts, their collective nature could not be erased, as the experience of subcontracting had affected every dispatched worker. Dictated by the dual logics of territorial power and capital, the rapid expansion of HSR lines 'brings the country together' to sustain its capitalist regime, but on the other hand, it 'brings the workers together', who are spatially diversified in production. These intense class conflicts which have emerged through the deepening of high-speed capitalism could provoke a new wave of destabilizing labour struggles.

INFRASTRUCTURE AND CLASS CONFLICT

The labour conflicts in China's HSR network illustrate the interconnections between the geographies of capitalism and labour and the potential for new labour insurgencies to gain ground, partly aided by the political profile large infrastructure projects take on. Through the restructuring of capital-labour relations by the state and monopolistic capital, a labour subcontracting system has emerged in the rail sectors. Large numbers of workers have been affected as the employers increasingly turned to subcontracted workers or dispatched labour whose labour rights were often seriously violated. At the point of contention, the affected rail workers were also connected, paradoxically, through the very same rail networks, facilitating the forming of a class-based spatial linkage to the various labour conflicts. The accumulated and shared grievances of workers often turned into widespread and collective actions that took both legal and non-legal forms to demand better socio-economic benefits and working conditions. These conflicts illustrate the spatial formation of the labour infrastructural power of workers in the HSR sector.

The study of HSR projects in China reveals some of the features and contradictions of China's infrastructural capitalism in this new era of monopolized capital. China's turn to infrastructure can be seen as a reaction to the 2008 economic crisis and the failings of neoliberal capitalism. Mega-scale infrastructure projects, such as HSR, also allowed the Chinese state to further expand and consolidate its territorial power, support new developments of high technology, and importantly, further enhance the capacities of an expansive state through its accretion of infrastructural power.

If the dual logics of territorial power and capital helped resolve the internal economic crisis and sustain further development of the accumulation regime, it also revealed the complexity and heterogeneity of China's emergent place within global capitalism.[55] China's contemporary form of capitalism is far from constrained within its own national territory. The operations of Chinese controlled capitals in many sectors now run far beyond its national borders and reach out to neighbouring Asian regions as well as continental Africa and South America. This invites further analysis of the territorial fluidity and complexity of China's capitalism and the current configuration of the global economy. The deepening state-led infrastructure development by China, both domestically and internationally, establishes the political conditions for the emergence of inter-state rivalry over market access and control through the competitive process of global capital accumulation.[56] As can be seen in the case of the infrastructure capitalism propelling the development of the high-speed rail network in China, these advances also create internal contradictions that intensify class conflicts and spur the formation of the infrastructural power of labour. It is here that one can also locate some of the struggles that are making a new Chinese working class.

NOTES

1   David Harvey, 'The urban process under capitalism: a framework for analysis', *International Journal of Urban and Regional Research,* 2(1-3), 1978, pp. 101-31.
2   China's railway network had covered 98 per cent of the cities with a population of more than 200,000, up from 94 per cent in 2012; 86 per cent for cities with a population of 500,000; and all provincial capitals in the country except for Lhasa were connected to the high-speed railway network in 2019. The average number of passengers taking China's high-speed trains each day rose from around 1.07 million in 2012 to 6.38 million in 2019, representing an average annual growth of 29.1 per cent. See: 'What will China's railway network be like in 2035?', *People's Daily*, 20 August 2020.
3   Ngai Pun and Peier Chen, 'Confronting global infrastructural capitalism: the triple logic of the "vanguard" and its inevitable spatial and class contradictions in China's high-speed rail program', *Cultural Studies*, 11 April 2022, online, pp. 1-22.
4   Neil Smith, *Uneven Development: Nature, Capital and the Production of Space*, second edition, Oxford: Basil Blackwell, 1990.
5   David Harvey, *The Enigma of Capital*, London: Profile Books, 2010, pp. 204-5.
6   David Harvey, *The New Imperialism*, New York: Oxford University Press, 2003, pp. 26-27.
7   Harvey, *The Enigma of Capital*, pp. 204-5.
8   David Harvey and Paik Nak-Chung, 'How capital operates and where the world and China are going: A conversation between David Harvey and Paik Nak-Chung', *Inter-Asia Cultural Studies*, 18(2), 2017, pp. 251-68.

9   Seung-Ook Lee, Joel Wainwright, and Jim Glassman, 'Geopolitical economy and the production of territory: The case of US-China geopolitical-economic competition in Asia', *Environment and Planning A: Economy and Space*, 50(2), 2017, pp. 416-36.

10 David Gregory, 'Introduction: Troubling geographies', in Noel Castree and David Gregory, eds, *David Harvey: A Critical Reader*, Oxford: Blackwell Publishing, 2006, pp. 1-25.

11 The 1949 China Revolution was never completed, and it was tragically ended at the end of the 1970s when China re-integrated – 'opened up' – into global capitalism and becoming part of it. Thus we reject the idea of capitalism as a linear progression for China or elsewhere. See: Lin Chun, *Revolution and Counterrevolution in China*, New York: Verso Books, 2021.

12 Brian Larkin, 'The politics and poetics of infrastructure', *Annual Review of Anthropology*, 42(1), 2013, pp. 327-43. See also: Biao Xiang and Johan Lindquist, 'Migration infrastructure', *International Migration Review*, 48(1), 2014, pp. 122-48.

13 By monopoly capital, we refer to its defining feature of the dominance of monopolistic firms which operate in oligopolistic industries and sectors; and also the corporate global value chains that are often facilitated by the financialization of capital and state power. See: Ernest Mandel, *Late Capitalism*, London: Verso, 1974.

14 Rail infrastructure was determined by speed and acceleration technology which determined design, construction, maintenance, and repair, especially for the operation of railway lines where speeds of 300 km per hour or above are reached.

15 Lee, Wainwright, and Glassman, 'Geopolitical economy and the production of territory'; and Jamie Peck and Rachel Phillips, 'The platform conjuncture', *Sociologica*, 14(3), 2020, pp. 73-99.

16 Michael Mann, 'Infrastructural power revisited', *Studies in Comparative International Development,* 43(3), 2008, p. 355.

17 Smith, *Uneven Development*. See also: Harvey, *The Limits to Capital*.

18 Raju J. Das, 'From labor geography to class geography: Reasserting the Marxist theory of class', *Human Geography,* 5(1), 2012, pp. 19-35. See also: Kendra Strauss, 'Labor geography 1: Towards a geography of precarity?', *Progress in Human Geography,* 42(4), 2018, pp. 622-30; Karen Strauss, 'Labor geography II: Being, knowledge and agency', *Progress in Human Geography,* 44(1), 2020, pp. 150-59.

19 Colin McFarlane, and Jonathan Rutherford, 'Political Infrastructures: Governing and Experiencing the Fabric of the City', *International Journal of Urban and Regional Research*, 32(2), 2008, pp. 363-74.

20 David Harvey, 'The right to the city', *International Journal of Urban and Regional Research*, 27(4), 2003, pp. 939-41.

21 Martha B. Lawrence, Richard G. Bullock, and Ziming Liu, 'China's High-Speed Rail Development', *International Development in Focus*, World Bank Group, 2019, available at: documents.worldbank.org.

22 'China Seen Cutting Local Government Bond Quota to Curb Debt', *Bloomberg News*, 1 March 2021.

23 Ngai Pun, *Migrant Labour in China: Post-Socialist Transformation*, Cambridge: Polity Press, 2016.

24 Minqi Li, *China and the 21st Century Crisis*, London: Pluto Press, 2015.

25 Jamie Peck and Jun Zhang, 'A variety of capitalism … with Chinese characteristics?',

Journal of Economic Geography, 13(3), 357-96; and 'Variegated capitalism, Chinese style: Regional models, multi-scalar constructions', *Regional Studies*, 50(1), pp. 52-78.

26   'What will China's railway network be like in 2035?', *People's Daily*, 2020.
27   Xin Qiu, *China 40 years Infrastructure Construction*, Berlin: Springer, 2020.
28   H. Xu, *The Rising Path of China's High-Speed Rail*, Hong Kong: Joint Publishing, 2018.
29   China State Railway Group Co., Ltd., *Audit Report*, 2019.
30   'China targets big expansion of high-speed rail network', *Argus blog*, 21 August 2020, available at: www.argusmedia.com.
31   Lawrence et al., 'China's High-Speed Rail Development'.
32   Zhe Sun, 'Technology innovation and entrepreneurial state: the development of China's high-speed rail industry', *Technology Analysis & Strategic Management*, 27(6), 2015, pp. 646-59.
33   Sun, 'Technology innovation and entrepreneurial state'.
34   The two-train collision in Wenzhou killed 40 people and injured 200 in July 2011, making it the most serious railway accident in a decade. The former Minster of Railways, Liu Zhijun, was given a suspended death sentence for taking bribes of 64 million yuan. Total liabilities for the Ministry of Railways increased to 2.79 trillion yuan in 2012.
35   Robin Bordie, Stephen Wilson, and Jane Kuang, 'The Importance, Development and Reform Challenges of China's Rail Sector', *Deepening Reform*, 2014, p. 477.
36   In the pre-reform Maoist period 'people-owned state enterprise' was meant in the sense that the ownership of the CRC belonged to 'all people' in China through the state. In the reform period as capitalist markets spread, the common discourse shifted to purely 'state-owned enterprise' to indicate state ownership and more direct control by the government bureau. This wording change also registered a shift in the social nature of the enterprise as, for example, more workers became contracted workers or dispatched agency workers and laboured in more exploitative and capitalistic work situations.
37   Hong Yu, 'Railway sector reform in China: Controversy and problems,' *Journal of Contemporary China*, 24(96), 2015, pp. 1070-91.
38   'China's rail bureaus renamed in corporate reform', *CGTN Business*, 21 November 2017, available at: news.cgtn.com.
39   Liu Rongfang, 'The role of state: High speed rail development in China', *Advances in Management*, 8(3), 2015, p. 1.
40   Liu Rongfang and Andy Li, 'Forecasting high-speed rail ridership using a simultaneous modelling approach', *Transportation Planning and Technology*, 35(5), 2012, pp. 577-90.
41   As the China Railway reported in its 2019 audit report, the Construction Fund after tax contributed to railway projects 49,804 million yuan in 2017, 54,372 million yuan in 2018, and 55,392 million yuan in 2019.
42   Rongfang, 'The role of state: High speed rail development in China'.
43   However, high-speed rail infrastructure embodied substantial fiscal risks when the government was incapable of handling borrowing on-budget. China's government debt had risen to 45.8 per cent of GDP by the end of 2020. China's total government debt-to-GDP ratio is expected to break the threshold of 60 per cent if large-scale local government bond sales continue to occur. Situations are worse in the economically 'backward' regions in China. More than 70 per cent of the fiscal revenues in Guizhou,

Qinghai, and three Northeast Provinces (including Liaoning, Jilin and Heilongjiang) will be used for debt service in the years to come. When local governments cannot pay off their existing debt, it will cause potential financial risk to the banking system, especially local banks. See: 'Beware of the Chinese version of the "European Debt Crisis" – the analysis and solutions on the local governments' debt risks', *National Institution for Finance & Development*, 2020, available at: www.nifd.cn.

44 Neil M. Coe, and David C. Jordhus-Lier, 'Constrained agency? Re-evaluating the geographies of labour', *Progress in Human Geography*, 35(2), 2010, pp. 211-33.
45 Sally A. Weller, 'Shifting spatialities of power: The case of Australasian aviation', *Geoforum*, 40(5), 2009, pp. 790-99. See also: Him Chung, 'The spatial dimension of negotiated power relations and social justice in the redevelopment of villages-in-the-city in China', *Environment and Planning A*, 45(10), 2013, pp. 2459-76.
46 An online post at a popular website on rail travel with the question, 'how do you feel working in the rail sector', received many answers from workers including railway drivers and attendants. Many railway drivers complained about the pay cut and overwork under the new payment policy. Available at: www.zhihu.com/question/24700434.
47 In general, this graded fine system comprises four categories, A, B, C, and D, with each category linked to a corresponding fine. For example, receiving a Category A means the railway driver will correspondingly receive a fine valued at 360 yuan.
48 Dispatched workers refers to the hiring of employees through and employment service agency. It is a common practice of irregular employment in China, with the workers being paid less than regular and unionized workers.
49 From a workers' self-produced magazine: *The Railroad Workers Bulletin*, 2016, pp. 15-17, available on-line in Chinese.
50 'Workers' self-report: An action in 2011', *The Railroad Workers Bulletin*, 10 December 2018. This is the source for the dispute discussed below.
51 According to the Interim Provisions on Labour Dispatch released by the Ministry of Human Resources and Social Security in January 2014, the number of dispatched workers employed shall not exceed 10 per cent of its total employment.
52 *Railroad Workers Bulletin*, 2016, pp. 15-17,
53 'Thousands of workers held massive gatherings outside the office of the Harbin Group', *Utopia*, 28 January 2016, available at: http://m.wyzxwk.com/content.php?classid=25&id=358465.
54 *China Judgments Online* is an official web site developed by the Supreme People's Court. It offers the largest collection of court judgements and decisions made in China. 1,905 results were found under the keywords of railway, labour dispute, and labour contract. Available at: wenshu.court.gov.cn.
55 Peck and Zhang, 'A variety of capitalism ... with Chinese characteristics?'.
56 Tom Goodfellow and Zhengli Huang, 'Contingent infrastructure and the dilution of 'Chineseness': Reframing roads and rail in Kampala and Addis Ababa', *Environment and Planning A: Economy and Space*, 53(4), 2020, pp. 655-74.

POLITICAL DIVISIONS AND NEO-FASCISM IN BRAZIL

ARMANDO BOITO

This essay reviews the current phase of the political history of Brazil, in which the neoliberal capitalist model is going through a period of instability and bourgeois democracy is showing signs of crisis. This situation is similar to that in other countries both in the centre and the periphery of the imperialist system. It identifies the political forces at play, outlines their main features, and analyzes the dynamics of the political process in Brazil. The underlying question is the following: can this crisis period also be characterized as a period of transition towards a new model of capitalism?[1]

The analysis brings to light issues that are worth drawing the readers' attention to right from the start; first of all, the flexible, and often shifting, cleavages in the Brazilian capitalist class, between a bourgeois fraction that is fully integrated into foreign capital through various connections and another that, though intertwined with and dependent on foreign capital, seeks to limit the internationalization of Brazilian dependent capitalism. The conflict between these two fractions of the capitalist class has played a central role in Brazil's recent political history. Closely related to this is the importance of the middle class in the political process, as it finds itself divided between rival political programs, and the secondary but important role of the popular movement during this period. This includes the political alliances or agreements that the popular movement has made or could make, and the dangers posed by these alliances.

More broadly, it is important to consider the base of support for the main political parties and their platforms, and the peculiarities of the Brazilian political regime and party system: the gap between the presidential election, on one hand, which, in practice, has been turned into a two-party process, and the elections for the legislative bodies and state governors, on the other, in which the participation of a wide variety of parties remains significant. Other institutional and ideological factors, intertwined in many ways with class conflicts, have played key roles in the political crisis that led to the overthrow of President Dilma Rousseff of the Workers' Party (*Partido dos Trabalhadores*, PT) in 2016, and the rise to power of what may be called 'Bolsonarism', in 2018. The two main factors were the growing intervention of the military and the judiciary in the national political process, and the deliberate deployment of racism and sexism in political and electoral mobilizations against the PT governments and their candidates.

THE PROBLEM

Since the political crisis of 2015-16, the political arrangement that had brought stability to the power bloc under the hegemony of the big internal bourgeoisie, and that had supported its neo-developmentalist policies, has been replaced by an arrangement based on the hegemony of the big bourgeoisie associated to foreign capital. However, this new hegemony has had several difficulties in asserting itself in a situation of political instability. The administration led by former Vice-President Michel Temer (2016-18), which replaced President Dilma Rousseff after her impeachment, was unable to establish what might be called 'hegemonic stability'. Instead, Temer's government operated under severe constraints due to the large number of corruption investigations and court cases led by the Federal Police, the Public Prosecutor's Office, and the judiciary. This was followed by the government of Jair Bolsonaro (2019-22). Though more stable than the Temer administration, it is the result of an unusual alliance between neoliberalism and neo-fascism – an alliance that neoliberal forces were forced to resort to because of the weakness, fragmentation, and decline of their traditional political parties. It was this recourse to neo-fascism that permitted the big associated bourgeoisie (that is, the fraction linked to foreign capital) to stop the PT, with its neo-developmentalist program, from returning to office in the 2018 elections. But this came at a cost: limitations on the rollout of neoliberal reforms, including changes in economic as well as social policy, and the continuing conflict between state institutions. For example, under Bolsonaro's leadership, the executive branch has been constantly threatening the Supreme Court, contributing to the political destabilization of the country.

Signs of the weakening of liberal democratic values and institutions in Brazil fully emerged during the crisis that eventually led to the *coup d'état* (disguised as impeachment) against President Rousseff. The beginning of the decline was the work of the Brazilian Social Democratic Party (*Partido da Socialdemocracia Brasileira,* PSDB), a party unrelated to any form of social democracy, and that was the vanguard of neoliberalism in Brazil. After its defeat in the October 2014 presidential elections by PT candidate Dilma Rousseff, then seeking re-election, the PSDB violated the rules of the democratic game by refusing to recognize the legitimacy of the popular vote and filing a series of complaints at the Electoral Court in an attempt to prevent the validation of the outcome of the election. Bolsonaro was not, therefore, the first to cast doubt on the reliability of the Brazilian electoral process. The refusal to accept the results of national polls and the discrediting of the structures and institutions of representation contributed to the political and ideological strengthening of the state bureaucracy, including its military branch. As elections and party representation are the foundations of bourgeois democracy, and since bourgeois dictatorships are bureaucratic or one-party regimes, the discrediting of voting and party representation tends to pave the way for political intervention by the civil and military branches of the state's bureaucracy. The judiciary and the armed forces increased their participation and weight in the national political process, each in its own way.

The impeachment of Dilma Rousseff in August 2016, the imprisonment of former President Lula da Silva in April 2018, and the subsequent exclusion of his candidacy, paved the way for the victory of Jair Bolsonaro in the elections in October. Each of these was an outcome of the intervention of those two institutions in the political process.

POLITICAL STABILITY DESPITE CHANGES IN HEGEMONY, 1995-2014

What were the main forces at play in Brazilian politics during this period? How can we examine their features and political practices? Why did these practices lead to the instability and crisis in Brazil today? To answer these questions, let us briefly clarify some conceptual issues.

Capitalist social formations, or historically existing capitalisms, are complex compositions of different modes of production in specific circumstances, and class conflicts are multipolar. The capitalist class can be politically divided into fractions, and the working classes are also heterogeneous. Our focus, here, is on the capitalist class.

This class is not a homogenous bloc involved in a simple, bipolar conflict between 'capital' and 'labour', and it is heterogeneous both in economic and in political terms. Capitalist firms can be different from one another for various reasons, and what increases the complexity of the phenomenon is the fact that the same firm or economic group can occupy distinct positions depending on the dimension being examined. The reasons for this heterogeneity are related to: a) the place or places these firms occupy in the process of valorization of capital as a whole – for example, banking, industrial, or commercial enterprises; b) their size – big or medium-sized capital; c) the origin of capital – whether foreign or local; d) the goal of production – e.g., for the domestic market or for export, and other features which may be structural or more or less circumstantial. For instance, the Covid-19 pandemic affected companies unevenly and had a differentiated impact on the position of different bourgeois segments vis-à-vis the Bolsonaro administration.[2] Economic heterogeneity is a permanent feature of capitalism, even though its forms have varied significantly throughout history and according to each country's position in the imperialist system. Economic heterogeneity opens the door to the rise of bourgeois class fractions. Depending on the context and the strategy of capitalist development defined at state level, *economic heterogeneity can be politically activated to foster the emergence of groups of companies converging around specific demands. These groups are what we call bourgeois (or capitalist) fractions – a phenomenon that is both economic and political at the same time.* To put it differently by way of an example, the existence of a banking sector in a capitalist country is not enough to demonstrate that there is a banking fraction of the bourgeoisie. To speak of such a fraction, this sector must be organized around a specific set of demands that is distinct from those endorsed by other sectors of the bourgeoisie.

To this, we add another three observations. As the definition above shows, the state plays an active role in shaping capitalist development policy. This active role does not, however, give it the prerogative to define public policy independently from social classes, fractions, and a myriad of interest groups. State agents that elaborate and implement capitalist development policy must take into consideration the possibilities determined by the stage of capitalism and the political balance of power between classes and class fractions in a given country.

The second observation is related to the fact that bourgeois fractions are not homogenous blocs without divisions. Despite the general unity that characterizes a group as a fraction of the capitalist class, each fraction can be affected by conflicts originating elsewhere. To give an example, a banking fraction of the bourgeoisie in a given country necessarily shares common interests; however, in spite of its broader unity, this fraction may be plagued by internal conflicts between medium and big banking capital and/or between national and foreign banking capital. These subgroups may be represented on the corporate level by different banking associations, as is the case in Brazil.[3] There is yet another complexity in the bourgeois fractions – one that does not, however, invalidate the use of this concept. Fractions are outcomes of the hierarchy of contradictions that divides the capitalist class.

If all banks were to prioritize their conflict with productive capital, they could form a banking fraction that would bring together foreign, national, small, and large banks despite the differences between the interests of these subgroups. However, if national banks were to start giving priority to their conflict with foreign banks, the banking fraction would dissolve and, in this case, we would witness the constitution of a new subgroup that could eventually join an internal or, more rarely, a national bourgeoisie.

The third and final observation stems from what has already been said: bourgeois fractions are not rigid, permanent formations.[4] They are flexible and may form and disband throughout the political process. In the context of a crisis, the escalation of the conflict with the popular classes may also lead different fractions of the bourgeoisie, previously divided by conflicts, to join forces. All the considerations mentioned here are related to each fraction's position regarding the features of the development policy selected by the state. This does not eliminate the possibility of companies within the same bourgeois fraction reacting differently to changes in government strategy, or even to specific economic or social policy measures.

In Brazil's recent political history, the main division within the capitalist class is that between the big internal bourgeoisie and the big associated bourgeoisie. The latter is the bourgeois fraction subordinated to imperialist domination, as this domination manifests itself in the current historical period. As for the big internal bourgeoisie, although it is not an anti-imperialist (national) bourgeoisie, it maintains a predominant relationship of unity with foreign capital, as well as, secondarily, a relationship of conflict with it.

Marxist analyses of contemporary Brazilian politics often ignore or underestimate the political weight of each of these fractions. Instead, analyses tend to prioritize a bipolar and oversimplified concept of class conflict. In the literature that does take these fractions into consideration, most analyses tend to focus on the conflict between banking (interest-bearing) and productive capital, rather than that between the internal and the associated bourgeoisie. In contrast with what is shown below, most authors do not view the conflict within the bourgeoisie as the conflict at the centre of Brazilian politics since the 1990s. Yet, this is the principal conflict because, even though the popular classes can influence the political process, their participation has been largely limited to localized struggles, and they have tended to be integrated politically into one of the bourgeois camps.

Between 1994 and 2014, the big associated bourgeoisie and the big internal bourgeoisie took turns as the hegemonic fraction within the power bloc. These swings were accompanied by a certain stability without major political disruptions. Changes in hegemony without political ruptures were possible because both conflicting fractions belonged to big capital, and the differences between them did not have a significant impact on the organization of the country's economy and society.

The 1990s began with a political crisis brought on by the first attempt to impose neoliberal capitalism in Brazil by President Collor de Mello (1990-92), which met the resistance of various segments of society and led to a political crisis and the forced resignation of the President.[5] In 1995, when Fernando Henrique Cardoso (PSDB) first took office, it was clear that the big associated bourgeoisie occupied the hegemonic position in the power bloc. This meant that the economic, social, and foreign policy of the Brazilian state would prioritize the interests of this fraction of the capitalist class. The Cardoso administration successfully implemented the program of the big associated bourgeoisie, which sought to impose the neoliberal capitalist economic model. The associated bourgeoisie and foreign capital were present in the banking, commercial, industrial, and agricultural sectors, which include firms of different sizes, but the sector of the associated bourgeoisie with the most political power is large capital. During the 1990s, then, the big internal capitalists occupied a subordinate position in the power bloc. That said, their interests were not ignored. The government's neoliberal social policy accommodated them: the various fractions of capital offered unanimous support to the policy of rolling back labour, social security, and social rights. However, neoliberal economic policy, which included opening the Brazilian economy even further to foreign capital and the attempt to secure primary fiscal surpluses to service the domestic public debt, ended up going against the interests of different segments of the big internal bourgeoisie. The deepening of trade liberalization during the two administrations led by Fernando Henrique Cardoso (1995-2002) was a source of conflict especially between the government and the industrial sector of the internal bourgeoisie. The policy of internationalizing Brazilian commercial banking – a market that, until then, had been reserved for large and medium-sized national banks – led the normally politically silent Brazilian Federation of Banks (*Federação Brasileira de Bancos*, Febraban) to criticize the government loudly, while the credit constraints imposed by the contractionary fiscal policy generated conflicts between the government and rural producers.[6]

The political program of the big internal bourgeoisie became dominant through the neo-developmentalist economic policy of the PT-led governments headed by Luíz Inácio Lula da Silva, between 2003 and 2010, and Dilma Rousseff, between 2011 and 2016. The term neo-developmentalism is used here because these governments sought to promote economic growth and reduce poverty through state intervention. This strategy of capitalist development modified, though not significantly, the economic, social, and foreign policy of the Brazilian state, while supporting the neoliberal economic model.[7] In essence, these governments pursued developmentalist policies as much as possible within the limits of the neoliberal model, and in line with the limited aspirations of an internal bourgeoisie that is not a national or anti-imperialist bourgeoisie. The state's intervention in the economy limited trade liberalization and the denationalization of the Brazilian economy, reduced poverty, and stimulated the domestic market. This strategy included strengthening the national banks, giving preference to local producers when sourcing government purchases, expanding subsidized credit for the industrial and agricultural sectors, raising the minimum wage, and adopting income transfer policies for low-income families as well as more generally.[8]

Although these measures produced positive outcomes, they were always limited by the constraints imposed by the economic model that the PT government had no intention of changing significantly. In the area of foreign policy, the PT administrations distanced themselves from US policy.[9] The Brazilian government's new foreign policy opened or expanded markets for large Brazilian companies, including the construction and banking sectors in South America, the Middle East, and across Africa. Important government initiatives in this area were the suspension of the negotiations for the Free Trade Area of the Americas (FTAA), Brazil's participation in the creation and consolidation of the BRICS Group, and the nationalist policy for the exploration of the pre-salt oil reserves deep under the South Atlantic Ocean.

Similar to the associated bourgeoisie, the internal bourgeoisie is distributed across several economic segments. It includes large national companies operating in the banking, industrial, trade, and agricultural sector, and firms of all sizes. Its most powerful segment, the big internal bourgeoisie, enjoyed political hegemony in the PT governments. In other words, the main division running through the Brazilian capitalist class in the recent period dislocated the conflicts between large and medium-sized capital, banking and industrial and other capital to a secondary position, though it remains present. In the six presidential elections held between 1994 and 2014, the partisan polarization between the presidential candidates of the PSDB and the PT – a polarization around which the entire Brazilian multiparty system was organized – represented, first and foremost, the conflict between the big associated bourgeoisie and the big internal bourgeoisie, and not essentially, despite appearances, the conflict between the popular classes, presumably represented by the PT, and the bourgeoisie as a whole, supposedly represented by the PSDB.

As was suggested earlier, none of this means that the working classes were absent from the national political process. The struggle of the working classes was present in both urban and rural areas throughout this period, with its highs and lows. However, this struggle remained generally fragmented and driven by short-term economic demands.[10] At the political level, as was mentioned above, the working classes ended up being integrated into one of the main bourgeois fractions. Throughout this period, no popular alternative project for the Brazilian economy and society emerged. It is, then, important to understand the dynamics of the transition from the period of hegemony by the big associated bourgeoisie to the hegemony of the big internal bourgeoisie. In the context of this transition, two political shifts occurred, which are key for understanding later developments in Brazilian politics; the first was a change in the popular camp. During Cardoso's second administration (1999-2002), the big internal bourgeoisie shifted from a right-wing position – which, despite some reservations, supported the neoliberal program of the 1990s – to a more centrist political position, in which it began to accept changes in economic and social policy, including a greater role for the state and some redistribution of income at the margin. At the same time, the PT abandoned its program for the structural reform of Brazilian capitalism, which aimed to create a social welfare state while strengthening state capitalism and replaced it with a more superficial and limited program of neo-developmentalism.[11] These two shifts converged and allowed both forces to come together into a heterogeneous, multi-class political front under the leadership of the big internal bourgeoisie. This front supported the neo-developmentalist policies of the series of governments led by the PT.

In addition to its economic policy centred on the interests of the big internal bourgeoisie, the social policy of neo-developmentalism also, if only secondarily, responded to the interests of the popular classes. The government adopted policies that benefited the working classes, broad fractions of the middle class, the peasantry, and workers from the marginalized masses,[12] including: policies for economic growth that created a large number of new jobs; real increases in the minimum wage; policies of social and racial quotas for universities and public services; a major increase in public sector recruitment processes and employment; financing programs for smallholder peasant production and reserving institutional markets for this production; income transfer programs; the expansion of basic public services; and a program to build water cisterns in semi-arid regions. The PT governments also launched programs designed to expand the citizenship of groups historically suffering discrimination and oppression, especially indigenous and black people, women, and LGBTQ+. The big internal bourgeoisie's neo-developmentalist policy finally gained mass support. There were several contradictions within this political front, and conflicts of various kinds and levels of significance followed. Even so, at times when the continuity of PT governments was at stake, such as during presidential elections, the various classes and class fractions in the alliance converged to defend the PT candidates. Class conflict and the economic conflict between different segments of the big internal bourgeoisie did not rupture the political unity of the neo-developmentalist front.

OVERTHROWING THE NEO-DEVELOPMENTALIST GOVERNMENT, 2015-16

Brazil experienced twenty years of political stability (1995-2014) – a relatively long period in the country's political history, in which one of the conflicting bourgeois fractions managed to establish its hegemony and maintain it securely, without causing a crisis in the political regime. The period that began with the crisis of the Rousseff administration and led to her removal from office is very different. This new situation can be explained by the intensification of the contradictions in the previous period – crisis is *not* the opposite of stability – and the emergence of new contradictions from, and within, the Brazilian political process. In order to analyze this issue we must determine, on the one hand, who mobilized against the PT government and why and, on the other, why the last PT government was unable to stop the advance of the forces supporting the judicial-parliamentary-media coup against Rousseff. Finally, it is important to investigate which trump cards the opposition used, and what were the weaknesses of the government and its base of support.

What essentially happened was this: the crisis of the second Dilma Rousseff administration, from 2015-16, was triggered by the political attack of the big associated bourgeoisie who mobilized to recover the hegemony it had enjoyed in the 1990s.[13] This bourgeois fraction had the active and, from a certain stage in the process, the radicalized support of the upper middle class.[14] It also managed to turn domestic medium-sized capital, whose interests were neglected by the PT governments, against the big internal bourgeoisie.[15] The big associated bourgeoisie sought, as we have already noted, to regain its hegemony within the power bloc and was able to maintain itself as the leading force of the coup that deposed of the Dilma Rousseff administration.

The politically conservative upper middle-class fraction opposed the social policy that had brought improvements to the standard of living of the popular classes. It viewed this policy as an increase in state spending on the back of middle-class taxpayers and a threat to the upper middle class's privileged status in Brazilian society. This fraction has an entire legion of domestic employees and service providers at its disposal: cleaners, cooks, nannies, chauffeurs, doormen, electricians, plumbers, and many others. During the PT administrations, numerous policy measures helped raise these workers' wages and, consequently, the cost of the services provided by them. What this fraction of the middle class found particularly upsetting was the extension of labour rights to domestic workers during the second administration of Dilma Rousseff, because it interfered with the employers' control of their domestic workers. In addition, members of the upper middle class notoriously posted countless messages on social media expressing their outrage when they noticed that manual labourers were frequenting spaces that had previously been, in practice, reserved for relatively rich people, such as airports, hotels, private health facilities, restaurants, and so on. Upper middle-class individuals and their professional associations filed numerous lawsuits to challenge the racial and social quotas. It has been abundantly shown that the five largest nationwide demonstrations against the Rousseff government and for the impeachment were primarily protests by the upper middle class.[16]

The owners and managers of medium-sized companies expressed their revolt against the policy of giving priority to large national companies for BNDES (the Brazilian development bank) financing, and also mobilized actively for the impeachment.[17] They were effectively used as pawns by the associated sector of big capital, which was fighting with the internal capitalists; however, the ambitions and interests of medium capital were, in fact, ignored by both sides.

The PT established a very different system of alliances from those traditionally proposed by European and Latin American communist parties, which prioritized closer ties between the organized workers and medium-sized domestic capital. The importance of medium capital in the impeachment is also apparent when we analyze the vulnerabilities of the PT governments in relation to the Brazilian party system, as is shown below.

The features of what may be called 'Lulaism', and the Brazilian party system, contributed to the success of the coup against Rousseff. To understand this, one must consider a hypothesis that most of the Brazilian left rejects: that 'Lulaism' is a type of populism. This rejection is found, for example, among communist intellectuals, who consider the concept of populism only in its Weberian version, and among intellectuals influenced by Trotsky, who conceive populism as a type of Bonapartism, when in fact the first is a superficially 'reformist political personalism', and the second is a 'conservative personalism'. Yet, Lulaism cannot be considered populism in the way that Weberians or Brazilian conservative and liberal social thought conceives the term – that is, as charismatic and demagogic leadership that deceives the uninformed masses. This conception is present in the foundational text of Helio Jaguaribe (1953),[18] and it is also present daily in the editorials of conservative newspapers. An alternative view of populism would see it as a political movement with a mass base, but that lacks mass party organization and is led from above by a superficially reformist leader. The masses support populist politics not because they are misinformed, but because their interests are met, albeit in a limited way, and because they are prisoners of an ideology that fuels the expectation that the bourgeois state can, and must, out of its own free will and initiative, improve the working and living conditions of the working classes. That is what Lulaism is.[19]

This is, in some way, a recycled version of the populist politics of the period 1930-1964 in Brazil but, this time, in new conditions and with a different social base. And here is the irony: the main leader of the previous populist period was Getúlio Vargas, a politician from the large landowning class, but backed mainly by the urban trade union movement. In contrast, the main leader of Lulaism is a politician emerging from trade unions in the manufacturing sector and drawing support primarily from workers of the marginal masses – the underemployed, domestic workers, street vendors, workers without a stable profession or steady employment and who make a living by performing odd jobs, and peasant farmers from agricultural regions in decline.[20]

The fact is that the vote for Lula and the other 'Lulista' presidential candidates – Dilma Rousseff, in 2010 and 2014, and Fernando Haddad, in 2018 – is not a partisan vote, but rather a vote highly focused on the individual candidate. The underlying motivation is political, and not personal, but this motivation is not clearly or necessarily present in the voters' minds, which makes a significant difference. Most of Lula's supporters vote for Lula and not for the PT. The proof is that in the Chamber of Deputies, the PT has never managed to obtain more than 17 per cent of the seats, and, in the Senate, the PT's performance has been even weaker. The PT has also not generally done well in the elections for state and municipal legislatures and executive positions. The Brazilian left does not give due importance to this phenomenon which, in fact, should be seen as intriguing: PT candidates won four consecutive presidential elections, but they have never come close to obtaining a majority in the Chamber of Deputies and the Senate. What is more, this is not the norm in Latin America. The Bolivian party Movimiento al Socialismo (MAS, Movement Toward Socialism) secured the majority of seats in the legislature in all the elections in which Evo Morales won the presidency, and it managed to do so again when current president Luís Acre was elected. The MAS has had a similar record in the subordinate bodies of the state apparatus: it even managed to win elections in two thirds of the municipalities in Bolivia. The situation of Peronism in Argentina (which, in our view, is not populist because it is a highly organized movement), and the Left Front in Uruguay is similar, although their performance is modest in comparison to the MAS.[21]

The outcome is that the PT governments have always had to deal with a National Congress that is distant from, or even hostile to, its economic, social, and foreign policy and the policy to expand the citizenship of women, black and indigenous peoples, and the LGBTQ+ population. Lula and Rousseff formed their base in the National Congress by seeking the support of conservative and opportunistic parties that were willing to abandon the government at the first sign of crisis. As a consequence of the populism that prevented the PT from securing the votes of the supporters of their own leader, unlike the Bolivian MAS, the PT remained vulnerable to the new type of coup we have seen recently in Latin America – the 'coup by impeachment' that, due to its apparent legality, comes at a low political cost for the coup-plotting right. This possibility is not available to the right in Bolivia, Argentina, or Uruguay. It is unsurprising, then, that Dilma Rousseff's conservative and opportunistic party base in the National Congress abandoned her in the political crisis that began in 2015 and voted against her during the impeachment proceedings of 2016.

The main party in the support base of the Rousseff administration in the National Congress, the Movimento Democrático Brasileiro (MDB, or Brazilian Democratic Movement), played a central role in the *coup d'état* that deposed the former president. Here, we address another aspect of the political process that facilitated the success of the perpetrators of the coup, which involves the medium internal bourgeoisie. The MDB was created during the military dictatorship with a political program and a type of agitation and propaganda that favoured the interests of medium capital in the struggle against the dictatorship. The dictatorship had united the big internal bourgeoisie and the big associated bourgeoisie behind a developmentalist policy at a time when, in contrast with the current period, imperialism supported and stimulated the industrialization of the biggest Latin American countries through foreign direct investment.[22] The MDB's discourse was democratic and moderately nationalist at the time, supported income distribution, and defended the need to expand the domestic market.

The MDB thus had an ambitious economic program. However, when the military dictatorship ended, the party changed, and it gradually became a clientelist or patronage party. It has since supported all governments, be they neoliberal or neo-developmentalist and, in exchange for its support, it expects these governments to award it public positions and pass specific measures that benefit its social base through amendments to the fiscal budget.[23]

On this, it is important to highlight two points. The mainstream media considers these amendments 'irrational', since they disturb the supposedly technical nature of the budget, which systematically favours big capital and financial capital. Even many left-wing intellectuals have incorporated this discourse, which rejects the idea that public funds might be allocated outside a select group of big companies, while parliamentary amendments often benefit small and medium-sized companies operating in the interior of the country. This change in the MDB suggests that medium capital gave up competing for political hegemony in the power bloc, and is content with the actions of a patronage party that occasionally caters to it, within the limits set by the interests of big internal or associated capital.

The position of Vice-President of the Republic under Dilma Rousseff was held by Michel Temer, one of the leaders of the MDB. Furthermore, with congressman Eduardo Cunha as the Speaker of the Chamber of Deputies, the party also controlled the Lower House of Congress. These positions gave the party, which had always tagged along with either the PSDB or the PT, unprecedented leadership in the crisis. It went from a patronage party to the organic party of big capital, especially associated capital.[24] This favoured the coup, which would not lead the neoliberal parties *par excellence* – the PSDB, Democratas, and so on – to take up the Presidency of the Republic replacing Dilma Rousseff. Aware of these circumstances, segments of the big internal bourgeoisie that had already been on a collision course with neo-developmentalism felt free to remain neutral vis-à-vis the coup or, alternatively, they could abandon the government. But let us now examine more closely the reaction of the classes and class fractions that, similarly to the big internal bourgeoisie, were part of the neo-developmentalist political front that supported the PT governments.

The neo-developmentalist political front was torn apart by the pro-coup attack. The big internal bourgeoisie, whose hegemony had been organized by the PT governments, once again revealed its oscillating political position vis-à-vis foreign capital. This group's opposition to the neoliberal program is selective, that is, it does not always or necessarily refer to the whole of that program. The part of the neoliberal program that suppresses workers' rights, depending on the conjuncture, can be accepted by this fraction of the bourgeoisie, and not just by the big associated bourgeoisie. The problem is that the economic policies of neoliberalism (credit, investment, foreign trade, and other policies) does not welcome the interests of the big internal bourgeoisie. The governments that apply this program in the periods of hegemony of associated capital can, therefore, sometimes count on the support of the big internal bourgeoisie, but sometimes there will be opposition to it. Something similar happened under the PT governments, and these governments had to deal with the pendular political position of the big internal bourgeoisie while they attempted to implement the neo-developmentalist program.

An especially important case involved FIESP (Federation of Industries of the State of São Paulo), which began actively participating in the pro-coup campaign in December 2015. It was mentioned above that state agents play an active role defining the strategy of capitalist development. This means that conflicts may arise between the government and the bourgeois fraction whose hegemony the government represents. The Rousseff administration distanced itself even further from the United States, and this seemed to cause concern among sectors of the big internal bourgeoisie. This distancing was visible in the following initiatives and decisions: the creation of the BRICS Bank in 2013; the insistence on strengthening Mercosur when the internal bourgeoisie indicated that it preferred its flexibilization,[25] and its firmness in maintaining the control of the state-owned oil company Petrobras over the pre-salt oil reserves, among other measures. All this went on as though the Dilma administration believed it was dealing with a national bourgeoisie, and not a mere internal bourgeoisie. José Dirceu, one of the PT's leading strategists, went as far as to argue that the PCB policy in the pre-1964 period, of forging an alliance with the national bourgeoisie to carry out a democratic revolution in Brazil, had become feasible in the twenty-first century.

Other sectors of the internal bourgeoisie stayed neutral in relation to the coup and, finally, some large companies remained loyal to the Rousseff government. This was the case of the large national private banks[26] and, to a lesser degree, the shipbuilding industry. Finally, it should be highlighted that an important portion of the big internal bourgeoisie was eliminated from the fight early on, in the first episode of the crisis, by the legal persecution of 'Operation Car Wash'. This operation used the so-called fight against corruption to fight large national companies. Brazilian heavy construction companies, which practically monopolized the public works market and the oil and gas chains, were criminalized and driven out of the market. This left the sector, which had benefited greatly during the Dilma Rousseff government, with its hands tied up politically, and in no position to stand up for the government. Operation Car Wash is an example of how one of the capitalist state's institutions – here, the judiciary – was turned into a political tool of one of the bourgeois fractions fighting for hegemony in the power bloc. It became a political instrument used by imperialist capital, the big associated bourgeoisie, and the upper middle class in the fight against the neo-developmentalist political front.[27]

As was already explained, two political camps were formed; each side brought together one of the bourgeois fractions and some popular classes or class fractions. Heterogeneity is not a feature only of the capitalist class; it is also present in the dominated classes. Contrary to what the common expression 'the working class' suggests, there is more than one working class: laborers, peasantry, petty bourgeoisie, middle class, and workers of the marginal mass – all of them important sectors in a dependent capitalism.[28] Each of these working classes has specific economic interests and different political tendencies and ideological dispositions. The complexity of the situation increases when we remember that these classes, in turn, can be subdivided into fractions or strata. Notorious cases include the middle class, whose upper, intermediate, and lower fractions tend to intervene in the political process differently, as well as the peasantry, whose different strata – the rich, the well-to-do, and the poor – also have their own specific demands and are susceptible to divisions in the political process.

Let us identify here a few positions found in the dominated classes. In Brazil's recent political history, the upper middle class supported the neoliberal program, whereas most of the lower middle class leaned towards the neo-developmentalist program. This was reflected in the polls and street protests. In the rallies for the impeachment of Dilma Rousseff, the upper middle class prevailed, whereas in the demonstrations held in defence of the former president there was a stronger presence of the lower middle class.[29] Most of the peasantry was drawn to the neo-developmentalist side. The interests of the better-off and rich peasants were contemplated in the policy of financing 'family farmers' and creating institutional markets for their products, whereas the specific demand of the poor and landless peasants and those with little land went unmet; their main demand is essentially the expropriation and distribution of land. As for the workers of the marginal masses, they formed the social base typical of Lulaism. Neo-developmentalism responded to their interests through income transfer policies, the expansion of public services (electricity, vocational training, quotas, and so on), and the policy of building popular houses and water wells in semi-arid regions, among others. In the presidential elections that took place between 2002 and 2014, trade unionists presented to the PT candidates lists including around ten demands.; one of them was the demand for an increase in the legal minimum wage that has existed in Brazil since the period of Getúlio Vargas. While salaried workers in the formal market benefited from the increases in minimum wage, the main demands they brought before the PT governments went unheard.[30]

The relationship between the PT governments with the different popular classes and class fractions did not lead to positive outcomes for the Rousseff administration during the crisis leading to her removal from office. The most organized workers were not the main ones to benefit from the government's neo-developmentalist policy. The popular sector that had gained the most from its social policies – the workers of the marginal masses – are not politically organized. They have a populist type relationship with Lula da Silva, and this is why they did not go out to defend the government from the attacks, even though they faithfully vote for Lulaism in elections. As for the labour unions, although they had the capacity to mobilize support for Rousseff, they remained practically neutral in the crisis. The leaders of the progressive trade union confederations appeared in the public events held in defence of Rousseff, but the big labour unions that could have multiplied the numbers at the protests in defence of the PT government remained absent. The surprising outcome of all this was that the richest minority of Brazilian society managed to mobilize far more people in their street protests, and this was decisive for the removal of Dilma Rousseff.[31]

The social base of the associated bourgeoisie and foreign capital – which remains attached to neoliberalism – was, by far, the most mobilized and committed social sector. Yet, the upper middle class was not the one who led the *coup d'état*, nor did it define the economic and social program of the political front that promoted the *coup d'état* of the impeachment. It was a bourgeois party that established this neoliberal program focused on the elimination of labour rights; it was Michel Temer's MDB that took over the presidency replacing Dilma Rousseff. Even so, the middle class with its massive street demonstrations was the main driving force behind that process.

NEO-FASCISM COMES TO NEOLIBERALISM'S RESCUE, 2017-22

The rise of neo-fascism in Brazil took place during a period of severe political instability. First, there was a crisis of the hegemony of the big internal bourgeoisie, in 2015-2016, which resulted in the overthrow of President Dilma Rousseff in August 2016. Even though the incoming Temer administration launched policies giving priority to the interests of foreign capital and the associated bourgeoisie, this government was not stable. It found itself under siege due to the investigations into corruption led by the Federal Prosecutor's Office, the Federal Police, and the judiciary. Temer was on the verge of resigning several times. In 2018, the last year of Michel Temer's administration and also a presidential election year, it was clear that no candidate from the traditionally neoliberal political parties, such as the PSDB, could win the election. It was in this context that the neo-fascist movement in support of Jair Bolsonaro took off. The success of this candidacy was a symptom of the instability of the political process during this period. At the time of writing, in mid-2022, another presidential election year, it is increasingly clear that the alternatives are either the victory of PT candidate Lula da Silva and his inauguration as President of the Republic, or a *coup d'état* by Jair Bolsonaro, in order to stay in power. In sum, this period is very different from the one where the political arena was polarized between the PT, a democratic, reformist party with a popular base, on one side and, on the other, the PSDB, a party espousing liberal policies and practices: that polarization was compatible with a long period of democratic stability in Brazil.

It is clearly controversial to classify the Bolsonaro administration as neo-fascist. Space limitations do not permit a detailed discussion of this issue, but let us say a few words by way of outline. The three most common descriptions of Bolsonaro's government and its base of support are: (a) right-wing populist; (b) traditionalist, and (c) neo-fascist.

The first description is by far the most common, since populism is said to be based on a personalist politics in which the leader appeals directly to the people and criticizes the elite.[32] However, this description is too generic, since capitalist societies encourage the personalization of politics throughout the entire ideological spectrum, making this a frequent phenomenon. In general, the personalization of politics is weakened only when the labour movement manages to organize mass parties.[33] Since personalism is a generalized phenomenon, those who speak of populism immediately feel the need to qualify it as left wing, right wing, and so on. This kind of qualification is not devoid of meaning, and it has some use as an initial and indicative characterization. However, as we know, denominations based on a presumably linear political spectrum going from the extreme left to the extreme right, with numerous political positions in between, are highly unsatisfactory. Let us take the case of Brazil today. Bolsonaro can be considered as populist as other leaders of the right – they tend to rely on personalism, appeal to the people, and criticize 'different kinds of elite'. This description could also be applied to Lula. So, how do we distinguish one from the other? To overcome the problem of using a vague classification based on a politician's supposed position on a linear political spectrum, we could try using more precise qualifiers. Would it be accurate to call Lula a popular populist? Could former judge Sérgio Moro be considered a liberal populist? Or other right-wing politicians? And how about Bolsonaro, would he be an authoritarian populist, a fascist populist, or something else entirely? In the end, Mussolini was also a populist in the general sense of the term. In other words, we come back to the question that the classification of Bolsonaro as a populist politician avoids addressing.

The characterization that associates Bolsonaro and Trump with traditionalism can be found, for example, in the book *War for Eternity*[34] and it has had some impact on thinking in Brazil and the US. This analysis underestimates the differences between the traditionalist ideologues from the first half of the twentieth century, and the ideologues of current right-wing politicians. Olavo de Carvalho and Steve Bannon, the names most closely associated with Bolsonaro and Trump respectively, are not, in fact, traditionalists. Teitelbaum recognizes these differences and calls them 'neo-traditionalists'. However, these differences suggest more of a rupture with traditionalism than a modification of this ideology. The key ideas of traditionalism are the rejection of modernity, its ideas and values, and even the idea of nationhood; the defence of the division of society into castes; the apology of domination by the religious caste; the vision that sees the workers as a caste of slaves moved by their basic urges; the conception of history as a repetition of cycles that go from the golden to the dark ages, with intermediate phases in between, and that start over again after a period of decline, following a circular path repeatedly.[35] Yet, these are some of the main ideas of traditionalism that current ideologues have abandoned or moved away from. They now defend the nation as a key agent for the restoration of civilization. They no longer argue for the organization of societies in castes, and it is their understanding that the custodians of the eternal values that must be restored are the workers.

When I classify the Bolsonaro government, and Bolsonarism specifically, as neo-fascism, it is my understanding that we are dealing with a variant of fascist politics and ideology. Fascism is a genus with several species.[36] The fascist movement is an active and mobilized movement of the intermediate strata of capitalist societies. The predominance of the petty bourgeoisie in the original fascism was replaced by the predominance of the middle class in neo-fascism. Although originally fascism was of petty bourgeois origin, it served as a means, but never as a passive instrument, for organizing the hegemony of the big monopolist and imperialist national bourgeoisie of central countries.[37] In contrast, neo-fascism serves to organize the hegemony of foreign capital and the associated fraction of dependent bourgeoisie. In all these cases, when we view fascism as a genus, what best describes it is a formula taken from Palmiro Togliatti: fascism is a reactionary regime of the masses.[38] Reactionism appears in anti-communism, in the petty bourgeois ideology, in the authoritarian criticism of democracy, in the defence of a pure and homogenous nation, in the traditional values of the patriarchal family, and so on. These are features of Bolsonaro's government and the movement that supports him; they can be considered a species within the fascist genus, together with the other species that we can call 'original fascism'.

The literature still lacks a detailed study of the process of fascistization in Brazil. Although we do not claim to fill this gap, we can identify a few steps of this process and some of the main actors. Neo-fascist movements began to organize in Brazil during the large right-wing protests led by the upper middle class in 2015 and 2016 to demand the removal of President Rousseff. Although they marched together with Bolsonarism against the PT government, not all the movements organizing these rallies were neo-fascist. Jair Bolsonaro, a congressman at the time, was a high-profile participant in these protests, and he had well-established links to groups that had been calling for a military dictatorship in the country. In 2017, Bolsonaro began travelling around Brazil making speeches and organizing political events. He strengthened his ties, which he has subsequently maintained, with self-employed truck drivers, a typically petty bourgeois base of his movement, and with capitalist landowners, especially in the centre-west and south regions of the country, where export-oriented agriculture is highly developed. The upper middle class felt threatened by the modest social gains of manual labourers and the lower middle class that were enabled by the social policies of the PT governments. Large landowners felt threatened by the peasant, indigenous, and rural Afro-descendent (*quilombola*) movements who had been fighting for land and for agrarian reform. Bolsonaro promised landowners that he would make it easier to buy and own weapons and would change the law to allow them to use firearms against peasants, indigenous, and quilombola communities occupying land that the landowners considered their own. In the first half of 2018, a new character entered the scene: big capital. The dynamic was as follows: presidential elections were scheduled in October 2018, and when big business realized that none of the candidates of the traditional neoliberal bourgeois parties was likely to win, it started to lend its support to the neo-fascist candidate.

Big business has profited greatly from Bolsonaro's electoral victory and from his government. Michel Temer had already given them a radical neoliberal reform of the Brazilian labour code (*Consolidação das Leis do*

Trabalho, or CLT) and a bold privatization program. Bolsonaro gave them a drastic neoliberal reform of the social security system and has been working to privatize the remaining giant state enterprises, especially Petrobras, Eletrobrás, and the post office network. The period of political instability is not over. In this year's electoral race (2022), Lula da Silva has a comfortable lead in all the opinion polls, and Jair Bolsonaro openly and frequently threatens to stage a *coup d'état* if he loses. Despite all the evidence, and like Donald Trump in the US, Bolsonaro claims that the Brazilian electoral system is unreliable. In other words, the need for neoliberalism to resort to fascism, which destabilizes democracy in Brazil, remains.

NOTES

Translation into English by Karen Louise Lang.

1. See, for example, Nancy Fraser and Rahel Jaeggi, *Capitalism – A Conversation in Critical Theory*, Cambridge: Polity Press, 2018.
2. Octavio Del Passo and André Valle, 'As frações burguesas na crise da Covid-19: apontamentos preliminares', *Brasil de Fato*, 2020, available at: www.brasildefato.com.br/2020/04/16/artigo-as-fracoes-burguesas-na-crise-da-covid-19-apontamentos-preliminares.
3. Ary César Minella, 'O Discurso Empresarial no Brasil: Com a Palavra, os Senhores Banqueiros', *Ensaios, fee*, 15(2), 1994, pp. 505– 546; Ary César Minella, 'Elites Financeiras, Sistemas Financeiros e Governo FHC', in Waldir José Rampinelli, Nildo Domingos Ouriques, eds, *No Fio da Navalha. Crítica das Reformas Neoliberais de FHC*, São Paulo: Xamã, 1997.
4. Francisco Farias, *Estado burguês e classes dominantes no Brasil (1930-1964)*, Curitiba: CRV, 2017.
5. Danilo Enrico Martuscelli, *Crises Políticas e Capitalismo Neoliberal no Brasil*, Curitiba: CRV, 2015.
6. Claudinei Coletti, Neoliberalismo e burguesia agrária no Brasil, *Lutas e Resistências*, 1, 2006, pp. 131-45.
7. Alfredo Saad- Filho and Lecio Morais, 'Brazil Beyond Lula: Forging Ahead or Pausing for Breath?', *Latin American Perspectives*, 38(2), 2011, pp. 31– 44; Lecio Morais and Alfredo Saad-Filho, 'Neo- Developmentalism and the Challenges of Economic Policy- Making under Dilma Rousseff', *Critical Sociology*, 28(6), 2012, pp. 789–98.
8. Armando Boito, *Reform and Political Crisis in Brazil: Class Conflict in Workers' Party Governments and the Rise of Bolsonaro Neo-fascism*, Boston: Brill, 2021, pp. 56-66.
9. Tatiana Berringer, *A burguesia brasileira e a política externa nos governos FHC e Lula*, Curitiba: Appris, 2015.
10. Paula Marcelino, 'Sindicalismo e Neodesenvolvimentismo: Analisando as Greves entre 2003 e 2013 no Brasil', *Tempo Social*, 29(3), 2017, pp. 201–27.
11. Armando Boito, *Política neoliberal e sindicalismo no Brasil*, São Paulo: Editora Xamã, 1999; Lincoln Secco, *História do PT – 1978-2010*, São Paulo: Ateliê Editorial, 2016.
12. Boito, *Reform and Political Crisis in Brazil*, pp. 56-66.

13 Boito, *Reform and Political Crisis in Brazil*, pp. 161-75.
14 Sávio Cavalcante and Santiane Arias, 'A divisão da classe média na crise política brasileira (2013-2016)', in Paul Boufartigue et al., eds, *O Brasil e a França na mundialização neoliberal – mudanças políticas e contestações sociais*, São Paulo: Alameda Editorial, 2019, pp. 97-126
15 Fernanda Perrin, *O ovo do pato: uma análise do deslocamento político da Federação das Indústrias do Estado de São Paulo*, Universidade de São Paulo (USP), Phd Thesis, 2020, available at: www.teses.usp.br/teses/disponiveis/8/8131/tde-16092020-205057/pt-br.php; Luciana Raimundo, *Bancos e o Estado no Brasil*: Estudo sobre a atuação dos *dealers no mercado de títulos públicos, na rede de financiamentos do BNDES e no financiamento eleitoral, 2003-2018*, Universidade Federal de Santa Catarina, Phd Thesis, 2021, available at: repositorio.ufsc.br/handle/123456789/226802
16 Cavalcante and Arias, 'A divisão da classe média na crise política brasileira (2013-2016)'.
17 Perrin, *O ovo do pato: uma análise do deslocamento político da Federação das Indústrias do Estado de São Paulo*.
18 Jaguaribe, Helio 'O que é o ademarismo', *Cadernos do Nosso Tempo*, 2, 1953.
19 Boito, *Reform and Political Crisis in Brazil*, pp. 67-88.
20 José Nun, *Marginalidad y Exclusión Social*, México: Fondo de Cultura Económica, 2001; Lúcio Kowarick, *Capitalismo e Marginalidade na América Latina,* Rio de Janeiro: Paz e Terra, 1975.
21 Armando Boito and Danilo Martushelli, 'A questão do voto partidários na esquerda latino-americana', São Paulo, Unpublished, 2022.
22 Fernando Henrique Cardoso and Enzo Faletto, *Dependência e desenvolvimento na América Latina – Ensaio de Interpretação Sociológica*, Rio de Janeiro: Editora LTC, 1970; Peter Evans, *A tríplice aliança – as multinacionais, as estatais e o capital nacional no desenvolvimento dependente brasileiro*, Rio de Janeiro: Zahar Editores, 1979.
23 In the Brazilian political system, deputies and senators in the National Congress evaluate, amend and approve the budget that comes from the Executive. Leandro Santos, *O PMDB no impeachment de Dilma Rousseff (2015-2016): Da Patronagem à Representação Orgânica?* State University of Campinas: Masters Dissertation, 2022.
24 Santos, *O PMDB no impeachment de Dilma Rousseff (2015-2016)*.
25 Berringer, *A burguesia brasileira e a política externa nos governos FHC e Lula*.
26 André Flores Penha Valle, and Pedro Felipe Narciso, *A burguesia brasileira em ação – de Lula a Bolsonaro,* São Paulo: Enunciado Publicações, 2021
27 Boito, *Reform and Political Crisis in Brazil*, pp. 153-60.
28 Nun, *Marginalidad y Exclusión Social*; Kowarick, *Capitalismo e Marginalidade na América Latina*.
29 Cavalcante and Arias, 'A divisão da classe média na crise política brasileira (2013-2016)'.
30 Boito, *Reform and Political Crisis in Brazil*, pp. 56-66.
31 Boito, *Reform and Political Crisis in Brazil*, pp. 176-85.
32 Nadia Urbinati, *Io, il popolo – Come il Populismo trasforma la democrazia*, Bologna: Il Mulino, 2019.
33 Umberto Cerroni, *Teoría marxista del Partido Politico*, Mexico: Cuadernos Pasado y Presente, 1977; Maurice Duverger, *Les partis politiques*. Paris: Librairie Armand Colin, 1951.

34 Benjamin Teitelbaum, *Guerra pela eternidade: O Retorno do Tradicionalismo e a Ascensão da Direita Populista*, Campinas: Editora Unicamp, 2021.
35 Teitelbaum, *Guerra pela eternidade*; Mark Sedgwick, *Against the Modern World: Traditionalism and the Secret Intellectual History of Twentieth Century*, Oxford: Oxford University Press, 2004
36 Boito, *Reform and Political Crisis in Brazil*, pp. 186-206.
37 Daniel Guérin, *Fascisme et Grand Capital*, Paris: François Maspero, 1965 [1936]; Nicos Poulantzas, *Fascisme et Dictature*, Paris: François Maspero, 1970.
38 Palmiro Togliatti, *Lezioni sul Fascismo*, Roma: Editori Riuniti, 2019 [1970].

CAPITALIST RESTRUCTURING, STATE TRANSFORMATION: LEO PANITCH AND CAPITALISM TODAY

STEPHEN MAHER AND SCOTT M. AQUANNO

With the death of Leo Panitch, editor of the *Socialist Register* for 35 years, the international left lost an irreplaceable guiding light. Apart from maintaining the *Register* as a unique, non-sectarian space for the free exchange of socialist ideas, his many contributions to Marxist political economy and social science will leave a lasting imprint on socialist theory and practice long into the future.

Above all, Leo's writing was exemplary of 'the unity of theory and practice'. Taking this seriously, for Leo, meant confronting the 'hard questions' about the limits and contradictions facing contemporary left forces and political strategies. Leo's socialism was one of 'sobriety', as he would constantly insist, by which he meant that we must base our analysis not on the world as we wish it was, but as it is. A primary concern for socialists, therefore, is to decipher the arrangement of social forces, the structure of capitalist class power, the specificity of state institutions, and the like, within a particular historical moment.

This emphasis on understanding how capitalism actually exists historically, and how it is restructured and practically reproduced over time, is expressed methodologically in what we have elsewhere referred to as the 'Institutional Marxism' which Leo, along with his co-author and lifelong friend Sam Gindin, developed across much of their work.[1] History, from this perspective, is not a matter of the working out of general economic laws, nor the functional equilibration of a closed system. Rather, it is a process of open-ended eventuation, shaped by human beings and the institutions they create, albeit within conditions not of their own choosing. Critically, that history remains a capitalist one is indicated by the systematic reproduction of its basic structural pressures: competition and class struggle.[2] The question 'what is capitalism' is thus inescapably one of 'what is capitalism *today*'.

On this basis, Panitch and Gindin crafted the most sophisticated analysis now available of how the imperial role of the American state in 'making global capitalism' arose from the complex interaction of the fundamental pressures of capitalism, the creative dynamism of individuals and classes, and the development of specific institutional forms of capital and the state. The result was a rich and historically grounded account of the interconnection between finance, globalization, and American hegemony. They showed that the rise of finance was hardly a harbinger of decline, but a structural foundation of the American empire, providing the basic infrastructure for the integration of the global economy. This was predicated on the restructuring of the US state, as the Federal Reserve and Treasury, especially, developed the capacities to manage the internationalization of capital.

Panitch and Gindin illustrated how this configuration of power, and the commitment of the American state, was essential for maintaining a globally integrated capitalism through the turbulence of the Great Financial Crisis. Yet the restructuring of capitalism in the wake of the crisis also led to the formation of a structure of corporate power which, in our own work, we have argued constitutes a new form of finance capital – a fusion of financial and industrial capital reminiscent of the system analyzed by Rudolf Hilferding in the early twentieth century. This regime is characterized by the unprecedented concentration, centralization, and diversification of power within a small number of giant asset management companies supported by a new 'risk state'.

A serious, concrete analysis of this form of capitalism today is the essential starting point for socialist politics – allowing us to locate ourselves at a moment in history, register its trends and fault lines, and sketch a way forward. An inherent consequence of the logic of Institutional Marxism is that socialism is by no means inevitable: in Leo's words, 'I'd even bet against it'.[3] Yet Leo's analysis was grounded in what he called a 'revolutionary optimism of the intellect': a search for openings within our historical present from which a brighter future might emerge.[4] This requires a profound optimism. It means looking at the world *as if* socialism is possible and seeking to identify opportunities to begin building the institutional capacities, rooted in the working class, that can cultivate the creative forces necessary to change the world. Leo's work is inspiring, not despite its 'sobriety', but *because* of it.

I

Panitch's work can be broken down into four periods.[5] The first, represented especially by his book *Social Democracy and Industrial Militancy* as well as his pivotal essay in the 1985/86 *Register*, focused especially on the limits of social democracy.⁶ Overlapping with this, as in his 1981 *New Left Review* article, 'Trade Unions and the Capitalist State', were his efforts to demonstrate that the corporatist arrangements fostered by capitalist states to negotiate incomes policies in the 1970s were not, as some believed, roads toward socialism, but were more likely to constrain and discipline trade unions.⁷ Thirdly, in a series of *Socialist Register* essays, written both on his own as well as with Sam Gindin – culminating in their magnum opus, *The Making of Global Capitalism* – he took on the question of the relationship between globalization and the American empire.⁸ Finally, he sought to identify, in the new 'democratic socialist' moment, possibilities for socialist advance.⁹

Across all these phases, Panitch made especially important contributions to Marxist state theory, picking up on the work of his mentor, and *Socialist Register* co-founder, Ralph Miliband, as well as that of Nicos Poulantzas. After the great strides made in developing the theory of the capitalist state over the 1960s and 1970s, this project was all-too-quickly cast aside. First, Theda Skocpol and her 'new institutionalist' confederates aimed to 'bring the state back in', albeit without its class foundations. Then, a so-called 'globalization theory' that saw states as having been circumvented by multinational corporations and transnational institutions sought to 'kick the state back out' as a relevant object of critical social scientific inquiry. 'I don't think I realised just how little time we had', Panitch wrote in 1999, or 'how contingent the further development of the Marxist theory of the state would be on immediately favorable political conditions. How quickly it all passed.'¹⁰

Despite changing academic 'fads', as Panitch put it, he remained committed to developing – and especially *concretizing* – state theory. It is truly difficult to capture today how anathema at the time were the arguments taken up by Panitch in a groundbreaking essay in the 1994 *Socialist Register*, and then in subsequent essays with Sam Gindin in the 2004 and 2005 volumes, asserting that states had not been supplanted by globalization, but were in fact the primary *authors* of it.¹¹ Far from having been bypassed by abstract 'networks' or 'flows' – or by a transnational capitalist class out in the ether – capitalist states were becoming more deeply integrated within an American informal empire. While the American state superintended 'the making of global capitalism', capitalist states everywhere had come to take on greater responsibility for reproducing the conditions for international accumulation within their own territories and securing the free movement of capital globally.

This conception was strikingly consistent with the concern Panitch expressed in his landmark 1977 essay on 'The Role and Nature of the

Canadian State' – that in delimiting the 'complex of institutions' which comprise the state, a 'fully developed' Marxist state theory must 'demonstrate concretely, rather than just define abstractly, the linkages between the state and the system of class inequality'.[12] Particularly important in this respect was Panitch and Gindin's theorization of the relationship between the 'internationalization of the state' and global finance. As against the many Marxist and social democratic theorists who saw financialization as a harbinger of decline, Panitch and Gindin demonstrated that it was in fact a material foundation of the American empire. The integration of global finance, they showed, was an essential condition for the emergence and regulation of a single global capitalism under the superintendence of the American state, rather than distinct regional or national capitalisms.

After World War II, 'inter-imperial rivalry', whereby capitalist empires exploited exclusive territories through the export of capital, was replaced by a condominium of states organized under the auspices of the American empire. The American state took responsibility for overseeing the world system – registered in the unprecedented step of rebuilding its major industrial rivals through the Marshall Plan, as well as setting up and managing the Bretton Woods regime. The densest imperial linkages increasingly ran not North-South, but rather between the countries of the advanced capitalist core. The free movement of investment was a major component of this: much more than mere trade, Foreign Direct Investment (FDI) transforms class structures and state formations. As American capital internationalized through increasing FDI, it became a class actor *within* each host country. Subsequently, other capitalist classes similarly internationalized, eroding any distinctly 'national' bourgeoisies.

The capital controls contained within Bretton Woods were not about limiting international integration, but rather providing a stable foundation for this to occur, just as the constraints on finance imposed through New Deal regulations had aimed not to weaken finance, but to strengthen it. By the 1970s, the 'baby had outgrown its incubator'.[13] Moreover, financial liberalization through the elimination of Bretton Woods controls and 'deregulation' was essential for resolving the decade-long 1970s crisis. As the post-war boom began to slow by the end of the 1960s, union wage militancy had increasingly squeezed profits, leading to a wage-push inflationary spiral and declining investment and growth – so-called 'stagflation'. Globalization helped to restore discipline, intensifying competition among workers for jobs while opening the vast low-wage workforce of the global periphery to exploitation. Financialization was not a problem for capital, but a solution.

Clearing the path for globalization was the unprecedented spike in interest rates engineered by Federal Reserve Chairman Paul Volcker in 1979, leading to a recession and skyrocketing unemployment which finally broke the back of the working class and tamed inflation. The 'Volcker Shock', as it became known, significantly concentrated state power within the highly autonomous, 'independent' Fed, substantially insulated from democratic pressures. As barriers to the free movement of capital were continually reduced, the need to manage a volatile financialized global capitalism led the Fed, as well as the Treasury, to serve as global 'firefighters in chief', addressing crises all over the world.[14] Indeed, one of the most significant contributions of *The Making of Global Capitalism* is its rich historical illustration of the close interconnection between the formation of the neoliberal state, the rise of finance, and US-led globalization: these are, in fact, three facets of the same process.

Although Panitch and Gindin did not undertake such an analysis, we have shown in our own work how the globalization of capital within American hegemony was articulated through changes in the structure of corporate power.[15] The emergence of a streamlined world of capital accumulation entailed the development of new organizational forms through which capital circulated as it became more mobile, competitive, and globally integrated, facilitating its movement across space and between sectors. Over the post-war era, the industrial corporation stepped out from the shadows of bank power to come under the control of 'insider' managers. At the same time, through a series of adaptive responses to the complexities of managing an increasingly diversified range of internationalized processes, operational control over specific businesses within multinational conglomerates was decentralized to divisional managers, while control over investment was centralized in the hands of top executives.

By the 1970s, this had led to the reorganization of corporate planning structures as internal capital markets, with top executives distributing finite pools of investment funds among competing business divisions. Senior managers effectively came to resemble investors, who increasingly saw corporate divisions as a portfolio of financial assets. Industrial corporations were thereby reconfigured as financial groups, blurring the line between financial and non-financial corporations. It is this deep corporate restructuring, and not their conversion into banks, that constitutes the financialization of the non-financial corporation. Moreover, as Panitch and Gindin suggested, financialization came at the expense of neither industry nor American power. Contrary to those who argued that this amounted to the 'hollowing out' of production, the result was to intensify competitive discipline to maximize profits, enhance margins, cut costs, and 'offshore' production.[16]

While control of the firm by 'insider' managers as opposed to outside investors during the post-war era had been supported by the fragmentation of shareholdings, the concentration and centralization of stock in the hands of large financial institutions over the neoliberal period supported the financialization of the non-financial corporation. This was fuelled by the pools of money-capital controlled by a new set of institutional investors, especially pension funds. Ironically, the growth of such funds reflected the economic strength of unions in winning gains for their members, becoming the largest single holders of corporate stock by the mid-1970s. While this led to speculation about the coming of 'pension fund socialism', these funds in fact ended up contributing to shifting the balance of class forces toward capital, intensifying financial pressure to restructure non-financial corporations. The result was a form of 'polyarchic financial hegemony', in which constellations of competing financial institutions exerted broad influence and discipline on industrial firms.[17]

The empowerment of finance was reflected in the doctrine of 'shareholder value', according to which corporate strategy should primarily be concerned with increasing stock prices. In keeping with this, industrial firms increased dividend payments and undertook stock buybacks to drive up share prices. Yet this did not come at the expense of investment, which actually *increased* relative to GDP, as did spending on R&D.[18] In fact, corporate investment and R&D spending only appear to have declined when seen as a percentage of profits, which is the measure William Lazonick and others have relied upon in making the case that finance has 'hollowed out' production.[19] Since corporate profits have been high, this misleadingly suggests a decline in investment, as corporations diverted a larger share of their income to buybacks and dividends. In reality, high profits – partly as a result of financial restructuring – allowed firms to pay out investors without jeopardizing their long-term competitiveness.

Corporate financialization and internationalization culminated in the replacement of the multidivisional conglomerate with a new multi-layered subsidiary form by the 1990s. Increasingly, industrial firms organized production by entering into subcontracts with other firms using cheaper labour, often based in the global periphery. MNCs thereby integrated subcontractors and their own divisions into highly flexible systems of production and investment.[20] Reliance on subcontractors intensified competitive pressures, holding down wages and restraining environmental and labour regulations, as well as making it easier for MNCs to relocate and restructure their operations. The multi-layered subsidiary form was the organizational structure through which capitalist globalization took place.[21]

II

Then came the Great Financial Crisis of 2008 – the deepest crisis of capitalism since the 1930s. In contrast to the Great Depression, it did not lead to the reversal of international economic integration, thanks mainly to the leadership of the US state in managing its global implications and maintaining a commitment to international integration. In fact, as Panitch repeatedly emphasized in the wake of the crisis, the Fed's central international role was actually reinforced by the extent to which states around the world turned to it for leadership and support – which it obliged by acting as a global lender of last resort, including extending unlimited swap lines of credit to foreign central banks. Meanwhile, investors flocked to dollars and Treasury bonds, reaffirming their status as 'safe-haven assets'. It would have been difficult to find a better demonstration of Panitch and Gindin's central thesis that the Fed had become the *world's* central bank.[22]

In the 2019 *Register,* Panitch and Gindin asked if, having weathered the economic crisis, the neoliberal state could withstand the chaos of a Trump presidency. Indeed, in international forums that had long served as venues for coordination among the core states of its 'informal empire', such as the G20, Trump repeatedly repudiated the historic US commitment to superintending global capitalism. As Panitch and Gindin remarked, it would be no small irony that central bank independence, 'explicitly designed by states and capital working together to protect the making of global capitalism from the progressive tendencies of democratic pressures on elected governments', should now safeguard global capitalism from the political *right*.[23] And yet, any doubts about the resilience of the neoliberal state were definitively answered when, in March 2020, the Fed extended all the emergency powers it had used in 2008 – and then some – to address the economic fallout from Covid-19.[24]

There could hardly have been a clearer illustration of how wrongheaded were hopes that an economic crash would inherently bring about the self-destruction of capitalism, or automatically benefit the working class, than the restructuring of financialized capitalism following the crisis. In the end, the crisis did not weaken capital, but strengthened it, with the full support of the 'democratic' state, and despite devastating consequences for workers. Insofar as one can speak of 'general tendencies' of capital accumulation, this was perhaps the most important for socialists. Moreover, the alternative of a more prolonged or severe economic crisis had the state not acted would have been even worse. As Panitch had pointed out earlier, 'it is through crises that capitalism historically has tended to recover its dynamism; where and when it is unable to do so, and where no viable socialist alternative or at least few means of democratic defense exist, the consequences are always appalling'.[25]

The reconstruction of the financial system was supported by the extension of state power over a wide range of 'economic' institutions through two interrelated phases of intervention. The first of these was *stabilization*, characterized by the ad hoc deployment of state power to manage the immediate fallout of the crisis. In this phase, the state effectively nationalized the primary organs of market-based finance, the decentralized system of credit creation that had evolved over the neoliberal period. Out of these interventions came the *consolidation* of a new 'risk state' through the internalization within the economic apparatus of a range of practices that became integral to the 'normal' functioning of the financial system. The risk state is defined by the extension of state power to risk-proof specific financial assets and support the major institutional pillars of market-based finance, especially the banks.[26] As we will see, the risk state constituted the basic infrastructure of a new architecture of financial power dominated by giant asset management companies.

The Fed sought to increase the stability of the banking system by reorganizing it around a handful of mega-banks integrated more closely with state power. As a result, the 'Big Four' banks – Bank of America, J.P. Morgan, Citibank, and Wells Fargo – emerged as foundations of a more robust financial order. Erasing the boundary between commercial and investment banks through merger or rechartering expanded the Fed's emergency liquidity-creating powers from commercial banks to the investment banks that were at the centre of the crisis. These banks were also extended additional state protection, and subjected to additional supervision, through the Dodd-Frank financial reform legislation. While their designation as 'systemically important financial institutions' implied that such banks had become 'too big to fail', they also faced new capital requirements, periodic 'stress tests', and a requirement to produce 'living wills' for how bank assets could be broken up and sold in the event of failure.

Central to the new risk state was continuous quantitative easing (QE), through which the Fed provided cash to financial institutions by purchasing mortgage-backed securities and Treasury bonds. As the Fed absorbed 'safe' assets, especially government bonds, from financial institutions, it pushed them to purchase other kinds of assets, especially stocks and corporate bonds. QE thus effectively de-risked not just the asset classes the Fed purchased, but others as well: the flow of money into 'riskier' assets served to support price inflation in these asset classes, reducing risk and boosting gains for such investments. Asset inflation, and the expansion of the Fed's balance sheet, were therefore two sides of the same coin. On the other hand, QE reduced the returns investors could receive on government and corporate bonds. With interest rates at or near zero, bonds and bank deposits yielded zero or even negative returns. Consequently, other forms of money-capital, especially equity, became more significant.

Meanwhile, inter-bank lending functions were internalized within the state economic apparatus through the creation of a new monetary policy system known as 'Interest on Excess Reserves' (IOER). Pouring trillions of dollars of liquidity into the financial system through QE made it impossible for the Fed to set interest rates. To resolve this dilemma, the Fed developed IOER, whereby it directly paid banks interest for depositing cash. Since banks would never lend to each other at a lower rate than that offered by the Fed, the latter became the benchmark rate across the financial system. Instead of merely influencing interest rates by managing the supply of liquidity, the Fed now directly supplied short-term capital to financial institutions. Private inter-bank lending markets were consequently displaced by the direct interposition of state power – dramatically de-risking these markets.[27]

Purchasing bonds from banks also meant that the Fed took on a new role in supporting government borrowing. This formed a circuit, whereby the Treasury issued bonds to finance government expenses, which were purchased by banks, before being purchased in turn from these banks by the Fed – thereby providing banks with cash. As with the neoliberal 'debt state', a large portion of government spending continued to be financed through debt as opposed to taxation.[28] However, while the debt state served to amplify the disciplinary power of finance on fiscal policy, the closed circuit of government bond exchanges between the Treasury and Fed amounted to the monetization of state debt, whereby the central bank finances state spending. By 2020, the Fed held nearly one-third of all outstanding US federal debt. Nevertheless, because the Fed purchased only a portion of state bonds, market discipline had by no means evaporated.

Core aspects of the neoliberal state had been preserved through all this, as Panitch and Gindin had insisted in their 2019 essay. Yet there were also important changes in the structures and capacities of the state, particularly in relation to the economic apparatus. While the Fed remained the leading agency within the economic apparatus, its strict inflation targeting regime, so central throughout the neoliberal period, was significantly relaxed. Moreover, the continuation of QE, after the immediate turmoil of 2008-2009 subsided, illustrated the extent to which the financial system had become dependent upon these 'emergency' measures. In fact, the de-risking of government bonds sharply accelerated as the Fed sought to fund consumption and support business amidst the unprecedented economic shutdown of the Covid-19 pandemic. What had at first seemed to be a radical extension of state power into the heart of the financial system was now organic to its routine functioning.

III

Panitch and Gindin were certainly correct that globalization, and the form of state power and class forces that supported it, not only survived the economic crisis, but were fortified by it. The 2008 crisis, however, *did* mark a fundamental change in American capitalism, with important implications for the organization of capital – and political power – across all states.

In the wake of the crisis, a small group of asset management companies displaced the banks as the most powerful institutions within contemporary finance. During the neoliberal period, institutional investors formed ephemeral alliances and exerted broad discipline over industrial firms. Now, the 'Big Three' asset management firms – BlackRock, Vanguard, and State Street – concentrated and centralized ownership power to an extent never before seen in the history of capitalism. They became central nodes in a vast network of corporate control that incorporated nearly every major firm from every economic sector.[29]

The rise of the Big Three was part of a broader transformation of corporate power. The separation of corporate ownership and control had, since the New Deal, been a central aspect of its organizational form: those who *owned* the firm (shareholders) were formally different from those who *controlled* the firm (managers). With the extreme concentration and centralization of ownership power in the hands of the asset management companies, this distinction broke down. The result was a new version of the *fusion* of financial and industrial capital that Rudolph Hilferding dubbed 'finance capital'.[30] Though widely misused, in Hilferding's usage the term does not simply refer to financial, much less bank, capital. Rather, finance capital emerges through the conjoining of financial and industrial capital, as a new form of capital established through their union – a synthesis which both preserves and negates the original industrial and financial forms (*aufhebung* in Hegel's terminology).

Through this fusion, financial institutions come to play a more active and direct role in the management of the industrial corporation. During the neoliberal period, markets for corporate control had mediated the relationship between shareholders and managers: though they did play an active role, shareholders could 'exit' by selling shares in under-performing firms. However, the new group of asset management firms are so-called 'passive investors'. This means they can only trade to reflect the changing weight of firms in an index, like the S&P 500 or the NASDAQ. As effectively *permanent* shareholders in all the largest and most important companies, they have to pursue more direct means of influencing corporate strategy. Unable to 'exit' firms in which they are invested, these financiers come to focus on increasing the creation of surplus value within the firms they own. By doing so, they aim to maximize the returns on their money-capital in the form of increased stock prices, as well as through dividends and other interest payments.

QE set in motion an interaction between state power and the 'asset management' form of financial organization whereby asset price inflation, the de-risking of equity, and the increasing size and diversification of asset management companies formed a self-reinforcing cycle. The asset inflation that resulted from QE created pressure on 'active' mutual funds, in which professional money managers attempt to 'beat the market' by strategically trading stocks. This became more difficult to do with the generalized increase of equity prices, which in turn made it harder to justify the management fees these funds charge their clients. Instead, 'passive' investment funds – once a niche segment of the market – became more appealing, as they could boast consistently robust returns alongside low management fees. Before 2008, 75 per cent of equity funds were actively managed; by 2020, more than half were passive, with nearly $6 trillion in equity under management.[31]

To be sure, passive management had been around for some time – Vanguard launched the first such fund in 1976. While State Street and Vanguard had a longer history with passive management, as the crisis unfolded, BlackRock successfully restructured its operations to become the most important player in this market. This took place especially through its landmark acquisition for $15 billion of Barclay's, along with its iShares passive funds. Meanwhile, State Street's Assets Under Management (AUM) increased by 41 per cent from 2004 to 2009, while those of Vanguard increased by 78 per cent. BlackRock's AUM grew in the same period by a barely believable 879 per cent – making it by far the largest global asset manager, with nearly $3.5 trillion in AUM, up from forty-first in 2004. Its AUM were nearly double those of the second-largest firm, State Street, with $1.9 trillion. By 2022, BlackRock's AUM had reached $10 trillion, while Vanguard had more than $8 trillion and State Street over $4 trillion.

Today, the Big Three are collectively the largest or second-largest shareholders in firms which comprise nearly 90 per cent of total market capitalization in the US economy. These firms have a combined market capitalization of nearly $45 trillion dollars. Even if one focuses only on cases in which the Big Three are the largest shareholder, the market capitalization of these firms substantially outstrips US GDP. The tremendous power of the Big Three is especially clear from the ownership structure of firms listed on the S&P 500, which tracks the largest companies within the American economy. The Big Three are the largest or second-largest holders of 98 per cent of S&P 500 firms, and own an average of over 20 per cent of any given company – an unprecedented scale and scope of ownership concentration.[32]

Asset management firms drew together the vast pools of money accumulated within expanding financialized pension funds, which, as we saw, had been an important foundation for the return of financial hegemony in the neoliberal period. The increasing externalization of the management of these pension funds meant that ever larger sums of money-capital were entrusted to professional asset managers.[33] The explosion of income and wealth inequality over the neoliberal period also contributed to the centralization of assets within the asset management companies. As the de-risking of equity diminished returns from other outlets, the low-cost investment model offered by asset management companies made investing in stock increasingly attractive. With nominal interest rates near 0 per cent, asset management companies constituted an institutional matrix whereby investing savings in the stock market could become nearly as secure and accessible as a bank deposit – and almost certainly more profitable.

Thus emerged a positive feedback loop, whereby the de-risking of equity drove the increasing size and diversification of asset management companies, which in turn supported these companies' role in allocating savings. As money flooded into the asset management companies, their growing size allowed them to further reduce management fees, since administrative costs per dollar under management declined as investment funds got larger. This essentially meant that these firms' profit margins increased alongside assets under management, even as management fees declined. Moreover, as the asset management firms grew, their investment funds became even safer, since this meant they were funnelling more and more savings into equity markets, thereby serving to perpetuate the inflation of stock prices; which, in turn, further encouraged the flow of still more money into the asset management companies, and so on.

Despite the extreme concentration of ownership, this regime of finance capital is intensely competitive. Asset management companies compete not only with one another, but also with all other outlets for savings, including banks, hedge funds, and private equity firms. To attract savings, these firms seek to maximize returns for clients: they must offer better returns, and lower risk, than their competitors. As we saw, such competition imposes limits on the fees these firms can charge, which is what led them to shift toward lower cost 'passive' index funds. Unable to increase fee rates, asset management firms grow through the continuous expansion of their AUM, as the fees they charge are typically calculated as a percent of this. Consequently, they also have an incentive to boost the value of the AUM they already hold. This leads asset management companies to actively pressure their portfolio companies on governance and strategic issues, including restructuring their operations and closing facilities that do not adequately contribute to profits.

Competitive pressures therefore drive asset management companies to maximize their direct control over financial and non-financial corporations: although they are *passive investors*, they are highly *active owners*. The especially long-term nature of passive funds leads asset management firms to form durable, collaborative relationships with firms in which they hold stakes. While the size of the holdings of pension funds and other institutional investors makes it difficult for them to trade without damaging the value of their own portfolios, the portfolios of asset management companies are even less liquid – as they are contractually barred from trading other than to track indexes. Unable to simply dump shares of under-performing corporations, asset management companies must find other means to influence firms. In the absence of the option to 'exit', therefore, competition takes the form of intervention.[34] And of course, backing up the power of these large shareholders is the possibility of their voting against management at shareholder meetings.

As the asset management companies are effectively permanent owners of the largest corporations in the economy, equally permanent interconnections condense between these financiers and industrial corporations. These relationships are organized through the asset managers' 'stewardship divisions', which centralize oversight of industrial corporations. This includes coordinating the asset management firms' shareholder voting strategies, as well as collaborating with portfolio companies to implement governance reforms, influence board composition, approve executive compensation, and supervise strategy. This relationship to industrial corporations is similar to that of the investment banks Hilferding analyzed – and is very different from the activism of 'active' investors, which have a relatively high portfolio turnover. While such active investors may exercise significant leverage over particular firms, this does not result in the formation of the kind of stable fusion between finance and industry characteristic of finance capital.

All of the asset management companies monitor their portfolio companies and reach out to them to discuss any concerns. In 2020, BlackRock held over 3,500 company engagements, covering nearly 65 per cent of global equity under management, while Vanguard engaged with companies representing 52 per cent of its US equity holdings.[35] Importantly, portfolio companies also recognize the power of the asset management firms by themselves requesting meetings to discuss strategies and plans, or to address unforeseen events which may impact the performance of the company. The expectation of routine coordination on the part of the asset management firms ensures that they are rarely surprised by strategic developments or operational issues, as well as that portfolio companies are clearly aware of the expectations and interests of the asset managers. Openly voting against management at a shareholder meeting is therefore a last resort, signifying a breakdown of 'normal' relations.

Nevertheless, asset management companies have frequently advanced and supported shareholder proposals to restructure corporate governance in order to further institutionalize investor power, building on the gains of the neoliberal years.[36] This has taken the form of demands for the elimination of 'classified shares', whereby some shares (usually held by managerial insiders) have more voting power than others – pushing instead for the principle of 'one share, one vote'. Similarly, they have insisted upon the right to nominate independent directors, and to approve them through a simple majority vote at shareholder meetings, while supporting independent board compensation and audits. Moreover, they have sought to expand the power of shareholders to bring proposals to meetings for a vote and have exercised significant oversight over executive compensation. At stake in these conflicts is nothing less than control over the corporation itself.

IV

In his 2021 *Register* essay, Samir Sonti raised the possibility that the rise of the new finance capital ('asset manager capitalism' in his terms) could pave the way for a new social democratic class compromise of sorts. This potential was expressed especially in the Biden administration's proposals for significant fiscal expansion and a more robust industrial policy. That these programs were, in part, crafted by BlackRock executive Brian Deese, who Biden appointed as head of the Council of Economic Advisors, and that BlackRock had issued reports supporting a more expansive monetary and fiscal policy, implied that the interests of the asset management firms now at the centre of the financial system were distinct from the traditional orientation of finance toward low inflation and fiscal austerity. As such, Sonti suggested that these firms could constitute the core of a 'liberal financial bloc', which could support 'an economic program capable of providing real relief for working people'.[37]

For Sonti, 'Bidenomics' was congruent with the interests of asset managers for several reasons. First, the de-risking of stocks and bonds through continued QE and low interest rates served to maintain asset price appreciation, thereby enhancing the competitiveness of passive management strategies. Moreover, Bidenism added to these long-running practices of the post-crisis risk state the call for an expansionary fiscal policy. The opening for such measures was made possible by the Fed's move toward a more accommodative approach to inflation following the 2008 crisis, meaning that the expansionary effects of government spending would no longer be counteracted by interest rate increases. Channelling state investment into strategic areas, such as infrastructure and R&D, aimed at encouraging private investment and enhancing competitiveness also boosted asset prices and aligned well with the logic of asset management.

Despite widespread comparisons of Biden's political program to that of Franklin D. Roosevelt, the extent to which any of this could serve as a basis for a renewed class compromise, let alone on the order of the New Deal, was always rather dubious. For one thing, as Sonti explains, the foundation of the entire logic is the ability to sustain low inflation. While an expansionary fiscal policy may tighten labour markets, and thus create an opportunity for workers to bargain for increased wages, to the extent that this results in price increases it actually collapses the entire strategy. Thus, the rhetorical support Biden extended for trade union rights was not complementary to the supposed interests of the 'liberal financial bloc', but directly antagonistic to them: as Sonti notes, 'to the extent, if any, that "Bidenomics" succeeds in empowering American workers, it may undermine an important condition of its own existence'.[38]

It is equally unclear how the moderate expansion of social programs Biden proposed, such as universal pre-kindergarten, affordable childcare, free community college, strengthening unemployment insurance, and expanding Obamacare fitted with the interests of asset managers. Indeed, the fiscal and monetary programs Sonti highlights are not really social democratic at all, but focused primarily on enhancing the competitiveness of American MNCs. Insofar as this rests on the globalization of production, the mobility of capital and the power of firms to 'exit' by closing plants and investing elsewhere will continue to serve as a powerful disciplinary force on workers. While the interest of these industrial firms is apparently not connected to the liberal capitalist bloc, as we have seen asset management companies are themselves competitively disciplined to press for the maximization of profits and share values, and therefore the exploitation of labour by the industrial firms they own.

An active fiscal and monetary policy is often seen as capable of leading to an increase in social spending, as well as tighter labour markets, which create openings for workers to push for gains. The problem with this logic is that the new finance capital is built upon maintaining competitive discipline on workers and industrial capital. Active fiscal and monetary policy can always only occur in the context of the maintenance of these competitive disciplines. Workers will not, therefore, automatically or incidentally benefit from this – which can only take place insofar as their docility, and low inflation, is preserved. The opportunities for workers to benefit from this policy regime are therefore not merely limited or contradictory, but fundamentally off the table. If the position of workers is to be bettered, this will not take place based on a confluence of interests with a 'liberal financial bloc', but through independent organizing, class formation, and confrontation with capital.

Enacting reforms that would substantially improve the lives of workers requires taking on capital to an extent that goes well beyond what one could imagine BlackRock or other asset management companies supporting. This involves a direct *challenge* to the interests of these asset management firms, which, at least in regard to social democratic reforms, are hardly distinguishable from the rest of capital. Soon after Biden's election, BlackRock initially appeared to recognize the need for some corrections in the current grotesque levels of inequality through changes to the tax system.[39] However, such openness to tax increases has very real limits. These firms' entire growth model relies on inequality, and the availability of surplus savings, to increase their AUM. Even their support for 'easy money' evaporates the moment the working class begins to mobilize, or inflation rises beyond certain limits. And of course, these firms remain deeply committed to globalization.

As inflation climbed to levels unseen since the 1970s, reaching over 9 per cent at the time of writing, the Fed moved once again to raise interest rates and taper new purchases of Treasury bonds. The Fed's resort to interest rate hikes to tame inflation does not invalidate the more accommodative approach it adopted after 2008; on the contrary, it merely proves – as should always have been obvious – that its tolerance for inflation is not unlimited. Nevertheless, the Fed's moves were especially noteworthy since price increases did not seem to stem primarily from wage-push dynamics, as in the 1970s. Nor had bond markets signalled a concern with long-term inflation. In effect, the Fed's rate hikes constituted a pre-emptive strike to prevent inflationary expectations from becoming entrenched, which could lead to workers demanding higher wages as well as prolonged economic stagnation.

Not only did BlackRock CEO Larry Fink explicitly support increasing interest rates, but he even challenged the assessment of Fed Chair Jerome

Powell that inflation was transitory, and insisted before the fact that the Fed would have to change policy.[40] This raises questions about the link between QE and low interest rates, on the one hand, and the market power of asset management companies, on the other. While easy money was a critical foundation for the rise of the Big Three, it is not clear that their continued financial dominance, and the regime of corporate governance constructed around it, intrinsically hinges on the continuation of monetary policy stimulus. Not only do a disproportionate share of BlackRock's profits come from its relatively high-fee actively managed funds, but it is also a leading provider of cash management services to the financial system, which will become more profitable with rising interest rates.

In any case, the attractiveness of passive management does not depend on low rates: even in the context of greater market volatility, active managers' ability to 'beat the market' is dubious. Moreover, the economies of scale established by the Big Three grant them considerable cost advantages, allowing them to offer extremely low-price investment products. There is good reason to believe, therefore, that low-cost, diversified, passively managed funds will retain a considerable competitive edge – and that the ownership power concentrated within the Big Three will be preserved. In fact, since passive management offers the safest path to invest in stocks, market uncertainty may actually increase these companies' ability to attract savings and build AUM. Meanwhile, the absence of generalized asset price appreciation may lead asset management firms to intervene even more forcefully in their portfolio companies in order to improve performance and extract value.

The risk of a stock market crash certainly threatens asset management firms, like all investors. Yet higher interest rates and greater market volatility may not weaken the new finance capital – and could even strengthen it. Similarly, such changes are virtually certain to fortify the commitment to globalization of all sections of financial and industrial capital, along with the American state. The power of asset management companies in this emerging context will only reinforce their portfolio firms' relentless pursuit of cost savings through the search for cheap labour, low-cost resources, and low taxes. Even BlackRock's much-vaunted focus on 'Environmental, Social, and Governance' (ESG) investing has been publicly reined in. While ESG always amounted to little more than greenwashing, a recent memo explained that the firm would endorse fewer shareholder proposals on environmental responsibility over the coming year than the prior one, because, in Fink's words, these were now too 'constraining' and 'prescriptive'.[41]

After a decade and a half of QE, a new policy paradigm that could succeed neoliberalism had yet to cohere. Despite Trump's rhetorical challenge to globalization, his failure to offer an alternative – even as he appeared willing to undermine electoral institutions – was notable. Subsequently, Biden's social reforms, which sought to signal a break with Trump without so much as restoring corporate tax rates to pre-Trump levels, were mostly defeated in Congress by Republicans, alongside a handful of Democrats. The Berniecrats, whose electoral victories had been so inspiring for the new generation of democratic socialists, were left to fight for the meagre rations Biden had offered, without any significant support from unions or wider social mobilization. Their defeat, along with mounting inflation, led to the earlier optimism around reform being overtaken by gloomy calls for recession – casting a pall over Biden's term in office and foretelling possible further dangers from the far right.

V

The formation of the new finance capital does not seem to have created space for a meaningful social democratic class compromise. Rather, this has served to entrench the consensus among all fractions of capital around globalization and class discipline. While the ascent of the new fraction of finance capitalists within the power bloc has come with some limited moves towards a more robust industrial policy, whereby the state would extend greater subsidies to corporations for advanced manufacturing and cutting-edge R&D, such initiatives are narrowly focused on improving corporate competitiveness within the context of free capital mobility, not reversing four decades of neoliberal devastation of working-class communities. The political paradox the left faces today is that even as the working class is as weak as it has ever been, winning substantive reforms and shifting the balance of class forces requires a truly radical confrontation with capital.

Carrying forward the project of building a genuine alternative demands winning people over to socialist ideas. The lesson, above all, that emerged from the experience of Sanders and Corbyn, as well as the limits subsequently faced by Momentum and the 'Berniecrat' insurgency, is that nothing like the base necessary to enact the wide-ranging reforms these forces have sought now exists. Nor, for that matter, can an electoral coalition – that ephemeral collectivity which is spontaneously assembled only to melt away – substitute for one. Electoral victories and individual reforms can be helpful, but in the absence of a base with deeper roots in working-class communities and organizations such gains are all too easily isolated, deflected, or absorbed. Such a base can ultimately lay the groundwork for going beyond merely supporting a progressive caucus within the Democrats to establishing a socialist party, which remains the indispensable 'fulcrum between class formation and state transformation'.[42]

Socialist strategy begins from the objective of taking the productive capacities of private corporations under public control and deploying them to serve social and ecological needs. While advocating more 'realistic' reforms, such as Employee Share Ownership or worker representation on corporate Boards of Directors, may seem safer in the context of the weakness of the left, such strategies actually embed workers *more* deeply in the logic of competitiveness. Even if workers receive a larger share of the gains, or a greater stake in shaping market strategy, the model of individual firms maximizing profits through market competition imposes strict discipline to reduce all costs – including wages, taxes, and regulations. The survival of the firm demands that all values which do not advance the cause of competitiveness must be sacrificed. This does not lead toward establishing social control over production, nor contribute to developing the economic coordination necessary to address the existential climate crisis, let alone build a more democratic society.

Of course, expanding social programs and trade union rights – not to mention supporting elections themselves in the face of threats from the far-right – are foundational mandates for the left. Yet such reforms alone are not enough. Preserving the gains of the past, as well as creating a more just future, requires deeper structural change, first and foremost challenging the capitalist globalization of recent decades. This means going beyond narrow critiques of financialization. It is not possible to separate a discrete group of 'industrialists' who have been victimized by financialization from 'financiers' who have benefited from it. While the internal restructuring of the firm converted industrial managers into financiers, globalization has made finance even more essential for industrial production. The current form of finance capital involves an especially close interconnection between financiers and industrial corporations.

Creating space for workers to win lasting gains necessitates breaking with globalization by imposing capital controls, which obstruct capital's ability to 'exit'. Yet this raises the question of what happens with the capital that stays home – and thus points to the need to democratize control over investment. Doing so entails going beyond calls to restore competitiveness by 'breaking up the banks', and focusing instead on the need to nationalize finance and run it as a public utility. Crucially, if nationalized financial institutions are to operate substantially differently from capitalist ones, market dependence must be replaced by social control through the development of new state capacities for democratically planning the allocation of investment. The obvious inadequacy of the ESG strategies promoted by asset management firms to address the climate emergency only further highlights the critical importance of this project of economic democratization and state transformation.

Despite the fact the Big Three have amassed such tremendous ownership power, simply calling for their nationalization would, on its own, amount to little. For one thing, they do not engage in anything like the kind of society-wide economic planning that would characterize socialism – relying on price signals and profitability to determine the allocation of investment. More problematically, their power is dependent upon voluntary contributions of capital. Pension funds and other investors would be unlikely to entrust the management of their capital to an institution which had been taken under public control with the explicit objective of reducing (even if not immediately eliminating) its reliance on competitiveness and monetary returns, turning instead to meeting social needs. Establishing meaningful social control over finance, therefore, requires capturing the underlying pools of money-capital that support the power of asset managers.

Clearly, this is not on the immediate horizon. But socialists can take the lead now in envisioning and creating institutions that can serve as the basis for larger change. Promising in this regard are struggles around establishing public banks.[43] Unlike private banks, which exist solely to valorize money-capital, public banks are deposit-taking institutions that can be chartered around meeting democratically established objectives: developing infrastructure such as public transit and community housing; improving access to credit for marginalized populations, preventing foreclosures, and allowing farmers to repurchase land; and providing capital to local businesses. While they must generate returns to reproduce themselves, they are able to fund loss-making or revenue-neutral projects, as well as offering below-market interest rates. As such, public banks offer a glimpse of the community self-governance and empowerment that could be possible within a democratic economy.

Public banks are a *supplement to*, rather than a *replacement for*, capitalist financial institutions. Whether they can form part of a strategy for a broader democratization of the state and the economy, while operating on the margins of financialized capitalism, is an open question. Community public banks must gain the support of city councils and state legislatures, and face intense opposition from capital. They must therefore be presented as non-threatening, thereby marginalizing socialists and socialist ideas in their conception and public presentation. Far from being held up as seeding a post-capitalist alternative, they are often chartered along narrow lines that leave them indistinguishable from their private counterparts. Community-elected boards and democratic deliberation about priorities all-too-often fall by the wayside. In the end, they can merely end up supporting profitability and competitiveness by reducing risk and inflating returns for big and small capital alike.

It would therefore be naive to see class consciousness and community solidarity as automatically resulting from the formation of public banks. The possibility that public banks could serve as a model depends upon socialists taking the lead in connecting them to community needs, as well as educating workers about their transformative potential and linking them to a wider and deeper struggle. The ultimate objective would be to establish an integrated system of local, regional, and national public banks, chartered with a mandate to support a green transition, which could, to some extent, replace the allocation of capital on competitive markets with conscious democratic decision-making. A central paradox of public banks, then, is that the socialist leadership necessary to integrate them within a transformative project of economic democratization tends to be undermined by the political and economic constraints they operate within.

VI

In contemplating the wreckage that is being left behind by the limits of Bidenism amidst the continued weakness of the left, Panitch's theoretical and strategic contributions continue to illuminate 'the socialist challenge today'. Even as the decades-long neoliberal onslaught broke workers' organizations and served up one defeat after the next, and even as other erstwhile New Leftists lamented the 'God that failed', Panitch continued to devote himself to illustrating the necessity of a democratic socialist society that would fall prey neither to the shortcomings of social democracy nor those of Soviet-style communism. It is the carving out of this political space that is the most precious legacy not only of Leo himself, but the entire New Left generation of which he was a part.

One of the things that was most impressive and inspiring about Leo was his seriousness about building socialism. He was committed to acknowledging the immense challenges entailed by the need to socialize the economy, and building the working-class forces and mass public support needed for anything like this to be possible. This commitment was at the heart of his classic essay in the 1985/86 *Register* criticizing the socialist 'realists', who, in the context of the defeat of Tony Benn's attempt to democratize the Labour Party and the rise of Thatcherism, retreated into a 'pragmatic' reformist politics. Amidst the historic defeat of social democracy, and the initiation of neoliberalism, Panitch called for a renewed radical commitment to socialist transition by establishing social control over the productive forces.[44]

Panitch argued the success of Thatcherism was, in large part, an outcome of the bankruptcy of social democracy – its acceptance of the structure of the capitalist state, its obsession with parliamentary debates and electoral timetables, its commitment to a politics of class harmony, and its neglect for building working-class capacities. Its defeat was facilitated by its failure to preserve existing gains through a transition to socialism, rather than acceding to neoliberal restructuring in the face of capitalist crisis and stagnation. But it was also enabled, Panitch insisted, by popular dissatisfaction with the highly bureaucratic and undemocratic nature of the welfare state it constructed. It was not, therefore, sufficient for socialists to call for restoring the 'Keynesian' welfare state. Rather, in order to meet the reactionary onslaught, the very real limits of social democracy had to be acknowledged head-on, and the need to transcend it reaffirmed. At stake for socialists was not a question of 'more' or 'less' state, but *a different kind of state*. What was needed was a fundamental *transformation* of the state, such that it fostered democratic participation in managing social services as well as the economy.

The renewed commitment to socialism that Panitch saw as necessary in that dark moment ran directly contrary to the widespread concern among the new group of socialist 'realists' with the 'immediacy of power', which led them to dilute their messages and moderate their strategies so as to achieve electoral victories and implement reforms. The narrow reformist politics that this led to, Panitch argued, would only make it more difficult to build the mass popular support that is an obvious precondition for taking the means of production under social control. Building such public support would not be possible if the limits of capitalist democracy could not be acknowledged, and the difficult questions about the nature of socialist democracy confronted. Because their politics was predicated on evading these issues, the growing number of 'realists' had 'no more managed to square the circle of how to transform capitalism while cooperating fully with it than did traditional social democracy'.[45]

Reading this essay today can feel like a prophetic warning for today's democratic socialists. As Panitch, and his co-authors, wrote in an essay in the 2020 *Register*, one of the most promising aspects of the new 'democratic socialist' movement was the willingness of the intelligent and committed young activists leading it to move beyond the organizational and political models of the past. A refreshing openness resulted: however inspiring 1917 certainly remained, it no longer animated the core identity of socialist politics. As these organizers and activists struggled to find a new form of political organization capable of giving concrete expression to the ideals of democratic socialism, they eschewed fatalism and asserted a political horizon beyond capitalism. More importantly, they initiated important and inspiring efforts to reconstitute the political and cultural identity of the working class, an objective with which Panitch was concerned throughout his political life.[46]

Yet as Panitch observed in *Searching for Socialism* (co-authored with Colin Leys), and across numerous essays in the last decade of his life, the programs put forward by the political leaders who had emerged from within centre-left parties in the US and UK to lead this socialist renewal lacked the clarity of purpose around socialist transition he had called for in his 1985/86 *Register* essay. This was not a matter of these figures' insufficient personal commitment to the cause of socialism, but rather a reflection of the balance of class forces, and the relative weakness of the left and labour. Still, these writings asked the hard questions about whether, and to what degree, the policies advanced by these figures could serve as stepping stones toward something more and far better.[47]

In the end, it was difficult to avoid the conclusion that the energy and commitment within Momentum and the Democratic Socialists America was more promising than the specific policies being advanced by these political candidates, however much their presence on the political stage had been an essential factor in leading the new socialist upsurge. The future of socialism in both the US and UK, therefore, would depend in that moment more on *politics* than *policy*, as the meaning and implications of any reforms would hinge on whether these new socialist activists would be able to use them to deepen class consciousness and identity, educate workers about the limits of the capitalist state and the imperative to transcend capitalism, and develop new organizational forms capable of articulating the power of the working class as a political agent and winning victories that would bring real change to people's lives – and ultimately transforming society.

These projects now face profound difficulties. In the wake of the defeat of Jeremy Corbyn's leadership of the Labour Party and Bernie Sanders' two presidential campaigns, the failure of Trump-era protest movements to leave any organizational legacy, and Biden's inability to pass even mild reforms, the pressure to focus on 'realistic' objectives, or simply winning elections, while forgoing any serious commitment to socialist transition can be overwhelming. Yet this does not lessen the urgency of a fundamental change in our social system, whereby capitalism's relentless drive for the infinite accumulation of surplus value is replaced by an economy oriented around meeting social and ecological needs. As Panitch held, this cannot be accomplished through the 'pragmatic' adjustment of socialist ideals. It requires a commitment to demonstrating the inability of capitalist democracy to meet the challenges of our time, and to envisioning a democratic socialist future.

The commitment to transforming the state, such that it becomes the central organ of a democratically planned socialist economy, rather than accepting its capitalist structure and seeking to wield its power through elections, is what sets socialists apart from social democrats. In the face of the growing influence of an extremist right, the understandable temptation is to revert to defending 'Keynesian' capitalism or the post-war social democratic welfare state. However, to take the lessons of Panitch's 1985/86 essay into the present, this would be to forget that it was the limits of the social democratic politics of class compromise which ultimately led these parties to spearhead neoliberal reforms. The vacuum left by this failure has today increasingly been filled by a radical and mobilized radical right wing. Reaffirming the *socialist* critique of the capitalist state is therefore more important than ever – and an essential starting-point for developing a serious alternative.

Such a call for a renewed commitment to socialist transition may seem utopian. Yet in the context of the mounting threat to organized human life posed by the ecological crisis, the real utopians are not those who dare to dream of a better world, but those who believe it is possible to keep things as they are. Despite the constant stream of catastrophic news across social media feeds and cable news channels, doom is not inevitable. The possibility for the fundamental social transformation so urgently needed is not foreclosed. It is up to us to maintain our optimism of the intellect, not deluding ourselves about how bad things are, but staying true to our commitment to searching for cracks in the current order from which a better future could bloom. It is well past time to turn the page on capitalist prehistory, so that a truly human history can begin. The next chapter in human development could be a socialist one. Whether or not this comes to pass depends on us.

NOTES

1   Stephen Maher, 'Escaping Structuralism's Legacy: Renewing Theory and History in Historical Materialism', *Science & Society*, 80(3), 2016, pp. 291-318; Stephen Maher and Scott M. Aquanno, 'Conceptualizing Neoliberalism: Foundations for an Institutional Marxist Theory of Capitalism', *New Political Science*, 40(1), 2018, pp. 33-50; Stephen Maher and Scott M. Aquanno, 'Institutional Marxism', in Clyde Barrow, ed., *Encyclopedia of Critical Political Science*, Cheltenham: Edward Elgar, forthcoming.
2   Leo Panitch and Sam Gindin, 'Marxist Theory and Strategy: Getting Somewhere Better', *Historical Materialism*, 23(2), 2015.
3   Leo Panitch, 'Still a Marxist After All', Phyllis Clarke Lecture, Toronto, 10 March 2009.

4   Leo Panitch, 'On Revolutionary Optimism of the Intellect', in Leo Panitch and Greg Albo, eds, *Socialist Register 2017: Rethinking Revolution*, London: Merlin Press, 2016.
5   See: Greg Albo, Stephen Maher, and Alan Zuege, 'Postscript', in Greg Albo, Stephen Maher, and Alan Zuege, eds, *State Transformations: Classes, Strategy, Socialism*, Chicago: Haymarket Books, 2022.
6   Leo Panitch, *Social Democracy and Industrial Militancy: The Labour Party, the Trade Unions, and Incomes Policy 1945-1974*, London: Cambridge University Press, 1976; Leo Panitch, 'The Impasse of Social Democratic Politics', in Ralph Miliband, John Saville, Marcel Liebman, and Leo Panitch, eds, *Socialist Register 1985/86: Social Democracy and After*, London: Merlin Press, 1985.
7   Leo Panitch, 'Trade Unions and the Capitalist State', *New Left Review*, 1(125), 1981.
8   Leo Panitch, 'Globalisation and the State', in Ralph Miliband and Leo Panitch, eds, *Socialist Register 1994: Between Globalism and Nationalism*, London: Merlin Press, 1993; Leo Panitch and Sam Gindin, 'Global Capitalism and American Empire', in Leo Panitch and Colin Leys, eds, *Socialist Register 2004: The New Imperial Challenge*, London: Merlin Press, 2003; Leo Panitch and Sam Gindin, 'Finance and American Empire', in Leo Panitch and Colin Leys, eds, *Socialist Register 2005: The Empire Reloaded*, London: Merlin Press, 2004; Leo Panitch and Sam Gindin, *The Making of Global Capitalism: The Political Economy of the American Empire*, London: Verso, 2012.
9   Stephen Maher, Sam Gindin, and Leo Panitch, 'Class Politics, Socialist Policies, Capitalist Constraints', in Leo Panitch and Greg Albo, eds, *Socialist Register 2020: New Ways of Living*, London: Merlin Press, 2019; Leo Panitch and Sam Gindin with Stephen Maher, *The Socialist Challenge Today: Syriza, Corbyn, Sanders*, Second Edition, Chicago: Haymarket Books, 2020; Leo Panitch and Colin Leys, *Searching For Socialism: The Project of the Labour New Left From Benn to Corbyn*, New York: Verso, 2020.
10 Leo Panitch, 'The Impoverishment of State Theory', *Socialism and Democracy* 13(2), 1999.
11 Panitch, 'Globalisation and the State'; Panitch and Gindin, 'Global Capitalism and American Empire'; Panitch and Gindin, 'Finance and American Empire'.
12 Leo Panitch, 'The Role and Nature of the Canadian State', in Leo Panitch, ed., *The Canadian State: Political Economy and Political Power*, Toronto: University of Toronto Press, 1977.
13 Panitch and Gindin, *The Making of Global Capitalism*, p. 121.
14 Panitch and Gindin, *The Making of Global Capitalism*, p. 248; Greg Albo, Leo Panitch, and Sam Gindin, *In and Out of Crisis: The Global Financial Meltdown and Left Alternatives*, Oakland: PM Press, 2010.
15 Stephen Maher, *Corporate Capitalism and the Integral State: General Electric and a Century of American Power*, New York: Palgrave, 2021.
16 Maher, *Corporate Capitalism and the Integral State*; Neil Fligstein, *The Transformation of Corporate Control*, Cambridge, MA: Harvard University Press, 1993; Claude Serfati, 'The New Configuration of the Capitalist Class', in Leo Panitch, Greg Albo, and Vivek Chibber, eds, *Socialist Register 2014: Registering Class*, London: Merlin Press, 2013.
17 John Scott, *Corporate Business and Capitalist Classes*, Oxford: Oxford University Press, 1997.

18 Author calculations based on data from the Federal Reserve Economic Database and the National Center for Science and Engineering Statistics.
19 William Lazonick, 'Profits Without Prosperity', *Harvard Business Review*, 1 September 2014; William Lazonick, 'The Financialization of the U.S. Corporation: What Has Been Lost, and How It Can Be Regained', *Seattle University Law Review*, 36(2), 2013.
20 Harland Prechel, 'Corporate Transformation to the Multi-Layered Subsidiary Form', *Sociological Forum*, 13(3), 1997.
21 Stephen Maher and Scott M. Aquanno, 'The New Finance Capital: Corporate Governance, Financial Power, and the State', *Critical Sociology*, 48(1), 2022; Stephen Maher and Scott M. Aquanno, 'A New Finance Capital? Theorizing Corporate Governance and Financial Power', in Judith Dellheim and Frieder Otto Wolf, eds, *Rudolf Hilferding's Critical Political Economy*, London: Palgrave Macmillan, 2021 (second edition 2022).
22 Leo Panitch and Sam Gindin, 'Trumping the Empire', in Leo Panitch and Greg Albo, eds, *Socialist Register 2019: The World Turned Upside Down?*, London: Merlin Press, 2018.
23 Panitch and Gindin, 'Trumping the Empire', p. 18.
24 Stephen Maher and Scott M. Aquanno, 'From Economic to Political Crisis: Trump and the Neoliberal State', in Rob Hunter, Rafael Khachaturian, and Eva Nanopoulos, eds, *Capitalist States and Marxist State Theory: Enduring Debates, New Perspectives*, New York: Palgrave, forthcoming.
25 Leo Panitch, *Renewing Socialism: Democracy, Strategy, and Imagination*, London: Routledge, 2002.
26 Our conception of the 'risk state' owes a substantial debt to the work of Daniela Gabor. However, our theorization differs in significant respects. See: Daniela Gabor, 'The Wall Street Consensus', *Development and Change* 26, 2021.
27 Marcelo Rezende, Judit Temesvary, and Rebecca Zarutskie, 'Interest on Excess Reserves and U.S. Commercial Bank Lending', *FEDS Notes*, Federal Reserve Board of Governors, 18 October 2019.
28 Wolfgang Streeck, *Buying Time: The Delayed Crisis of Democratic Capitalism*, London: Verso, 2014.
29 Benjamin Braun, 'Asset Manager Capitalism as a Corporate Governance Regime', in Jacob Hacker, Alex Hertel-Fernandez, Paul Pierson, and Kathleen Thelen, eds, *The American Political Economy: Politics, Markets, and Power*, Cambridge, UK: Cambridge University Press, 2021; Jan Fichtner, Eelke M. Heemskerk, and Javier Garcia-Bernardo, 'Hidden power of the Big Three? Passive index funds, re-concentration of corporate ownership, and new financial risk', *Business and Politics* 19(2), 2017.
30 Rudolf Hilferding, *Finance Capital: A Study of the Latest Phase of Capitalist Development*, 1911; Maher and Aquanno, 'The New Finance Capital: Corporate Governance, Financial Power, and the State'; Maher and Aquanno, 'A New Finance Capital? Theorizing Corporate Governance and Financial Power'.
31 Kevin McDevitt and Michael Schramm, 'Morningstar Direct Fund Flows Commentary: United States', Morningstar, 2019; Amy Whyte, 'Active Managers Kept Losing Out to Passive, Even After Markets Crashed', *Institutional Investor*, 25 January 2021.
32 Authors' calculations based on Orbis database.

33 Stephen Maher, 'Stakeholder Capitalism, Corporate Organization, and Class Power', in Simon Archer, Chris Roberts, Kevin Skerrett, and Joanna Westar, eds, *The Contradictions of Pension Fund Capitalism*, Ithaca, NY: Cornell University Press, 2017.
34 This contrasts with the conclusion drawn in Benjamin Braun, 'From exit to control: The structural power of finance under asset manager capitalism', working paper, Max Planck Institute for the Study of Societies, SocArXiv, 12 October 2021, available at: osf.io/preprints/socarxiv/4uesc.
35 BlackRock, *Investment Stewardship Report*, 2021; Vanguard, *Annual Investment Stewardship Report*, 2020.
36 Ian R. Appel, Todd A. Gormley, and Donald B. Keim, 'Passive investors, not passive owners', *Journal of Financial Economics* 121, 2016; Vanguard, *Semi-Annual Engagement Update*, 2019.
37 Samir Sonti, 'The Crisis of US Labour, Past and Present', in Greg Albo, Leo Panitch, and Colin Leys, eds, *Socialist Register 2022: New Polarizations, Old Contradictions*, London: Merlin Press, 2021, p. 137.
38 Sonti, 'The Crisis of US Labour', p. 137.
39 Matt Egan, 'US economy can 'definitely withstand tax hikes, BlackRock's Rieder says', *CNN*, 17 March 2021.
40 Saqib Iqbal Ahmed, 'BlackRock CEO Fink does not see inflation as transitory', *Reuters*, 14 July 2021; Brian Stewart, 'BlackRock's Larry Fink: Higher Interest Rates Will "Help a Lot of Savers"', *Seeking Alpha*, 18 January 2022.
41 BlackRock, '2022 climate-related shareholder proposals more prescriptive than 2021'.
42 Leo Panitch, 'The Revolution Party', *Constellations*, 24, 2017.
43 Thomas Marois, *Public Banks: Decarbonization, Definancialization, and Democratization*, Cambridge: Cambridge University Press, 2021.
44 Panitch, 'The Impasse of Social Democratic Politics'.
45 Panitch, 'The Impasse of Social Democratic Politics', pp. 81-88.
46 Maher, Gindin, and Panitch, 'Class Politics, Socialist Policies, Capitalist Constraints'.
47 Panitch, Gindin, and Maher, *The Socialist Challenge Today*; Panitch and Leys, *Searching for Socialism*.

MASS PARTIES, DUAL POWER, AND QUESTIONS OF STRATEGY: A DIALOGUE WITH LEO PANITCH

PANAGIOTIS SOTIRIS

The original design of this panel for the 2020 Historical Materialism conference in Turkey was meant to include Leo Panitch as one of the presenters.[1] His absence makes this an even sadder moment as this is a debate that would have benefited from his insights.

I shared a panel with Leo in 2012 in Athens, between two momentous national elections. One might say that this was the beginning of a 'Greek Moment'. Namely, the moment when the entire world realized that the immense social and political crisis in Greece, and the mass movement that had an almost insurrectionary dynamic, had initiated tectonic changes in the relations of political representation. These changes seemed so great that the rise to power of a party of the non-social-democratic left, with a programme that suggested the possibility of rupture with the embedded neoliberalism of the European Union, suddenly seemed possible.

Syriza came to power in 2015. However, the expectation of this electoral victory and of the measures that a left government in power was supposed to implement had already had a subduing effect on popular mobilization in the period between the 2012 and the 2015 elections. It soon became evident, however, that Syriza was prepared neither for the difficulty and complexity of this challenge, nor for the extent and violence of the blackmail that Greece's lenders, namely the Troika of the European Union (EU), the European Central Bank (ECB), and the International Monetary Fund (IMF), could and would exercise. The 'Greek Moment' was followed by the 'Greek Tragedy': the capitulation of the Syriza leadership to the Troika's programme of austerity, despite a tremendous show of strength and defiance from the part of the subaltern classes in the highly polarized July 2015 referendum. Four years of EU diktats and austerity implemented by Syriza followed; and that paved the way for the authoritarian neoliberalism of the current Greek government under the leadership of a renewed political right.

Greece was not the only place where the left reaching political power looked like a possibility. For a short time Podemos in Spain, which emerged from the dynamics of protest and contestation generated by the Spanish crisis sequence before and after the 2011 Indignados movement, seemed to offer another possibility for a radical left movement. But Podemos ended up as the junior partner in a coalition government with the Socialist Party and is now caught in a downward spiral of electoral decline and fragmentation. And of course, there was also the case of Britain, where Jeremy Corbyn managed to create a very impressive dynamic around the possibility of left-wing leadership in the Labour Party gaining governmental power, a breakthrough envisaged by generations of left-wing militants. But in Britain, too, the result was defeat, and the current attempt by a revanchist leadership to erase almost all elements of a left wing in the Labour Party. Finally, in a different register, Bernie Sanders' two failed attempts to win the nomination of the Democratic Party for president in the US also led to an important mobilization of the American left with the emergence of the Democratic Socialists of America (DSA). This unexpected left organizational momentum in the historically barren terrain of the US is now stalled and strategically at a loss.

THE POLITICAL IMPASSE OF THE LEFT

These political sequences all pose an important challenge: by which means can the left take state power through a democratic election and begin the process of social transformation historically described as socialist transition? And the challenge is even more difficult if we think of the following two contrasting observations. On the one hand, the entire history of working-class movements points toward the dangers associated with any reliance on a parliamentary road to socialism, from German social democracy to the tragic defeat of Popular Unity in Chile. On the other hand, all the possible 'rupture sequences' of the current era, both in Europe but also Latin America, have included large social movements, widespread social contestation, political crisis with elements of hegemonic crisis, and the formation of fronts that had the potential for large scale electoral victory. This is not to deny the possibility of political sequences based on the collapse of the state and forms of more or less violent insurrection. But so far this has not been the case in the social formations we are discussing, and it would be theoretically rigid and politically sectarian to expect all political breaks to conform to an insurrectionary ideal-type.

Panitch followed all these developments and wrote about them.[2] And although one could disagree with some of his tactical positions (and I was at times of dissenting opinion), his analyses demonstrated a deep understanding of all the difficulties and dangers associated with the potential forms of left-wing governance after an electoral victory. At the same time Panitch was acutely aware of the complexity of the challenges associated with any process of socialist transformation and the inadequacy of the theoretical and strategic resources of all the tendencies of the left, especially in regard to the question of the state. The following passage, from a text co-written with Sam Gindin for the 2017 *Socialist Register*, exemplifies this awareness:

> Socialists have since paid far too little attention to the challenges this poses. While the recognition that neither insurrectionary politics to 'smash the state' nor the social democratic illusion of using the extant state to introduce progressive policies became more and more widespread, this was accompanied with a penchant for developing 'market socialist' models in the late 1980s which has subsequently been succeeded by a spate of radical left literature that – in almost a mirror image of neoliberalism's championing of private corporations and small business firms against the state – weakly point to examples of cooperatives and self-managed enterprises as directly bearing socialist potential.[3]

What were the political and transformative limits of the experiences that Panitch continually raised in his quest for a radical yet feasible socialist project? These limits are located, for Panitch, in the relational yet pervasive materiality of the state. We can briefly state several of the central propositions on the limits that capitalist states pose.

The state cannot be reduced to a simple coercive apparatus. In its integral form, to borrow Antonio Gramsci's definition, the state includes all its political, organizational, ideological, knowledge-producing aspects, and even the civilizational features of a given social formation. The state constantly undermines the potential for change on the part of the subaltern classes being, in a sense, the condition of their subalternity. The state ceaselessly produces discourses and strategies for the reproduction of capitalist accumulation. As the state is at the centre of social reproduction, it is crucial to reproducing the social division of labour and the class fractions this division produces; and the state undertakes these roles even if this means guaranteeing its extensive privatization. The state materializes all the forms of racism and the perpetual recreation of persons in a 'constant state of exception' in border-zones, no-man's lands, and detention centres. The state imposes austerity and at the same time creates new 'private spaces' of capitalist investment and accumulation. The state is responsible for the 'internalization' of capitalist internationalization (as Nicos Poulantzas already stressed in the 1970s).[4] This is obvious in the many ways that European integration led to the inscription of neoliberal capitalist internationalization into the very institutional and constitutional fabric of European states. And the state is accountable for the extreme expansion of the coercive apparatuses of the state including the police, prisons, militarized arms of repression, and the new forms of digital surveillance.

Panitch's constant interlocutor on these questions has always been Poulantzas. To this day Poulantzas's *State, Power, Socialism* represents the culmination of the last great theoretical and strategic debate in the Western left.[5] There are two points in Poulantzas's book that made it an exceptional contribution. First, Poulantzas develops a rich analysis of how the state produces discourses, strategies, and histories – an analysis closest to Gramsci's notion of the integral state. Second, although Poulantzas disavows 'a dual power' strategy, distancing himself both from Lenin and, surprisingly, Gramsci, what he suggests is actually close to a dual power strategy. He insists on autonomous social movements and subaltern organization – an insistence informed by his understanding of the relational complexity of the state and the experiences of working-class movements in the twentieth century – while at the same time problematizing the very notion of dual power.

Let me clarify a point here. The limits we have pointed to so far with regard to left strategy are grounded in the fact that taking governmental power does not mean conquering political power and an ability to actually use state power as means of transformation. Simply put, the materiality of the state is the materiality of capitalist class strategy, including strategies of international relations and in particular strategies of internationalization of capitalist accumulation. Even if we think of this 'materiality' in terms of the relational conception of the state that Poulantzas suggested (the state as 'the condensation of a class relation')[6] we are still dealing with a condensed, 'materialized' class relation of forces *in favour* of capital. This fact poses extreme constraints on the ability to simply 'use' the state for alternate ends. In this sense, the state is the material condensation of social relation of forces, but it is also the materialization of an 'excess' of force on the part of capital exemplified not only in the functioning of the repressive apparatuses of the state against social movements, but also in, for example, the dependence of treasuries on taxation and sustaining accumulation, or the entire logic of 'independent' central banks, insulated from any democratic control, in the measures they adopt in order to preserve the value of the currency and finance.

To counter these structural limits, socialist governments must have autonomous movements and autonomous organizations of the masses to apply pressure, overcome obstacles (institutional, juridical, political), and enhance real legitimacy to back socialist measures as opposed to simple legality. Such movements and organizations would even, to a certain extent, push for exceptional institutional ruptures – a kind of 'progressive popular state of exception' – and create the kind of social mobilization that would support and persist through difficult transition processes.

The crucial question is how to think through such a strategy. Let's follow Poulantzas on this point:

> *Transformation of the state apparatus tending towards the withering away of the State* can rest only on increased intervention of the popular masses in the State: certainly through their trade-union and political forms of representation, but also through their own initiatives in the State itself. This will proceed by stages, but it cannot be confined to mere democratization of the State.[7]

However, Poulantzas delivers an important warning: simply relying on autonomous movements can also lead to statism via a different road in that 'a unilateral and univocal shift of the centre of gravity towards the self-management movement would likewise make it impossible, in the medium turn, to avoid techno-bureaucratic statism and authoritarian confiscation of power by the experts'.[8] At the same time, Poulantzas warns that simply trying to quarantine the state by means of 'counter-powers' from below can also lead to a 'neo-technocratic talk of a State which is retained because of the complex nature of tasks in a post-industrial society, but which is administered by left experts and controlled simply through mechanisms of direct democracy. At the most basic level every left technocrat would be flanked by a self-management commissar.'[9]

Poulantzas does not simply propose a 'synthesis'. Rather, he points to the need to 'open up a *global perspective of the withering away of the State*',[10] which comprises for him two articulated processes of 'transformation of the State and unfurling of direct, rank-and-file democracy'.[11] This strategy runs into, according to Poulantzas, two dangers: first, the *'reaction of the enemy'*[12] makes imperative a continuous mass movement; and second, the potential dangers associated inherent in the articulation between two parallel forms of power – 'a left government and a second power composed of popular organs'.[13] Poulantzas used Portugal as an example, insisting the 'even when two forces of the Left are involved, the situation in no way resembles a free play of powers and counter-powers balancing one another for the greatest good of socialism and democracy' and 'quickly leads to open opposition, in which there is a risk that one will be eliminated in favour of the other'.[14] Poulantzas thought that in the case of Portugal this led in the end to 'social-democratization'.[15] Poulantzas had in mind here the particular sequence of the Portuguese revolution in the period between April 1974 and November 1975, where one could see this coexistence of forms of government with the participation of forces of the left and organs of 'popular power', from the radical segments of the armed forces to forms of workers control, before the final defeat of the most radical tendencies in November 1975.[16]

One could also think of the much later example of Argentina, where the radicalism of the *piquetero* movement, the importance of the December 2001 uprising, the extensive network of assemblies, and the wave of occupied factories that followed the economic collapse of 2001 acted as catalyst for government change, but this was not transformed into an autonomous political dynamic.[17] At the same time, Poulantzas also warned of a more general danger entailed by the elimination of representative institutions in the name of 'direct democracy' as opening the possibility for a 'new type of authoritarian dictatorship'.[18] Poulantzas's plea was to face and embrace these risks – or risk capitulation to liberal democracy. However, if we look at the strategic questions posed for the contemporary radical left, it is clear that we are often failing even to contemplate these risks, despite their centrality to any project to recompose a radical left.

The question of political power at a moment of radical transformation refers to an *exceptional situation*. In contrast to a left populist conceptualization of a strategy for power that is based on the discursive construction of 'the people', and hence is an electoralist approach, it is only social movements with truly destabilizing potential that make possible the kind of political mobilization and shifts in relations of representation that can even pose the question of governmental power. Working towards this possibility means treating social movements and their autonomous organizations as potential 'counter-powers'.

Consequently, I would like to insist that the extent to which in a period of increased protest and contestation a form of dual power or counter-power emerges from below is both an indication of a dynamic that can pose the question of power, and also a way to push developments in that direction. This means that we should not treat dual power as a 'moment' but as a permanent modality of any process of profound social and political transformation: permanent dual power is a crucial aspect of any 'revolution in permanence', to use this old phrase by Marx and Engels from 1850,[19] in the sense that there is a constant need to struggle against the 'survival' or even 'persistence' of capitalist social forms and also against the continuous possibility of right-wing counter-offensives.

If we look at these forms of popular self-organization and even 'counterpower' from below, we can see how they also represent forms of a new politicization. It is obvious that a hegemonic crisis implies that large segments of the subaltern classes no longer recognize themselves in existing political discourses and strategies. Such moments of political uncertainty, as well as intense struggle, carry with them both the violent changes on one's life induced by the social crisis, but also with the intensity of the mobilization, new collective identities and solidarities emerge along with new spaces of participation and discussion. Such a process is the only way to induce almost 'existential' changes to the political orientation and self-perception of the subaltern, which can even take the form of new political relations of representation and collective engagement quite beyond simple electoral dynamics.

CHANGING CIRCUMSTANCES, EDUCATING MOVEMENTS

There is also another crucial aspect to such radical moments of political contestation: the *learning or educational function* that such processes and forms of counterpower or dual power have. They are educational in the Marxist-Gramscian sense of Marx's third thesis on Feuerbach, that the educators must also be educated in the process of changing circumstances and ourselves. Learning here is in two different senses. One is how movements become sites of knowledge with regard to envisioning new social and political configurations – learning how institutions or enterprises actually function while at the same time collectively discussing the possibility of alternative forms. The other is how movements transform the persons involved in ways that go beyond militancy as they create at the same time the conditions for new forms of engagement and further militancy. This is exactly the kind of politicization that can help the left in power overcome the many constraints it will face.

Panitch was well aware of this prefigurative dynamic and potential of contemporary movements, and the dialectic between movements, class formation, and individual transformation in any feasible radical left politics:

> Developing alternative means of producing and distributing food, health care and other necessities, depends on autonomous movements moving in these directions through takeovers of land, idle buildings, threatened factories and transportation networks. All this, in turn, would have to be

supported and furthered through more radical changes in the state that would range over time from codifying new collective property rights to developing and coordinating agencies of democratic planning. At some points in this process more or less dramatic initiatives of nationalization and socialization of industry and finance would have to take place.[20]

Panitch saw political organizations not as 'electoral machines' but as potential laboratories of new intellectualities and capacity-building for workers of all backgrounds and abilities, enabling profound processes of ideological transformation. He insisted that any process of social transformation requires new forms of engagement and solidarity, profound changes in worldviews and behavioral patterns, and a readiness to accept new ways of living, working, and consuming. Such a politics of class and individual transformation is, moreover, the only way to envisage, discuss, and set in motion new ways of participatory running of both enterprises and socialist administration. Althusser stressed a not dissimilar position in the 1970s:

> [T]he slogan 'union of the people of France', is not synonymous with the slogan of the Union of the Left. It is broader than it, and different in nature; for it does not designate just the union or united action of the political organizations of the Left, parties and trade unions … Why address the popular masses in this way? To tell them, even if still only as a hint, that they will have to organize themselves autonomously, in original forms, in firms, urban districts and villages, around the questions of labour and living conditions, the questions of housing, education, health, transport, the environment, etc.; in order to define and defend their demands, first to prepare for the establishment of a revolutionary state, then to maintain it, stimulate it and at the same time force it to 'wither away'. Such mass organizations, which no one can define in advance and on behalf of the masses, already exist or are being sought in Italy, Spain and Portugal, where they play an important part, despite all difficulties.[21]

The emphasis on mass participation and self-organization points to another important contention that Panitch continually raised in his texts: the fact that, so far, we have mainly seen class-focused rather than class-rooted movements. The only way to have political movements of the left that are really rooted in the realities of the subaltern classes and the complexities of the contemporary condition of labour is to treat movements as potential sites of dual power and not simply as background to electoral politics. This could also mean – and I point to my previous point – actually treating movements as ways to learn from the collective ingenuity of the subaltern, something absent from varieties of 'left populism' and, of course, many of the historical forms of 'left vanguardism'. In a sense, such an approach deals with two important preoccupations: (a) how to actually engage the subaltern classes in politics and learn from them instead of simply discursively interpolating them as political subjects; and (b) how to transform subordinate classes, or more precisely to encourage processes of collective 'self-transformation', with regard to their attitudes, mentalities, and collective identities in order for them to both engage more actively and endorse the profound changes involved in the process of transformation.

Does this mean that we abandon the question of the state? Not at all: it would be impossible to initiate socio-economic ruptures without confrontations with capital in regard to measures such as nationalizations, rationing of resources, capital controls, and increased workers' rights, and thus without the use of state power. It is more a question of the need to deploy an almost 'exceptional' use of state power that, to a certain extent, pushes beyond the existing constitutional order and on the basis of social mobilization creates the conditions of an emergent 'constituent process'. A political rupture of this sort would require, moreover, profound changes inside the state, especially with regard to democratic control and oversight over repressive apparatuses such as the police, armed forces, and the judiciary. We are firmly – if simply – saying that a strong state is not all it takes, and it depends on wider democratic forces and processes emerging.

Does this mean playing the forms of counterpower against the force of the state, as if these new forces were their own form of 'checks and balances'? No, I think that however contradictory this process might be, it has to be treated as a dialectic of experimentation and collective problem-solving rather than of balance between old and new institutional practices, in the sense that movements from below should be encouraged to experiment with new social configurations and ways to organize social life which then could be generalized, thus enhancing and expanding the transformation process. We would want, in other words, the forms and practices of the movement, and in particular their participatory and direct democratic drive, to also be incorporated into the state – precisely as a means to induce profound transformation in state practices that are highly original and, in the last instance, explicitly experimental.

There is always, of course, the question of violence and whether sections of the state itself will react violently against any process of change – a question which also stresses the importance of popular mobilization, but also of popular presence in such apparatuses. This is an open question and beyond the scope of this discussion. Suffice it to say that there may be moments when movements realize what Georges Labica described as the impossibility of non-violence.[22]

Panitch also paid great attention to the question of economic policies. In regards to the programmes of the 1970s when, for example, the Tony Benn wing of the British Labour Party proposed the nationalization of a great segment of strategic enterprises and the extension of planning agreements between the state and industry; or when Swedish Social Democracy was discussing the Meidner Plan to increase the social ownership and management of large corporations and introducing forms of workers' participation; or when various forms of an 'Alternative Economic Strategy' raised by the British left were also being discussed across Europe and North America; Panitch was constantly engaged in these debates and directing attention not just to the policy programme but also to the kinds of political agencies and struggles over the state that would be required.[23]

In contrast, contemporary left programmes seem rather minimalist. Indeed, apart from redistributive measures, such as wage and pension increases, changes in taxation, extra spending for health and education, reinstatement of trade union rights, and calls for maintaining public sector participation in utilities, one cannot easily identify more radical proposals for socializing strategic sectors of the economy, radically democratizing the state, nor ideas about the political ruptures necessary to transform social relations of production. It is as if the scope of left politics has been reduced to anti-austerity, anti-privatization, and anti-authoritarian demands, rather than articulating elements of a renewed socialist strategy. Even more radical proposals, as with regard to breaking away from the euro, mainly dealt with it in terms of more democratic control over monetary policy, economic sovereignty, and better macroeconomic conditions for growth. The element of transformation of relations and forms of production and distribution toward a non-market horizon are not even discussed, apart from stating a general preference for public ownership.

However, the kinds of debates that Panitch often made reference to and constantly engaged in about 'non-reformist reforms', a notion initiated by Andre Gorz's interventions in the 1960s,[24] or similar debates about structural reforms of the economy and the state across the European Communist parties and left in the 1970s and into the 1980s, are often missing today. And despite the fact that the leaderships of those parties took more or less 'reformist' positions, it would be wrong to dismiss these debates as 'reformist', because they nevertheless had a strategic and programmatic horizon that is missing today.[25]

This brief summary captures important aspects of the impasse of left politics. The constraints of the market, the embedded character of the fetishistic conception of economic relations and practices, the difficulty to think beyond a capitalist market and liberal democratic state, are some of the main difficulties of any process of social transformation – and we could of course debate whether post-capitalist and not just state-capitalist forms actually ever emerged out of the experiences of the 'socialist revolutions' of the twentieth century. At the same time, we have all the 'traces of communism', to borrow Althusser's phrase, emerging within struggles, solidarity initiatives, forms of democracy from below, self-management initiatives, cooperatives and, of course, the many discourses and campaigns emerging with regard to a different functioning of public services and social provisioning. There is, as well, all the knowledge of persons engaged in struggles and movements, the resources of militant expertise that typically remains untapped or even ignored. These experiences and new initiatives suggest, in a certain sense, another way of rethinking dual power and the possibility for the emergence of deeper social transformations.

Another aspect to insisting on the possibility for a profound social transformation is its necessity for survival. It is obvious that the limit of any efforts to initiate a 'Green Transition' is the incompatibility between ecological sustainability and capitalist accumulation. One might observe that this is the limits of all 'Green New Deals' in practice, and, in a quite direct way, it is socialism that is the only possible survival strategy. This conclusion forces us to present a set of profound ruptures with capitalist logic as necessary measures towards a new sustainable economic model if we are to avert an impending climate disaster. The central questions of a Green Transition, moreover, bring forward not technical exigencies but social, political, ideological, and cultural ones. That is, there is the necessary adjustment of societies to new forms of production and consumption and, in a broader sense, a civilizational change. All these can only be thought through in terms of socialist strategy and, indeed, the kind of strategic debate that is more than needed today. Such strategic thinking is the only way to ensure that alliances are created with those segments of the subaltern classes that are going to bear the social costs of adjustment involved in a Green Transition, whether from the loss of well-paid union jobs or paying the extra costs of 'green taxes' on fuel and heating.

GLOBAL CAPITALISM AND STATES

Any discussion of potential processes of social transformation requires a profound rupture with imperialism. Panitch (alongside his often co-author, Sam Gindin) has offered important insights into the current functioning of US-led imperialism and the inter-connections between neoliberalism, internationalization of capital, and imperial aggression, stressing the inter-connection between these processes.[26]

In cases of countries of the European Union (EU), such as Greece, it is important to understand that both the euro and, more broadly, the limited sovereignty imposed by membership of the Union, is by itself a material constraint on any process of social transformation, or even a simple distancing from neoliberal orthodoxy. Both the Greek case, and to a certain extent the Portuguese and the Spanish cases as well, point to the enormous violence – financial, institutional, and monetary – inscribed at the heart of European integration that was unleashed upon these countries in the 2010s in the form of austerity programmes. Indeed, Panitch and Colin Leys demonstrated the significance attributed to the EEC by the British left as far back as the 1970s as a constraint to any socialist project.[27] Although the EU does not follow the classical gunboat imperialism that many of its states pursued in the past, it can be coercive in other ways, as with fiscal discipline, with its less powerful members, and is quite capable of adopting military solutions in some of its international relations.

If we look at the current conjuncture, the EU has rallied itself behind the worse case of Atlanticist bellicosity in the name of supposedly protecting the democratic freedoms and sovereignty of smaller states from authoritarian regimes and military aggression. It hardly needs pointing out that the EU itself is on its way to becoming even more repressive and profoundly anti-communist. The further deepening of ties between the EU and NATO is adding a militarized dimension to the authoritarian neoliberalism that now characterizes capitalist states. A broader conclusion follows. In the current conjuncture, with new international alignments emerging, with the US leading the 'West' (in the sense of combining the G7, the EU, and traditional Pacific allies), as well as a Eurasian linkage between Russia and China and a large number of states from the Global South seeking a multi-polar world order, it is important to rediscover some form of democratic sovereignty as a necessary condition for any process of social transformation. It is also to insist on the need for a new conception of independence, of non-alliance, of refusing to enter into militarist 'camps' fuelling a new arms race. This poses the challenge, as Panitch insistently raised, of a new anti-imperialism to accompany the necessary anti-capitalism, a strategic break that would prevent independence from becoming isolation and instead forming new practices of international solidarity.

QUESTIONS OF STRATEGY WHEN TIME IS SHORT

In a certain sense, this discussion of dual power and socialist strategy seems out of touch with the reality of the current political conjuncture of the core capitalist states in Europe and North America. After all, in Greece Syriza has evolved into a social democratic party, unable even to take advantage of the current discontent against the right-wing New Democracy government of Kyriakos Mitsotakis. Jeremy Corbyn is no longer leader of the British Labour Party, and was suspended for a lengthy period, and Labour now has a leadership from the right intent on returning to a Blairite politics. The US left is at a juncture of deep strategic uncertainty, and a repetition of the Bernie Sanders campaign seems only a faint possibility. And while the Jean-Luc Mélenchon campaign in France was an inspiration and is drawing the broad left together in the NUPES alliance (Nouvelle Union Populaire Écologique et Sociale), strategic debate within the French left is at its lowest point in recent history.

Yet, for all this, we do not have the luxury of avoiding thinking about strategy. We see the reluctance, and even denial, with regard to the strategy debate, exemplified in how Daniel Bensaïd's plea for a 'return to strategy' in the end remained unanswered.[28] The invocation of a rhetoric of 'anti-neoliberalism' and 'alter-globalization' since the late 1990s meant that, in the end, movements like Syriza in Greece (or Podemos in Spain) were totally unprepared for the challenges ahead of them. At the same time, these political breakthroughs of the left proved incapable of exercising the kind of political pedagogy that is necessary to have a society ready for the kind of confrontation that any process of radical social change entails.

This failure shows that we need to have this debate on the politics of social transformation in the current moment, draw all the necessary conclusions and lessons about dual power and much else, and treat these varied experiences of the left as experiments and essential aspects of a learning process. Our failures also point to the need to have political organizations that could be the spaces of such learning processes, another debate we need to have. For now, we can agree that viewing political parties as exclusively electoral machines and instruments of government is, in fact, the royal road to the next disaster. The same goes for the self-justifying rhetoric of the political sects that insist that they are always right on the political capitulations to come and the errors of political compromises with the political alliances of united fronts. We need, in other words, the ambitious optimism to develop new organizational forms that can be laboratories of militant intellectualities and 'factories of strategy'.[29]

It is appropriate to end here, in a note of agreement, with Panitch and Leys's words from *Searching for Socialism*:

> In face of the contradictions being generated by twenty-first century capitalism, discovering and developing new political forms adequate to addressing them, and the popular capacities needed to overcome them, will take time. And yet, given the scale and intensity of these contradictions – political, economic, cultural, and not least ecological – time is short.[30]

NOTES

1. This essay stems from my presentation at a panel in honour of Leo Panitch at the Historical Materialism Conference, 'Systemic Fragilities and Counter-Strategies', Istanbul, April 2022.
2. For example, see: Leo Panitch and Sam Gindin, *The Socialist Challenge Today: Syriza, Sanders, Corbyn*, London: Merlin Press, 2018.
3. Leo Panitch and Sam Gindin, 'Class, Party and the Challenge of State Transformation', in Leo Panitch and Greg Albo, eds, *Socialist Register 2017: Rethinking Revolution*, London: Merlin Press, 2016, p. 53.
4. Nicos Poulantzas, *Classes in Contemporary Capitalism*, London: New Left Books, 1975.
5. Nicos Poulantzas, *State, Power, Socialism*, London: Verso, 1980.
6. Poultanzas, *Classes in Contemporary Capitalism*, p. 26
7. Poulantzas, *State, Power, Socialism*, p. 261.
8. Poulantzas, *State, Power, Socialism*, p. 262.
9. Poulantzas, *State, Power, Socialism*, p. 262.
10. Poulantzas, *State, Power, Socialism*, p. 262.
11. Poulantzas, *State, Power, Socialism*, p. 263.
12. Poulantzas, *State, Power, Socialism*, p. 263.
13. Poulantzas, *State, Power, Socialism*, p. 264.
14. Poulantzas, *State, Power, Socialism*, p. 264.
15. Poulantzas, *State, Power, Socialism*, p. 264.
16. On the Portuguese revolutionary sequence see: Raquel Varela, *A People's History of the Portuguese Revolution*, London: Pluto Press, 2019.
17. On the dynamics of social and political antagonism in Argentina in that period see: Pablo Heller, *Argentina 2000/2004. Fabricas Occupadas*, Buenos Aires: Ediciones Rumbos 2004; Marina Sitrin, ed., *Horizontalism. Voices of Popular Power in Argentina*, Oakland: AK Press, 2006; Collectivo Situaciones, *19&20: Notes for a New Social Protagonism*, New York: Autonomedia, 2011
18. Poulantzas, *State, Power, Socialism*, p. 264.
19. Karl Marx and Friedrich Engels, *Collected Works, Volume 10*, London: Lawrence and Wishart, 1975-2004, p. 287.
20. Panitch and Gindin, 'Class, Party and the Challenge of State Transformation', p. 55.

21 Louis Althusser, 'On the Twenty-Second Congress of the French Communist Party', *New Left Review,* 104, 1977, p. 11.
22 Georges Labica et Franscis Sitel, 'De l'impossibilité de la non-violence. Entretien avec Georges Labica: Interview with *Critique Communiste*', *Contretemps*, 16 September 2009, available at : www.contretemps.eu.
23 Stephen Maher, Sam Gindin and Leo Panitch, 'Class Politics, Socialist Policies and Capitalist Constraints', *Socialist Register 2020*, Merlin Press 2019.
24 André Gorz, *Stratégie ouvrière et néocapitalisme*, Paris: Editions du Seuil, 1964.
25 See for example the extensive debates on the state at the end of the 1970s, debates that were not simply theoretical but also strategic. See *inter alia* the texts collected in: *Discutir el Estado. Posiciones frente a una tesis de Louis Althusser*, Mexico D.F. : Folios Ediciones 1982.
26 Leo Panitch and Sam Gindin, *The Making of Global Capitalism: The Political Economy of American Empire*, London: Verso, 2012.
27 Leo Panitch and Colin Leys, *Searching for Socialism: The Project of the New Labour Left from Benn to Corbyn*, London: Verso, 2020.
28 Daniel Bensaïd, 'On the return of the politico-strategic question', 2006, available at: www.marxists.org/archive/bensaid/2006/08/polstrat.htm
29 Antonio Negri, *The Factory of Strategy: Thirty-Three Lessons on Lenin,* New York, Columbia University Press, 2014.
30 Panitch and Leys, *Searching for Socialism*, p. 255.

LEO PANITCH ON BRITISH LABOURISM AND THE PROSPECTS FOR A 'LABOUR NEW LEFT'

MADELEINE DAVIS

Written with Colin Leys and published in 2020, *Searching for Socialism* turned out to be Leo Panitch's last major work. Nobody had expected this to be so. Yet there was symmetry in his return to what had been perhaps his most enduring and formative preoccupation – the analysis of labour parties and their role in class politics. Published in the aftermath of Jeremy Corbyn's defeat in the 2019 British general election and replacement as Labour leader, the book traced Corbynism back to the 'project of the Labour new left championed by Tony Benn and designed to transcend the limits of parliamentary socialism', in the process giving the authors an opportunity to revise and revisit the analysis advanced in 1997's *The End of Parliamentary Socialism*.[1] This concept of the 'Labour new left' denoted a position, emerging in the 1970s, that, while sharing a broadly New Left analysis of British Labourism as defined by its structural integration and subordination within the British class and national system that continually frustrated efforts to transform it into a 'broadly mass and democratic' party capable of acting as a vehicle for socialism, nevertheless 'took the view that there was no alternative but to attempt precisely such a transformation of the party'.[2] Much of Leo's political energy in the last few years was directed to understanding, nurturing, and educating those tendencies within and around the Corbynite left that he judged might prove capable of continuing those attempts. It was a role he relished and for which he was supremely suited, not only because he radiated an exceptional personal warmth and disarming intellectual curiosity, but because he personified and carried, by virtue of his own intellectual and political development, the links, the history, and the analysis on which such a transformative project depended. This essay attempts to take the measure of Leo's contribution to thinking about the problems of British Labourism and the prospects for a 'Labour new left', as a way to record, perhaps to help retain, that sense of continuity that came to an abrupt end with his too early and unexpected death at the end of 2020.

THE NEW LEFT, 'LABOURISM' AND THE LIMITS OF SOCIAL DEMOCRACY

Had E.P. Thompson had his way, *Parliamentary Socialism*, the 1961 book that launched Ralph Miliband's career and the strand of broadly Marxist analysis of British 'Labourism' which Leo Panitch, Colin Leys, and others would develop, might have been called Green Corn. The reference was to a speech by Ramsay MacDonald, Labour's first Prime Minister, in 1924, in which he said he had no expectation of fulfilling socialist pledges because 'it would be cutting green corn'.[3] Rejecting the title as 'too recherché', Miliband replied to Thompson's suggestion (made in comments to Miliband on the draft manuscript) that he should state the theoretical argument of the book more explicitly, by saying 'what I mean is that if one accepts neither crass parliamentarism nor the straightforward revolutionism of the Leninist kind (the first being silly and the second inappropriate) one is involved in an argument of great complexity'.[4] Yet the terms and premises of this argument remained opaque in the published text. As sympathetic commentators at the time and since have noted, while *Parliamentary Socialism* offered a detailed narrative of the Labour Party's 'integration into parliamentary politics ... becoming more pronounced, assuming more specific forms, and producing new tensions',[5] its explanatory framework was 'buried and undeveloped' and the political conclusions to be drawn from the analysis were ambiguous.[6] Nor was Thompson alone in finding the thrust of the analysis worryingly pessimistic.[7] Yet while the book might easily be interpreted as writing off the Labour Party, Miliband himself saw it as an intervention on the side of forces within and outside it, in the trades union movement and the youthful radicalism of the post-1956 New Left and Campaign for Nuclear Disarmament: a 'groundswell of militancy'[8] that might be mobilized to defeat Gaitskellite revisionism and secure the transformation of the party that he had referred to in a 1958 essay as 'the transition to the transition'. As he had then put it:

> There is so much which is wrong with the organised Labour movement, and with its only serious political expression, that Socialists often tend to forget all that is right with it. It is enough to compare it with the Labour movement in the United States, or with the divided and demoralised working class movement in France, to realise the asset, actual and potential, which it represents. At the present time, what is mostly wrong

with it is that it only contains a minority of Socialists. Above all else, and beyond all other political commitments, this, it seems to me, is the first problem to which socialists must address themselves in the period of the transition to the transition. There are some who yearningly look for a short cut. There isn't one. Now is the time to get *in* and push.[9]

This reflected an early New Left experiment with 'parallellism', or more prosaically, a 'one foot in, one foot out' strategy toward Labour, seeking to capitalize on the 'movementist' possibilities of new forms of extra-parliamentary activism such as CND and the New Left-sponsored 'left clubs' network to affect a 'break back' of ideas into the Party. It implied embracing multiple forms of left activity which, as John Saville, Miliband's closest collaborator at this time and later co-founder of the *Socialist Register*, explained, might

> … inevitably, take new organisational forms, sometimes wholly within the Labour Party, sometimes without, sometimes half-in half-out – (i.e. involving many Labour Party people and seeking to influence the party, but not restricted to or limited by it) … At the same time, a genuine forward move involves a) replacement of the present leadership of the party, and b) the development of political forms which will enable the Left to grow within the Labour movement.[10]

By the time Miliband met Panitch, then a graduate student at the LSE, in 1967, his position had changed.[11] Factors included the exhaustion and fragmentation of the early New Left amid a sombre reassessment of its mobilizing ambitions, frustration with the record of the 1964-70 Labour government led by Harold Wilson, and the focus of Miliband's intellectual work shifting to a more general theory of 'the state in capitalist society'. This was, of course, to be the title of his 1969 book, preparatory lectures for which had induced Panitch to switch to a Political Sociology Masters and set him on a course that would shape his future career. There had also been an accumulation of New Left critical analysis of British Labourism and its role in the dual crises of the British economy and state. Much of this was broadly complementary to Miliband's analysis, at the same time as it was theoretically more explicit and politically more uncompromising. Tom Nairn's essays on 'the nature of the Labour Party', presented within the sweeping historical and theoretical schematic of the 'Nairn-Anderson' theses, keynotes of the revamped *New Left Review*, figured the Labour Party and labour movement as profoundly subordinate and corporatist.[12]

'Labourism' as Nairn deployed the term encompassed 'the pre-eminence of trade unions, the inherent weakness of indigenous British socialism and the Labour left, the acceptance of parliamentarism, and the failure of intellectuals to forge a counter-hegemonic ideology'.[13] Crucially, within the Labour Party itself, the myth of 'broad church' unity masked a structural subordination of the left within it: 'the extreme and constant inner tension generated by Labourism has never exploded. Its own inherited inadequacies, and the evident lack of any practical alternative to the Labour Party, have tied the socialists of the left wing remorselessly into the pathological internal dialectic of Labourism.'[14] Meanwhile, Perry Anderson's essay 'Problems of Socialist Strategy' addressed head-on the conundrum that Miliband had told Thompson was at the heart of *Parliamentary Socialism:* neither the 'short but sheer' path of traditional models of revolution nor the 'long and winding' one of social democracy offered strategic perspectives adequate to the British case. What for him was required was a 'hegemonic party', proposing, as he put it, a 'coherent global alternative to the existing social order and represent[ing] a permanent drive towards it'.[15]

Increasingly then, prominent New Leftists were coming to regard the existence of Labour as, on balance, obstacle rather than asset.[16] Here is Miliband in 1966 restating the problem:

> The Labour Party remains the 'party of the working class', and ... there is, in this sense, no serious alternative to it at present. This, of course, has always been the central dilemma of British Socialism, and it is not a dilemma which is likely to be soon resolved. But the necessary first step in that direction is to take a realistic view of the Labour Party, of what it can and of what it cannot be expected to do. For it is only on the basis of such a view that socialists can begin to discuss their most important task of all, which is the creation of an authentic socialist movement in Britain.[17]

By 1967, Saville was asserting, with characteristic directness, that: 'Labourism has nothing to do with socialism ... the Labour Party has never been, nor is it capable of becoming, a vehicle for socialist advance, and ... the destruction of the illusions of Labourism is a necessary step before the emergence of a socialist movement of any size and influence becomes practicable'.[18] Practical initiatives to work toward such a movement that were supported by the *Register*'s editors – for example the set-up of a network of Centres for Socialist Education in collaboration with Ken Coates, expelled from Labour in 1965 – were now framed in terms of the long haul:

... the question is not at present one of parties and political combinations, but of a broad and sustained effort of socialist education, cutting across existing boundaries, free from formula-mongering, and carried on with patience and intelligence by socialists wherever in the Labour movement or outside they may be situated. Such an effort is not an alternative to an immediate involvement in concrete struggle but an essential element of it.[19]

This generalized hardening of perspectives on Labour was lent new impetus as the transnational New Leftism of the late 1960s took inspiration from revolutionary movements around the world. Thus a 1968 interview with Michael Foot carried out by the editors of *New Left Review* gave them the opportunity to ask:

Are you ever troubled by the thought that possibly your function as a Left MP is really just to give people the illusion that there is some sort of struggle for socialism within the Labour Party? Do you ever worry that maybe you're tempting people into a trap, into what can only be the graveyard of any hope for socialist change?[20]

When in 1972 *Parliamentary Socialism* was reissued (at which point Labour was again in opposition), Miliband left the text unchanged, but added a postscript excoriating the record of Labour in office. Characterising Labour as at best 'a party of modest social reform in a capitalist system within whose confines it is ever more firmly and by now irrevocably rooted', he now stressed the *functionality* of its role in managing and containing class conflict.[21] Far from 'get in and push', he now saw the 'dissipation of paralyzing illusions' about its true role and purpose as an indispensable prerequisite in preparing the ground for an alternative formation.

What has, of course, to be emphasized here, however, is less the shift in tactics than the essential continuity of the strategic and theoretical perspective. Panitch and David Coates in 2003 identified three key emphases as characteristic of the Milibandian perspective from its inception:

... *first*, the centrality of parliamentarism to the theory and practice of Labour politics, and its deleterious consequences for the party's capacity to act as a successfully reformist agency when in office. It stressed, *second*, the functionality of the Labour Party's periodically radical rhetoric to the long term stability of the British class structure and its harmful consequences for the creation and consolidation of a radicalized proletariat. *Third* ... the inability of socialists within the Labour Party to do more than briefly (and episodically) radicalize the rhetoric and policy commitments of the party in opposition, and the deleterious consequences of that inability for the creation of a genuinely potent socialist party in Britain.[22]

Alongside these one might add subordination of class to national interests, particularly emphasized in the work of Tom Nairn.

Panitch's doctoral work pursued strongly complementary themes to these, from the first with a sharp eye to the broader comparative lessons to be drawn about the role of Labour and social democratic parties in managing capitalism. The first Wilson government's embrace of incomes policy provided a starting point and contemporary relevance for his thesis, awarded in 1974 as *The Labour Party and the Trade Unions: A Study of Incomes Policy Since 1945 with Special Reference to 1964-70*. In 1971 he published a piece entitled 'Ideology and Integration, the Case of the British Labour Party' that shifted the explanatory focus away from the pre-eminence of parliamentarism. In language more explicitly sociological, he emphasized instead the 'strain in its ideology which has *throughout its history* been aggregative and has minimized the party's class role'.[23] Labour ideology, he argued, was 'essentially integrationist': holding a view of society as 'basically unified', with socialism seen as the logical outcome of social maturation, its dominant traditions consistently rejected, and subverting class struggle and class analysis in favour of themes of community and nation. And yet:

> Although the party's ideological history facilitates its ability to act as an integrative party, it faces an inhibiting structural constraint in its association with trade unions. While the party ideology does not see capital and labour as permanently antagonistic forces and therefore promotes policies which integrate the demands of both these classes, the trade unions, by virtue of their very functions in industry, cannot accept this position without strain … The result is conflict between the unions and Labour Party over the very integrative character of the party and over party policy towards the economy and industrial relations.[24]

Labour's embrace of incomes policy, then, in Panitch's PhD published in 1976 as *Social Democracy and Industrial Militancy*, became an example par excellence of this integrative function, a function which consists 'not only of representing working class interests but of acting as one of the chief mechanisms for inculcating the organised working class with national values and symbols and of restraining and reinterpreting working class demands in this light'.[25]

The final chapters of Panitch's PhD and subsequent book were completed in Canada, Leo having returned in 1972 to take up a post at Carleton University in Ottawa. His relationship, both intellectual and personal, with Miliband developed as the two continued to pursue complementary interests. Miliband regularly encouraged Panitch to apply for posts in the UK, at one point commenting 'England hath need of thee, my friend, considering how quite thoroughly the unions have been screwed in the latest deal'.[26] The context was renewed adoption by the 1974-79 Wilson-Callaghan government of variants of incomes policy and wage restraint to help manage economic crisis, the second general election of 1974 having given Labour a slim majority. Intellectually, both now painted on larger canvases, expanding and generalizing some of the key arguments of their studies of Labourism to develop what would later come to be recognised as a distinct 'Milibandian' school of analysis with implications and influence for Marxist political thought more broadly. Panitch drew on and went beyond the Miliband-Poulantzas debate in an important theoretical introduction to a 1977 collection he edited on *The Canadian State: Political Economy and Political Power*[27] and made key interventions in an emerging scholarly debate on corporatism.[28] Some part of the explanation for proclivities toward corporatism in liberal democracies, he noted, was to be found 'in that dominant ideological strain within social democracy which rejects the notion of the class struggle as the dynamic of social change'.[29] With others, including David Coates, Greg Albo, Sam Gindin, and Colin Leys, he would also go on to pursue a more systematic engagement than had Miliband with political economy. A turn to 'a more general political sociology of social democracy and the state' was then followed, as Coates and Panitch themselves would later explain, by forays into 'intellectual territory that Miliband did not explore – rounding out this Marxist political sociology with a series of studies in international and comparative political economy'.[30]

This collective body of work, partially inspired by close study of the British Labour Party, in turn generated new frameworks for the analysis of Labour politics, much of this work being carried on by Coates and Leys. The *Socialist Register*, founded by that branch of the post-1956 New Left most explicitly concerned with questions of political organization, remained a key forum for discussion of the problems and prospects of Labour and Labourism. Panitch's personal distance from day-to-day British developments was at times a source of frustration to him, and perhaps gave the interventions he did make to these debates something of a detached quality. As he put it in the preface to a Verso collection of his essays in 1986, his central theme over the preceding 15 years had been 'the irreducible importance of political and ideological structures in determining the limits and possibilities of working class advance'.[31] In relation to Labour, and in line with the position outlined in Miliband's postscript, it was mostly the limits that were emphasized, as corrective to what he and Miliband saw as understandable but misplaced revivals of 'paralysing illusions' about the possibility of its transformation. Yet this pessimism was overstated, and both would be led back by their search for effective agencies to a more positive assessment of the prospects for a revitalized left within Labour.

FROM THE SICKNESS OF LABOURISM TO THE NEW LABOUR LEFT

'It has in no sense been the argument here that the integrative ideology has been ubiquitous in the Labour Party. To say that it is dominant necessarily implies that it is dominant over something else. That something else is the Labour Left, which has repeatedly challenged the integrative premises and policies of the Labour leadership.'[32]

An interesting feature of the Milibandian analysis of Labour is that some of its key authors have also been its most consistent chroniclers. For David Coates, to whose selection of and commentary on a collection of key *Register* essays this essay is significantly indebted, such restatement and exegesis has been a necessary exercise to correct the 'misleading and hostile' presentation of its key arguments; 'a pattern of disagreement and distortion [of the Milibandian analysis] that has been there from the outset'.[33] It is not hard to substantiate this claim, even looking beyond the examples Coates himself cites. Not surprisingly, it has been the broadly Marxist perspective of the analysis that has often irked critics most. Panitch's 1976 book was reviewed in only mildly patronizing tone by Labour historian Henry Pelling; introducing it as 'pretentiously titled', he remarked that '[Panitch's] only long-term solution for Britain appears to be an economy planned in a thorough going socialist fashion; and it must be disappointing to him that the British electorate does not see things his way'.[34] More savage was a review of Panitch and Leys' 1997 *The End of Parliamentary Socialism* by Bernard Crick in the *New Statesman*.[35] 'Nice old trendies' Leys and Panitch, harking back 'nostalgically to 'student politics; and the fantasy 'alternative economics of the 1970s' re-presented

> … the familiar grand narrative of socialism betrayed: the subtitle is 'From New Left to New Labour', a ludicrous and arrogant antithesis. The latter, for all its faults and uncertainties, is a modulation of a large, democratic political party. The other is a mental construct of two journals, the *Socialist Register* and *New Left Review* … under the delusion that their far-too-

late Marxism gives them an authoritative insight into the minds of 'the people' (from the tenured safety of Canadian university departments).

The book's dedication to Miliband (who, apparently 'once famously argued that parliamentary socialism was proving the death of true socialism') afforded the opportunity for a final swipe: 'Intellectuals such as these, rarely thinking politically if at all, confused the grassroots activists of the old Labour Party. One does not ask for repentance, silence would be enough.'[36]

Crick's review recycled some of the most persistent misrepresentations characteristic of those inclined to dismiss the Miliband-inspired analysis as the 'we wuz robbed' school of Labour history, resting on assumptions of some kind of latent socialist majority or consciousness among the working class and the linked idea of leadership 'betrayal'.[37] In its denigration of meddling intellectuals peddling a 'far too late Marxism' among the susceptible foot-soldiers of Labourism, it also gestured toward the limits of a 'broad church' which maintained socialism as shibboleth and source of periodically useful radical rhetoric, even at times programmatic content, but whose dominant figures were 'not interested in developing a socialist strategy; did not believe in it, considered it irrelevant or actually harmful to the Labour Party and to Britain's problems'.[38] Certainly, as that last quote demonstrates, the Milibandians were frequently scornful of the role party leaders, including many identified with the left, played in defusing and diverting socialist oppositional currents. But their analysis continually stressed the *weakness* of such currents, not only in relation to the structures of Labourism but in relation to the fundamental task of creating and mobilizing mass support for socialism that those structures evaded: 'the whole thrust of the Milibandian argument on the working class and socialism was that the fusion between the two was one that had to be created, and that such a creation required clear and unambiguous political leadership of the kind that the Labour Party systematically declined to offer.'[39] Preoccupied above all with the question 'is activity within the party a precursor of the creation of a mass base for socialist politics, or a debilitating distraction from that creation?', it was also an argument unapologetically addressed to socialists themselves.[40] From this perspective, perhaps a more cogent criticism might have been that the pessimism of the analysis, although in some respects superficial and always allowing for the possibility that – recalling Nairn's words – the contradictions might explode to break the cycle, has sometimes prevented its exponents fully recognising the potential of various currents until after their moment had passed. Such is arguably the case with the 'Labour new left'.

When on May Day 1997 Panitch and Leys completed *The End of*

Parliamentary Socialism, the ending they referred to was any pretence that the Labour Party, which on the same date achieved a stunning electoral victory immediately claimed by Tony Blair as an unambiguous vindication of the 'modernizing' project of New Labour, stood for a commitment to the achievement of socialism through parliamentary (or indeed other) means. The book was framed as a challenge to the narrative of Labour history upon which Blair's 'modernization' depended. Against this narrative, which blamed attempts by adherents of 'old style socialism' to capture control of the party as responsible for its 'wilderness years' of opposition from 1983-1997, the authors sought to recover and reconstruct an alternative project of party transformation and democratization more genuinely modernizing and creative than Blair's own:

> What is at stake here is the rationale and justification for the Labour 'modernisers' project. If as they intend, the legacy of Thatcherism is to be accepted as a kind of settlement akin to Conservative accommodation to the legacy of the Attlee governments in the 1950s, the Labour new left project of the 1970s and 80s must be made historically meaningless.[41]

In substance, the book is a careful and sympathetic historical reconstruction of (ultimately defeated) attempts by a diffuse alliance of socialists, involving Labour leftists, constituency and social movement activists, trade union militants, and intellectuals, with Tony Benn as its chief spokesman, to revitalize and transform the Labour Party. 'The Labour new left saw that "parliamentary socialism" after reaching its apogee in the post-war settlement, had come to an end. They wanted to replace it with democratic socialism; New Labour would replace it with parliamentary capitalism.'[42]

If the political and historical importance of the 'Labour new left' was clear in the 1997 text, the concept itself is quite compressed and complex in its meaning. Indeed, in both the 1997 book and its 2020 restatement there is some slippage in use between this formulation and an alternative formulation of the 'new Labour left'. Commentaries on *Searching for Socialism* have tended to identify the 'Labour new left' primarily with Bennism as a left faction within Labour, losing something of the complexity of Panitch and Leys' interpretation of the latter. To understand this complexity, we need to go back to earlier work in the Milibandian vein, recognizing that that the concept of the 'Labour new left' has something of the quality of a retrospective reconstruction and defence of phenomena whose meaning and significance was contested at the time. At least as important for our purposes too is the role the concept has played in terms of Panitch's developing analysis of the limitations and possibilities of (labour) party structures and the particularities of the British case.

CONSTRUCTING THE LABOUR NEW LEFT

For Panitch and Leys in 2020, the overarching significance of the New Left currents that emerged after 1956, becoming enlarged and enriched by the new radicalisms of the late 1960s, lay in their recognition that the prime strategic goal was the creation of a new popular base for democratic socialism.[43] Strands of New Leftism with which Panitch most identified were those that remained (as opposed to a 'culturalist' emphasis) committed to thinking through questions of political organization and agency; here, party organization was not rejected but the inadequacy of existing parties (and indeed conceptions of party) pointed to the need for fundamental transformation or the emergence of new party forms. As we have seen, both the record of Labour governments in office and the accumulation of Marxist critique of Labourism led Miliband and Panitch by the early 1970s to discount the possibility of Labour's transformation. At the end of 1974 Miliband wrote Panitch that he was actively seeking 'to work toward the formation, in due course and with all possible caution and preparation, of an independent socialist party of a kind which has never been in this country'. In 1976 the *Register* published Miliband's call to 'move on' from the question of Labour's transformation to serious discussions of a new party.[44] The kind of democratic socialist party Miliband envisaged was one that, unlike extant far left parties, would seek electoral legitimation and representation within existing institutions at the same time as being involved in the 'many different forms of action, pressure and struggle' necessary for the attempt to bring about 'radical transformation of the existing social order in a socialist direction'.[45] In other words, a party embracing a 'dual power' strategy of socialist reformism of the kind that he articulated in *Marxism and Politics*, as he discussed at a more theoretical level the prospects for such a party in government to implement a transformative program against the interests of capital. Critical would be its ability to mobilize wide popular support through a 'complex network of organs of popular participation operating throughout civil society and intended not to replace the state but to complement it'.[46] Miliband's own efforts to build toward the conditions for such a party in the mid-1970s were unsuccessful; encountering 'almost universal scepticism' among even close contacts on the British left, they were diverted into the creation of a relatively short lived network of Centres for Marxist Education from 1975.[47]

It was in a sense ironic that Miliband's most developed arguments for a new formation should be articulated as the Bennite 'Labour new left' was taking shape, and when others sharing his general perspective were becoming newly interested in the prospects for Labour's transformation into something like the kind of socialist reformist party he advocated. For this was a period when intense industrial militancy and left-wing pressure on Labour from within and without produced a shift: Labour regained power in 1974 committed to a raft of interventionist economic measures, and with left MPs Tony Benn and Eric Heffer in control of a new Department of Industry. Becoming known as the Alternative Economic Strategy (AES), this agenda drew significantly on the arguments and analysis of economists and activists associated with the New Left.[48] It was against this developing context that Ken Coates' spirited critique of Milibandian pessimism, published in the *Register* in 1973, argued that the surge of militancy and radicalization of key unions made it wrong to talk of defeat for socialists within Labour when 'the battle lines are just beginning to form'.[49] Having arrived, however, at a position of determined rejection of the Labour Party, Miliband was relatively slow to revise it (from 1977 Miliband would spend a considerable part of his time in North America and it would not be until 1983 and the effective defeat of Bennism that he would return to the issue in the *Register*).

Ken Coates had seen the ground being laid for a renewed left challenge from within the party during its period of opposition; by the time Panitch revisited those arguments at length in 1979, his reflection on the 1974-79 Labour government reaffirmed a more pessimistic view. Rather than charting in detail the emergence of what he would later see as a Labour new left, he drew on his earlier analysis of structural limits to explain how the potential of union militancy had *necessarily* been defused by Labour in office. Stressing in particular 'the limitations which the requirements of defensive and electoral unity place upon changing the Labour Party', and noting that the left so often shouldered the burden of this unity, he restated his view that the 'problem with the Labour Party is not that it has sought to bring the working class to power by peaceful means. Rather the fact that it has not seen its task as bringing the working class to power has determined the kind of parliamentarism it practices.' Thus Labour in power had 'blocked the political remobilization of the working class necessary to socialist advance'.[50] Agreeing with Ken Coates that the task of beginning again outside Labour was a Herculean one, and that there was little historical evidence for its success, he doubted that the alternative was any easier. For, '[w]here are the examples of a transformed social democratic party?'[51]

As he posed this question, a fresh perspective on the issues was being afforded by activists of new social movements, especially feminists. Panitch would repeatedly acknowledge the impact of Hilary Wainwright's discussion of the problems of socialist political organisation in 1979's *Beyond the Fragments*. Wainwright's analysis was somewhat in the 'dual power' vein: stressing the potential of autonomous grassroots organizations and the consciousness-raising achievements of the women's movement, she called for a political alliance between socialist activists within and outside Labour to develop 'the strength which can be gained from ways of organizing that provide for both sharp action and joint debate'.[52] Wainwright didn't use the term 'Labour new left' and the role of left parliamentarians was not prominent in her analysis, which instead saw some of the functions of a socialist party being assumed by a variety of 'industrial, community and cultural organisations': 'it is as if the different parts of a piece of cloth – a political organisation – were being woven creatively and with ad hoc contact between the weavers, but without anyone having a master plan.'[53] Thus the question of what kind of coordination was needed was an open one. By 1981, when battles over Labour's constitution and internal democracy, since 1973 fought and coordinated by the Campaign for Labour Party Democracy (CLPD), provoked a crisis and defection of rightist MPs to form the Social Democratic Party (SDP), some New Leftists were reconsidering their position of critical distance from Labour leftism. In the *New Left Review*, Mike Rustin laid out the case for renewed effort within Labour on the basis that the Bennite left, adopting a collectivist (as opposed to individualist) conception of the party's representative function, was explicitly recognizing and taking on those problems of party structure that New Leftists had repeatedly identified.[54] At around the same time, discussion of *Beyond the Fragments* morphed into preparation for the launch of a new Socialist Society supported by figures from *New Left Review*, the women's movement, and the wider socialist left. Miliband, who had recently met and been impressed by Benn, was centrally involved, describing it as an attempt to organize 'some kind of independent socialist intervention ... by way of publications, research work etc.; and also to help the Bennite left, or the left which Benn is presently leading, in their struggles in the Labour Party, but from outside (even though some people in the planning process are Labour Party members)'.[55] By January 1982, when the Socialist Society was formally launched, Benn's bid to become Deputy Leader of Labour had been defeated, a setback that would be followed by worse as the Falklands War entrenched and emboldened Thatcherism in its second electoral term.

Discussion of the lessons to be drawn from Labour's catastrophic electoral defeat in 1983 produced a realignment on the left. Amid fractious debates, the emphasis of the Milibandian analysis shifted from critiquing the limits of

Labour leftism to challenging positions that became associated with *Marxism Today,* dubbed 'the new revisionism' by Miliband.[56] This realignment produced the first of three key moments in the (re)construction of a Labour new left, now defended as offering an alternative route for a left fightback and analysis of Thatcherism. In a 1983 essay Miliband had already rejected the analysis that blamed Labour's defeat on changes in the character and composition of the working class on one hand (an argument he thought misconceived), and divisions in the Labour Party on the other.[57] The vilification of Benn and the party's left wing as wreckers of Labour's electoral chances led him to a reassessment and defence of the revitalized and activist left in the party that was Benn's support base. Miliband recognized that this activist left, oriented to the grassroots, conceived the struggle within the party in different terms, and 'with the purpose of achieving predominance and turning the Labour Party into a socialist party free from the constrictions hitherto imposed on it by its leaders'.[58] Though he judged the chances of success to be slim, he admitted he had underestimated the challenge this activist tendency had been able to pose – thus 'the question whether the activists can push matters further and achieve the conquest of the Labour Party is more open than I had believed'. In the event, the other scenario he outlined was realized – 'the election of a new Leader ... able to combine a vocabulary that would please the left on the one hand with a sufficient degree of flexibility over policy on the others to reassure the Right and the Centre'. His judgement that such a scenario would involve 'a massive defeat for the left in the party' and a purge of leftist elements would prove prescient.[59]

This defeat had largely been accomplished when Panitch, who the same year assumed co-editorship of the *Register,* contributed to its double issue on *Social Democracy and After* a detailed and distinctive critique of the 'new revisionism' and the acquiescence of parts of the socialist independent left to the 'unity' agenda of Neil Kinnock, a major plank of which was indeed the extirpation of the new Labour left. An especially notable element of his critique was to identify the new revisionist perspective as resting on a simplistic understanding of the link between politics and class structure; 'a crude determinism which moves directly from socio-economic changes to the orientation of the electorate, without a serious examination of the role of the party as an intervening variable'. In the British case, Labour had consistently declined to assume the responsibility of a mass working-class party to educate, mobilize, and extend class consciousness; indeed, the practice of Labourism was in no small measure complicit in the withering away of the party's own class base.[60]

Despite – and because of – the marginalization of Bennism within Labour, the mid 1980s saw an intensification of support for him in the 'independent left' that had formed the Socialist Society. His value as a national figure for the socialist left was stressed to him by Miliband: 'you are now the only voice that can effectively project the case of the left on a national scale.'[61] Indeed Miliband now took on a key support role for Benn, corresponding often, commenting on drafts of speeches, and offering to get together a kind of think-tank of left academics. Calling itself the 'Independent Left Corresponding Society' (ILCS), this involved key figures from the Socialist Society and NLR, including Wainwright, John Palmer, Perry Anderson, and Robin Blackburn, drawing in left-wing economists Andrew Glyn and Robin Murray, and making some tentative common cause with the Socialist Campaign Group of MPs (among whom was Jeremy Corbyn) and the Trades Union Congress (TUC) left.[62] Panitch was kept up to date and participated when he could, also hosting Benn in Toronto. Tensions and ambiguities between the New Left/independent left and Labour identities in these relationships persisted – the ILCS remaining wary of being harnessed to Labour left organizations even as they sought to harness Benn's leadership qualities for the broader socialist left. But joint activity moved on, at Miliband's suggestion (and with some help from Panitch in persuading Benn),[63] to the reinvigoration of the Socialist Society and the joint organization with the Campaign Group of what would become a series of socialist conferences in Benn's Chesterfield constituency.

Given the scale of the left's crisis in the late 1980s and beyond, such initiatives were small scale and marginal, but they nevertheless kept open a space for dialogue and cooperation, acting also as a vector for the modest but significant influence of New Left intellectual perspectives among receptive Labour MPs. This could not be said to amount to a 'Labour new left' tendency in the sense of an organized and identifiable group, but in any case the term was not yet used, even when in 1988 the *Register* published Panitch's powerful retrospective of the development and defeat of the 'new radical opposition', a 'new Labour left' emerging out of the party's own contradictions. In the context of the 1988 volume's theme, *Problems of Socialist Renewal East and West*, the essay put flesh on the bones of the editors' contention that the Labour Party provided the 'most dismal example of social democratic crisis … and the repression of a movement of socialist renewal in and through that party has only intensified its continuing debilitation'.[64] It contained much of the analysis that the 1997 and 2020 books drew on, also contextualizing the new Labour left's challenge in relation to other left turns in social democratic parties in the 1970s.

The special significance of this new Labour left was that it addressed not simply intra-party democracy but also and explicitly the 'nature of democracy in the state'; 'it gradually set itself the task of transforming the ideology and organization of the Labour Party as the critical means of transforming the British state and society', in the process moving 'towards a new conception of socialist party politics' that pointed beyond social democratic parliamentarism and Leninist vanguardism.[65] Synthesizing analysis from the previous decade, Panitch gave a compelling account of how a range of forces and factors combined to produce this conception. Especially key was the political focus of new activists schooled in local and 'municipal socialism' moving into Labour with a commitment to use the resources of the local and central state to demand and extend effective democracy and to 'turn the Labour Party into an agency of social and political mobilization'.[66] Benn's significance, demonstrated via an analysis of his interventions and speeches through the 1970s, lay in his conviction that Labour must embrace and serve the energies generated by extra-parliamentary activism and in his willingness to act as focus and figurehead for this remobilization. He was also credited with a prescient anticipation of the potential for a right-wing attack on the very foundations of the post-war settlement, deploying a narrative promising 'freedom from the state' while legislating for greater disciplinary control. Unless an exhausted social democracy could be surpassed, its limited gains would be susceptible to rollback.

New Labour leftism, Panitch argued, differed from previous left Labourism in several key ways. Where the latter assumed 'near majoritarian' electoral support from a traditional class base, the former, a product of electoral and membership crisis, understood that the task was one of remobilization and reconstruction of class identities in conditions of heterogeneity. Where left Labourism exhibited 'parliamentary paternalism', directed toward maintaining a minority group of parliamentarians committed to the extension of welfarism and nationalisation through a benign and centralizing state apparatus, the new Labour left's socialism 'was inflected towards the participationism of 1968'.[67] Benn's great contribution was in his understanding of the limits of 'parliamentary paternalism', in his rejection of it, and in the alternative modes of political practice he tried to put on the agenda. This, Panitch emphasized, was of much greater significance than Benn's advocacy of the AES:

> The heady debates among socialist economists concerning the ambiguous nature of Planning Agreements, the National Enterprise Board and the import and exchange controls advanced under the Alternative Economic

Strategy missed the main point. For in so far as the policy changes were directed at merely electing a Labour Government to carry them through from on high, they portended in themselves little indeed. For they did not by themselves address the central political question of the structural changes in party and parliamentary politics, as well as in the ideological orientations of the leadership, that could open the means to their implementation. The main question was not only whether a Labour Government would have either the will or the courage to go ahead with the enunciated policy once it became clear what else it would involve, but how they could transform their own managerialist practices to mobilizing ones so as to retain their popular mandate even if they could be elected on this basis.[68]

As was the pattern, by the time Panitch's analysis was published he could once more point to the deep-rootedness and resilience of 'parliamentary paternalism' not, this time, able to defeat this challenge outright, but to 'turn its struggle inward', exhaust its energies in inner-party factionalism, and feed a media narrative that conflated the democratic socialist agenda of the new Labour left with the sectarian entryism of Militant (a Trotskyist faction organized around the newspaper of the same name) to demonize and delegitimize such efforts. Thus he closed the essay with the observation that 'new attempts at socialist renewal of that project will have to concentrate less on reforming the Labour Party and more on building a long-term independent campaign for a democratic socialism that transcends the limits of parliamentary paternalism'.[69]

The 1988 essay was originally to be part of a book project; 'a larger study of the attempt to change the Labour Party'.[70] The project was shelved until the Blair ascendancy, as we have seen, produced the second of three key moments in this counter-narrative of Labour's transformation. The 1997 book took up the narrative, now benefiting from the impact of Panitch's collaborations and his reading of the by now much enlarged corpus of Marxist theory of the state. Colin Leys traced the development of the discourse of party 'modernization' that produced New Labour, while Panitch's restatement of the analytical framework showed a deeper assimilation of Hilary Wainwright's insights into alternative conceptions of power, and the possibilities and limitations of hybrid 'movement–party' organization, as well as reflecting his own experiences of activism.[71] The term 'Labour new left' now implied, perhaps more strongly than the 'new Labour left' had, the possibilities and potential for such a hybrid, a political alliance unifying Labour leftism and the extra-parliamentary left. In the epilogue to the second edition of the book, published in 2001 and written with David Coates, these possibilities were closed off. Heavy emphasis was placed on the closing down by New Labour of the space, the language, and terms in which to debate, indeed it was in this closure that its novelty was seen to reside: 'what is above all regarded as antiquated and no longer acceptable is the party as a contested terrain, as an arena of democracy and as an incubator of popular democratic capacities.' Not only had the project of 'parliamentary socialism' been killed off, so too had the project to democratize the party as a precondition for democratizing state and society. 'Every previous phase of the party's history was characterised by prolonged struggles between the leadership and recognisably distinct, organised and programmatically informed left oppositions. New Labour has restructured the party so that virtually no room is any longer allowed for this.'[72]

There was yet to be a third moment, however, for the renewal of the 'Labour new left' in the unexpected, almost accidental, accession of Jeremy Corbyn to the Labour leadership. By his own admission, Panitch had in the interim 'lost interest in British politics' and in a 2020 interview credited his reengagement to contact with young activists influenced by the analysis of *The End of Parliamentary Socialism*.[73] Yet he overstated the extent of his previous disengagement from the British scene, for he had maintained links with Labour leftists, some of whom, such as Jon Lansman, a former organizer for Benn mentioned in the 1997 book, now appeared at the centre of Momentum, as well as with Ed Miliband, to whom he remained personally close, during and after his period as Labour leader. His research and insights on the struggles within the British Labour Party had also remained a cornerstone for his developing work. In *The Making of Global Capitalism*, the major study of the political economy of American empire co-written with Sam Gindin and published in 2012, the role that social democratic governments, including that of Blair, played in internalizing neoliberalism within their own Third Way projects remained a key theme.

That such a marginal figure as Corbyn, protégé of Benn and veteran of the Campaign Group, about whose non-existent leadership prospects Tony Blair had joked in 1996, could be propelled to the leadership by virtue in part of reforms enacted by Ed Miliband as Labour leader, was an irony not lost on Panitch. He and Leys took on, in short order, an updating of the analysis to understand and to try to shape this moment: 'The question now was whether the cycle of resistance and neutralisation would once again be repeated, or whether the Labour Party could after all become the agent of democratic-socialist advance in the UK.'[74] The answer was clear before the book came out. If aspects of its portrayal of Corbynism can (and have been) subjected to critique,[75] the overall analysis was important and necessary, not least as interpretation of the Corbyn moment, and Corbynism itself, became something of a battleground. Against accounts that portrayed Corbynism as either left-populism or 1980s far-left revivalism, Panitch and Leys' analysis authoritatively established its direct continuity from earlier manifestations of 'Labour new leftism'. Drawing directly on that experience, they attempted to alert the new generation of activists mobilizing in Momentum to the opportunities and pitfalls inherent in models of left organization that still reasserted themselves, and to the need to prioritize tasks of political education and re-mobilization. Crucially too, in line with the internationalist project and reach of the *Register,* and with the development of Panitch's own corpus of collaborative work, the analysis situated Corbynism within an overview of global movements on the left as they reacted to the structural adjustments imposed to meet the requirements of global capitalism in crisis. In the context of a 'marked turn on the left from protest to politics'[76] instantiated in such developments as the election of Syriza and emergence of Podemos as well as a wider resurgence of interest among young activists in the possibilities of democratic socialism, Corbyn's election was seen as opening the way to remobilization hitherto blocked by the peculiarities of the British party and electoral system as well as the internal dynamics of Labourism. Could a 'party of a new kind' after all emerge from the Labour Party's contradictions?

As before, such hopes, which as ever went against the grain of the underlying analysis, were frustrated. Corbynism's own limitations and divisions, and difficulties negotiating the politics of Brexit, combined with the predictable hostility of the PLP (Parliamentary Labour Party) and mainstream media to ensure that 'resistance and neutralisation' again prevailed. The many obstacles to the project, astutely surveyed by Colin Leys in an essay in the 2019 *Register*, proved insurmountable.[77] Keir Starmer's leadership, which has seen the suspension of Corbyn from the party, which at the time of this writing requires of Labour MPs 'unshakeable support for NATO' and seeks to ban front-benchers from attending picket lines, seems bent on resuming, if not exceeding, prior attempts to marginalize and defeat leftists in the party. Yet this resort to old reflexes looks in some ways both desperate and anachronistic and may yet prove misjudged. If a straightforward 'Labour new left' conversion or capture of the party seems unlikelier than ever, legatees of the New Left, Bennite, and Corbyn projects are again discussing how best to 'move on', inside and outside of the party.[78]

STILL SEARCHING FOR SOCIALISM

Through his writing and his activism, Leo Panitch did more than almost anyone of his generation to articulate and extend a New Left-inspired, democratic socialist critique of the Labour Party and social democracy. A tireless educator, his insistence on sober understanding of political and ideological structures never outweighed his enthusiasm for dialogue and his hope in the capacities of new generations of activists. In his many interviews through the locked down months of 2020, Leo patiently and indefatigably rehearsed the history of attempts to transform the Labour Party by democratic socialists, of the opposition these faced, and the reasons for their failure. This essay has attempted to complement that history by tracing the development of the concept he and his co-authors arrived at – the 'Labour new left' – as shorthand for this attempt, in the context of his own intellectual and political development. Initially expressed as a 'new Labour left', it captured the novelty of Bennism as a permutation of Labour leftism sufficient to require 'moving on' from the 'in or out of Labour' debates and some reassessment of an established New Left critique of Labourism. Expressed as 'Labour new left', the emphasis shifted somewhat to the significance of extra-parliamentary and social movement politics and their implications for conceptualizations of party organization, as well as denoting the influence of independent socialist (New Left) ideas within Labour. Conceptually, the term 'Labour new left' also keeps open the notion of a significant and longstanding current of democratic socialist thought that cannot be contained within the 'old/fundamentalist left' versus 'new/revisionist Labour' binary. A position from which to critique New Labour in 1997, itself developed from a defence of Bennism in the context of Thatcherism and the 'new revisionism', became by 2018 a position from which to defend and radicalize the Corbyn insurgency. Revealing its continuity with this earlier current and parallels with wider left remobilizations, this sought to reclaim the Labour Party as a space of contestation where possibilities for systemic change can be discussed. Leo was apt to date the origins of the Labour new left to the mid-60s and the crisis of Keynesian social democracy, but arguably its intellectual roots stretch back much further, through earlier New Left arguments for industrial democracy and attempts at 'parallellism', and to those pre-existing currents of libertarian and democratic socialist thought that the post-1956 New Left revived. I think he'd have liked the idea, but might have thought thinking forward, and in more concretely political terms, more useful. As he put it in one of his final interviews:

> I think increasingly people can see that the old corporatism is not possible. They can see from the crisis of ecological devastation that without democratic economic planning we are not going to be able to resolve our contemporary problems and we're going to have a host of new ones. So,

I think in some ways the chances [for democratic socialist advance] are greater provided we can develop the institutional capacities, as well as the organizational ones, to begin to remake the class through the process of remaking the politics.

In preparing this essay I have benefited from conversations with Patrick Diamond, Nicolas Jara Joly, Colin Leys, Karl Pike, and Hilary Wainwright. I am extremely grateful for comments on the draft by Colin, Greg Albo, and Sam Gindin.

NOTES

1. Leo Panitch and Colin Leys, *Searching for Socialism: The Project of the Labour New Left from Benn to Corbyn*, London: Verso, 2020; Leo Panitch and Colin Leys, *The End of Parliamentary Socialism: From New Left to New Labour*, London: Verso, 1997.
2. Panitch and Leys, *Searching for Socialism*, p. 6.
3. Even, he said, were he to be Prime Minister for 50 years, 'the pledges I have given you from my heart would still be unfulfilled, not because I fainted or failed, but because the corn was still green', comments by E.P. Thompson on the draft manuscript of *Parliamentary Socialism*, Miliband papers, Leeds University Special Collections.
4. Letter from Ralph Miliband to E.P. Thompson, not dated but probably early 1961. See also: Michael Newman, *Ralph Miliband and the Politics of the New Left*, London: Merlin Press, 2002, pp. 76-7 and p.102, fn. 47.
5. Ralph Miliband, *Parliamentary Socialism: A Study in the Politics of Labour*, second edition, London: Merlin Press 1972, p. 14.
6. David Coates, ed., *Paving the Third Way: The Critique of Parliamentary Socialism*, London: Merlin Press, 2003, p .73. See also: Newman, *Ralph Miliband*, p. 77.
7. Newman, *Ralph Miliband*, p. 77.
8. Miliband, *Parliamentary Socialism*, p. 350.
9. Miliband. 'The Transition to the Transition', *New Reasoner*, 6 (Autumn), 1958, p. 48, available at banmarchive.org.uk/new-reasoner/the-autumn-1958/the-transition-to-the-transition.
10. John Saville, 'Apathy into Politics', *New Left Review*, 4, 1960, p. 9. For fuller discussion of early New Left perspectives see: Madeleine Davis, 'Labourism and the New Left' in John Callaghan, Steven Fielding, and Steve Ludlam, eds., *Interpreting the Labour Party: Approaches to Labour Politics and History*, Manchester: Manchester University Press, 2003, pp. 40-42.
11. Leo Panitch recalled their first meeting in: 'Ralph Miliband, Socialist Intellectual 1924-1994', in Leo Panitch, ed., *Socialist Register 1995: Why Not Capitalism?*, London: Merlin Press, 1995.
12. Tom Nairn 'The Nature of the Labour Party I', *New Left Review*, 27, 1964; 'The Nature of the Labour Party II', *New Left Review*, 28, 1964. Interestingly, while these pieces contained few references to Miliband's text, their author had sent him a draft with a plea for advice.
13. Davis, 'Labourism and the New Left', p. 44.
14. Nairn, 'The nature of the Labour Party I'.

15 Perry Anderson, 'Problems of Socialist Strategy', in Perry Anderson and Robin Blackburn, eds, *Towards Socialism*, London: New Left Books, 1965.
16 Note, however, that some key New Left figures maintained a different emphasis. Thompson's work, by contrast, had its focus on the working class making itself as much as it was made, and the work of Raymond Williams traced similar developments through cultural formations.
17 Ralph Miliband, 'The Labour Government and Beyond', in Ralph Miliband and John Saville, eds, *Socialist Register 1966*, London: Merlin Press, 1966, p. 24.
18 John Saville, 'Labourism and the Labour Government', in Ralph Miliband and John Saville, eds, *Socialist Register 1967*, London: Merlin Press, 1967, reprinted in Coates, 2003, p. 91.
19 Miliband, 'Labour Government and Beyond'. For a fuller discussion of the Centres for Socialist Education see: Madeleine Davis, "Among the Ordinary People': New Left Involvement in Working-Class Political Mobilization 1956–68', *History Workshop Journal*, 86 (Autumn), 2018, pp. 133–59.
20 Michael Foot, 'Credo of the Labour Left', *New Left Review*, 1(49), 1968.
21 Miliband, *Parliamentary Socialism*, p. 376.
22 David Coates and Leo Panitch, 'The Continuing Relevance of the Milibandian Perspective', in Callaghan, Fielding and Ludlam, eds, *Interpreting the Labour Party*, p.73.
23 Leo Panitch 'Ideology and Integration: The Case of the British Labour Party', *Political Studies*, XIX(2), 1971, p. 187.
24 Panitch, 'Ideology and Integration', pp. 199-200.
25 Leo Panitch, *Social Democracy and Industrial Militancy: The Labour Party, the Trade Unions and Incomes Policy, 1945–1947*, Cambridge: Cambridge University Press, 1976, conclusion, excerpted in Coates, *Paving the Third Way*, p. 121.
26 Ralph Miliband to Leo Panitch, 29 April 1976, Miliband papers, Leeds University Special Collections.
27 See: Clyde W. Barrow 'From the Canadian State to the Making of Global Capitalism', in Greg Albo, Stephen Maher, and Alan Zuege, eds, *State Transformations: Classes, Strategy, Socialism*, Chicago: Haymarket Books, 2022.
28 Leo Panitch, 'The Development of Corporatism in Liberal Democracies', *Comparative Political Studies*, 10(1), 1977; 'Recent Theorisations of Corporatism: Reflections on a Growth Industry', *British Journal of Sociology*, 32(2), 1980; 'Trade Unions and the Capitalist State', *New Left Review*, 125, 1981.
29 Panitch, 'The Development of Corporatism', p. 72.
30 Coates and Panitch, 'The Continuing Relevance of the Milibandian Perspective', p. 76.
31 Leo Panitch, *Working Class Politics in Crisis: Essays on Labour and the State*, London: Verso, 1986, preface.
32 Panitch, *Social Democracy and Industrial Militancy*, p. 130.
33 Coates, ed., 'Introduction', *Paving the Third Way*, p. 1.
34 Henry Pelling, 'Review of *Social Democracy and Industrial Militancy: The Labour Party, the Trade Unions, and Incomes Policy, 1945–1974* by Leo Panitch', *The Journal of Economic History*, 37(3), pp. 835-36.
35 A clipping of Crick's review resides in a file of Miliband's personal papers relating to *Parliamentary Socialism*, although Miliband himself died in 1994.

36 Bernard Crick, 'Review of Panitch and Leys, *The End of Parliamentary Socialism*', *New Statesman*, 14 November 1997. Crick had earlier engaged much more usefully with aspects of the development of New Left thinking, in his 'The Rediscovery of Democratic Socialism', *Government and Opposition*, 23(4), Autumn 1988, pp. 424-39.
37 Coates and Panitch, 'The Continuing Relevance of the Milibandian Perspective', p. 71.
38 Leo Panitch, 'Socialist Renewal and the Labour Party', in Ralph Miliband, Leo Panitch, and John Saville, eds, *Socialist Register 1988: Problems of Socialist Renewal East & West*, London: Merlin Press, 1987, reprinted in Coates, *Paving the Third Way*, 2003, p. 215.
39 Coates and Panitch, 'The Continuing Relevance of the Milibandian Perspective', p. 75.
40 Coates and Panitch, 'The Continuing Relevance of the Milibandian Perspective', p. 82.
41 Panitch and Leys, *The End of Parliamentary Socialism*, p. 4.
42 Panitch and Leys, *The End of Parliamentary Socialism*, p. 4.
43 Panitch and Leys, *The End of Parliamentary Socialism*, p. 12.
44 Ralph Miliband to Leo Panitch, 16 December 1974, Miliband papers; Ralph Miliband, 'Moving On', in Ralph Miliband and John Saville, eds, *Socialist Register 1976*, London: Merlin Press, 1976.
45 Miliband, 'Moving On', p. 139.
46 Ralph Miliband, *Marxism and Politics*, Oxford: Oxford University Press, 1977, p.188. For a useful summary of his perspectives at this time, see also: Newman, *Ralph Miliband*, pp. 234-37.
47 Newman, *Ralph Miliband*, pp. 239-46.
48 David Coates, 'Labour's New Left Then and Now', in Matt Beech, Kevin Hickson, and Raymond Plant, eds, *The Struggle for Labour's Soul: Understanding Labour's Political Thought Since 1945*, second edition, Oxfordshire, UK: Routledge, 2018, p. 24.
49 Ken Coates, 'Socialists and the Labour Party', in Ralph Miliband and John Saville, eds, *Socialist Register 1973*, London: Merlin Press, 1973, p. 177.
50 Coates, *Paving the Third Way*, p. 159.
51 Leo Panitch, 'Socialists and the Labour Party: A Reappraisal', in Ralph Miliband and John Saville, eds, *Socialist Register 1979*, London: Merlin Press, republished in Coates, *Paving the Third Way*, London: Merlin Press, 2003, pp. 159-79.
52 Hilary Wainwright 'Moving Beyond the Fragments' in Sheila Rowbotham, Lynne Segal, and Hilary Wainwright, eds, *Beyond the Fragments, Feminism and the Making of Socialism,* third edition, 2013, London: Merlin Press, p. 296.
53 Wainwright, 'Moving Beyond the Fragments', p. 299.
54 Mike Rustin, 'Different Conceptions of Party: Labour's Constitutional Debates', *New Left Review*, 126, 1981.
55 Newman, *Ralph Miliband*, p. 271.
56 Ralph Miliband, 'The New Revisionism in Britain', *New Left Review*, 150, 1985.
57 Ralph Miliband 'Socialist Advance in Britain', in Ralph Miliband and John Saville, eds, *Socialist Register 1983*, London: Merlin Press, 1983, republished in Coates, *Paving the Third Way*, London: Merlin Press, 2003, pp. 181-198.
58 Miliband, 'Socialist Advance in Britain', p. 194.

59 Miliband, 'Socialist Advance in Britain', pp. 193-95.
60 Leo Panitch, 'The Impasse of Social Democratic Politics', in Ralph Miliband, John Saville, Marcel Liebman, and Leo Panitch, eds, *Socialist Register 1985/86: Social Democracy and After*, London: Merlin Press, 1986, republished in his *Working Class Politics in Crisis: Essays on Labour and the State*, London: Verso, 1986 pp. 13-16.
61 Letter, Ralph Miliband to Tony Benn, April 1985, Miliband papers.
62 See: Newman, *Ralph Miliband*, pp. 300-301.
63 Newman, *Ralph Miliband*, pp. 304-5.
64 Ralph Miliband, Leo Panitch, and John Saville, 'Problems and Promise of Socialist Renewal', in Ralph Miliband, Leo Panitch, and John Saville, eds, *Socialist Register 1988: Problems and Promise of Socialist Renewal East & West*, London: Merlin Press, 1988, p. 4.
65 Panitch 'Socialist Renewal and the Labour Party', pp. 327-28.
66 Panitch, 'Socialist Renewal and the Labour Party', p. 335.
67 Panitch, 'Socialist Renewal and the Labour Party', p. 340.
68 Panitch, 'Socialist Renewal and the Labour Party', p. 342. For a recent account of the AES that stresses the limits of its radicalism see: Baris Tufecki, *The Socialist Ideas of the British Left's Alternative Economic Strategy*, London: Palgrave, 2020.
69 Panitch, 'Socialist Renewal and the Labour Party', p. 363.
70 Panitch, 'Socialist Renewal and the Labour Party', fn. 1.
71 For her developing analysis see especially: Hilary Wainwright, *Arguments for a New Left*, Oxford: Blackwell, 1994; Hilary Wainwright, 'Once More Moving On: Social Movements, Political Representation and the Left', in Leo Panitch, ed., *Socialist Register 1995: Why Not Capitalism?*, London: Merlin Press, 1994. More recently see: Hilary Wainwright, 'Rethinking Political Parties', *Transnational Institute*, 8 February 2008, available at: www.tni.org.
72 Panitch and Leys, *The End of Parliamentary Socialism*, p. 290.
73 'Interview with Leo Panitch: Labour's New Left: From Benn to 2024', *Novara Media*, 12 May 2020, available at: www.youtube.com.
74 Panitch and Leys, *Searching for Socialism*, p. 2.
75 See, for example Matt McManus 'Wherefore Art thou Socialism?' A Review of *Searching for Socialism*, available at: www.historicalmaterialism.org.
76 For discussion of the turn from protest to politics see: Leo Panitch and Sam Gindin, 'Class, Party and the Challenge of State Transformation', in Leo Panitch and Greg Albo, eds, *Socialist Register 2017: Rethinking Revolution*, London: Merlin Press, 2018, p. 36.
77 Colin Leys, 'Corbyn and Brexit Britain: Is There a Way Forward for the Left?', in Leo Panitch and Greg Albo, eds, *Socialist Register 2019: A World Turned Upside Down?*, London: Merlin Press, 2020. Leys' analysis here is notably circumspect about the prospects for Corbynism, contrasting, perhaps, with Panitch's tendency to optimism, despite the thrust of his own analysis.
78 See especially the interview with James Schneider conducted by Hilary Wainwright and published as 'Finding a Way Forward: Lessons from the Corbyn Project in the UK', in Greg Albo, Leo Panitch, and Colin Leys, eds, *Socialist Register 2022: New Polarizations, Old Contradictions*, London: Merlin Press, 2023. Schneider's proposal for a 'Left Bloc' might be seen both as drawing on and trying to transcend the 'Labour new left' formulation.

AGAINST PESSIMISM: A LIFE ON THE LEFT

LEO PANITCH
INTERVIEWED BY RAFAEL KHACHATURIAN

It would not surprise readers of the Socialist Register to see Leo Panitch described as one of the most dedicated and tireless intellectuals on the Western left. Upon his death in December 2020, the outpouring of tributes from colleagues, students, and interlocutors with whom Leo engaged over the past five decades was a testament to the intellectual and political legacy he left behind.[1] From his early works on the political economy of the Canadian state and the impasse of social democracy in Britain and across Europe, to his later studies of American empire, culminating in the magisterial The Making of Global Capitalism co-authored with his long-time writing partner and political comrade Sam Gindin, the questions that Leo asked were always deeply grounded in the contemporary dilemmas of socialist politics. Just as importantly, Leo's extended editorial tenure with the Register helped bring to the fore new voices on the left – in a true internationalist spirit – from across the world, in the process cultivating a space for incisive analysis and critique.

Leo's intellectual work – as a scholar, teacher, editor, and activist – was always motivated by a fundamental commitment to emancipatory politics and the socialist project. His politics were first formed during his undergraduate years at the University of Manitoba and continued into his graduate studies under Ralph Miliband at the London School of Economics. In the years that followed, Leo's research placed him amidst a nascent movement of scholars in political sociology and political science who drew on Marxist social theory to analyze the capitalist societies of the advanced industrial world. Much of his influential research on the limits of social democracy and the centrality of the nation-state to globalization cannot be understood apart from this background, formed in the Marxist debates about the capitalist state of the 1970s. Even as that research trajectory, forged in the crises and social unrest of the late 1960s and 1970s, waned by the late 1980s, Leo's writing continued to bring the insights of New Left debates on the state, class, and imperialism to bear on the new form taken by capitalism after the end of the Cold War. In the years after the 2008 financial crisis, the intellectual tradition kept alive by Leo and his many colleagues, collaborators, and students found new audiences among the revitalized socialist movements in Western Europe, Latin America, and North America. Through the advances and setbacks of this period, Leo continued to maintain the same political standpoint – that of the engagé intellectual – that he imbued as a young scholar and activist, as he recounts in this interview.

The overarching theme that cut across all Leo's writing, teaching, and political work was the struggle to find new pathways out of capitalism to socialism. As with Miliband, this political project was always understood as a series of obstacles to be overcome, inescapable dilemmas to be confronted, and working-class capacities for self-governance to be built. It was oriented around the need to transcend the two primary twentieth-century alternatives to capitalist crises and retrenchment: social democracy and communism. To this was added the growing worry since the 1980s about the forces gathering on the political right, stretching from Margaret Thatcher to Donald Trump and a host of other hard-right political figures. The commitment to searching for a new socialist trajectory in this difficult context is reminiscent of Gramsci's much earlier exhortation to the Italian left to pick itself up in the wake of a series of defeats and amidst the rise of fascism:

> We should take a look at the little that we have done and the enormous amount of work we still have left to do; this should help to dissipate the thick, dark cloud of pessimism which is oppressing the most able and responsible militants, and is in itself is a great danger. It may in fact be the greatest danger we face at present, given that its consequences are political passivity, intellectual slumber, scepticism about the future. ... The truth is that we, as a party, have already taken some steps forward in this direction: we have nothing left to do but to take note of what we have done so far and to bravely continue ...[2]

These sentiments are echoed in Leo's final book, *Searching for Socialism: The Project of the Labour New Left from Benn to Corbyn*, authored with long-time collaborator and former co-editor of the *Socialist Register* Colin Leys.[3] As that book concludes:

> In the face of the contradictions being generated by twenty-first-century capitalism, discovering and developing new political forms adequate to addressing them, and the popular capacities needed to overcome them, will take time. And yet, given the scale and intensity of these contradictions –

political, economic, cultural, and not least ecological — time is short. This is the central dilemma for democratic socialists, not just in Britain but everywhere.[4]

This sober acknowledgement of the scale of the challenge, as well as of the absence of historical guarantees or easy answers, is typical of how Leo approached the question of political strategy under the conditions of contemporary capitalism. He passed along these lessons — perhaps best captured in Gramsci's well-known phrase, 'to live without illusions without becoming disillusioned' — to the many younger scholars and activists whom he mentored and inspired.

INTELLECTUAL BEGINNINGS

Rafael Khachaturian (RK): What were your main intellectual influences in your youth, both at the University of Manitoba in Canada and as a graduate student in Britain?

Leo Panitch (LP): My influences go back even before college and didn't come from intellectuals, initially. I grew up in North Winnipeg, in a working-class, socialist political culture. Along with Seattle, Winnipeg had been one of the sites of the two great general strikes in 1919, after World War I, and it left the legacy of a political culture which still reverberated with my generation. I was born in 1945. It was largely a social democratic legacy, although in a significant sense, a communist one as well. In my family, it was a social democratic legacy, which one found not only in the ethnic communities. The Ukrainians had a Labour Temple built the year of the general strike, which was a centre of communist education. Paul Robeson used to visit to speak and sing there. But there was also a social democratic milieu, which in my case, because I was Jewish, was also often Labour Zionist and Yiddish. That is, it was not religious. It was largely secular, and it was very oriented to Yiddish literature. This was distinct from the communists, who were mostly not (or only briefly) Zionist, and rather had Bundist backgrounds.

Intellectually, I went to a parochial Jewish school, in day school right up to grade seven and then night school until grade ten. I was taught by intellectuals who were Eastern European authors, writers, and poets. I look back now, and I think about how many of them were close to being mad. They were putting up with little brats when they had previously been major journalists or intellectuals. Some of them had come via South America. One of them had a big influence on me. After I came back to Canada from London I was on the radio a lot speaking about general issues, and had also published a book called *The Canadian State: Political Economy and Political Power*.⁵ I suddenly got a Yiddish note from this guy who had taught me in grades six and seven, and it said, 'Your ideas impress me very much'. I never saw him again, but after he died his wife sent me a very impressive unpublished manuscript about the Marranos making their way to Brazil.

In any case, while these people were intellectuals, my father and mother only had grade school educations. They came to Winnipeg right after World War I. My mother was an orphan. My father's family had come before the war and had left behind his relatives. My father, in particular, was a self-educated socialist. I've often thought that my fourth-year honours students in political science know less about politics, and certainly less about Robert's Rules of Order, in organizing a meeting, than my father did. He was a furrier, a cutter and sewer of fur coats, which was the aristocracy of the needle trade because of the expensive materials. At one point, I think he was the president of his local furriers' union branch. So, it was a political-intellectual milieu.

By the time I got to university, which was the early sixties, I think probably the greatest influence on me was a man called Cy Gonick, who founded what is now the oldest independent socialist magazine in North America next to *Monthly Review*, called *Canadian Dimension*. Gonick had just returned from Berkeley's economics department to teach at Manitoba. He was infused with the free speech struggle and the anti-Vietnam war. That said, early on at university, probably in my second year, I was in the library reading Marx's Preface to *A Contribution to the Critique of Political Economy*, which I don't think much of now, and I whispered to Sam Gindin, who I met in first year university economics and have known ever since: 'I think I'm a Marxist.' I don't know to what extent I really was. Later, I had won a Commonwealth Scholarship to go to the UK, and I remember reading, and not being very critical of, John Kenneth Galbraith's *New Industrial State*, and Anthony Crosland's *The Future of Socialism*, both of which remain classic social democratic statements, especially Crosland's.⁶

RK: Were you, at that point, already beginning to think from a Marxist perspective?

LP: I'm not sure that's true. Apart from some of Marx, I had read some Marxist literature but not a great deal. I'd gotten a B from an economic historian for a paper I did on Lenin, which shocked me. I remember also reading and writing a paper on Louis Hartz, the American political scientist of political development also influential in debating Canada's political system, where I think I was very sympathetic to him.⁷ I immersed myself more clearly in Marxist political sociology only when I got to London, not knowing that such a thing existed because previously I had just done political science and economics. My professor, Cy Gonick, the economist who I'd done the paper on Hartz for, was astonished that I was writing and being influenced by Marxist political thought. Based on that paper on Hartz, he was sure I was a liberal. I think I was open to all kinds of influences, even if at some point I thought Marxism made enough sense for me to say, 'I think I'm a Marxist'. Of course, even before I got to London, I was broadly influenced by the intellectual milieu of the sixties as well.

RK: In your piece commemorating Ralph Miliband's passing in 1994, you described your first encounter with him in a lecture room.[8] You wrote of an eye-opening moment in 1967 when you first heard Miliband lecture on the topic that would later become *The State in Capitalist Society*.

LP: What does a working-class Jewish kid know about university? I was the first person in my family to go to university, and you either became a lawyer or a doctor if you went to university. I'd done well at university and had been nominated for a Woodrow Wilson Fellowship and a Rhodes Scholarship, neither of which I won. Instead, I won a Commonwealth Scholarship. I intended to go to the UK for just a year, and then come back and go to law school. I was certainly interested then in the notion of economic planning, which was why I was reading Galbraith and Crosland. When I wrote up my Commonwealth statement for that year away, I said I wanted to study planning.

You couldn't choose the university you went to, only put preferences down. I was sent, bizarrely, to Leeds, because there was a fellow named Albert Hanson who had written a book on planning in India.[9] Luckily, when I arrived he was in Berkeley for that year. The other famous political scientist who was at Leeds was John Peter (J.P.) Nettl, who had written a biography of Rosa Luxemburg and a critique of American behavioural political science.[10] But he'd been killed in a plane crash that summer in Pennsylvania. There was no one to study with there, and they tried to convince me to not do an MA but instead start a PhD program. Since I still wanted to go to law school, I didn't want to do that. I convinced the Commonwealth Scholarship people and the London School of Economics to let me in, because I wanted to be in London anyway. But because I had still said I'd study planning for that year, the people at the LSE stuck me in a public administration program. It was the most boring thing I'd even encountered in my life. There was a very famous professor there named Peter Self. But I was about to blow my head off.[11]

I encountered another Canadian, a guy from Winnipeg, to whom I said, 'I don't think I can stand this, I'm going to have to pack it in.' And he said, 'Oh, come up and hear these lectures by this guy Miliband on the fourth floor'. Miliband was doing the lectures that were to become *The State in Capitalist Society* and there, I said to myself, 'Oh, this is it'. I didn't know what it was called, but it had a very powerful effect on me, obviously.

LSE offered an MA in political sociology, which I immediately switched into. The influences were broad there too. I enrolled in a seminar with Robert McKenzie, who very famously wrote the book *British Political Parties*, which was an apologia for parliamentary elitism.[12] Miliband's *Parliamentary Socialism* was partly intended as a response to McKenzie.[13] In that seminar, I read Robert Michels, Moisei Ostrogorsky, and all the great classical literature on parties, writing a critique of some of them along with McKenzie, which was intellectually very stimulating. Obviously, Miliband's lectures and the informal seminar he was running, called 'The State in Contemporary Capitalism', which I attended even after not doing coursework anymore, were also very interesting at the time.

Most of the readings that Miliband assigned in that seminar are in the footnotes of *The State in Capitalist Society*. One read C. Wright Mills' *The Power Elite*, who was a friend of Ralph's, as well as more mainstream literature in political sociology, from Shmuel Eisenstadt to Jürgen Habermas. I must say, there weren't a lot of introductions to the Marxist classics. One read those on one's own. I read the three volumes of Isaac Deutscher's trilogy on Trotsky, which was itself an education, although I was never tempted by the Trotskyist groups that became very fashionable among students at the LSE and more generally.[14] Ralph himself had never been either in a communist party or a Trotskyist. As a young man, he had been influenced by Trotsky's critique of Stalin and was very close friends with the Deutschers. But he himself was never actually a member of the Communist Party, unlike E.P. Thompson or John Saville.

Ralph and I became friends very quickly. I had a little Morris Minor convertible that I'd bought for 100 quid the first year I was in England. I was at a meeting, a big meeting in downtown London in support of Rudi Dutschke, who was a German anti-war student activist who had been hurt in an assassination attempt. Dutschke was in London, and I'd been attending Ralph's lectures for the better part of a year. As I was leaving, he was sitting at the back of the room, about to take the subway or bus home. I said, 'Do you want a lift?' and drove him home. Our friendship grew out of that. He quickly invited me and my wife to dinner and so on. But what then impressed me about Ralph was that he was involved in working-class education through the sixties. In the wake of the break-up of the British Communist Party, his intellectual alliance with Thompson, Saville, and Lawrence Daly, who was the miners' leader, was very much oriented by their differences from the *New Left Review*. They were very much oriented to engaging in socialist education with working-class people, and they'd get off on that as much or more than from the brilliant students they had at the LSE.

POLITICS AND THE ACADEMY

RK: There's a moment in the time you're describing in which the conventional schematic distinction, between politics as normative and the social sciences as value neutral, begins to blur.

LP: Not only does it blur, but there's an explicit and profound rejection of it. Of course, your research is governed, motivated, and stimulated by your values. People who think it isn't are the ones who are not very conscious about how they creep in. Those who realize that it is want to make sure that they aren't sweeping the influence of their values under the carpet. They're open and explicit about it. It matters more that they get the empirical historical stuff right, because it's actually going to affect their orientation politically, whereas someone who is value-neutral has nothing other than his reputation in academe, and thus no political stake in getting it right. When your research is oriented to its strategic implications, you've got to really make sure that you're not finding inconvenient facts and burying them, because that's going to affect whether your strategy is right or wrong.

It's important that people understand that these were engagé intellectuals. Ralph used to say, privately to me, of the people he'd be debating at the university, both in Britain and when he would come to North America to lecture: 'These people aren't my colleagues. They're my enemies.' He didn't mean that he was competing with them academically. He meant it in the sense that they had a different political project. Although Ralph never said this explicitly, *The State in Capitalist Society* was actually a response to Crosland's *The Future of Socialism*, and the influence that it had on 1950s social democracy. He was trying to challenge all of Crosland's premises, such as that whereas capital had directly controlled the state until World War II, that was no longer the case, that labour counterbalanced it, and that finance was no longer a power in the capitalist economy. If you look at the way in which *The State in Capitalist Society* is constructed, it's very much an attempt to empirically disprove those premises.

I think people too often forget that the literature that launched the Marxist theory of the state in the late sixties was very much being written by engagé intellectuals who were thinking in terms of its implication for political strategy. This also applies to Poulantzas, who was writing his first major book, *Political Power and Social Classes*, as a critique of the crude kind of monopoly capital theories that you would hear at Communist Party meetings or read in the not-very-sophisticated Communist Party literature in France. This is very important to understand about those figures.

RK: There was much at stake politically in many of these discussions about the state. Even though it tended to sometimes take an abstract tone, it nevertheless had a concrete political intent.

LP: Yet they were simultaneously *dis*connected intellectuals, coming out of an era of disenchantment, and break with the two great political movements of the left up to that point. Moreover, they were critical of the labour movement. One of the reasons Poulantzas became so despondent toward the end of his life was that he was swimming against the current of the French Communist Party. Others like Miliband or Thompson didn't have a natural political home. Miliband had been a member of the Labour Party on the left and had spoken at the 1953 Labour Party conference calling for the common ownership of the means of production. Of course, very famously, he had written *Parliamentary Socialism,* and that reflected the most critical perspective on the Labour Party, and he had very little engagement with it except that he would knock on doors at election time for it. By 1973, for the second edition of *Parliamentary Socialism*, he wrote in the preface that the greatest of illusions that socialists in Britain succumb to is the belief that the Labour Party could be changed into a socialist party.

On the other hand, he'd never been a member of the Communist Party and had no time for the Trotskyist sects. He'd tried to find a way to launch a new kind of socialist movement. But he and others weren't connected to one that provided an institutional framework.

RK: Your point about disconnection and disenchantment echoes Perry Anderson's critique of Western Marxism.[15] What do you make of the claim that Marxist research on the state, in particular, suffered from this tendency towards abstraction and academicism throughout the seventies that it never really recovered from?

LP: That depends on where you were sitting. In my view, that was true of the very famous, and I think damaging, piece by Gold, Lo, and Wright in the *Monthly Review*.[16] Although Erik [Olin Wright] was always an engaged intellectual in his local community, that piece was a classically academic piece. Theda Skocpol's critique, although motivated by social democratic illusions, and I think anti-communist and anti-Marxist animus, was also very academic.¹⁷ I think you could say that Bob Jessop's work is academic, but I don't think that is true of many, many others, including myself, not to speak of Miliband and Poulantzas. Theirs was not academic work. It was *in* academe and had an enormous influence on students at the time, but I don't think it suffered from that.

One might point to the critique of the *New Left Review* that Thompson or Miliband would have had, with Miliband warning Thompson away from the merger between *The New Reasoner* and *Universities and Left Review* that produced the *NLR* because he felt that they had a fascination with French and continental intellectual culture that was salon-oriented rather than working-class education-oriented. Specifically, the animus with which Thompson wrote *The Peculiarities of the English*, against Anderson, reflects that.¹⁸

Yet, I don't think that line of critique was entirely fair either. If you go back and look at the *New Left Review* in the late 1960s, they had a regular series of very interesting bullets and articles related to ongoing struggles. Of course, Ralph always kept very close relations with the *New Left Review* people, much more than Thompson, including with Tariq Ali. They had met in the great debate over Vietnam at Oxford, where they had taken the side of the pro-North Vietnam position. Perry was more of an abstract theoretician, but Ralph and Tariq were very close friends and close to the Fourth International, and the IMG [International Marxist Group] in Britain.

So, to take up your question, I think that tendency toward abstraction was especially the case with graduate students who got into this, but I certainly don't think it applied to Miliband and Poulantzas, nor to me. In editing *The Canadian State*, my Preface and Introduction to it came out of a seminar at Carleton University in the mid-70s, which was attended by trade unionists and activists in the Indigenous Peoples' movement. Some of the people who contributed to it were not academics. That Preface states: 'Whether Marxist theory in Canada will prove capable of generating its own further development will in no small measure depend on the future development of the Canadian working class.' And so, a good many of us who are engaged in this important intellectual work of trying to make Marxism better were at the same time motivated by what effect it could have on political strategy. Certainly, I never saw myself primarily as a teacher, although I ended up being a pretty good one and having a lot of influence. I always thought of myself as lucky enough to get a job which paid me for doing political work.

RK: A number of your books, including *Social Democracy and Industrial Militancy* and *From Consent to Coercion*, have examined the course of British and Canadian trade unions over the post-war decades.[19] Was there a receptivity to these more radical ideas among the trade union movement and activists in the New Left?

LP: Yes and no. If you look back at the book I did on the Labour Party and the end of parliamentary socialism, there's even a passage in there about how a lot of the Labour New Left activists, like the Bennites, would say that they've been influenced, obviously, by *Parliamentary Socialism*, but also by *The State in Capitalist Society* as undergraduates.[20] I think Ralph's work did influence that generation, as previous social democratic activists in the 1950s tended to see the state as neutral. Their thinking was: We come up with a policy, we are elected as a government, and then the state will implement it. Remember, a lot of trade unionists in that period, who Ralph in particular would have known, were influenced by, or had come out of, or some of them were still in, the Communist Party, so they had their own intellectual influences. I don't know which way the influence ran, in other words. Some of the later generation of trade unionists would definitely have been influenced by reading some of the debate around *The State in Capitalist Society*.

RK: As you say, much of the Marxist literature on the state in the late 1960s was a critique of the main tenets of liberalism and pluralism in the advanced capitalist world. Specifically, the assumptions of state neutrality, where the rise of managerial capitalism allegedly no longer required seeing the state as an instrument of class power.

LP: The best of those intellectuals who took a pluralist view, mostly in debate with the elite theorists, especially with Mills, ultimately recanted. I'm thinking of Robert Dahl, above all, who was highly influenced by his own students' arguments. The pluralists were also often more complex than others would think. Dahl's first published essay was on the debates around workers' control in Britain around the time of the nationalization of key industries under the 1945 Labour government.[21] He revisits the debates at the trade union congress in the 1930s around workers' control and industrial democracy, and is implicitly critical of establishing the nationalized industries on the basis of boards that are made up of technocrats, financiers, and engineers. Perhaps in the context of the Cold War, and of an era of trade union strength, he becomes a pluralist and is critical of Mills and elite theory, writing *Who Governs?* in response to it.[22] Someone like Dahl, in American terms, is a pretty radical guy. He would certainly have been a member of a social democratic party or a socialist party in Europe, had he lived there. Some of his writing on planning is technocratic, but some of it isn't. Dahl and Lindblom's *Politics, Economics, and Welfare* is another important book that I read as an undergraduate and was very impressed with.[23]

My MA thesis included a critique and humorous expose of Gabriel Almond and Sidney Verba's famous book *The Civic Culture*, a massively funded empirical study of the attitudes of party members and activists in five democracies. One common question posed in all of these surveys is asking Democrats whether they would mind if their daughter married a Republican. You find that they wouldn't, and then they ask members of the Christian Democratic Party in Italy if they would mind if their daughter married a Communist, and you find that they would. From this, they come to the conclusion that the United States has a tolerant political culture and Italy has an intolerant political culture. That is the level of scholarship one is talking about here.

LOOKING BACKWARD

RK: Why the relative petering out of Marxist research in political sociology and political science by the early to mid-eighties?

LP: I think that has more to do with the disciplines, the problematic politics of the academy, and the epoch, than it has to do with those of us who remained engaged with those types of questions. Intellectual life goes through fashions, including the intellectual capital that for a while was associated with post-modernism and post-structuralism, and that was part of it. People did get tired of the Miliband-Poulantzas debate, and I think that the fallout of the piece by Gold, Lo, and Wright had a lot to do with that. There was something like a certain academicization. For example, rational choice Marxism was less overtly political. Now, that's not to say that real advances in Marxist conceptualizations of class weren't made through that — they were. I think Erik Olin Wright and Guglielmo Carchedi made very, very important conceptual advances. But the American Sociological Association became, for people like Erik and even Michael Burawoy, their political home. Arguably, the ASA is one of the more significant factions of social democratic politics in the United States.

Moreover, this marginalization also had to do with the shift in the balance of class forces, with a labour movement that was beaten back and defeated. It is true that with the defeat of trade unionism in the early eighties, with the rise of Reaganism and Thatcherism and its great success, in the face of that reaction, a lot of left-wing political sociologists and political scientists and economists embraced social democracy naively, and their politics became that of the Varieties of Capitalism school, pointing to the Swedish welfare state and the strength of the German labour movement. Increasingly, their political horizon became involved with making a case to neo-classical economists that you could square the circle – that you could have a welfare state and be export competitive within capitalism – and they saw themselves as doing political work. They were naïve about the trajectory of what was going on in social democracy in Europe. Someone like Fred Block, who wrote an outstanding, path-breaking essay on the state, one that is close to my own work in terms of state elites taking the lead in organizing the capitalist class and figuring out appropriate policies, very rapidly turned into someone who was trying to make a case for social democracy within American academe in the face of Reaganism.[24]

This was hardly reactionary. You find this all over the place, as the default position when you find yourself in an argument with someone who says socialism is impossible, which I agree it may well be, to say, 'well there's something like it in Sweden'. Bernie Sanders does this himself, of course. But it's based on wishful thinking about what's going on in other places. I love Erik (Olin Wright), and I think he had made great advances, but I'm very critical of what he had to say about participatory democracy in Brazil, or the social planning networks in Quebec. It's a bit like the Webbs going to Russia in 1932, and coming back and saying, 'I've seen socialism and it works,' because they weren't exposed to any of the horrors that were going on or asking hard questions. That was true of most people who went to study the participatory budgets in Porto Alegre. They listened to the cadre of the PT [Workers' Party] in the local area telling how wonderful everything was and weren't asking the hard questions about what was not working.

Still, for a lot of people, and Frances Fox Piven stands out very much here, the point of what we do is not so much to win over our colleagues. People like her continue to produce generations of intellectuals who share that perspective. Even though she is not from quite the same intellectual camp as us, the theory and being an engaged political intellectual with a sharp class sensibility was never lost to her.

RK: Back in 2010, Block and Piven pointed to the 'analytic amnesia' of American political science, including the American Political Science Association's task force on inequality, arguing that scholarly conversations about inequality in American politics were unknowingly revisiting a lot of the debates in political sociology from the sixties and seventies.[25] In particular, they suggest that there was a disciplinary forgetting of Marxist responses to the elite theories that are now largely informing the discourse on inequality. How would you summarize the lasting legacy of this moment, and its impact on political sociology and political science?

LP: I really think that in a lot of circles the Marxist discussions of the state did not fully go away in the 1990s. Clyde Barrow's 1993 book *Critical Theories of the State* is a reprise of that scholarship.[26] Peter Bratsis and Stanley Aronowitz organized that interesting conference on Miliband and Poulantzas at CUNY in 1998.[27] And certainly, in my case, that scholarship ended up influencing the reception that my writing on the globalization of the state received. Looking back on my first essay in *The Canadian State*, 'The Role and Nature of the Canadian State,' I do wish I had at that point developed that into a more general theory rather than just try to apply it to Canada. Consider also the superficial way in which globalization was received, in which people would come to the astonishing conclusion that capital was bypassing states. My 1994 *Register* essay, 'Globalization and the State,' which was quite celebrated, was written very much under the influence of what I had integrated from the Marxist theory of the state.[28] The beginning of that piece references Immanuel Wallerstein and Perry Anderson as both saying that capital has escaped the state. From the mid to late nineties, globalization theorists like William Robinson had also adopted a notion that states were controlled by a trans-national capitalist class. Those of us who were rooted in really trying to figure this out were never taken in by that claim.

But one has to be careful not to overblow the influence of that Marxist scholarship on the state. It's not as if those of us who were engaged in trying to develop and improve Marxism, and to understand why the world is still capitalist, were ever hegemonic in any country's discipline. Maybe we had, for a time, a hell of a lot of influence on Canadian political science, but that drifted away. It was never hegemonic, but always a countercurrent. Certainly, it really was a minor stream in American political science and even political sociology. If you were studying to become a political scientist, or even in terms of what most undergraduate students were taught, it was still some version of either psephology or civics, all through that period. Even though that strain continued with the Caucus for a New Political Science, one shouldn't make too much of it in terms of the entire discipline. You also have to remember that some of what we were doing was picked up in other disciplines, such as geography, influencing people like David Harvey, Neil Smith, and Erik Swyngedouw. A lot of the Marxists who perhaps were no longer in political science departments were to be found in geography departments, through the eighties and nineties. It depends where one was looking, in other words.

I remember being at the conference of Europeanists in Washington circa '83 or '84. There was a very large panel with a range of people, for which I was the discussant, along with Claus Offe. I was quite close with Claus then.

I probably shouldn't have been, but I was extremely critical of their politics and of the very shoddy claims I felt they were making. It kind of silenced the room, that anyone would be that unacademic, I guess. I remember Claus saying to me afterwards, 'No, you really can't behave like that in an academic meeting,' but I think this was true of Ralph as well.

I didn't separate my life like that. It was easy for my generation not to do. It's much harder of course for yours, but there was a cache when I got hired in 1972 about being a Marxist and about being Ralph Miliband's student. There was a certain frisson that went with that, even amongst mainstream intellectuals. It was easy for me to get a job, and I could behave in university in a way that I wasn't embarrassed about, because it was like, 'Look, we're doing this because we're trying to get this theory to be useful to political change'.

NOTES

Unlike many hundreds who learned from him, I was never Leo's student or colleague. My connection to him was established some eight years ago, when I was still a graduate student, after he contributed a review essay on Thomas Piketty's *Capital in the Twenty-First Century* to *Perspectives on Politics*, where I was then working as an Editorial Assistant. Leo and I corresponded occasionally in the years that followed, mostly regarding my dissertation on conceptualizations of the state in twentieth-century American political science and their relationship to Marxist political theory. We would intermittently run across each other at conferences like the Left Forum and Historical Materialism, where he was a mainstay. Over dinner and drinks during a visit to Toronto in January 2019, I floated the idea of interviewing Leo for my project, which by then was becoming a book. Ever supportive, Leo generously agreed. Shortly after we spent time discussing his intellectual formation, his recollections of working with Ralph Miliband, and his retrospective lessons from that creative period for Marxist political thought. After Leo's passing, it felt only natural to approach the editors of the *Socialist Register* about publishing the interview. This is an edited version of our conversation.

1   See for example: Greg Albo, Stephen Maher, and Alan Zuege, eds, *State Transformations: Classes, Strategy, Socialism*, Chicago: Haymarket, 2022; Stephen Maher, 'Leo Panitch and the Socialist Project', *Jacobin*, 23 December 2020; Sam Gindin, 'Leo Panitch Was a Sober Optimist and an Anti-Utopian Utopian', *Jacobin*, 27 February 2021.
2   Antonio Gramsci, 'Against Pessimism', *L'Ordine Nuovo*, 15 March 1924 (trans. Natalie Campbell).
3   Leo expounded upon the affinity between his own intellectual approach to socialist strategy and that of Antonio Gramsci in: Leo Panitch, 'On Revolutionary Optimism of the Intellect', in Leo Panitch and Greg Albo, eds, *Socialist Register 2017: Rethinking Revolution*, London: Merlin Press, 2016.
4   Leo Panitch and Colin Leys, *Searching for Socialism: The Project of the Labour New Left from Benn to Corbyn*, London: Verso, 2020, pp. 254-55.

5   Leo Panitch, ed., *The Canadian State: Political Economy and Political Power*, Toronto: University of Toronto Press, 1977.
6   John Kenneth Galbraith, *The New Industrial State*, Boston: Houghton Mifflin, 1967; Anthony Crosland, *The Future of Socialism*, London: J. Cape, 1956.
7   Among Hartz's best-known works are *The Liberal Tradition in America: An Interpretation of American Political Thought since the Revolution*, New York: Harcourt, 1955; and *The Founding of New Societies: Studies in the History of the United States, Latin America, South Africa, Canada, and Australia*, New York: Harcourt, Brace & World, 1964.
8   Leo Panitch, 'Ralph Miliband, Socialist Intellectual,1924-199', in Leo Panitch, ed., *Socialist Register 1995: Why Not Capitalism?*, London: Merlin Press, 1994, pp. 1-21.
9   A. H. Hanson, *The Process of Planning: A Study of India's Five-year Plans 1950-64*, London: Oxford University Press, 1966.
10 J.P. Nettl, *Rosa Luxemburg*, London: Oxford University Press 1966; Nettl and Roland Robinson, *International Systems and the Modernization of Societies: The Formation of National Goals and Attitudes*, New York: Basic Books, 1968.
11 Self was a scholar of conventional British public administration, whose publications included *Whither Local Government?*, London: Fabian Publications, 1950; and, with Herbert J. Storing, *The State and the Farmer: British Agricultural Policies and Politics*, London: Allen & Unwin, 1962. Later he was well-known for his critiques of neoliberal public administration, such as *Government by the Market? The Politics of Public Choice*, Basingstoke: Macmillan, 1993; and *Rolling Back the Market: Economic Dogma and Political Choice*, Basingstoke: Macmillan, 2000.
12 Robert McKenzie, *British Political Parties: The Distribution of Power Within the Conservative and Labour Parties*, New York: St. Martin's Press, 1963.
13 Ralph Miliband, *Parliamentary Socialism: A Study in the Politics of Labour*, New York: Monthly Review Press, 1964.
14 Isaac Deutscher, *The Prophet Armed: Trotsky, 1879-1921*, New York: Vintage, 1954; *The Prophet Unarmed: Trotsky, 1921-1929*, New York: Vintage, 1959; *The Prophet Outcast: Trotsky, 1929-1940*, New York: Oxford University Press, 1963.
15 Perry Anderson, *Considerations on Western Marxism*, London: New Left Books, 1976.
16 David A. Gold, Clarence Y. H. Lo, and Erik Olin Wright, 'Recent Developments in Marxist Theories of the Capitalist State, Parts I and II', *Monthly Review* 27 (October and November), 1975.
17 Theda Skocpol, 'Political Response to Capitalist Crisis: Neo-Marxist Theories of the State and the Case of the New Deal,' *Politics & Society* 10 (1980), pp. 155-201.
18 E.P. Thompson, 'The Peculiarities of the English', in Ralph Miliband and John Saville, eds, *Socialist Register 1965*, London: Merlin Press, 1965, pp. 311-62.
19 See Leo Panitch, *Social Democracy and Industrial Militancy: The Labour Party, the Trade Unions and Incomes Policy, 1945-1974*, Cambridge: Cambridge University Press, 2009; and Leo Panitch and Donald Swartz, *From Consent to Coercion: The Assault on Trade Union Freedoms*, Toronto: University of Toronto Press, 2008.
20 Colin Leys and Leo Panitch, *The End of Parliamentary Socialism: From New Left to New Labour*, London: Verso, 1997.
21 Robert A. Dahl, 'Worker's Control of Industry and the British Labor Party', *American Political Science Review* 41 (1947), pp. 875-900.
22 Robert A. Dahl, *Who Governs? Democracy and Power in an American City*, New Haven: Yale University Press, 1961.

23 Robert A. Dahl and Charles E. Lindblom, *Politics, Economics, and Welfare: Planning and Politico-Economic Systems Resolved Into Basic Social Processes*, New York: Harper, 1963.
24 Fred Block, 'The Ruling Class Does Not Rule: Notes on the Marxist Theory of the State', *Socialist Revolution* 33 (May-June), 1977, pp. 6-28.
25 Fred Block and Frances Fox Piven, 'Déjà Vu, All Over Again: A Comment on Jacob Hacker and Paul Pierson, "Winner-Take-All Politics"', *Politics & Society* 38 (2010), pp. 205-11.
26 Clyde W. Barrow, *Critical Theories of the State: Marxist, Neo-Marxist, Post-Marxist*, Madison: University of Wisconsin Press, 1993.
27 Stanley Aronowitz and Peter Bratsis, *Paradigm Lost: State Theory Reconsidered*, Minneapolis: University of Minnesota Press, 2002.
28 Leo Panitch, 'Globalization and the State,' *Socialist Register* 30 (1994), pp. 60-93.

Also Available

Socialist Register 2022: New Polarizations Old Contradictions – The Crisis of Centrism
Edited by Greg Albo, Leo Panitch and Colin Leys

The 58th annual volume takes up the challenge of exploring how the new polarizations relate to the contradictions that underlie them and how far 'centrist' politics can continue to contain them. Original essays examine the multiplication of antagonistic national, racial, generational, and other identities in the context of growing economic inequality, democratic decline, and the shifting parameters of great power rivalry. Where, how, and by what means can the left move forward?

Contents:
Simon Mohun: A contemporary portrait of neoliberalism: The rise of the one per cent
Walden Bello: At the summit of global capitalism: The US and China
Ingar Solty: Market polarization means political polarization: Liberal democracy's eroding centre
Bill Fletcher Jr.: Trump and the dangers of right-wing populism in the US
Marcus Gilroy-Ware: What is wrong with social media? An anti-capitalist critique
Adolph Reed Jr., Touré F. Reed: The evolution of 'race' and racial justice under neoliberalism
Samir Sonti: The crisis of US labour, past and present
Sam Gindin: American workers and the left after Trump: Polarized options
Jayati Ghosh: Pandemic polarizations and the contradictions of Indian capitalism
Vishwas Satgar: Epidemiological neoliberalism in South Africa
Ilya Matveev, Oleg Zhuravlev: Loft offices and factory towns: Social sources of political polarization in Russia
Ana Garcia, Virginia Fontes, Rejane Hoeveler: The far right, corporate power, and social struggles in Brazil
Samir Gandesha: Identity crisis: The politics of false concreteness
David Harvey: The double consciousness of capital
James Schneider interviewed by Hilary Wainwright: Finding a way forward: Lessons from the Corbyn project in the UK

ISBN 978-0-85036-773-7 paperback
978-0-85036-772-0 hardback

Socialist Register 2021: Beyond Digital Capitalism – New Ways of Living
Edited by Leo Panitch and Greg Albo

As digital technology became integral to the capitalist market dystopia of the first decades of the 21st century, it refashioned both our ways of working and our ways of consuming, as well as our ways of communicating. And as the Covid-19 pandemic coursed through the world's population, adding tens of billions of dollars to the profits of the high-tech corporations, its impact revealed grotesque class and racial inequalities and the gross lack of public investment, planning and preparation which lay behind the scandalously slow and inadequate responses of so many states.

Contents:

Ursula Huws: Reaping the whirlwind: Digitalization, restructuring, and mobilization in the Covid crisis

Bryan D. Palmer: The time of our lives: Reflections on work and capitalist temporality

Larry Lohmann: Interpretation machines: Contradictions of 'artificial intelligence' in 21st century capitalism

Mathew Cole, Hugo Radice & Charles Umney: The political economy of datafication and work: a new digital Taylorism?

Grace Blakeley: The big tech monopolies and the state

Tanner Mirrlees: Socialists on social media platforms: Communicating within and against digital capitalism

Derek Hrynyshyn: Imagining platform socialism

Massimiliano Mollona: Working-class cinema in the age of digital capitalism

Joan Sangster: The surveillance of service labour: Conditions and possibilties of resistance

Jerónimo Montero Bressán: From neoliberal fashion to new ways of clothing

Sean Sweeney & John Treat: Shifting gears: Labour strategies for low-carbon public transport mobility

Benjamin Selwyn: Community restaurants: Decommodifying food as socialist strategy

Pat Armstrong & Huw Armstrong: Start early, stay late: Planning for care in old age

Pritha Chandra & Pratyush Chandra: Health care, technology, and socialized medicine

Christoph Hermann: Life after the pandemic: From production for profit to provision for need
Robin Hahnel: Democratic socialist planning: Back to the future
Greg Albo: Postcapitalism: Alternatives or detours?

ISBN 978-0-85036-761-4 paperback
978-0-85036-762-1 hardback

Socialist Register 2020: Beyond Market Dystopia – New Ways of Living
Edited by Leo Panitch and Greg Albo

How can we build a future with better health and homes, respecting people and the environment?
Connecting with and going beyond classical socialist themes, each essay in this volume combines analysis of how we are living now with plans and visions for new strategic, programmatic, manifesto-oriented directions for alternative ways of living.

Contents:

Stephen Maher/Sam Gindin/Leo Panitch: Class politics, socialist policies, capitalist constraints
Barbara Harris-White: Making the world a better place: restoration and restitution
Amy Bartholomew/Hilary Wainwright: Beyond the 'barbed-wire labyrinth': migrant spaces of radical democracy
Katharyne Mitchell/Key Macfarlane: Beyond the educational dystopia: new ways of learning through remembering
Birgit Mahnkopf: The future of work in the era of 'digital capitalism'
Michelle Chen: A new world of workers: confronting the gig economy
Yu Chunsen: All workers are precarious: the 'dangerous class' in China's labour regime
Ursula Huws: Social reproduction in twenty-first century capitalism
Alyssa Battistoni: Ways of making a living: revaluing the work of social and ecological reproduction
Nancy Holmstrom: For a sustainable future: the centrality of public goods
Karl Beitel: The affordable housing crisis: its capitalist roots and the socialist alternative
Roger Keil: Communism in the suburbs?
Owen Hatherley: The retroactive utopia of the socialist city

Nancy Fraser: What should socialism mean in the twenty-first century?

ISBN 978-0-85036-752-2 paperback
  978-0-85036-753-9 hardback

Socialist Register 2019: A World Turned Upside Down?
Edited by Leo Panitch and Greg Albo

Since the Great Financial Crisis swept across the world in 2008, there have been few certainties regarding the trajectory of global capitalism, let alone the politics taking hold in individual states.

This has now given way to palpable confusion regarding what sense to make of this world in a political conjuncture marked by Donald Trump's 'Make America Great Again' presidency of the United States, on the one hand, and, on the other, Xi Jinping's ambitious agenda in consolidating his position as 'core leader' at the top of the Chinese state.

Contents:

Leo Panitch/Sam Gindin: Trumping the empire
Marco Boffo/Alfredo Saad Filho/Ben Fine: Neoliberal capitalism: the
  authoritarian turn
Ray Kiely: Locating Trump
Doug Henwood: Trump and the new billionaire class
Nicole Aschoff: America's tipping point: between Trumpism
  and a new left
Elmar Altvater/Birgit Mahnkopf: The Capitalocene: permanent capitalist c
  ounter-revolution
Alan Cafruny: The European crisis and the left
Aijaz Ahmad: Extreme capitalism and 'the national question'
Jayati Ghosh: Decoupling is a myth: Asian capitalism in the global disarray
Sean Starrs: Can China unmake the American making of global capitalism?
Lin Chun: China's New Internationalism
Ana Garcia/Patrick Bond: Amplifying the contradictions:
  the centrifugal BRICS
Adam Hanieh: The contradictions of global migration
David Whyte: 'Death to the corporation': a modest proposal
Umut Ozsu: Humanitarian intervention today
Colin Leys: Corbyn and Brexit Britain: Is there a way forward for the Left?

ISBN 978-0-85036-735-5 paperback
  978-0-85036-736-2 hardback

Socialist Register 2018: Rethinking Democracy
Edited by Leo Panitch and Greg Albo

This volume seeks a re-appraisal of actually-existing liberal democracy today, but its main goal is to help lay the foundations for new visions and practices in the development of socialist democracy. Amidst the contradictions of neoliberal capitalism today, the responsibility to sort out the relationship between socialism and democracy has never been greater. No revival of socialist politics in the 21st century can occur apart from founding new democratic institutions and practices.

Contents:

Sheila Rowbotham: Women: linking lives with democracy
Martijn Konings: From Hayek to Trump: the logic of neoliberal democracy
Alex Demirovic: Radical democracy and socialism
Dennis Pilon: The struggle over actually existing democracy
James Foley & Pete Ramand: In fear of populism: referendums and neoliberal democracy
Sharryn Kasmir: Cooperative democracy or competitiveness? rethinking Mondragon
Adam Hilton: Organized for democracy? Left challenges inside the Democratic Party
Natalie Fenton & Des Freedman: Fake democracy, bad news
Nina Power: Digital democracy?
Tom Mills: Democracy and public broadcasting
Ramon Ribera Fumaz & Greig Charnock: Barcelona en comu: urban democracy and 'the common good'
Leandro Vergara-Camus & Cristobal Kay: New agrarian democracies? The pink tide's lost opportunity
Michelle Williams: Practising democratic communism: the Kerala experience
Paul Raekstad: From democracy to socialism, then and now
Ian McKay: Challenging the common sense of neoliberalism: Gramsci, Macpherson and the next left

ISBN. 978-0-85036-733-1 paperback
978-0-85036-732-4 hardback

www.merlinpress.co.uk